ASA Monographs 24

Reason and Morality

Edited by
Joanna Overing

Reason and Morality

Tavistock Publications
London and New York

First published in 1985 by
Tavistock Publications Ltd
11 New Fetter Lane, London EC4P 4EE

Published in the USA by
Tavistock Publications
in association with Methuen, Inc.
29 West 35th Street, New York, NY 10001

Typeset by Keyset Composition,
Colchester
Printed in Great Britain
at the University Press, Cambridge

British Library Cataloguing in Publication Data

Reason and morality. — (ASA monographs; 24)
1. Rationalism
I. Overing, Joanna   II. Series
153.4′3   BF441
ISBN 0-422-79800-2
ISBN 0-422-79810-X Pbk

Library of Congress Cataloging in Publication Data

Main entry under title:
Reason and morality.

(ASA monographs ; 24)
Papers from an ASA conference
held at the London School of Economics
in Apr. 1984.
Includes bibliographies and index.
1. Ethnophilosophy – Congresses.
2. Reason – Cross-cultural studies – Congresses.
3. Cultural relativism – Congresses.
I. Overing, Joanna.
II. Association of Social
Anthropologists of the Commonwealth.
III. Series: A.S.A. monographs ; 24
GN468.R32 1985   301′.01   85–12637

ISBN 0-422-79800-2
ISBN 0-422-79810-X (pbk.)

Contents

List of contributors

Joanna Overing — Senior Lecturer in the Social Anthropology of Latin America, London School of Economics

Raymond Firth — Emeritus Professor of Anthropology, University of London

Edwin Ardener — University Lecturer in Social Anthropology; Fellow of St John's College, Oxford

Sybil Wolfram — Fellow and Tutor in Philosophy, Lady Margaret Hall, Oxford; Lecturer in Philosophy, University of Oxford

Paul Hirst — Professor of Social Theory, Birkbeck College, University of London

Mark Hobart — Lecturer in Anthropology with reference to South East Asia, School of Oriental and African Studies, University of London

David Parkin — Professor of Anthropology, School of Oriental and African Studies, University of London

Ladislav Holy — Reader in Social Anthropology, University of St Andrews

Jonathan Parry — Senior Lecturer in Social Anthropology, London School of Economics

Michael Saltman — Associate Professor of Anthropology, University of Haifa

Anne Salmond — Senior Lecturer in Anthropology, University of Auckland

Preface

The ASA conference on the topic to which this volume is devoted, originally entitled 'Rationality and Rationales', took place in April, 1984 and was in celebration of the Malinowski Centennial year. Appropriately it was held at the London School of Economics where, in 1927, Malinowski was appointed to the first chair in Social Anthropology at the University of London. It was Malinowski's insistence that there is no fact without theory. The contributors to this volume, in following the lead of Malinowski as supreme ethnographer, reverse his insight to read: there is no decent theory without data. It is through detailed comparative ethnography and thereby through the experience of multiplicity that Social Anthropology can contribute to the on-going debate about rationality, and in so doing help to reformulate ways of asking about such standard philosophical issues as translation, relativism, universalism, truth, knowledge – and human nature.

The contributors to this volume question the tendency of many ethnographers and philosophers to adhere uncritically to a received philosophy of mind and human nature. They are also sceptical about the notion that human nature is already charted and *as such* comprised of specific features that are universally shared. Through sensitive ethnography we see that some cultures may have more sophisticated theories of human nature than our own, or ones that are equally interesting and 'valid'. While we might recognize that aspects of Western scientific knowledge of the material world are superior to other knowledges, we cannot assume the same about Western theories of mind, society, and social behaviour. It would be self-defeating to compare 'modes of thought' in the conviction that the intellectual capacities of humankind are already known absolutely and that the forms of correct reasoning are definitively exemplified in the thoughts of the anthropologist and the Western scientist. The contributors are therefore uneasy about the idea that our own notion of humankind in its enthronement of Reason can provide a firm basis from which to judge the capacities either of ourselves or other human beings.

We need always to keep in mind when studying the knowledge of others the ethnography of our own theories of human nature and to be reflective about them, a never-ending corrective process in the tasks of understanding and translating.

I wish to give warm thanks to Professor Sir Raymond Firth for opening the conference by presenting his contribution, 'On Intelligibility', to us in full. I also wish to thank Professor George Stocking (Chicago), Professor Bernhard Lang (Gütenberg), Dr Misha Penn (Minnesota), Professor Ioan Lewis (LSE), Dr Paul Heelas (Lancaster), Dr Michael Brunowski (Posnan), Dr Robert Thornton (Capetown) and Dr Judith Oakley (Essex), all of whom presented excellent papers to the conference, but which unfortunately are not included in the volume because of the dictates of space and coherency of theme. The ASA is particularly indebted to its guests Professor Andre Paluch from Cracow and Mrs Helena Wayne, daughter of Malinowski.

A debt of gratitude is due to Dr Peter Loizos and Dr Michael Sallnow who were jointly responsible for the local arrangements. The chairpersons of individual sessions were Professor Ernest Gellner, Dr Peter Riviere, Dr Raymond Apthorpe, Dr Nigel Barley, Professor David Pocock, Professor Emiko Ohnuki-Tierny, and Professor John Davis. These were joined by Dr Ivan Karp in a final summing-up session, chaired by the conference convenor, who thanks them and the contributors for their support and enthusiasm. Thanks are also due to the British Academy, the ASA, and the British Council for helping with the transportation costs of two of our paper-givers and one of our guests. Finally, I am grateful to Deborah Spring of Tavistock Publications for her invaluable assistance in putting this volume through the press.

Joanna Overing
December 1984
London

Joanna Overing

1 Introduction[1]

The debate

The recent debates in Britain on rationality,[2] which revolve around reflections on the epistemological presuppositions of anthropological fieldwork, and include the hoary issue of comprehending in general 'other minds', began in 1970 with the publication of Bryan Wilson's edited volume, *Rationality*. This collection of essays by philosophers, sociologists, and anthropologists used as a focus the 1964 article by Winch, 'Understanding a primitive society', which challenged Evans-Pritchard's contention (1934, 1935, 1937) that Azande beliefs about witchcraft and oracles are logical (they obey universal laws of logic), but mistaken. Very briefly, Winch argues that our sense of reality is a social construction based on the conventional discourse of our society, the corollary of which is that unrelated language communities may well have incommensurable world views and rationalities.[3]

The predominant position over the years has been against Winch and in agreement with Evans-Pritchard, i.e. that Azande beliefs are fictitious, though as logical in argument (and in the same way) as those of Western science. The debate has been carried through more by philosophers than by anthropologists and has therefore increasingly narrowed to focus upon internal issues raised in the analytic philosophy of science rather than those emerging from ethnographic fieldwork. In *Rationality and Relativism* (Hollis and Lukes 1982), a follow-up volume to *Rationality* where the positions of the philosophers have become more refined and strongly drawn, much attention is given to the question of the empirical verifiability and truth-value of strange beliefs and to the problem of which universals of mind, perhaps *a priori* ones, we must assume to exist for the translation of strange beliefs to be possible. With a few notable exceptions,[4] it was agreed by these philosophers that the cognitive skills developed by Western scientists are – on the criteria of truth-value and power over the physical – superior to all others in the history of the world, and such skills should therefore be the yardstick by which we measure and judge all others.[5] Hollis and Newton-Smith go so far as to label mistaken beliefs, those that the methods of Western science would not validate, as 'irrational beliefs' (Hollis 1982: 69; Newton-Smith 1982; Hollis and Lukes 1982: 12). With a wave of the empiricist's wand the status of 'rationales' in human experience has thus been consigned to the category of 'the wrong and the daft', and the question of the form and purpose of such rationales in human social life appears no longer to be of interest.

Less focused, and therefore broader in scope, are two other collections of essays that also form a critical part of the history of this particular debate, the 1973 collection of essays, *Modes of Thought*, edited by Horton and Finnegan, and *Philosophical Disputes in the Social Sciences*, edited by S. C. Brown, and published in 1979. In the latter volume an essay by Horton entitled 'Material-object language and theoretical language: towards a Strawsonian sociology of thought' anticipates in *Rationality and Relativism* much of the discussion on 'bridgeheads'[6] into the thought of others. In *Philosophical Disputes* an important section is also addressed to Karl-Otto Apel's article, 'Types of Social Science in the light of human cognitive interests'. Apel, whose views are associated with the Frankfurt School of social theorists, calls in question the neutrality of all science by arguing that the type of understanding being sought reflects particular value-laden cognitive interests. This is a topic missing from the other volumes on rationality, reflecting the fact that the concern with investigator reflexivity is more Continental than British in tradition. The Horton and Finnegan volume, *Modes of Thought*, has in contrast to other collections considerable anthropological content, and as such was little discussed in *Rationality and Relativism*. It is also pertinent to note the shift within anthropology itself in its formulation of issues. Reflection upon the topic of rationality is not the same today as it was in 1973. In *Modes of Thought*, as the title indicates, a major concern was over the delineation of distinct 'modes of thought' differentiating 'the modern' and 'the traditional', 'the scientific' from the 'non-scientific'. In brief, whatever the issue, there remained in the early 1970s a conviction that the West was a highly rational place, while 'traditional' people lived a more poetic, mystical, less rational and more restricted world of thought.[7] The crisis of faith within science had not yet left its mark.

The Hollis and Lukes volume addresses itself to the crisis of faith within philosophy, initiated by its own historians and sociologists, over the empiricist's paradigm of rationality.[8] Within science the idea of a 'single world' is being challenged. For instance, both Kuhn (1964) and Feyerabend (1975, 1978) have forcefully argued against the belief of Western science in a unified objective world unaffected by the epistemic activities of the scientists themselves; rather, they say, the world, from the perspective of our know-ledge of it, is how we view it through the paradigms we create. Richard Rorty has recently portrayed the moral commitment of Western philosophy to

Reality, Truth, Objectivity, and Reason as 'a self-deceptive effort to eternalize the normal discourse of the day' (Rorty 1980: 11). In a powerful critique, Rorty rejects philosophy's search for the rational foundations of knowledge. The faith of Western science in a universal rationality is being shaken, and as Hollis and Lukes comment (1982: 1), 'recent upheavals in the philosophy of science have turned the historian or sociologist of science into something of an anthropologist, an explorer of alien cultures'. Such 'anthropology' of science unnerves many philosophers, and most of the contributors to *Rationality and Relativism* argue against what Hollis and Lukes label 'the temptation of relativism' within the philosophy of science. In so doing, they are defending their control of reality construction, one based on Reason, the ideal of Objective cognition, and a bedrock of Reality.[9]

It is important to stress the point that the issues of rationality, relativism, translation, and commensurability as discussed in the Hollis and Lukes volume are being defined by analytic philosophers who have a particular view of science and humankind to defend. Their discourse on relativism, and definition of it, suits their interest in maintaining a particular world view within the philosophy of science. The position of extreme relativism that they have attacked (see Hollis and Lukes 1982) is one that threatens their definition of humankind, science, and reality; but it is also a red herring, as are the styles of reasoning and practices of other cultures which in fact do not interest them. Extreme relativism as they discuss it is a stance no anthropologist would seriously hold. We wish to encourage, in Hirst's words, 'points of contact' between cultures, not discourage them, or the idea of them. Our business is, after all, 'translation'.

The social sciences have traditionally thought themselves dependent upon the natural sciences; but the battle going on today within the philosophy of science frees social inquiry from such dependency. Those who are involved in social inquiry can now ask interesting questions about translation and relativism which have previously been banned by the thought police of philosophy. We do not need to agree with the authority of such traditional distinctions as 'the rational' and 'the irrational' and the notion of knowledge to which they are attached. We can now raise such issues as the role of paradox and faith in social thought and practice, about which we know little: both are probably more powerful forces in society than logic and reason (also see Gellner 1982: 184). In short, our questions can now be framed by *our* knowledge interests, and not those of the philosophers of science who must get their own house in order. Our knowledge interests have to do with understanding the theories, knowledge, ethical thought, and practices of other cultures, and not with defending a particular notion of rationality, humankind, and Western science.

It is unfortunate, but because of the interests they are defending, the philosophers in this debate on rationality have not, on the whole, been especially helpful to anthropology. Indeed, it sometimes appears that the entire canon of rationality would be as useful to the field anthropologist in the chore of understanding how a specific people (with perhaps the exception of analytic philosophers) use ideas and formulate them as would a plan of the London underground railway. Anthropological concerns are considerably different from many of those of philosophy. Usually the philosophers are not asking social questions; usually anthropologists are not asking for universal criteria of truth. Anthropologists *are* asking about *moral universes*, their basic duty being to understand the intentions and objectives of actors within particular social worlds, as well as what these actors say, understand, believe truth and those worlds to be, a task in metaphysical description.[10] The anthropologist deals as a matter of course with multiple theories of mind and knowledge, while traditionally many philosophers have been concerned with one, and one moreover that equates truth with value-free facts about the material world. The facts of the ethnographer, the truths we describe, are in contrast almost always tied explicitly *to a world of values*.

In modern Western science the empiricist's proposition is that truth is amoral and facts are autonomous from value. This understanding of truth is in sharp contrast to the belief systems of other societies where it is normal for truth to be tied to other truths that are social, moral, and political in scope (see Gellner 1973: 170 ff., Henry Myers Lecture 1974). However, since Kuhn's publication of *The Structure of Scientific Revolution* (1964), philosophers of science are having greater difficulty in separating out the world of values from the task of science and the grounds for knowledge itself. If for no other reason, the proximity of human progress to human frailty cannot be dismissed. The more technology 'develops', the more it menaces our human frailty, as the tragedy of Bhopal so tragically attests. The entrenched clauses of the empiricist's mechanical, neutral, and formal picture of the world are being unravelled, therefore, for many reasons, and there is confusion within science about its own knowledge interests. Thus, the view that morality is a domain to be looked at as an aside, separate from the pursuit of knowledge through Reason and empirical findings, is a belief that is being seriously questioned within science.

The contributors to this volume do not view morality as a separate area to be opposed to thought and reason. We thus speak of the moral aspects of thought, reason, and truth, as well as of practice. Part of our aim is to be aware of and to rectify our own privileging of rationality through a formalism that was premised on the doctrines of the rationalist paradigm dictated to us as the proper one for 'objective' inquiry by the philosophers of science. They themselves are no longer sure of this program. Thus, we are now free to pursue knowledge other than that tied directly or solely to reason.

To be very simplistic but to the point, I for one consider it unthinkable to claim that a Piaroa of the Venezuelan rain forest is irrational when he says that rain is the urine of the deity, Ofo Da'a. The Westerner asserting that rain is H_2O and the Piaroa saying that it is the urine of a deity are doing so on similar grounds: both are relying on the knowledge of the supreme authority of their society, respectively the scientist and the shaman, on the nature of water.[11] What is more, the one truth does not necessarily go against the truth of the other. Faith in many worlds may or may not negate a faith in one.[12] This is simply another way of saying that issues about the 'true' are easily confused; for there are among others empirical truth, rhetorical truth, social truth (e.g. a marriage rule), and metaphoric truth, on all of which there is now a large literature by certain philosophers of science.[13] Kenneth Burke (1966, 1969) is one of the more interesting writers on the creative role of rhetoric and tropes in the construction of reality. Through metaphor and the linking of incongruous concepts, one can see things in startling new ways. Rhetoric, in its use of tropes, creates categories of thought and persuades through felt identifications which overcome real differences of substance and interest. This is done through verbal modes which are not subject to empirical confirmations. Such 'entitlement', the summarizing and making sense of complex events, affects the ways people *act* in society; for in creating social truths rhetoric structures reality (see Crocker (1977) on Burke's understanding of rhetoric). The notion of truth like that of rationality is elusive and without meaning when not in the context of asking *true (or, equally, rational) toward what end?* All truths have their moral aspect, for instance.[14] To hope to find universal and independent criteria of truth is a hopeless and Quixotic goal when the task is to understand knowledge actors have of their moral universe and their standards of validation with respect to it, which as often as not includes the world of nature. In summary, by focusing on the issue of the cognitive powers of Western thought in controlling and knowing about the world of materiality, many British writers on rationality have strongly biased the picture of humankind's rationality and knowledge towards that mechanical world and away from the social. It is an incomplete depiction of cognition. The power of actors' *thinking as social and moral beings* is neglected and thereby denigrated absolutely. Rationality then becomes a matter of ranking, and certain thought is considered absolutely superior to all others. The question of rationality as a value which has different ends in human history and experience is rarely raised, and hence the issues become very confused indeed.

The contributors to this volume are in part reacting to the way in which the debate on rationality has been formulated over the past decade; but they are also responding to the question of what is the 'state of the art' in anthropology in the mid-1980s. It is a time when no new 'isms' are in view, a shaky but nevertheless healthy period of change when issues must be reconsidered, re-evaluated, and certain ones rediscovered. No contributor is suggesting the possibility of a new 'ism'; rather each is stressing the complexity of social experience, a position contrary to that of the faithful to a particular 'ism' where significant experience is inevitably reduced to one specific aspect privileged over all others. The declaring of 'isms', as Ardener remarks in his contribution to this volume (pp. 48–56), is a mark of Modernism: each 'ism', no matter what the subject, through manifesto, tolerates no rivals in its appropriation of the future as its own. It is Ardener's conclusion that in anthropology the modernist switch is now off. He suggests that with Functionalism, Malinowski switched 'Modernitas' on. Structural-Functionalism, then Structuralism followed Functionalism as expressions of the Modern in anthropology, until it eventually fragmented into Structural Marxism and flirtations with Hermeneutics, collapsing as a force within the discipline by the late 1970s. The span of Modernism in anthropology, Ardener suggests, was from 1920 to 1975. Thus we have no new 'isms', no *avant garde*; for, as Ardener observes (this volume, p. 62) to be a Modernist is now to be backward-looking. Moreover, the expropriation of the future by Modernists has led only to a number of undesirable conditions in the present. In Ardener's words, 'Modernism, Early, Middle, or Late, is a set of ideas and concepts that derives from the folk-thought of the industrial countries in the era of the expanding world' (ibid.). It reflects the optimistic phase of the scientific, industrial, and social revolutions following from the Enlightenment (this volume, pp. 48–9). The fact that social anthropology has already become transformed by the *experience of multiplicity* in the world makes it accidentally one of the branches of knowledge most prepared to experience the enormous conceptual changes that are involved in the collapse of Modernism in the West (Ardener, this volume, pp. 62, 65), and in so doing to generate its own valid approaches outside Modernism and the rationalist paradigms.

The set of controversies to which the contributors address themselves, sometimes directly, other times more indirectly, and the positions in general they take on them can be summarized as follows.

1. What is the place of reason in the social life of humankind? The general response to this question is to demote reason from its throne toward the end of achieving a more balanced view of the social and the formulation of social thought.

2. What is the place of the unreasonable, the contradictory, the emotional, and the chaotic in human social life? We tend to see these factors as having at least as much influence as reason over behaviour and thought, and thus as much topics for study as 'the reasonable' in cultural life.

3. What is the nature of a general human rationality? None of us seems to know what this would be, but several contributors, Hirst, Hobart, and Wolfram, directly express a wariness over postulating one. We are all more confident in the task of exploring particular 'rationalities' or 'rationales', the success of which does not depend upon the assumption of *specific* universals that might provide us with a 'bridgehead' into these 'rationales'.

4. Are there such things as incommensurable world views? If the value of this volume lies anywhere it is in the ethnographic detail through which are revealed a number of world views or metaphysics which are very different from our own. Understanding and communicating their content are not seen by us as an impossibility, but one of the more critical chores of the anthropological endeavour.

5. How efficacious are typologies of 'modes of thought' or 'cognitive styles'? Such typologies are not a concern of the contributors, particularly one so broad in scope and political in tone as only to distinguish 'rational scientists' from 'traditional others'.

6. Is modern Western thought cognitively superior? We firmly question such superiority when the subject of thought is not physical kind but humankind and moral relationships. Humility comes only through an acquaintance with the epistemologies and ontologies of other cultures, an acquaintance achieved through rich ethnography which is acquired by taking seriously what others say about their social worlds. We do tend to see all ontologies, including that of the scientist, as by definition bound by metaphysical presuppositions and therefore value-laden.

7. How possible are value-free investigative methods? The consequence of a certain humility in face of other theories of mind and social action is caution over any assumption giving superiority to the cognitive baggage of the investigator in the task of understanding these other theories. Our own analytical tools are far from being value-free and their use can therefore easily distort and denigrate the social thought of others, particularly that of 'alien' others, or, even worse, work against its being revealed.

8. How valid is the assumption of the absolute authority of hierarchical oppositions, as reason over emotions, and langue over parole? The contributors are especially wary of such postulations and recognize that the authority of any particular logic or ranking is both moral and social.[15] One concern common to many papers in this volume is precisely this, the question of the moral, social, political, and legal power of received logics and their imposition by one people upon another.

The ASA Conference of 1982, published as *Semantic Anthropology* and edited by D. Parkin, raised many of these questions, but phrased them differently; for they were not addressed to the rationality debate *per se*, but to issues relating to the premises of structuralism, a rationalist programme *par excellence*. Thus, this publication should be seen as a continuation of the discussion begun at that time. The 1982 conference concluded with the participants asking about the benefits of a dialogue between anthropologists and philosophers. Who helps whom in such a discussion, for instance? From the 1984 conference we might conclude that we need a grander framework, but not the one within which the philosophers work, while philosophers need the kind of 'therapy' that a sensitivity to ethnographic counter-examples may provide. The fact that philosophers and anthropologists have been unable to generate constructive discourse on, for example, the 'rationality' problem, says something about both disciplines. What is there, we might ask, in the thinking of both their respective 'cultures' which has led to such dis-agreement? This is an 'anthropological' question, if there ever was one, and we hope that the philosophers take our present discussion as a spirited attempt to explore the reasons for the present lack of a 'bridgehead' between the two disciplines. What is very clear is that those philosophers who do have a strong anthropological background, such as Gellner (e.g. 1973, 1982) and Wolfram (see Wolfram in this volume),[16] and who are therefore highly sensitive to the issue of the relationship of thought to systems of morality, have a good deal to tell us.

The following sections are an elaboration of the set of controversies listed above as discussed by the contributors of this volume.

Sense and sensibility: the dethronement of Reason

Several contributors to the volume, Hobart, Hirst, Parkin, Firth, and Wolfram, dwell upon the ambiguity of the notion of rationality in Western thought, especially as it is variously defined in recent debates on the topic. Both Hirst and Hobart (Hirst, this volume, p. 87; Hobart, this volume, p. 105) note that we are presented with a bewildering array of definitions of ration-ality from opposed philosophical doctrines, each of which gives its own epistemological guarantees and legislation. Philosophers tell us that ration-ality is universal to humankind and that all social interpretation must rest on its assumption. For instance, Hollis, who places an *a priori* constraint on what a 'rational man' can believe about his world (1982: 83) states that:

> 'some beliefs are universal among mankind. There are, because there have to be, percepts and concepts shared by all who can understand each other, together with judgements which all would make and rules of judgement which all subscribe to. If understanding is to be possible, there must be, in Strawson's phrase, "a massive central core of human thinking which has no history".' (Hollis 1982: 75)

As Rorty remarks in his critique of the philosophical notion of 'foundations' of knowledge, 'analytic philosophy is still committed to the construction of a permanent, neutral framework for inquiry, *and thus for all of culture*' (Rorty 1980: 8, my italics).

One problem with such a construction is the difficulty of determining which elements of 'reason' we are to take as forming the 'massive central core of human thinking'. If rationality cannot be variable, the philosophers' defini-tions of it most certainly are. We can well ask with Hobart (this volume, p.

108) and Hirst (this volume, pp. 87) on what grounds are we then to assume the universal efficacy of reason in human affairs and thought when faced with a virtual war among philosophers of competing standards of reason, and thereby of truth and knowledge? A further and related problem is that rationality itself is not free of faith, the aspect of human experience it most abhors. Underlying rationalism, especially in its more dogmatic dress, are questionable and easily challenged assumptions about human beings, knowledge and order, the world, and the relationship of language to the world, presuppositions that can look both quaint and ethnocentric to the social theorist (see Hobart, this volume, p. 109; Hirst, this volume, pp. 86–7; Barnes and Bloor 1982; also see Rorty 1980).

Ultimately, all social inquiry is directed by the investigator's specific understandings of human nature. As Wolfram remarks in her plea for more attention to be paid to the topic of *ir*rationality, it is not fashionable today to be irrational (Wolfram, this volume, p. 71). And this is perhaps the point. Since the seventeenth century the force of Western philosophy and thought has been against the efficacy of unreason, faith, or experience in the attainment of knowledge.[17] Not only knowledge but human nature itself became identified with Reason as its salient characteristic. As space was denied for sensibility in the quest of science for its mastery of knowledge, as validation procedures were seen to be structured by logic, so too it became the case for human nature. Parkin unfolds (in this volume, pp. 135–37) a hierarchy of values in Western folk usage arising from a popularization of Descartes' views on mind and body that has critically affected the direction of social inquiry. Even the grand debate on rationality and relativism, he argues, is couched epistemologically in dichotomies embedded in Western folk usage which have a very specific historical explanation. From mind versus body or mind versus heart – a popularization of Descartes – we move easily to reason over and above emotion (sense over and above sensibility), intellect over and above living or experience, objectivity over and against subjectivity, the mental over the physical or sensations, the intellect over the will, society over the individual, the universal over the particular, rules over creativity, langue over parole, competence over performance, and so on. Emotions and idiosyncratic creativity are seen as parasitic upon reason and rules. The implications of the embeddedness of such a folk hierarchy of values, where reason is classified as universal and emotions as individual, are clear. In social analysis, in accordance with this logocentric hierarchy of values (see Derrida 1976), we study reason, which is a matter of group behaviour, and not emotions, which pertain to the individual alone. Society works rationally, if individuals do not. As Parkin illustrates, transitivity in Western folk dichotomies slides easily into epistemological dogma. Or another way of seeing this process is to view it as one where the dogmas of the philosophy that explained the success of natural science filtered down into folk understanding of human nature, which in turn fed into the development of the analytical categories within the 'poor cousin' of natural science, the social sciences. Whichever way you have it, the picture is not a flattering one.

In the 'Finale' to his *Introduction to a Science of Mythology*,[18] (1981) Lévi-Strauss presents as elegant an apologia for the reign of reason, for our subject matter to be the logical and the rational parts of culture, as we could find in our discipline. For Lévi-Strauss, the development of the absolute superiority of scientific knowledge (in contrast to the illusions of philosophy and the arts) was possible because of its attachment to Reason, or 'sense', and success in anthropology as in the natural sciences proceeded to the extent that all other modes of knowledge were ignored. A true modernist, Lévi-Strauss believes the success of science, and therefore structuralism, to rest on the denial or the superseding of the past (see Ardener, this volume, p. 48). But in a remarkable two pages in the midst of this apologia (1981: 636–37), Lévi-Strauss bows to his critics and to new trends in the philosophy of science by saying that future progress in all science is dependent upon recovering a great wealth of knowledge that science itself began by sacrificing, i.e. forms of thought that it previously considered as being irrational and beyond the pale (Lévi-Strauss 1981: 637). Science, he says, is 'rediscovering the inexhaustible lessons of the realm of *sensibility*' (Lévi-Strauss 1981: 637, my italics). He suggests further that:

'While it is true that seventeenth-century thought, in order to become scientific, had to set itself in opposition to that of the Middle Ages and the Renaissance, we are now beginning to glimpse the possibility that this century and the next, instead of going against the immediately preceding ones, might be able to achieve a synthesis of their thought with more remote times, whose themes, as we are now beginning to realize, were not entirely nonsensical.' (Lévi-Strauss 1981: 637)

The aim of the contributors to this volume is to explore the possibility of such a synthesis in social inquiry.

In *Magic, Science and Religion*, Malinowski defines magic and religion as modes of behaviour built up of reason, feeling, and will, a fusion of experience necessary for the investigator to understand (1948: 24).[19] Firth in this volume goes further than Malinowski by seeing anthropological under- standing to be dependent upon the ability of the investigator to capture both the sense and the sensibility of behaviour in general – whether it be behaviour that is 'religious', 'magical', or otherwise. The anthropologist, Firth suggests, unfolds the *intelligibility* of behaviour, and not so much its 'rationality'. He goes on to stress that the cognitive process does not act in isolation. He argues that if all behaviour, including thinking, is a blend of reason and other aspects of the self – such as reactions of aesthetic delight, fear, love, anxiety – the implication for social inquiry is that an investigator emphasis upon rationality is misplaced. The issue of rationality is not irrelevant to understanding; but *it is not the prime issue* (Firth, this volume, p. 33).

Each of the contributors to this volume is exploring ways of overcoming the temptations of reason that historically pervade out analytic consciousness. To show the intelligibility of the social behaviour of others, we argue that we must pay attention to multiple expressions of experience and knowledge. To do this, we must beware the tyranny of our own language as it slices up the world, and the assumptions about society and human nature ordering such slicing. These assumptions which inevitably colour our investigations are attached, after all, to specific moralities belonging to Western eighteenth- and nineteenth-century sensibilities. To comprehend ourselves and the degree to which we are blinded by the constraints of the past we need more archaeology of this past, as both Parkin and Hobart present us with in their contributions.

Unreasonable thought, reasonable emotions: the problems of practical knowledge

'much of the emptiness of current social science arises from the attempt to study social and psychological questions with an entirely false ideal of "objectivity" which misses . . . the questions of the greatest importance of moral reflection.' (Putnam 1978: 93)

Here Putnam is expressing his discomfort with the propaganda of Western science which equates science and reason.[20] He sees it as an influence that has led philosophers and investigators of the social in general to neglect or distort other forms of knowledge, particularly practical or moral knowledge which requires for its understanding the 'full capacities of feeling and imagination' (Putnam 1978: 5, 85, 91).

As mentioned above, in so-called traditional societies, beliefs, knowledge, and actions are frankly and inextricably stuck to morality.[21] To render intelligible most aspects of social behaviour, the anthropologist must use evidence ranging over activity which is verbal, non-verbal, emotional, and so forth. Both Holy and Firth in this volume, in speaking on the wide range of evidence required for such understanding, view the dogma of investigator neutrality as naïve, unnecessary, and improbable. Basically their argument is that if one's aim is to understand the beliefs and actions of others on any other than a trivial level, the anthropologist *as an individual* must also be able to react to the reactions of others in a complex way using his/her 'full capacities of feeling and imagination'. They both say that accuracy depends upon the creativity, intuition, and reflexivity of the investigator, as well as upon his/her reasoning and systematic attention to empirical detail. Firth suggests that 'an anthropological interpretation should attempt neither to obliterate the self of the anthropologist nor to obtrude it' (Firth, this volume, p. 34).

Several contributors to the volume, in their analyses of specific behaviour, found that they could understand this behaviour only through sensitivity to a broader context of activity, which included experience that the Westerner might place fully on the side of 'sensibility' as opposed to 'sense'. Firth unfolds the intelligibility of an explosive and ill-mannered emotional outburst on the part of a Tikopian against his father, a chief. What at first appeared to be 'irrational' behaviour took on a different face, a blend of reason and affective reaction, when placed within the context of grief over a death, the love for a son, anger at an unintended slight, jealousy over the rights of siblings, religious duty, and a powerful dream. Overing shows that Piaroa kinship classification, which appears whimsical in application and is highly irrational according to any canons of Western logic and cognitive rationality, is perfectly understandable as a classificatory process that is used, among other things, to express moral judgement on qualities of relationship. The Piaroa kinship terms, or as Overing rephrases them, 'personal kind terms', have heavy metaphysical and related moral loading that allows for their powerful use in the highly flexible areas of the social structuring of emotions and the playing out of political battles. Holy is able to show with considerable elegance the rationales of contrasting Berti models of gender relations, respectively male and female, through his own sensitivity to silence and talk, to different aspects of male and female social existence among the Berti, to their moral judgements of responsibility and irresponsibility, and to conceptual-affective reactions to particular myths on the origin of gender relationships. Parkin shows the power of Giriama divining performance to be based on the persuasive artistry of the diviner which involves an aesthetic moving together and co-ordination of judgement, emotion and body. Parkin argues that it 'is this aesthetic moving together which gives sense to divination', for it 'reduces conflict between judgement, emotion, and the body and so presents them as an appropriate response to disorder' (Parkin, this volume, p. 147). As such, it is a rationality, Parkin suggests, whose intelligibility derives from a coherence of mind, body, and emotion.

Because each of these analyses depended upon the understanding of complex emotional, judgmental and aesthetic responses associated with 'cognitive process', it is relevant to ask whether such understanding dwells in the realm of subjective or objective methodology. Ways of gaining knowledge are here at stake, and the answer is far from clear. As noted above the 'folk' ideology of social inquiry, which distinguishes objective knowledge and less privileged areas of human activity, places emotions on the side of unreason, subjectivity, and the individual, with thought on the side of reason, objectivity, and the group. Yet as we all know, and as the analyses just mentioned demonstrate, thoughts can be disorderly and emotions structured. The expression of emotion is to a certain or even large extent a social matter, and some philosophers are now talking of 'the grammar of emotions' and their rationality (see A. Rorty 1980a: 2, 4, 5; 1980b: 104, 107; Averill 1980: 39–40, 46). The expression of emotions, as language, can be understood, learned, and communicated.[22] Indeed the Piaroa, with whom I lived, gave formal lessons to their children on the proper expression of emotions, which the Piaroa consider part and parcel of the process for acquiring 'thought' (Overing 1985). And just as one can be taught formal logic, one can be taught to master dreams. This is done in many societies where dreams are viewed as a crucial source of knowledge. Dreams, which Firth describes as existing in the interface between social norms and individual interest (this volume, p. 41), can bring order and enlightenment as well as terror. Emotions can also be partially intellectual in source, as Lévi-Strauss observes in his definition of anguish as the frustration of the symbolic faculty and laughter as due to its satisfaction (Lévi-Strauss 1981: 681)!

Wolfram deals with aspects of the problem of distinguishing the reasonable and the unreasonable. As she notes (and Hirst makes the same point), a decision can be rational by the canons of logic, but morally irrational, despicable by moral code. A man can give the most logical reasons for being mean to a wife, mistress, or neighbour. As Parkin argues, decisions are always framed by personal values and inner states, and a 'reason' through imaginative creativity can always be found for acting in a particular way (in this volume, pp. 140, 141–42). In other words, one can usually discover the premises from which to argue rationally for the correctness of most decisions. Hirst demonstrates that the standards of validity and styles of reasoning used in inquisitorial procedures during witch-hunting trials of sixteenth- and seventeenth-century Europe were also 'rational' according to most modern meanings of the term. Premises, and arguments from those premises, have force within the conceptual scheme in which they are set – as too does morality, a hoary topic for discussion below.

Wolfram, however, argues that it is often the case that it is not clear what the claim is when it is denied or affirmed that beliefs are irrational. Wolfram notes that not much attention is paid by logicians to the distinction between believing and asserting, a lack which has led to muddles in the debate on rationality. It is not surprising that she comes to the conclusion that the assertion with intent of both contradictory and false statements is a very common social activity which may or may not be irrational: 'someone may assert p, which is false, as a kindness, a courtesy, a joke, to avoid a quarrel, to win a vote, to get a proposal accepted, to insult, provoke, bewilder, mislead, and so on' (Wolfram, this volume, p. 76). She argues that causes of assertions must be sought in the realm of objectives, while the causes of beliefs in the treatment of evidence. Either can be irrational, Wolfram argues, but

'the ethnographer intent on investigating native beliefs has to find his way through courtesies, deception, mystification, displays of superiority, tall stories, Lewis Carroll humour, and the many other possible uses besides that of imparting beliefs to which assertions may be put.' (Wolfram, this volume, p. 82)

The notion of rationality as decontextualized thought, the ideal of objective cognition which places thinking outside the realm of intentions and morality, is a barren one which at the same time frames questions about human activity in a very peculiar and ultimately pointless way. When we project our own historical dualisms and *a priori* arguments about human nature upon others, as Hollis tautologically argues is necessary to the task of translation (Hollis 1970, 1982), we can never know whether what we understand of others is merely ourselves and the projection of our own common-sense understanding of the world or in fact says something about these others. To move around the impasse, we must begin by being more aporetical about our own conventional package of ideas centring on the nature of humanity. Our tendency to apotheosize Reason, the dominating force that both structures and limits the very questions we ask, is the aspect of ourselves where doubt should begin.

Roads to other worlds and the illusion of fact over value

The issue of the psychic unity of mankind has for the most part been defined in terms of Reason alone. So too have the related issues of translation and commensurability. As the above sections illustrate, many contributors to this volume emphasize the point that reason alone will not enable us to render intelligible most of the behaviour of others with which we are concerned. All of the contributors who speak on the topic of 'bridgehead' arguments (Hirst, Overing, Hobart, and Firth) are highly sceptical of postulating or assuming a set of universals based on a particular philosophical formulation of a cultural-neutral cognitive reference point (e.g. 'laws of thought'). But they all assume that 'points of contact' into other cultures exist that would go far beyond mere 'cognitive process'. Possibilities for such communication would be modes of thinking and feeling that would include the understanding of a range of moral and aesthetic judgements, principles of cooperation and fighting, categories of truth and falsity, the good and the bad, the comic and the tragic, the ugly and the beautiful, the emotions of love, grief, hate, anger, and envy (especially see Firth, this volume, pp. 35–6). In other words, the area of common understanding is most likely broad and complex. But none of the contributors would give priority to one area over another, such as reason over emotion, nor assume a particular universal. As Hirst remarks (this volume, p. 87), 'the [extreme] anti-relativist must explain how our common human nature underlies and is not subverted by very real cultural differences'. On the other hand, the *limiting* of the 'bridgehead' argument to 'laws of thought', 'material-object language', and perceptions of the world of the physical (as did the Hollis and Lukes volume) is biased towards the presuppositions of Western science and self-serving to the goals of analytic Western philosophy. Why else would it be assumed that 'laws of thought' are prior to 'morality', operate separately from it, and are more basic to human nature? As a general principle, we assume that it is no more nor less difficult to learn the social products of thought than the social products of emotion. *Many would go further and say that the distinction itself is a wrongheaded one.*

The extension of potential areas of mutual understanding between members of different cultures has serious implications for the credibility of the traditional distinction between objective and subjective methodologies. This is particularly the case when no priority is placed upon any one particular inner state, such as thinking or feeling, that is, when neither one nor the other is viewed as the bedrock of human nature. We must understand the products and the expression of various types of inner episodes that continually affect one another. Moreover, intellect and emotions alike are both individual and shared. From this perspective the dichotomy contrasting the objective with the subjective is an unclear one based upon a confusion and illusion of our own Western making.

To express the objectivity of the structural method, Lévi-Strauss in his *Introduction to a Science of Mythology* deliberately erases all human agency, both himself as investigator and those who tell myths, from his analysis of myths, an investigation that he sees as being of 'objectified thought', a pattern of conditions of truth that he argues 'takes on the character of an autonomous object, independent of any subject' (1969: 11). His argument for the object- ivity of his approach is basically that he is investigating reason, the con- straining structures of the mind that are universal to humankind, and not idiosyncratic to either himself or the Amerindian teller of myths. To express his intent to erase all subject, himself included, he uses the pronoun 'we' to refer to the author of his work as humankind, instead of the personal pronoun 'I'. Underlying Lévi-Strauss's claims for objectivity are the assumptions and discourse of a neo-Kantian philosophy where the following dualisms hold:

Knowledge

objectivity	subjectivity
science	art, religion
truth	fiction
universals	the particular
thinking	living
object	subject
no human agent	human agency
intellect	emotions
pure reason	unreason
group	the individual
'we'	'I'

All that is required to shatter the substantiality of this set of dualisms, upon which the assumption of objectivity and discourse on it is conventionally and ideologically based, is a deconstructive reversal that shows the possibility of rearranging and blurring certain aspects of these two series.[23] For example, once the category of emotions is placed on the left side of the series, the root paradigm of 'objectivity' (and of 'fact/value') disintegrates. The original diagram can be thoroughly deconstructed in a shorthand way to illustrate a reversal of hierarchies to be depicted as follows:

Knowledge

objectivity	subjectivity
science	art, religion, morality
truth	fiction
fact	value
emotions	intellect
reason	unreason
living	thinking
universals	the particular
group	the individual
human agency	no human agency

Within the framework of this paradigm, one can claim the objectivity of an approach that included the structuring of emotions on similar grounds to those of Lévi-Strauss in investigating reason, i.e., their universality.

None of us is suggesting that the new set of oppositions is one to hold or that it is a 'better' one; for it is constructed through a discourse based on many of the same assumptions underlying the neo-Kantian one. The hierarchical oppositions of the first series assume the priority of the first term (reason) and place the second (unreason) in relation to it as a complication, negation, or disruption of the first. None of us would give priority to emotions over intellect, for instance, as the second series suggests. Nevertheless, to demonstrate the effect of hierarchical reversal has a point. The purpose of a deconstruction is to illustrate the instability of any hierarchical opposition upon which the foundation of a universal is intended.[24] Hierarchical oppositions, such as reason over unreason, are dependent upon reductionism. Reversing hierarchy discloses such reductionism and the ideological imposition upon which the dichotomy was based. It does not so much reveal a new stable point or an indeterminacy, but the multiple aspects of elements and their interconnectedness (see Culler 1983: 134). Emotions are placed in the neo-Kantian 'objectivity' paradigm on the side of unreason, chaos, and the individual. In reversing the hierarchy, it is being said that in the original paradigm only certain aspects of emotions were focused upon; for emotions and their expression can also be on the side of truth, reason, order, and shared group knowledge – while thought has its chaotic and individual side. The outward manifestation of the inner 'states' of intellect and emotions have many attributes in common. The same can be said for aesthetics, intentions, and moral judgment.

It is because the root paradigm of 'objectivity' omits both human agency and the products of all inner processes except the mental that Firth suggests (this volume, p. 34) that it is not meaningful to classify anthropology as 'science' or as 'art'. Most of the contributors feel that the credibility of their analyses is dependent upon the extent to which they are both aware of and take into account human agency. Indeed, as Hobart insists, empirical rigour is impossible without taking cognizance of human agency which would include both the anthropologist's awareness of self, as well as 'the other' using language, reflecting upon its products, and acting in society. It is rationalism, which defines science in terms of the bedrock of pure reason, that ignores such data on the grounds of 'subjectivity'. The human agent, though always there, is therefore ignored. It is obvious that such an omission diminishes one's understanding of most social action and very likely distorts it as well. Ardener notes that structuralism, in converting life into genre and experience into text, failed to generate a practice for social anthropology (this volume pp. 52–3). In using the original set of hierarchies as a looking-glass of reality, one sees only those aspects of practice deemed 'reasonable' by the theory underlying it.

Other theories of knowing – and communicating them

An excellent antidote to the power of our Western hierarchical oppositions and the theory of knowledge upon which they ride is an acquaintance with other theories of knowledge and ontologies. The central concern of several of the contributors, Salmond, Hobart, Parkin, Parry, and Overing, is the description of other theories of knowledge and/or the world. Other cultures have their own understanding of, and theories about, the relation between emotions and thought, between knowledge and thought, between consciousness, will, the passions, reason, and social behaviour. The categories through which members of other cultures discuss such matters and act upon them are far from being identical to our own, but they overlap sufficiently for us to understand and learn them. To do so *is* difficult and requires, as Salmond says (this volume, p. 245), a richness of ethnographic detail that goes far beyond what is normal in anthropology.

What is common to all the schemes of human nature and reality the contributors describe in this volume, in contrast to a Kantian theory of knowledge, is that 'pure' knowledge is never separated from moral or 'practical' knowledge. Parry in his contribution talks about a Hindu science based upon a Sanskritic learning tradition where there is no epistemological divide between moral and technical knowledge. He describes Sanskritic learning and the *Shastrik* textual tradition within it as a highly developed science that is also a theology which devaluates the empirical world as illusion and equates real knowledge with knowledge of the metaphysical. It is believed, he says, that the *Shastras* contain the last word on both science and salvation, and science within this tradition does not therefore constitute an autonomous domain apart from religion. All authentic knowledge, including scientific knowledge, is within the Shastras, texts the words of which are in verse and of the gods, and which have the power of the gods. In this epistemology knowledge is not to be discovered, but recovered from the most ancient texts; for it is they that have been the least damaged by the progressive degeneration of time.

As we have seen with Western science, ideas of truth, and how to go about attaining it, and ideas about human nature are not separate matters. Other theories, based on an understanding of reality different from that of conventional science, usually do not assume that humans are above all either prescriptively or essentially rational, or that emotions are radically distinct from intellect. As Parkin describes for the Giriama and Salmond for the Maori, the distinction between body, reason, and emotion as we make it is inappropriate in these cultures. In both Maori and Giriama semantics there exists a rich vocabulary to speak about aspects of mind, body, and emotions; but as thought and feeling have the same source in bodily parts, the same terms refer ambivalently or polysemically to both inner states. For instance, the subtle and elaborate Giriama vocabulary used to express emotions also links emotional states and expresses intentionality; and Giriama terms for thinking are etymologically rooted in these same terms. Mind–heart and mind–matter distinctions presupposed in Western logic and philosophy are understood differently in Maori and Giriama theories of existence (Salmond, this volume, pp. 246–47; Parkin, this volume, pp. 143–46).

It is made clear in the above contributions that presuppositions about the world affect both styles of reasoning about it and ideas about the grounds for knowledge of it (also see Hacking 1982). For this reason (among others), Hobart in his contribution argues against the universality of the rationalists' 'laws of thought'. He compares Western 'laws of thought' with Balinese ideas of logic and use of inference, and shows that Balinese epistemology is highly subtle and sophisticated (Hobart, this volume, pp. 110, 112). Hobart describes a 'Kuhnian-type theory' as being built into the Balinese theory of knowledge, and he notes that in Balinese epistemology language is recognized as polysemic and double-edged, always affected by perceptions, interests, and intentions of both speakers and listeners. Highly sensitive to the diverse grounds of empirical knowledge, the Balinese are in daily life more punctilious than we are in expressing the relativity of any truth (Hobart, this volume, p. 113). Despite many similarities between the Western and the Balinese theories of knowledge, there are crucial differences that can largely be understood in terms of the different metaphysical assumptions about the world upon which the two theories are framed. The Balinese view the world as a transforming one, and in a continual state of becoming something else. The Piaroa, whose cosmology Overing describes in this volume, view the cosmos as comprised of multiple worlds interacting with one another and thereby in constant transformation (also see Overing 1982). Piaroa metaphysical con-

cepts of space and time are radically different from our own, and uncertainty
about identity is a daily ontological problem for the Piaroa, one which they
endlessly discuss. Hobart argues that transforming worlds fit ill with a law of
identity, a law of non-contradiction, and a law of the excluded middle. He
comments (this volume, p. 117) further that 'even if one allows the laws of
thought as the formal preconditions of intelligibility, they still need to be
applied to the world to which utterances refer'.

In the debate on rationalism, the analytic philosophers have ignored the
knowledge interests and the perspectives of the people who are actually
involved, and therefore logic and rationality are still very much open
questions. Self-claimed rationalists, as Hobart remarks (this volume, p. 116),
assume a prescriptive (or formal) view of logic the universality of which has
yet to be demonstrated. They have nevertheless largely defined the issues of
relativism, translation, and commensurability in terms of this prescription.
Feyerabend (1975) defines incommensurability as two world views based
upon totally different universal premises. On this level one would expect even
the philosophers to agree with the anthropologists: the metaphysical ideas of
the cultures we are describing are incommensurable to our own and to each
other. The critical question to ask and which still must be investigated is to
what extent do premises affect styles of reasoning? The analytic philosophers
involved in the rationality debate have not seriously tackled this question,
mainly it seems on the grounds that non-scientific premises are wrong and daft
(Hollis 1982), and therefore not worth while. However, if they do not do so,
they cannot answer the questions they are asking about logic and the nature of
man, and all remains an 'as if' or 'if so' land of possible worlds, but not actual
alternative ones. As Hobart observes (this volume pp. 115–17), most
'rationality' problems are in fact a problem in communicating metaphysical
principles different from our own. The evidence thus far, therefore, seems to
stand on the side of premises affecting logic, though this too is an assumption
that must be taken with care. As Hirst and Salmond in this volume show,
standards of validity, or arguing and showing that are 'rational' in accordance
with Western concepts of rationality can be conjoined with metaphysical
notions very different from our own. However, there is no reason why several
styles of reasoning cannot exist in the same culture, with appropriate style
being dependent upon what is being reasoned about.

Various contributors to the volume (Holy, Salmond, Hobart, Firth, and
Overing) are concerned with the problems arising in 'translation' due to the
privileging of a rationality that is in accordance with the rationalists' scheme
of reality and mind. In particular, they are questioning certain notions underlying formal analysis and much interpretation of figurative language. As all
five contributors argue, to render 'symbols' and 'metaphor' intelligible
requires learning alien metaphysical and moral presuppositions about the
world which underlie their use. It also demands paying attention to ordinary
language use, the pragmatics of ordinary speech acts, and their context.

Translation is not of words or even of sentences and single statements, but is the communication of another way of understanding things about the world. Words and sentences fit into a particular style of reasoning that gives them meaning as they sit within a network of other words, concepts, thoughts, and actions (on the impossibility of direct translation see Quine 1960; Feyerabend 1975: 287; Hacking 1982; Barnes and Bloor 1982). It is not the word or the statement about which we should be anxious ('the tapir is our grandfather', 'my brother is a parrot'), but an alien style of reasoning and judging based upon a set of universal principles about the world that are different from our own.

Too often we superimpose a particular logic on our data, distorting it, before we have sufficient knowledge to communicate it appropriately. For this reason, Overing argues that the formal semantic analysis of kinship domains in its method and assumptions about the world is an impediment to knowledge of the outsider's comprehension of the use of kinship terms in most 'traditional' cultures. While formal analysis can impose an order with only minimal knowledge of a domain, it also precludes the possibility of learning the metaphysics of others. 'Truth' in formal analysis, as in all brands of structuralism, lies beneath the surface on the level of the unconscious and emerges through the sophistication of the investigator's techniques, not through the acquisition of others' knowledge or learning their presuppositions about the world. To use the methods of structuralism can lead one therefore to underestimate the sophistication of others in the construction of their worlds; for through them the content, form, and richness of these worlds are reduced to a cognitive process, that of analogic thought made manifest through classification. The predication of Piaroa kinship terms, about which Overing writes, takes one to an alien world of explanation and abstract theory construction about difference and similarity in society and the cosmos. Once these principles of explanation are understood, so also can be the predication. Neither the predication nor the alien world of explanation could be learned or expressed through formal analysis.

To reiterate, the issues of relativism, translation, and commensurability in the debate on rationality have been defined by analytic philosophers who have a particular view of humankind and science to defend. Their definition of commensurability, unlike Feyerabend's (one of their real opponents, as opposed to the anthropologist or a Balinese), is in terms of a rationality they say is a human universal and upon which their own paradigm of science depends. If this rationality does not fit, then incommensurability follows; but as they argue, incommensurability is an impossibility, since for them their form of rationality is a human universal. Such discourse on rationality has suited the knowledge interests of these analytic philosophers, and is one based on their own ideas about truth and the set of dichotomies underlying it that they wish to defend.

Beyond modernism and the authority of logics

The issues of this volume are not a matter to be confined to ivory tower rhetoric; for one can no longer be naïve about the relation between the will to knowledge and truth and the will to power, between science and politics. It is Foucault's message that all knowledge is political, that truth does not exist outside power, and that each society has its own regime of truth, the types of discourse accepted as true (Foucault 1981: 27; also see Sheridan on Foucault 1980). Most of the contributors to this volume speak on the power implications of the hierarchical oppositions of the rationality paradigm. Several stress the political significance of the received understanding of rationality – and also question its authority.[25] The authority of a way of thinking and control that is being questioned goes far beyond that which has to do with major or minor skirmishes within science and philosophy. Saltman, Parkin, and Salmond each discuss the immoral effects of the imposition on others of Western rationality as 'superior'. Ardener, in describing Marxism as the archetype of Modernism and the highest stage of Capitalism, notes its continuous success in inspiring bureaucracies and élites to greater and more rigid technical control, a rationally cool success that 'makes it the epitome of the transmutation of the life of politics into genre' (this volume, p. 65). Not only through technology, but also through the myth of its own cognitive superiority which opposes itself to the 'irrationality' of other, the West has imposed its own political, legal, medical, and educational power throughout many parts of the world. Ways of being attached to moralities and epistemologies different from our own are being destroyed without the effort being made to learn first *what* is being destroyed, all in the name of reason, truth, and knowledge. The recovery of disappearing epistemologies is one of the most vital and challenging goals within anthropology. This cannot be taken care of within the context of museums, where the cult of the object is our only concession to the intrinsic worth of these cultures.

Saltman, who discusses the imperialist power of legal rationalism, observes that lawyers of the positivist persuasion base their authority upon the distinction between the validity of their own rational, judicial decision-making process and the invalidity of 'customary law' which is based upon particular moralities. The 'informal' legal systems are labelled by legal rationalists, on the grounds of 'irrationality', as 'defective'. Saltman argues that what is 'rational' is being dictated as an ideological charter by a legal élite in its own self interest. It is Saltman's understanding that in so far as social scientists have the right critically to assess social phenomena, legal practitioners and their ideology are fair prey for critical evaluation as powerful creators of social facts. Saltman examines two instances, eleventh- and twelfth-century England, and the recent history of the Busoga of Uganda, where legal systems based on principles of social order became similarly transformed into systems based on legal rationalism. He argues that the transformation from a legal rationality based on axioms of social order and morality to a formal system grounded upon axioms relating to concepts of power, authority, and the sovereignty of the nation-state to which legal positivism is committed reflects a general trend in modern history towards legal rationalism, but one that is by no means as inevitable as the legal positivists assume.

Informal or 'speculative' systems can undergo formalization without recourse to a power-based axiom – if allowed to do so. Saltman presents the cases of the Kipsigis of Kenya and the kibbutz as both developing alternative forms of systematic legal reasoning (rationalities) based upon axioms defending shared ideological and moral commitments contrary to those of legal rationalism. One definition of rationality, the pursuit of mutually coherent ends by appropriate means (Weber's 'Zweckrationalität' or pur- posive rationality),[26] applies equally to both the positivist and the alternative legal processes. By this definition, as Saltman notes, 'rationality is inextric- ably linked with and relative to specific substantive contexts' (Saltman, this volume, p. 237). For whose interpretation of means and ends is accepted as the most efficient and therefore appropriate (see Parkin, this volume, p. 138)? Hirst makes a similar point when he relates the highly rational standards of validity and legal reasoning of the inquisitorial legal élite to the 'repulsive and ghastly' assumptions and practices of forensic demonology (Hirst, this volume, p. 101).

Salmond argues in her contribution that power relations in colonial and neo-colonial contexts are such as to preclude serious attempts to learn the rationalities of 'the other'. She notes that Europeans from their first arrival in Aotearoa prejudged Maori thought in intellectual evolutionary terms as unreliable, childish, beastly, and philosophically worthless. Seen as devoid of knowledge, the Maori were assumed to be living in epistemological darkness and waiting only to be enlightened by the rationality of the civilized West (Salmond, this volume, p. 256). Westerners then went about abolishing Maori ideas and practices.

Salmond speaks also of the practical political dangers to the peoples of the 'third world' of irresponsible armchair speculations on traditional thought by Western academics, and of typologies created by anthropologists themselves when such typologies arise out of insecure ethnographic detail (Salmond, this volume, p. 260). Supposedly based on 'the facts', these typologies, such as 'the logical' and the 'pre-logical', 'the abstract' and the 'less abstract' and 'more mystical', the 'cognitive conservative' and the 'cognitive superior', have pre-judgement built into them, one that supports both the truth of our own paradigm of rationality and human nature and the type of power rel- ations assumed by it.[27] Salmond concludes that Western thought is therefore often, through the premise of its own intellectual superiority, more *closed* than that of the 'traditional' 'to radical cross-cultural reflection and thorough- going inquiry, and the process of opening Western knowledge to traditional rationalities has hardly begun' (Salmond, this volume, p. 260).

Parry also raises the subject of the legitimacy of typologies, and in particular of the antithesis between 'oral' and 'literate' cultures, the dichotomy his contribution questions. Parry argues on knowledge grounds that simple oppositions are precisely that – simple. Underlying them are mechanistic assumptions about the world, which are false. As Parry observes, the development of particular rationalities can be understood only when one has a good deal of knowledge about both the metaphysics and the politico-economic conditions with which such development is associated. Parry remarks that 'literacy . . . reveals as much about the specific conditions under which ['rational empiricism'] is likely to occur as the Neolithic Revolution reveals about the conditions likely to produce Stevenson's "Rocket"' (Parry, this volume, p. 221). Overing argues elsewhere (1983) that much of our 'observation' language in anthropology, and the use of such terms as 'kinship-based' societies, 'magic', 'mythology', 'shaman', are coloured by nineteenth-century morality and evolutionary assumptions about human nature and human progress. All these labels denote 'lesser', because they are associated with a low level of technological 'advancement'. They also refer to social roles, frameworks of thought, symbols, systems of morality which are all areas of life and related theory that may well be more sophisticated than the same areas of life and related theory in our own society. Ardener notes (this volume, p. 65) that although Western language was 'stretched' by the rapid territorial expansion that took place in the age of discovery, it is nevertheless the case that the 'deconstruction' of these 'stretched' (but still Western) concepts is necessary 'to accommodate the hitherto unaccommodated cultural representations of the muted majority of the World'. Thus, in Ardener's view (this volume, p. 65), the movements connected with language and relativism were the true motors of the epistemological break from Modernism, a child of colonialism, in social anthropology. He concludes by querying how anthropology can in fact ever be 'logically' possible within the vocabulary provided by the present age (this volume, p. 67). In this volume, Overing discusses more specifically the implications of reducing traditional usage of terminology and related theory of personal relationships to our own very weak language of 'kinship'. In so doing, indigenous theory constructions are not only misunderstood, but not seen to exist.

Several of the contributors, then, recognizing the relationship between power and knowledge, as well as the inevitable attachment of each and every knowledge to particular moralities, argue against the notion of a value-free social science on the grounds that such an idea is naïve and leads to an abrogation of responsibility. It also indicates both the passive acceptance of the ideological charter of power and power relations embedded within the Western paradigm and discourse on rationality and truth, and a willingness for one's knowledge to be manipulated by holders of power who operate within this discourse. Several of the papers in this volume are self-consciously not value-free. In commenting on the belief in the cognitive superiority of

Western thought, Salmond states against the rationalists: 'I do not accept the proposition that technological control is a final form of wisdom, nor that other forms of thought do not count' (Salmond, this volume, p. 259). Parkin speaks of the alienation of the Giriama patient rendered passive and mute under the authority of the Western-trained doctor, who literally 'embodies the power of an imposed Western rationality'. Both Hirst and Wolfram observe that there is no problem in judging some actions, standards of credibility and validity as more irrational, evil, and inefficient than others or in noting that some 'rational' action is very damaging to others. Hirst argues strongly against a relativism that does not take such responsibility and equally against the idea that one must use the rationalist's or the empiricist's standards of validity and meta-arguments to do so. We can accept the fact that our own knowledge lacks foundations in independent criteria of validity without having to accept each and any view as valid (Hirst, this volume, p. 89).

In this volume in general it is argued that it is a mistake to separate the issue of morality from the pursuit and grounds of truth. All practice and thought, including science, have their normative and ethical aspects. The implication of this assertion is that 'post-modern' Western knowledge can no longer be naïve about the authority of specific logics and their control by particular élites. In anthropology we deal in our investigations with a broad range of élites who have the power of knowledge – Brahmans, wizards, and in-quisitors, as well as philosophers, scientists, and ourselves. Some of the contributors argue that because all knowledge has power implications, it is the right, the need, or the duty of the anthropologist (as is equally the case for those whose inquiry is of the material world) to comment openly and self-reflectively upon those implications relevant to the particular body of knowledge that one claims as one's own. If judgment *is* to be assumed to be part of the anthropological endeavour, the anthropologist must also justify the standards used for such judgment. Morality is a very tricky business indeed, and because of the separation of fact from value in traditional Western science, Western scientists are not particularly sophisticated or knowledgeable about it. This volume at least raises some of the issues, although I think most of us feel extremely humble in face of the possibility of answers.

Notes

1 I wish to thank Mark Hobart, Ron Inden, David McKnight, and David Parkin for their spirited discussion of an early draft of the Introduction. None of them is responsible for any mistakes or views in the finished version.
2 See Ulin (1984) for a recent and interesting discussion of the history of this debate.
3 Contrast Ulin (1984) and Skorupski (1976) on their respective interpretations of Winch on translation and his use of the Wittgensteinian notion of 'language-game'.

4 The set of problems were quite differently perceived by the contributors Barnes, Bloor, and Hacking.

5 Hollis and Lukes (1982: 18). Also see Lukes (1973), Horton (1973). This position is most unempirical on their part and stems not from observation but from pre-supposition. Contrast Lukes of 1973 with his stance in 1982 (pp. 301–2), where he speaks of social inquiry being, in contrast to the natural sciences, inherently perspectival. This is because social inquiry deals with moral and political judgment, while, in his view, the natural sciences do not.

6 The term 'bridgehead' is, so far as I know, first used by Hollis (1970) in this debate.

7 Especially see Wilson (1970b: xi, xvi–xvii) and Gellner's statement (1973: 173, 175, 178–9) on the total lack of sociological realism of such an assumption that is at any rate based on the propaganda of Western science about itself.

8 It is interesting that in their discussion of the present-day opposition to the rationalist paradigm, Hollis and Lukes (1982) do not mention obvious continental thinkers such as Derrida and Foucault. As Scholte remarks (1984: 961), they never 'sufficiently radicalized the problem of rationality to see it for what it is: an Occidental obsession.' Nor do they speak of Lévi-Strauss, the anthropologist who would be most sympathetic to their cause.

9 Hollis's rhetoric fits the seriousness of the battle. For instance, he labels the notion of the social construction of reality, a 'dry rot' highly disturbing to the rationalist's view of the world (see Hollis 1982).

10 Strawson in *Individuals* (1959) distinguishes between 'descriptive metaphysics', which 'is content to describe the actual structure of our thought about the world', and 'revisionary metaphysics', which 'is concerned to produce a better structure' (p. 9). R. G. Collingwood's use of the term metaphysics in his *Essay on Metaphysics* (1940), comes the closest to the way anthropologists would use the term. He defines metaphysics as the explication of the 'absolute pre-suppositions' underlying the characteristic thought of this or that period of history.

11 See Boyd (1979: 31) and Putnam (1977: 120, 132) who both argue that deference to the knowledgeable expert is a general principle of rationality.

12 Both Kripke and Putman have argued that water is necessarily H_2O, and that water is therefore a proper name of a specific substance (see Schwartz 1977: 28). There are, however, many aspects of 'waterness', e.g., its destructiveness as well as its chemical composition.

13 Many philosophers on metaphor are talking about the use of metaphor in science as an important aspect of the process of creating new theories of the world, and therefore new understandings of it. See, for example, Ricoeur (1968), Boyd (1979), Feyerabend (1975), Black (1962), Kuhn (1979), Goodman (1968), P. de Man (1978), on the topic of metaphor and scientific inquiry.

14 Derrida speaks of the duplicity of all truths. See Culler on Derrida for a clear discussion and overview of his work (Culler 1983).

15 See Barnes and Bloor (1982) who say that the authority of all logics is both social and moral.

16 Gellner can just as correctly be labelled as an anthropologist with a philosophical background.

17 See especially the works of Foucault and Derrida. Also see the *Encyclopedia of Science* (1967) on 'Rationality', where Rationalism is described as a position which opposes 'reason' and 'experience'.

18 See Lévi-Strauss, *The Naked Man* (1981).

19 Ever broad in approach, Malinowski warns us that to understand the 'mental attitude' of others, anthropologists must observe 'the imponderabilia of actual life', that is, both the behaviour and words of others, and their sentiments and desires (1961:18–19).

20 See Gellner (1973: 179) on the propaganda of the empiricist whose aim is to legitimize his mechanistic view of the world.
21 See Gellner (1973).
22 The literature on emotions is a vast one, and the topic is just as complex, controversial, and confusing as the one of 'rationality'.
23 See Derrida (1981) on the effect on dogma of deconstructive reversals.
24 See Culler (1983: 93 ff., 126–34) on deconstructive reversal.
25 See Parkin (1984: 362) on the corrective value of deconstruction in exposing the falsity of such political and academic axioms.
26 It is obvious that consideration of Weber's work underlies much of the discussion of the contributors to this volume. However, to deal explicitly with Weberian thought in any systematic manner, both on the subject of typologies and upon the issue of a value-free sociology, would demand a separate and different volume from this one.
27 Also see Needham (1972: 188) who criticizes the ethnocentrism of ethnographers who continue 'to adhere uncritically to a received philosophy of mind'. Scholte (1984), in a critique of rationalist typologies of cognition, observes that rationalism entails evolutionism.

References

APEL, K.-O. (1979) Types of Social Science in the Light of Cognitive Interests, In S. C. Brown (ed.) 1979, *Philosophical Disputes in the Social Sciences*. Sussex: Harvester Press.

AVERILL, J. R. (1980) Emotion and Anxiety: Sociocultural, Biological and Psychological Determinants. In A. Rorty (ed.) *Explaining Emotions*. Berkeley: University of California Press.

BARNES, B. and D. BLOOR (1982) Relativism and the Sociology of Knowledge. In M. Hollis and S. Lukes (eds) *Rationality and Relativism*. Oxford: Basil Blackwell.

BLACK, M. (1962) *Models and Metaphors*. Ithaca: Cornell University Press.

— (1979) More about Metaphor. In A. Ortony (ed.) *Metaphor and Thought*. Cambridge: Cambridge University Press.

BOYD, R. (1979) Metaphor and Theory Change: What is 'Metaphor' a metaphor for? In A. Ortony (ed.) *Metaphor and Thought*. Cambridge: Cambridge University Press.

BROWN, S. C. (ed.) (1979) *Philosophical Disputes in the Social Sciences*. Sussex: Harvester Press.

BURKE, K. (1966) *Language as Symbolic Action*. Berkeley: University of California Press.

— (1969) *A Rhetoric of Motives*. Berkeley: University of California Press.

COLLINGWOOD, R. G. (1940) *Essay on Metaphysics*. Oxford: Clarendon Press.

CROCKER, J. C. (1977) The Social Functions of Rhetorical Forms. In *The Social use of Metaphor*. University of Pennsylvania Press.

CULLER, J. (1983) *On Deconstruction*. London: Routledge & Kegan Paul.

DE MAN, P. (1978) The Epistemology of Metaphor. *Critical Inquiry* 5: 13–30.

DERRIDA, J. (1976) *Of Grammatology*. Baltimore: Johns Hopkins University Press.

— (1981) *Positions*. Chicago: University of Chicago Press.

EVANS-PRITCHARD, E. E. (1934) Lévy-Bruhl's Theory of Primitive Mentality. *Bulletin of the Faculty of Anthropologists* (Faud I University, Cairo) **11,** pt 1: 1–36. University of Egypt.

— (1935) Science and Sentiment. *Bulletin of the Faculty of Anthropologists* (Faud I University, Cairo).

— (1937) *Witchcraft, Oracles and Magic among the Azande*. Oxford: Clarendon Press.
FEYERABEND, P. (1975) *Against Method*. London: New Left Books.
— (1978) *Science in a Free Society*. London: New Left Books.
FOUCAULT, M. (1981) The Order of Discourse. In Robert Young (ed.) *Untying the Text* New York: Routledge & Kegan Paul.
GELLNER, E. (1973) The Savage and the Modern Mind. In Horton and Finnegan (eds) *Modes of Thought*. London: Faber & Faber.
— (1982) Relativism and Universals. In Hollis and Lukes (eds) *Rationality and Relativism*. Oxford: Basil Blackwell.
GOODMAN, N. (1968) *Languages of Anthropology*. Indianapolis: Bobbs-Merrill.
— (1978) *Ways of Worldmaking*. Brighton: Harvester Press.
HACKING, I. (1982) Language, Truth and Reason. In M. Hollis and S. Lukes (eds) *Rationality and Relativism*. Oxford: Basil Blackwell.
HESSE, M. (1980) The Strong Thesis of Sociology of Science. In M. Hesse, *Revolutions and Reconstructions in the Philosophy of Science*. Brighton: Harvester Press.
HOLLIS, M. (1970) The Limits of Irrationality. In B. Wilson (ed.) *Rationality*. Oxford: Basil Blackwell.
— (1982) The Social Destruction of Reality. In Hollis and Lukes (eds) *Rationality and Relativism*. Oxford: Basil Blackwell.
HOLLIS, M. and LUKES, S. (1982) Introduction. In Hollis and Lukes (eds) *Rationality and Relativism*. Oxford: Basil Blackwell.
HORTON, R. (1973) Lévy-Bruhl, Durkheim and the Scientific Revolution. In R. Horton and R. Finnegan (eds) *Modes of Thought*. London: Faber & Faber.
— (1979) Material-Object Language and Theoretical Language: towards a Strawsonian sociology of thought. In S. C. Brown (ed.) (1979) *Philosophical Disputes in the Social Sciences*. Sussex: Harvester Press.
HORTON, R. and FINNEGAN, R. (1973) (eds) *Modes of Thought*. London: Faber & Faber.
KUHN, T. (1964) *The Structure of Scientific Revolutions*. Chicago: University of Chicago Press.
— (1979) Metaphor in Science. In Ortony (ed.) *Metaphor and Thought*. Cambridge: Cambridge University Press.
LEVIN, S. Standard Approaches to Metaphor and a Proposal for Literary Metaphor. In A. Ortony (ed.) *Metaphor and Thought*. Cambridge: Cambridge University Press.
LÉVI-STRAUSS, C. (1969) *The Raw and the Cooked*. New York: Harper & Row.
— (1981) Finale. In *The Naked Man*. English translation by Jonathan Cape. New York: Harper & Row.
LUKES, S. (1973) On the Social Determination of Truth. In R. Horton and R. Finnegan (eds) *Modes of Thought*. London: Faber & Faber.
— (1982) Relativism in its Place, in M. Hollis and S. Lukes (eds) *Rationality and Relativism*. Oxford: Basil Blackwell.
MALINOWSKI, B. (1948) *Magic, Science and Religion*. Garden City, N.Y.: Doubleday.
— (1961) *Argonauts of the Western Pacific*. New York: Dutton & Co.
NEEDHAM, R. (1972) *Belief, Language and Experience*. Chicago: The University of Chicago Press.
NEWTON-SMITH, W. (1982) Relativism and the Possibility of Interpretation. In Hollis and Lukes (eds) *Rationality and Relativism*. Oxford: Basil Blackwell.
ORTONY, A. (ed.) (1979) *Metaphor and Thought*. Cambridge: Cambridge University Press.
OVERING, J. (1982) The Paths of Sacred Words: Shamanism and the Domestication of the Asocial in Piaroa Society. Presented in symposium on 'Shamanism in Lowland South American Societies: A problem of Definition'. J. Overing, Organizer, 44th International Congress of Americanists, Manchester.
— (1983) Translation as a Creative Process: the power of a name. Presented at SSRC

Symposium, University of St Andrews, on Comparative Methods in Social Anthropology, 15–18 December.
— (1985) There is no End of Evil: the guilty innocents and their fallible god. In D. Parkin (ed.) *The Anthropology of Evil*. Oxford: Basil Blackwell.
PAIVIO, A. (1979) Psychological Processes in the Comprehension of Metaphor. In A. Ortony (ed.) *Metaphor and Thought*. Cambridge: Cambridge University Press.
PARKIN, D. (1982) Introduction. *Semantic Anthropology*. London: Academic Press.
— (1984) Political Language. *Annual Review of Anthropology* **13**: 345–65.
PETRIE, H. (1979) Metaphor and Learning, In A. Ortony (ed.) *Metaphor and Thought*. Cambridge: Cambridge University Press.
PUTNAM, H. (1977a) Is Semantics Possible? In S. Schwartz (ed.) *Naming Necessity and Natural Kinds*. Ithaca, NY: Cornell University Press.
— (1977b) Meaning and Reference. In S. Schwartz (ed.) *Naming Necessity and Natural Kinds*. Ithaca, NY: Cornell University Press.
— (1978) *Meaning and the Moral Sciences*. Boston: Routledge & Kegan Paul.
QUINE, W. V. O. (1960) *Word and Object*. Cambridge, Mass.: Harvard University Press.
RICOEUR, P. (1978) *The Rule of Metaphor*, translated by Robert Czerny. London and Henley: Routledge & Kegan Paul.
— (1981) *Hermeneutics and the Human Sciences*, edited and translated by John B. Thompson. Cambridge: Cambridge University Press.
RORTY, A. (ed.) (1980a) *Explaining Emotions*. Berkeley: University of California Press.
— (1980b) Introduction. In A. Rorty (ed.) *Explaining Emotions*. Berkeley: University of California Press.
RORTY, R. (1980) *Philosophy and the Mirror of Nature*. Oxford: Basil Blackwell.
SAPIR, D. (1977) The Anatomy of Metaphor. In D. Sapir and C. Crocker (eds) *The Social Use of Metaphor*. Philadelphia: University of Pennsylvania Press.
SCHOLTE, B. (1984) Reason and Culture: the Universal and the Particular Revisited. *American Anthropologist*, vol. 86, no. 4: 960–65.
SCHWARTZ, S. P. (1977) Introduction. In S. P. Schwartz (ed.) *Naming, Necessity and Natural Kinds*. Ithaca: Cornell University Press.
SEARLE, J. (1979) Metaphor. In A. Ortony (ed.) *Metaphor and Thought*. Cambridge: Cambridge University Press.
SHERIDAN, A. (1980) *Michel Foucault: The Will to Truth*. London: Tavistock.
SKORUPSKI, J. (1976) *Symbol and Theory*. Cambridge: Cambridge University Press.
STRAWSON, P. F. (1959) *Individuals*. London: Methuen.
ULIN, R. C. (1984) *Understanding Cultures*. Austin: University of Texas Press.
WILLIAMS, B. (1967) Rationalism. In *The Encyclopedia of Philosophy*, vols 7 and 8. New York: Macmillan.
WILSON, B. R. (ed.) (1970a) *Rationality*. New York: Harper & Row.
— (1970b) A Sociologist's Introduction. In Bryan R. Wilson (ed.) *Rationality*. New York: Harper & Row.
WINCH, P. (1964) Understanding a Primitive Culture. *American Philosophical Quarterly* **I**: 307–24.
WITTGENSTEIN, L. (1953) *Philosophical Investigations*, translated by G. E. M. Anscombe. New York: Macmillan.

Raymond Firth

2 Degrees of intelligibility

It is almost 60 years since in the autumn of 1924 I came as a graduate student to the London School of Economics, to read in economics. But in New Zealand as an amateur anthropologist I had read *Argonauts of the Western Pacific* with admiration, and soon decided to throw in my lot with anthropology under Malinowski's guidance. If I say little about Malinowski on this centenary occasion it is because I have already written fairly fully about him, as in a recent essay in which I tried to relate his theories to his personality (Firth 1981; see also 1957). But here I do want briefly to indicate once again the nature of my debt to him in ethnography.

Malinowski's field work has been generally regarded as providing the prototype for modern anthropological field research. I think this is correct, though not in the way often imagined. It has been argued (e.g. Gluckman 1963: 245; Evans-Pritchard 1981: 197; see also Leach 1982: 26) that Malinowski's essential achievement in field work – 'the source of his strength and originality' – was to have lived for a long time in Trobriand villages and to have worked through the Trobriand language without interpreters. I think this is mistaken. Malinowski was distinguished in this, unlike most professional anthropologists of his time. But he did not invent long-period stay in the field, direct observation, working in the vernacular, or the collection of vernacular texts, as the records of many early missionaries and administrators attest. Nor did they fail to collect data on everyday life. Before I had ever heard of Malinowski I had done a little field work by direct observation in rural areas of New Zealand (1924: 1, 23). I had grown up in the tradition of scholars such as Elsdon Best and Te Rangihiroa (Peter Buck), who spoke Maori fluently, lived for long periods among Maori people, and recorded both everyday and esoteric data, mostly in Maori. They published many vernacular texts – some untranslated, because as Best wrote, he believed translation destroyed the poetic quality of songs and invocations.

What Malinowski did was not just to borrow and improve these technical skills; his real contribution was to supply principles of systematic, intensive collection and interpretation of field data to a degree of sophistication not known before. Using an associational or contextual theory of meaning, the sheer analytical power that he brought to bear in enquiry into social relationships illumined both field observation and the subsequent ordering of material. Both his penetrating understanding of ethnographic data and his more general theoretical stance of functionalism took time to develop. The latter in particular had its roots in his Cracow academic experience, as the studies by modern Polish scholars are tending to reveal (Paluch 1981; see also Symmons-Symonolewicz 1959: 12). But it was effectively aided in crystallization by Malinowski's personal relation to many British and European thinkers of the period, with their various emphases on behavioural studies, on associational definition, on the querying of hitherto accepted scientific stereotypes and moral norms. In the field, part of Malinowski's sensitivity was his realization of the significance of the field worker as a factor in the situation he was observing. His diaries were never meant for publication, and the egocentrism and irritation with his human subjects that they reveal are probably more common to field anthropologists than many of us have been willing to acknowledge. But in his published work, while he rather ostentatiously threw his own difficulties and failures into relief, he raised at least by implication some of the important issues involved in what has come to be known as reflexive anthropology. So in line with his thought one moved easily to the position, as I expressed it nearly fifty years ago, on the last page of *We, The Tikopia* – 'the assumptions due to the conditioning and personal interest of the investigator must influence his findings' and that bias should be consciously faced (1936: 599). With the hindsight of half a century Adam Kuper's shrewd – if sometimes highly coloured and over-simplified – version of the history of British social anthropology has justly praised the unprecedented richness of Malinowski's material. Kuper has allowed Malinowski's grasp of the complexities of social reality to have the status of 'almost, (to) a theory' (1983: 17). I suspect that the 'almost' is a reflection of Kuper's taste for 'grand theory', and it is true that Malinowski himself writes of his 'innocence of any ultimate theoretical assessment' of the institutions of *kula* and of Trobriand agriculture (1935: i, 455). But grand theory, like a grand piano, is for concert platform performers, and many of us are content with less sonorous instruments. For the anthropologists of Malinowski's seminars there was plenty of inspiration – for criticism as well as acquiescence – at less 'ultimate' levels. Malinowski's insistence on the importance of the way of posing a problem (*Problemstellung*), his distrust of conventional definitions, his penetrating exploration of the significance of minute behavioural items, his treatment of verbal statements as material for social analysis, not merely as factual evidence, his trenchant pronouncements on what he saw as the fundamentals of human cooperation – all this shot through with his emphasis on no fact without theory, that is, without a relation to general rules – stood out in refreshing contrast to so much else at the time. Perception of defects in his approach was not lacking, but pursuit of these, it was felt, could wait till the more positive gains from his approach could be realized.

The problem of thought process

A recurrent theme in anthropology has been the relation between the thought processes of an anthropologist and of the people he or she studies. Malinowski himself had no doubt that the type of mind and logical faculties of a Trobriander were like his own – granted, as he insisted, that belief and dogmatic thinking are 'alogical' in both cases (1948: 320). But the swirl of hermeneutics since his day has carried the controversy much further, into the nature of reality, the character of meaning, the contrast between rationalist and empiricist approaches, the significance of awareness or unawareness in modes of thought.

The central definition of rationality has been explicitly dealt with from many angles – from early socio-philosophical studies by Max Weber, L. T. Hobhouse, or Talcott Parsons, to later anthropological and sociological enquiries by S. F. Nadel (1951), Bryan Wilson (1970), Martin Hollis, Steven Lukes, and their colleagues (1970, 1982) and Maurice Godelier (1972). More than thirty years ago, in his *Foundations of Social Anthropology*, Nadel raised many of the issues which lie at the root of the matter. As a concept, rationality has had rough handling from several sides. Broadly speaking, rationality may be said to be concerned with the ordering of ideas, the quality of relation between antecedent and consequent at an abstract level – with the relation between premise and inference. Expected of this relation is an element of consistency, exemplified by the lack of contradiction. But another sense of rationality is concerned also (or alternatively) with the nature of the antecedents or premises from which the reasoning begins, or with which it is associated. This is where in anthropology some confusion has arisen. Anthropologists are very familiar with the way in which unexpected inferences or statements presented to them can be traced back to premises or beliefs that do not correspond to empirical reality as defined in well-recognized scientific terms. Whether such premises are characterized as rational or not may depend upon the analyst's view of the epistemological status of science, among other things. But as Malinowski was at pains to point out, the operation of unscientific non-rational thought not subject to verification can apply to all of us – as even Lévy-Bruhl tended to accept in the end, to judge from his posthumously published notebooks. But however unacceptable the premises, the reasoning from them may seem so straightforward that the conclusions clearly follow. Much anthropological exposition deals with just such situations. If anthropologists were faced by a reasoning process of totally different type from their own, an 'alternative logic' in the mental operations of the people they study, then as Martin Hollis (1970: 218) and others have pointed out, how could they ever have access to it? Well before the time of Lévy-Bruhl, most anthropologists have tended to adopt the comfortable pragmatic position that while the premises of thinking may not be shared by them and the people under study, the basic reasoning processes are broadly shared or at least understood. Steven Lukes's expression 'context-dependent rationality', despite arguments brought to bear upon it, seems useful here (1970: 208), implying that the statements of people can make sense if their social conditions and their 'knowledge' of the world be properly studied.

In discussion of such issues the views of Evans-Pritchard have been significant, especially in his defence of Lévy-Bruhl, who, he avers, has been much misunderstood by other anthropologists. Evans-Pritchard's own work, especially his powerful analysis of Zande magic and witchcraft, provided a valuable, clear statement about comparative thought process. But his reflections on Lévy-Bruhl's work have been less helpful. His initial summary of Lévy-Bruhl's position (1934) gave a useful précis, but did not in fact interpret this very differently from the judgment of many of his colleagues at the time. His examination of the 'more serious methodological deficiencies' in the work – over-mystification of primitive thought, over-rationalization of civilized thought; lack of attention to variation in primitive culture and to historical dimension of civilized culture – can be found in essence in other criticism that he dismissed as ineffective, especially in the critique by Marcel Mauss when Lévy-Bruhl read his paper on La Mentalité Primitive before the Société française de Philosophie on 15 February 1923 (Evans-Pritchard 1934: 7–8; Mauss 1923). Recently Evans-Pritchard has been represented as arguing that what Lévy-Bruhl was saying was not that 'primitives' were unintelligent but that their beliefs were unintelligible to us. They are reasonable people, but they reason in social categories different from ours; they are logical, but the principles of their logic are not ours, not those of Aristotelian logic (1981: 123; see also 1965: 78–99). The juxtaposition of 'beliefs', 'categories', and 'principles of logic' leaves some questions of their relative status open. It is also in strong contrast to a passage in Evans-Pritchard's original commentary on Lévy-Bruhl, making a strong, indeed surprising, claim to comparable reasoning.

'As Lévy-Bruhl has seen, primitive thought is eminently coherent, perhaps over-coherent. . . . Beliefs are co-ordinated with other beliefs and with behaviour into an organised system. Hence it happens that when an anthropologist has resided for many months among a savage people he can foresee how they will speak and act in *any* [my italic] given situation. I have tested this fact again and again in Central Africa where I found that my questions to the peoples among whom I carried out ethnological research eventually became more and more formalities since I was able to supply the answers to my questions before I asked them, often in almost the identical phraseology in which the replies were afterwards given. For once we have understood wherein lie the interests of a primitive people we can easily guess the direction which their thinking will take, for it presents the same intellectual characters as our own thinking.' (1934: 19)

One can see what he meant, but this proleptic view of field research is not altogether reassuring!

Intelligibility

In considering rationality another problem arises. The cognitive process does not operate in isolation. In practice, as Mauss pointed out in his critique of Lévy-Bruhl (1923: 28), rational judgment and rational action are interwoven – some would say, inextricably – with elements of impulse and feeling. Where elements of status involvement or strong reactions of grief or anger enter into conduct, it seems pointless to debate whether or not such conduct is rational. What does seem significant is whether it can be seen as *intelligible*, i.e. capable of being understood by an anthropologist from another cultural setting but with curiosity to enquire as to meanings. Steven Lukes has written (1970: 196) that I myself have found the issue of rationality irrelevant. This is not so; I think it can provide a useful opening for enquiry. But I do not think it to be the prime issue, and would give preference to intelligibility. For while rationality is the imputation of a quality to mental process, intelligibility is the imputation of a relationship between authors of mental process, in its behavioural mani-festations. And it is in relationship between anthropologist and people studied – a two-way process – that much of our concern lies. Of course such a position opens up another set of basic questions. What is meant by 'under-standing'? Is it intellectual comprehension by reasoning process alone? Must 'understanding' go beyond purely mental appreciation and be demonstrated by subsequent concrete action? How far is understanding a parallelism rather than a penetration of motive? Is this comprehension after all nothing but a projection of the anthropological self upon the recorded sense data, another instance of egocentric anthropology, the solipsist trap into which we all can fall?

We are familiar with some of the varied answers to these questions. For myself, I see no escape from philosophic doubt on most of these issues. For me there is no fount of certainty in knowledge, but only a continual attempt to refine the intellectual areas of debate. I am not greatly taken with the language of models. But anthropological interpretations are like economists' models in one way – they do not state (except for shorthand presentation) *why* people behave in such-and-such a way; they contend only that the inter-pretations are consonant with the behaviour in an *as if* kind of manner. But granted the *as if* in anthropology – and some of my colleagues would eliminate the *if*, believing that they have more certitude about the ultimate nature of things – certain assumptions are needed for viability in our work.

Assumptions

I assume first that there is a reality in the behavioural phenomena of the Tallensi, Tikopia, Trobrianders, Tswana, and so on that is accessible to observation; that granted some social conditioning of perception occurs, sensory bridges can nevertheless be established between observer and observed. At its crudest, this seems an unnecessary point to make. But in more subtle form it has been suggested that the societies an anthropologist purports to describe are his/her own creation. This notion is close to a kind of secular mysticism – the claim that ultimately the Knower and the Known are One – and it ignores a lot of empirical parameters. True, the terms of description are the anthropologist's own, as is the framework in which the description is couched. But as has often been emphasized, the reports of observation are not simply a series of refractions of the anthropologist's own personality. An anthropological interpretation should attempt neither to obliterate the self of the anthropologist nor to obtrude it. I do not wish to be seen as simply an apostle of the concrete. But I am prepared to maintain the assumption of social entities/individuals separate from an observer but capable of interaction with an observer and with one another; and of being able to be observed, described, commented upon, interpreted. I maintain also that there can be degrees of faithfulness or accuracy in such report, depending upon the carefulness, pertinacity, systematic method, ingenuity, and flair of the reporter. In such broad contention I am an empiricist, though by strict construction my acknowledgement of the value of analogical or intuitional leaps in interpretation would rule me out from philosophical empiricism, which claims to rely solely upon the evidence of the senses. (Martin Hollis has made this point to me in private correspondence.)

In this connection it has been argued that anthropology is an art, not a science. Here I am reminded of arguments in economics around the turn of the century, where after much debate it seemed to be agreed that the subject was both abstractly scientific and humanistically or pragmatically oriented. As I pointed out in examining the question a quarter of a century ago, the labels are not important; what is important is to try to see more clearly what is meant when they are used (1958). Here it is well to recall a comment by S. F. Nadel, himself an artist in the sphere of music. Nadel argued that in field work a sympathetic intuitive understanding was a necessary ingredient, a 'vocational qualification' – for him, to be able to make jokes at which the people laughed was the (rather heavily Germanic) *summa cum laude* of achievement in this direction! But just as some faculty of intuition is indispensable to the creative scientist, so its operation does not make a physicist a mystic, he said, nor an anthropologist a novelist. The sparks of comprehension, Nadel wrote, are not the steady light of scientific understanding (1951: 17–19). To this I would add that a systematic comparison of anthropological monographs (by indigenous as well as by alien observers) with novels by indigenous writers about the same or similar societies, would clarify the issue further.

A second assumption about intelligibility is that in the encounters between oneself as an anthropologist and the people studied there are great areas of similar basic experience of the external world. Many types of social relation have comparable expression in word and act. Such an assumption may run counter to the emphases put by some anthropologists upon relativism and the predominance of cultural conditioning. But I am among those who would argue that comparable dispositions can be identified among all human beings – e.g. starting from defence of personality on the one hand, and urge to communicate, on the other. I would argue too that while the forms of defence or of communication vary greatly according to social setting, often in symbolic ways, they are recognizable as such and can be interpreted by careful study. The resultant institutional categories and patterns are comparable. But while this assumes some likeness in modes of thinking and feeling between anthropologist and subject, it makes no statement on how far elements of reasoning alone are involved.

One shared domain where the logic of process may be grasped almost immediately by an anthropologist is technology – not in its detailed operation, necessarily, but in the principles of relation of antecedent to consequent in operations. I would argue too that economic processes are not just a western invention, but that prudent manipulation of resources in production, exchange and consumption may be discerned in transactions of people in very different types of society, whether of peasant monetary type or other rural non-monetary type, as well as in more complex industrial societies. Reactions of a community to scarcity can be envisaged by an alien observer in terms which allow of comprehension, prediction and cooperation in decisions taken. When in 1952 the Tikopia were faced by acute food shortage after a tropical cyclone, the technical, economic and social measures they took to meet the situation were easily understood by the resident anthropologists, who were able in joint discussion to help in means of relief, using the Tikopia social framework (Firth 1959: 56–105). In a less secular sphere, in what may be called the logistics of ritual, the organization of personnel and supplies to fulfil an obligation of religious worship can be readily appreciated by an anthropologist. Such appreciations may of course differ from one anthropologist to another. When a Nuer master of ceremonies cut a wild cucumber in half, Evans-Pritchard and other commentators were impressed by its significance as a sacrifice surrogate. Granting this, I have also suggested (1963a: 20) that a cucumber is cheaper (i.e. more readily conceded) than the cow for which it ostensibly stands. But the relative weight of symbolic or economic elements in the action is not the point here: my point is that all the themes of symbolic representation, of offering or of sacrifice of material object, and of prudent substitution of less for more valuable property are familiar both to Nuer and to us, members of very different types of society, from our experience at some level. In such contexts too an anthropologist becomes aware of a range of moral judgements, categories of truth and falsity, good and bad, right and wrong, of which he can feel the force and appreciate the application – even though, as with a revenge killing, he may share neither the premises nor the conclusions. All this is very familiar to us. But to cite a further example from recent literature – a very telling demonstration of logical process at pragmatic level is Edwin Hutchins's analysis of a Trobriand land dispute (1980). If a bit over-elaborate in its use of artificial intelligence methodology, this is still a masterly dissection of a mass of carefully recorded evidence about the implications of statements, their relation to cultural codes, and the kind of cognitive process Trobrianders display in litigious conference. It is an analysis that clearly shows the command of understanding that can be reached by consistent probing of a sustained kind.

It is important to note too that intelligibility is a two-way process. The people among whom we work are often anxious that we should understand the reasons for their actions or opinions. They assume that we have similar thought processes to theirs – to judge from their exposition – and on this basis proffer information in causal terms. They clearly have an expectation that when furnished with the correct premises either party can draw the same conclusions and act upon them accordingly. Most field anthropologists will have had the experience of being instructed to carry out a sequence of operations in a ceremony, with each step lucidly explained as a consequence of that which went before.

Mere multiplication of instances does not mean that intelligibility can be assumed without question for all areas of conduct. But the very operational viability of an anthropologist in the field – the ability to conform to social norms with local approval, to foresee and participate in on-going ceremonial activity, or on the other hand to explain in the vernacular what some foreign custom or attitude means – all this depends upon the existence of an extensive shared area of common understanding.[1]

Language and thought

Our common assumption in anthropological analysis has been that language provides clues to thought. As a general assumption this is surely valid; but it has its limitations. Relations between thought and language are extremely complex, and what passes for modes of thought in many anthropological discussions is often no more than modes of linguistic expression. Cognitive anthropology is essentially an inferential study. While thought can flow freely, behaviour, including verbal behaviour, is apt to be more constrained (though sometimes the reverse is true). Thought itself is not directly communicative; it can be turbulent, erratic, inchoate; but in order to communicate, behaviour, including speech, must be relatively coherent, ordered, sequential. Patterns of speech are not necessarily patterns of thought; they can be patterns for expression of thought, but they may also at various levels be patterns for concealing some aspects of thought. The gap between thought and utterance means that our assertions about cognition, systems of thought, patterns of knowledge, the symbolizing process, should be treated as tentative, not tested summations of mental process. Anthropologists may try to escape the dilemma of inference by talking of collective representations, symbols, codes, as if they were independent of the conditions of formulation, which are ultimately those of individual utterance in social context. It seems legitimate to postulate that all these category formulations and rules do reflect mental process in some way. The isolation of principles of identity, complementarity, binary opposition, and so on does surely represent a perception of the structures of basic human ordered thought. Yet at some point all these assertions about what people think, believe, or know have got to be hooked into some body of evidence of a behavioural kind, especially of personal utterance. I do not want to seem captious. But what I want to emphasize is that in this field we are working with gross, crude analytical tools, involving wholesale inference, much speculation, and some introspective analogy. Our generalizations should be accordingly modest.

In the anthropological preoccupation with language and linguistic models over nearly two decades, my own engagement has been fairly limited. But for much of this time I have been occupied, with the special help of a Tikopia colleague, in preparing a Tikopia-English dictionary.[2] I have found it a pedestrian job in some ways but also fascinating to peer into the meanings of words. To make a dictionary is a task I can strongly recommend to any anthropologist with a taste for humility. We may 'speak the language' with some fluency, but having to face the selection of some thousands of glosses in assigning fairly precise yet succinct 'meanings' to vernacular words demands a scrutiny of defining qualities and perception of subtle categories that show up one's deficiencies in information and understanding. I illustrate from an example.

Many of my colleagues are more competent than I am to discuss the epistemological status of figurative language. But in dictionary-making one constantly encounters the problem of whether or not any given lexeme is to be regarded as literal or figurative in meaning, and indeed, how significant is such a dichotomy. An anthropologist, even as dictionary-maker, may not have the sheer time needed to get adequate contextualization to identify precisely the most critical indices of definition in an expression. *Te tafe, te matangi o te moana ki raro* – a current (at sea) is a wind of the ocean below – is to me a vivid and understandable metaphor, in its likeness between impalpable forces and contrast between the spheres in which they operate. But I cannot always claim to have isolated exactly the criterion that is basic to the Tikopia comparison. Take the statement: *A tama tāngata e somo i paito e muna a pou o paito* – of male children growing up in a house it is said they are posts of the house. Is this an intelligible statement? I would think so: sons are to the social household what posts are to the physical house, a major support. (We have an analogous expression – 'a pillar of society'.) But ignoring what some may regard as the chauvinistic male tone of the epigram, in this strongly patrilineal group structure, one must realize that a major house post in Tikopia is more than a structural support to the building. It is a conventional back-rest for seated men, especially men of rank; and in the traditional society it was often a material symbol and putative abiding-place of an ancestor or god, and a site for libation and offering for household welfare. So a post (*pou*) was and still is associated with respect and power. Hence *pou* is preserved in a range of figurative descriptions. The 'man of the house' as husband and father is its *pou*, in contrast to juniors and women. A man's mother's brother, a principal social support, may be sung of as his *pou*, as may a visiting chief because of some genealogical connection giving point to the dignity he brings with him and reflects upon the house. A whale is the *uru pou*, head post, of the ocean spaces. Finally, in an ancient song, *pou* was interpreted to me by a Tikopia commentator as the male organ. (He said rather apologetically: 'You know the mind of a man!' – meaning that I was familiar with the prolific sexual imagery drawn from the material environment.)

Now all these figurative expressions, I would think, are intelligible to us from their associations. But just what do they represent to Tikopia? They involve bundles of rather imprecise criteria: solidarity, stoutness, uprightness of timber; supportive function; status; focus of social interest and respect; power of somewhat indeterminate kind. There is a definite association with males in the instances I have cited, but only one is with sexual maleness, and ritually a house post often represented a female deity. So while I think I have the correct drift of the Tikopia metaphor, it is in rather vague terms of prominent, major, often supportive role in a situation, and not in more precise defining criteria. Of course it may be that for Tikopia the figuration is also imprecise – but much more enquiry than I could spare would have been needed to establish if this be so. Two points seem to me to be significant about these sons and posts. One is the very approximate nature of much anthropological understanding of even simple analogic propositions. The other point is the necessity of making imaginative leaps to comprehend or supply the synapses in the terms of the analogy – and yet the need to control these leaps by close observance of the contextual cultural detail, both verbal and non-verbal. (On the question of how far figurative analogic expression may provide an avenue to further knowledge – a position dear to theologians – I keep to a relatively mundane view.)

An expressive act

The major focus in modern cognitive and semantic anthropology, on linguistic data as object of and aid to interpretation, has been necessary and productive. But anthropologists are often called upon to interpret a combination of verbal and non-verbal behaviour. The situation may be complicated by the fact that one is dealing not simply with culturally coded actions, elements in a system of communication, but also with very personal, individual expressive acts, with focus on medium as much as on message. I illustrate this from an incident in Tikopia in 1929, in which I myself was involved and which set me a problem of intelligibility in a vivid way.[3]

I was writing in my house when I was called: 'Friend! Come! Pa Rangifuri (eldest son of the local chief and a good friend of mine) has become angry!' The word I have rendered as 'angry' was *teke*, which can take a range of glosses, from being unwilling to do something to making strong objection, even culminating in violent behaviour. Sometimes this seems formal, sometimes it seems out of control by the person concerned. This message left the degree of objection open, but when it was also reported that this much respected senior man had been seen striding to his house in a greatly disturbed state people inferred that he was angry, though they were as yet ignorant of the cause. The whole village was concerned. When we got to his house we found him highly agitated. He and I greeted each other with the usual pressing of noses, as publicly recognized friends, but for him this was an unusually perfunctory gesture, and he paid me little attention. He was uttering brief incoherent statements: 'I'm going off to sea'. . . 'They said their axe should cut first'. . . 'But was it for a dirge, no! It was for a dance!' Men were trying to soothe him down by respectful gestures, and to enquire the reason for his agitation. Tears were streaming down his cheeks, his voice was high and broken, his body quivered from time to time. Gradually it appeared that he had burst out from the house of his father the chief without the decorum proper to a son and a commoner taking leave from authority. As he calmed down it was taken for granted by the other men present that the first priority was the re-establishment of normal social relations by an apology to his father. To save Pa Rangifuri's face a neutral person of some status was needed to take him by the wrist and lead him to the chief's house. This role was deputed to me, as his friend and a relative outsider; had I not been there I knew that a Tikopia man of rank from outside the family circle would have undertaken the task, so I complied. Under instruction, I led him off, with merely token resistance, and he apologized formally in a lament chanted at his father's knee, with wails of submission. Publicly, he made no attempt at justification, and amicable relations were soon restored.

The background to his outburst then became clear to us. My friend's son had been lost at sea some months before (as I knew) and he had wanted to make preparations for a celebratory mortuary rite, the formal burial of graveclothes in memory of the dead boy. But when he had gone to ask his father for an axe to begin to cut down trees to make barkcloth for the graveclothes the old chief had temporized, and he had thought his father was refusing him, so threw himself out of the house. (As it emerged later, in private, he had put this down to manipulations by his brothers, whom he had suspected of wanting a dance festival to precede the mourning ritual, so making their drain on family resources take priority.) His father now explained that he had not refused the request for the axe, that he had had something else on his mind, and that if his son had only waited, permission to go ahead with the funeral preparations would have been given to him. After this, the axe was handed over, and the way to the funeral rites was now open.

But how did these matters become intelligible to me? While many elements in this striking situation could be seen as products of rational thought, some aspects of my friend's actions could hardly be described as rational. He was clearly moved at some stage by very strong emotion, which blocked him from more reasoned discussion with his father and led him to stalk off in almost speechless anger.

Language was an essential factor in the interpretation. With nine months' experience in Tikopia I was able to understand instruction and explanation adequately, i.e. my actions in response to what was said to me seemed to accord with Tikopia expectations. But the most important contribution to my appreciation was a long private talk I had with my friend the following day. I discovered that unwittingly his action had been triggered off by a dream. The spirit of his dead son (who he felt had abandoned him in going off to sea) had appeared to him and after some distressing dream episodes had asked to be provided with proper graveclothes. '*Ke ne muna ki a kuou ke fakamasamasa?*' – 'Did you say that I should be made dry?' This dream utterance was the culminating point of a poignant narrative in which verbal and other images illustrated the father's affection for his dead son and desire for reconciliation.

The dream had its logical elements. Though the boy's body had not been recovered, dry wrappings appropriate to a normal burial on land could be interred, together with valuables consonant with his rank as grandson and heir presumptive to a chief. At the conceptual level, the provision of dry garments and wrappings could be held to appease the spirit and restore it to a state of equable intercourse with his past society and the world beyond. Sociologically, this was a rational proceeding too, since rites for the lost dead, notionally rescued from the indefinite open ocean spaces and given a grave on shore, had a cathartic value in putting a term to mourning, which with its taboos had disrupted normal routine for some months past. The provision of dry garments fitted in with other social norms, since wet garments are appropriate only to technical operations such as fishing or bathing, and changing into dry clothing is synonymous with restoration to bodily comfort and social respectability (see Firth 1967: 136).

But the whole situation blended rational and non-rational elements. Sensitized by his vivid dream, my friend reacted to his father's apparent rejection of his request in a way which I came to understand, though initially it seemed unintelligible. It was a way that other Tikopia too seemed to understand, perhaps more quickly than I did. To bury dry garments in a grave from which a body was lacking, and to sit down and wail in mourning for the dead before rising to dance in a festival of enjoyment were procedures of which they approved. In the disentangling of antecedents and consequents language was a vital ingredient. But important semantic indices were also given by the non-verbal bodily signs – the quivering, the tears, the nose of a kinsman pressed to the distressed man's thigh, my hand round his wrist, his gestures as he told me his dream.

I can now make some very summary points about the intelligibility of this incident, and the whole general issue of interpretation.

Summary

1. Interpretation of this incident was not just a matter of cognitive anthropology in any narrow sense. Elements of reasoning were certainly present in my friend's attitudes and arguments, as in other people's judgments upon them – reasoning about priorities, the logistics of ritual activity, the proprieties in conduct. But strong elements of feeling and of willing were combined with the reasoning, in what may be conceived as fusion of reason and affect.

2. The subtle intermingling of rationality and non-rationality came out in the dream experience. To the father it was a spiritual visitation, quite painful yet in a way also comforting since it put him once again in touch with his lost dead son. To the anthropologist it was an involuntary effort of the psyche to come to terms with a traumatic emotional situation in a figurative way which could give it some semblance of order and some resolution by activity. Dreams and their allied spirit medium representations have long seemed to me, in Kelantan as in Tikopia, to be fruitful areas for anthropological study, since they appear at the interface between social norms and individual interests. Material of this kind can indeed help one to understand the degree of significance attached to social norms in the life of the individual. To the old complaint that we should keep clear of psychology I would reply that we need not less but more adequate psychology, if only to understand better how social norms are envisaged and interpreted by individual action; the values

attached to them; and how the nuances of symbolic expression are created and transmitted through personal channels.

3. Much behaviour, non-verbal and verbal, can be regarded as signals, i.e. with intent to communicate messages about the state or intentions or views of the person issuing them. But a communication model alone may be inadequate for understanding the behaviour. Some aspects of action may be essentially expressive rather than communicative, concerned primarily with the self rather than with the other. Often there would seem to be a subtle blend of both.

4. Whatever be the logical status of the verbal and non-verbal acts that an anthropologist is studying, at some point one may have to adopt some empathy, not merely sympathy, with the people involved. Unpalatable as such an admission may be, much of our direct interpretation in the field shows a projection of one's own ideas as a social being on to the actions of one's object of observation, also a social being. In the case just discussed I had to assume that anger and agitation were reactions to antecedent circumstances of frustration and opposition, and that the demonstration was expressing this. What those circumstances were could be elucidated. How much of status affront, calculation of future benefit, memory of former sibling antagonism was commingled with grief and bitterness about the loss of a son, I could not know with precision. But my comparative experience of frustration, albeit very different in context and scale, made such a combination comprehensible to me. Yet while I see no grounds for denying an assumption of some empathy with the people we observe, I do not think this means that an anthropologist is simply imposing his/her own ideas upon the situation. To inventory is not to invent the culture one is studying. An anthropologist is often in a position to test an interpretation by later checking. If one is an active participant in a situation, clues from other participants may both guide towards interpretation and confirm or modify it.

5. Interpretation is not a simple one-way process, like sucking information out of a bottle with a straw. It is a process in motion, a multiple operation of give-and-take. 'Understanding' can be problematic for locals as well as for anthropologist, and in consequent discussion and speculation the anthropologist may become a source of opinion or a testing-block for local assertion.

6. Interpretation, understanding, meaning are often spoken about by anthropologists as if they come in complete packages, all or nothing. My argument to the contrary is that since many social phenomena we study are extremely complex, interpretation is not a holistic affair. We should not be afraid of saying we only partly understand. The time factor is often important. What we call 'events' are not neatly tailored to fit the time frame of the anthropologist's period in the field. So one may see only a partial sequence, and not appreciate the full development. One may perforce base one's interpretation on abstraction from a very limited set of examples, with incomplete range of

variation or incomplete context. To put it bluntly, when generalizations are made, for instance, about the symbolic significance of objects such as cucumbers, milk trees, house posts, or pangolins, these should not be read as necessarily the eternal verities of thought for the particular society, but as contingent figurations, abstractions from specific statements or specific acts observed, the products of particular individuals, with currency perhaps quite limited in time and place.

7. The time dimension of our inferences is important in another way, in that we have to think of interpreting not just static bundles of reasoned or emotional action, but a behavioural flow, often with turbulence. There is constant readjustment of the elements to one another. The concept of network has taken the fancy of some anthropologists and sociologists, from Radcliffe-Brown onwards. Now the connections of ordinary elements in a network are not constantly altering. But one might borrow from polymer chemistry the notion of macromolecules in complex networks of physical entanglement, with fluid properties. There appears to be a new discipline of rheology (from the Greek term for motion of liquids, literal or figurative), concerned with the flows and deformations in the constitutive behaviour of any polymeric liquid. Can we look forward to a rheological anthropology, which will focus upon the progression of events in communities, as a complex behavioural flow, not smooth but commonly interrupted by the agitation, disorder, and spasmodic turbulence of individual or special group expression? We need more than the episodic character of the Tikopia illustration I have just given, or the dramatic emphasis of a Kenneth Burke or a Victor Turner, and more too than a Marxist assertion of historical inevitability. We need a conception of social change in which there is continued if turbulent flow between structural demands and personal wants, between conformity to codes and individual assertion, between mundane pragmatic interests and the call to more figurative, symbolic modes of expression. An introduction of the time perspective once again aligns anthropologist with historian, a relationship that I have always considered to be profitable to both.

8. So far I have been discussing mainly what may be called secular phenomena, not calling for any notably different sets of assumptions about the reality involved. Problems of another order arise in the religious field, where the issue of rationality, even intelligibility, can become acute. For here, though the issue is often muted, assumptions about the nature of the phenomena divide anthropologists deeply. As we know, on the one side are those who look on conceptions of the spirit and of the divine as purely human constructs, of an elaborate imaginative and aesthetic order, but products of the human condition. On the other side are those who see such ideas as manifestations, however obscure and distorted, of the relation of God to man, an apprehension, intuitive or by revelation, of a mystery that lies behind all the ritual and imaginative constructions. Ultimately there can be no reconciliation of such contrasted interpretations. But in intermediate phases

the task of seeking intelligible relationships in the phenomena has been pursued by many anthropologists with considerable success, as ASA monographs edited by Richard Werbner on regional cults and by John Davis on religious organization and religious experience, or the volume on sacrifice produced under the contrasted auspices of Michael Bourdillon and Meyer Fortes, or the interpretations of Biblical myth by Edmund Leach, have all amply demonstrated. A holistic approach to the history of anthropological theory may well show how many apparently neutral generalizations about religion and allied matters in actuality have been shaped by or have been consonant with the author's specific preconceptions about the nature of ultimate reality and the forces by which human activity is controlled. Up to the present, the fiction of neutrality has been well preserved, and there are distinct advantages in continuing it. But this is another issue.

9. Finally, what of the future? In the forty years or so since Malinowski died there have been very great advances in social anthropology, if only in bringing to the surface issues that previously were latent or put aside for more urgent needs. The result may seem to some as if the age of innocence has given way to the age of ambiguity, and it is still uncertain whether the knowledge of good and evil has paid off. Field work, for example, is represented no longer as a simple gathering of information but variously as initiation, as the enactment of a fiction, as dramaturgy, as the decipherment of an unwritten text, as unravelling of a puzzle, a mystery. It may be any or all of these depending on circumstances, including the reactions and imagination of the field worker. But essentially these 'encounters of the human kind' are attempts of the self to understand the behaviour of the other, by interpreting the particular in terms of the general, itself in process of constant re-formulation. This is so for all human interaction. What distinguishes anthropological enquiry is the object of the communication, the kind of questions to which answers are sought, and the methods of systematic observation by which they are pursued. In these respects I look to advancing sophistication as time goes by. On one point I have special concern. Whatever the swirl of theory, we are committed to the core of our discipline, a sound ethnography according to our lights, an ethnography inspired by theory but grounded in solid empirical data. 'Respect for the material' is one of our canons. And to secure this, however the anthropologist may get immersed in the life and way of thought of his subjects, he/she must preserve enough detachment to remain in control of the intellectual framework of the enquiry. If at this stage the intelligible pre-supposes the rational I think this is a predicate of the scientific enterprise.

Notes

1 If this seems to point in the direction of Adolf Bastian's *Elementar-Gedanke* or Malinowski's model of culturally conditioned 'basic drives' I would say only that

historically there is some common ground but that my approach is more pragmatic and more specific. Malinowski's heroic attempt, e.g. to provide a 'scientific theory of culture' was too formalistic and too simplicist to meet modern efforts to unravel the very complex web of human interaction, with its many symbolic patterns not at all clearly relatable to 'basic' human endowment, needs or ideas.

2 From a phonological standpoint I have examined Tikopia phonemes L and R (rarely found together in a Polynesian language), with comment on the phonoaesthetic quality of L words (Firth 1963b). In semantics, I have explored the concept of *pali*, akin to taboo, with some account of how I came to recognize its meaning (Firth 1966). See References (Firth 1985).

3 Long ago, as an illustration of the dynamic aspect of social organization, I gave a more detailed account of this incident (Firth 1971 (1951): 61–72); here I want to bring out some methodological issues not there discussed.

References

EVANS-PRITCHARD, E. E. (1934) Lévy-Bruhl's Theory of Primitive Mentality. *Bulletin Faculty of Arts* (Fuad I University, Cairo) **II**, pt. 1 (extract): 1–36.

— (1965) *Theories of Primitive Religion*. Oxford: Clarendon Press.

— (1981) A History of Anthropological Thought (ed. André Singer). London: Faber & Faber.

FIRTH, R. (1924) The Kauri-Gum Industry: Some Economic Aspects. Wellington, New Zealand: W. A. G. Skinner, Government Printer.

— (1936) *We, The Tikopia: A Sociological Study of Kinship in Primitive Polynesia*. London: Allen & Unwin.

— (1957) Introduction: Malinowski as Scientist and as Man; The Place of Malinowski in the History of Economic Anthropology. In Raymond Firth (ed.) *Man and Culture*. London: Routledge & Kegan Paul. 1–14, 209–27.

— (1958) Social Anthropology as Science and as Art. Dunedin: University of Otago.

— (1959) *Social Change in Tikopia*. London: Allen & Unwin.

— (1963a) Offering and Sacrifice: Problems of Organization. *Journal Royal Anthropological Institute* **93**, pt.1: 12–24.

— (1963b) L and R in Tikopia Language. *Oceanic Linguistics* II, no. 2 (Winter): 49–61. Honolulu: University of Hawaii.

— (1966) The meaning of *pali* in Tikopia. In C. E. Bazell *et al.* (eds) *In Memory of J. R. Firth*. London: Longmans. 96–115.

— (1967) *Tikopia Ritual and Belief*. London: Allen & Unwin.

— (1971) *Elements of Social Organization* (1951). London: Tavistock.

— (1981) Bronislaw Malinowski. In Sydel Silverman (ed.) *Totems and Teachers: Perspectives on the History of Anthropology*. New York: Columbia University Press. 103–37.

— (1985) *Tikopia-English Dictionary: Taranga Fakatikopia ma Taranga Fakainglisi*. Auckland, New Zealand: Auckland University Press; London: Oxford University Press.

GLUCKMAN, M. (1963) *Order and Rebellion in Tropical Africa*. London: Cohen & West.

GODELIER, M. (1972) *Rationality and Irrationality in Economics* (translated by Brian Pearce). London: NLB.

HOLLIS, M. (1970) The Limits of Irrationality. In Bryan R. Wilson (1970): 215–20.

HOLLIS, M. and LUKES, S. (eds) (1982) *Rationality and Relativism*. Oxford: Basil Blackwell.

HUTCHINS, E. (1980) *Culture and Inference: a Trobriand Case Study*. Boston, Mass.: Harvard University Press.

KUPER, A. (1983) *Anthropology and Anthropologists: The Modern British School*. London: Routledge & Kegan Paul.

LEACH, E. R. (1982) *Social Anthropology*. London: Fontana.

LÉVY-BRUHL, L. (1923) La Mentalité Primitive. *Bulletin de la Société française de Philosophie* 23e Année, no.2: 2–48.

— (1931) La Mentalité Primitive. (Herbert Spencer Lecture, delivered at Oxford 29 May 1931). Oxford: Clarendon Press.

LUKES, S. (1970) Some Problems about Rationality. In Bryan R. Wilson (ed.) *Rationality*. Oxford: Basil Blackwell.

MALINOWSKI, B. (1935) *Coral Gardens and Their Magic*, 2 vols. London: Allen & Unwin.

— (1948) Baloma, the Spirits of the Dead in the Trobriand Islands (1916). In Bronislaw Malinowski, *Magic, Science and Religion and Other Essays*, selected with Introduction by Robert Redfield. Glencoe, Ill.: Free Press. 125–227.

MAUSS, M. (1923) Discussion in Lévy-Bruhl (1923), 24–29.

NADEL, S. F. (1951) *The Foundations of Social Anthropology*. London: Cohen & West.

PALUCH, ANDREJ K. (1981) The Polish Background to Malinowski's Work. *Man* **16**: 276–85.

SYMMONS-SYMONOLEWICZ, K. (1959) Bronislaw Malinowski: Formative Influences and Theoretical Evolution. *Polish Review* **4**, no 4: 1–28 (reprint).

WILSON, BRYAN R. (ed.) (1970) *Rationality*. Oxford: Basil Blackwell.

Edwin Ardener

3 Social anthropology and the decline of Modernism

The discussion of Modernism as a Western cultural movement, expressed in a number of tendencies in art and thought that are now perceived to be in decline or collapse, is widespread in general literary circles. It is, perhaps, dangerous for social anthropologists to intervene, but they have a genuine interest, if only because of the involvement in these developments of some of the theories popular in social anthropology in the last decade or so. At the same time, there has been a trajectory in social anthropology itself which needs a name and which I am prepared to relate to Modernism. This paper was originally conceived for a general intellectual audience, and I have delivered its theme to at least one such. I am preserving the somewhat broad-brush treatment, as I do not expect its argument to be other than provisional. I do, however, address some genuinely puzzling matters.[1]

To begin with, something characteristic of the twentieth century, but which derives from the second half of the nineteenth century, *has* been in decline of late – something that can be summarized as a belief in the once-for-all distinction between the present age (called 'Modern') and the past. Yet, if that something is to be called Modernism, there are as many versions of it as there are speakers and subjects. It resembles one of those indigenous concepts with which we are so often concerned in our fieldwork. In the second part of this paper the essentials of a definition of Modernism are laid out in the only way possible – by constructing a general pattern from its various expressions in different fields and disciplines. Readers can turn straight to this if they wish. The term is there exemplified, rather than defined, from certain ways in which social anthropology developed. From this it seems clear that 'Modernism', if it is applied to social anthropology, has its own particular meaning, and some important discrepancies occur between its understanding there and in neighbouring fields. Perhaps those between social anthropology and literary criticism are most interesting and striking. A main purpose of this paper is to suggest that Structuralist approaches which are called 'Post-Modernism' (i.e. *not* Modernism) in literary circles, are far from 'Post-Modern' in social anthropology, but are a late stage in Modernism itself, albeit an interestingly marked one.[2]

No general or consistent definition of Modernism is usually required or offered by those who engage in literary or artistic debate. It would seem on the face of it, therefore, that it is quite hopeless to relate the uses of a term like this to our own aspirations for precision. There are two points to bear in mind here. The first is that it is a well-known feature of social anthropology that its own general ideas also, in fact, lack precision of definition. Over many years of trying to examine what social anthropology is about, I have been forced to the conclusion that there is no account of the intellectual history of social anthropology in the usual terms ('Functionalism', 'Structural-Functionalism', 'Structuralism', and so on) that would command universal support.[3] Yet these terms are consistently used. Social anthropology clearly falls into the artistic spectrum in its habits of self-nomenclature. The second point, and it is an explanation of the first, is that social anthropology is part of the movement of 'Modernism' itself, and we are both subject and object of any discussion of it. The announcement of Functionalism by Malinowski was, as we shall see, a typically Modernist act, which leads us to ask how subjects like social anthropology do partake of general social movements. Furthermore, general movements of this kind are ultimately all we have in the way of a past, in the unthinking memories of our successors. In a study of our own society they are the equivalent of our own myths. So any discussion of this subject is related to the history of social anthropology as we live it daily.

'Modernist' declarations always come to us in the quite specific dress of their own subjects or fields, yet there is (underlying all the specificity) a surprising generality of tone, metaphor, and expression. For this reason I do not intend to give a definition of 'Modernism' now, but to allow its nature to emerge from its appearance in social anthropology. A few points may, however, be anticipated. One is that Modernism was a movement of manifestos. Modernists declared new ages, created of new forms, and in some cases the manifestos were themselves all that the new age consisted of. Other movements had previously proclaimed new ages but usually as a restoration of past virtue: the new ages proclaimed by Modernism are totally new, and associated with extremely specific technical ends, as we shall see. It 'knows' that there are historical movements, and it undertakes to label new ones in advance, as it were. Not surprisingly, some of them did not 'happen' – another mark of Modernism – and that is the reason why there cannot be any definition of it that is based on common content, only one based on common aspirations. It is a myth not a philosophy. Resting as it did on a denial – better, on a superseding – of the past, it is clearly a reflection of the optimistic phase of the scientific, industrial and social revolutions that followed the Enlightenment. This is not the Romanticism of the first phase.[4] It is cool, it is rational, it supersedes history but it is the very peak of history, it is active, it is organized, it is able to solve, it is able to redefine – it is indeed the 'very model of a modern Major-General'. Although we should scrutinize carefully the credentials of any movements defined as 'Modern', such was the force of the historical tendency that even the weaker brethren were borne up by it. In the words of President Kennedy (a Modernist if ever there was one!), 'When the tide comes in even the beached boats are lifted'.

These remarks have not yet provided a definition, but they have touched on the reason why Modernism goes undefined: it has for long been the water in which the ordinary intelligentsia, goldfish-like, has swum – and as everyone knows, 'Fish are the last to discover water'. I know no better expression of the Modernist condition than these words of Ortega y Gasset (who was also an early critic):

'The very name is a disturbing one; this time calls itself "modern"; that is to say, final, definitive, in whose presence all the rest is mere preterite, humble preparation and aspiration towards this present. Nerveless arrows which miss their mark!'[5] (1961: 25)

Functionalism and structuralism

Let us start with what lies at the heart of Modernism in our subject. Malinowski, an anglicized Pole whose centenary fell in 1984, was associated with the anthropological movement, method, or outlook we know as 'Functionalism'. This, I shall propose, is the form that Modernism took at its developmental stage in social anthropology. Malinowski was a person of such personal charisma that he was felt by his contemporaries to have invented Functionalism. He encouraged this view. Indeed he said:

'Let me confess at once: the magnificent title of the Functional School of Anthropology has been bestowed by myself, in a way on myself, and to a large extent out of my own sense of irresponsibility. The claim that there is, or perhaps that there ought to be, a new school based on a new conception of culture and that this school should be called "functional", was made first in the article s.v. "Anthropology" in the 13th edition of *The Encyclopaedia Britannica* (1926). Among the various tendencies of modern anthropology, I there claimed a special place for "the Functional Analysis of Culture". And I briefly defined this method as follows: "This type of theory aims at the explanation of anthropological facts at all levels of development by their function, by the part which they play within the integral system of culture, by the manner in which they are related to each other within the system, and by the manner in which this system is related to the physical surroundings. It aims at the understanding of the nature of culture, rather than at conjectural reconstructions of its evolution or of past historical events."

'I was fully aware then that I was speaking of a New Movement, which hardly existed, and that in a way I was making myself into the captain, the general staff, and the body of privates of an army which was not yet there. The only thing which I can claim in extenuation of this act of self-appointment was that it was not done without some sense of humour.

"Oh, I am the cook and the captain bold,
And the mate of the Nancy brig:
And the bo'sun tight
And the midship mite
And the crew of the captain's gig . . ."
(. . . and, as many of my colleagues would suggest, for the same reason
. . .).'[6] (Malinowski 1932: xxix–xxx)

At this stage Functionalism had obviously many idiosyncrasies which were related to the interests of Malinowski as a person. Many of these were discussed by Leach in 1957 and in various writings since (see Jarvie 1963; Leach, Jarvie, and Gellner 1966).[7] It takes some delicacy of analysis to sift out its essential features, as we shall see later. For the moment we note only its most striking one – its phenomenal success. Between approximately 1920 and his death in 1942 Malinowski completely rearranged social anthropology, while his pupils occupied a dominant position from 1945 to at least 1970. High Functionalism is the name used here for the period of Malinowski's own activity. The second, post-war period, has come to be known as Structural-Functionalism, or the period of Consensus. The latter had special features which we shall deal with, and it was finally challenged by other views, some short-lived (e.g. Transactionalism), and one in particular very powerful. This was Structuralism, which itself was also an expression of Modernism and which passed through its own trajectory of rise and fall, ending in frag-mentation among movements of a quasi-Structuralist type – Structural Marxism, flirtations with Hermeneutics and the ideas of Ricoeur, Derrida, Lacan, and the like. Most of these interests declined in the later 1970s and with them Modernism, in the social anthropological sense, is over (see *Figure 3.1*). The rest of this paper is essentially an amplification of this argument.

Of course, the ideas of the period are not, in some simple way, now abolished from the scene. Intellectual movements crystallize in persons and places, countries, and university departments. They become embodied or located. They continue their spread to other persons, or places, or into other intellectual fields. Thus the New Archaeology has virtually retraced the steps of Structuralist Anthropology, and although it is a movement of the 1980s, its sources are of the 1950s, 1960s, and 1970s.[8] Structuralist Anthropology took its own title and early models from the Structural Linguistics of a generation before that. Indeed Saussure's *Cours*, a nowadays much misunderstood

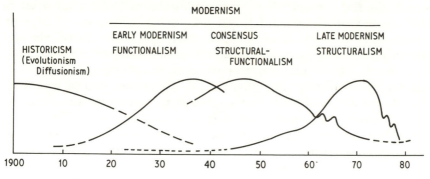

MODERNISM

| | EARLY MODERNISM | CONSENSUS | LATE MODERNISM |
| HISTORICISM (Evolutionism Diffusionism) | FUNCTIONALISM | STRUCTURAL-FUNCTIONALISM | STRUCTURALISM |

1900   10   20   30   40   50   60   70   80

Figure 3.1   Trajectories in British social anthropology

founding text of Linguistic Structuralism, came into being at the very moment (1916) that Functionalism was being gestated in Social Anthropology. The out-of-phaseness of such developments in different disciplines is common-place. Yet their actual contemporaneity produces effects that create still more confusion. Thus, Anthropological Structuralism was affected by the later Transformational Linguistics of Chomsky, with which it coexisted. The later Lévi-Strauss has thus some obvious affinities with Chomsky, greater in some respects than those with Saussure. The stress on structures located in the mind, and vocabulary of 'transformation', are obvious examples.[9] Similar 'time-warps' occurred as soon as other disciplines in their turn borrowed from Lévi-Strauss, as we shall see.

For non-anthropologists this is confusing, but for anthropologists an additional confusion occurs as a result of receiving echoes at second or third hand from other subjects of its own terms and concepts. It would frequently be better if each new application had a new name, for the ultimate sources of terms are not in the end irrelevant. Sometimes issues which have been thought through already somewhere else are raised as novelties in one context. They will probably not have been solved, but perhaps clear objections will have emerged that must be taken into account. Some issues may have turned out to be blind alleys. For an example of terminological echoes, consider the following. An article on 'The Post-Structuralist Position of Anthropology' was published in 1978 by Kirsten Hastrup, discussing a paper in which the term had been proposed, which was itself delivered in Oxford by myself in 1973 (Ardener 1978, 1980). Professor Godelier rose at that meeting and announced himself also to be a Post-Structuralist. The 1973 presenter described the application of the term as part of a technical argument. When Professor McCabe (a literary critic) calls himself a Post-Structuralist therefore, or when the *Daily Telegraph* attempts to define Post-Structuralism, we are in a different world.[10]

We have no right to make adverse criticism of this, when we in our turn examine the development of Lévi-Strauss's thought amid the ruins of his often wilful misunderstanding, not only of ethnographic sources, but of a dozen contemporary thinkers; or when Lukes finds the sources for Durkheim's *Elementary Forms of Religious Life* defective, or misconstrued as evidence. Do Durkheim's findings thereby rest on no evidence, or does his 'evidence' no longer matter? To use an idea from the 1973 paper I referred to, we would often be best advised to 'cut the painter' linking us to our stimulating authors, and to let the doomed *Titanic* steam on its way, while we row our own course. That advice is easier to give than to take, it would seem: hitching a ride from these impressive vessels is extremely tempting to many, especially when one's own barque is in the doldrums!

Genre and life

The development of anthropological ideas is of interest in illuminating this phenomenon. Anthropology at the creative stage consists of the transmuting of a certain kind of experience into a certain kind of text. For a time, only the actual or a similar experience can produce such texts. Later, however, people become skilled in imitating the texts themselves. What was once *life* becomes simply *genre*. Similar processes occur in literature as well as in anthropology – indeed there they are endemic. Thus, although *Jane Eyre*, a great novel which pulsates with its creator's own pugnacious life, remains greater than its shadow, *Rebecca* (or the winner of the Betty Trask Award for romantic novels, or its other ultimate genre successors), many readers can hardly tell the difference, and many will prefer the newer texts. Anthropology passes through this transformation quite commonly. After great innovations even the pupils are great, but soon what once required genius is now performed or 'thought' merely as a matter of professional course. *As experience is made text, life becomes genre.* Within a genre *texts* generate texts. There are therefore two kinds of texts, or texts brought into being in different ways.

LIFE

EXPERIENCE $\longrightarrow$ TEXT
TEXT $\longrightarrow$ TEXT

GENRE

Figure 3.2

It is an irony that Lévi-Strauss really did show us how texts create text. He is, we may go so far as to say, the great anthropologist of genre, for The Myth as Text is the very apotheosis of genre. Nevertheless, Myth is, in its oral state, continually restored to life by 'mute inglorious Miltons', and this actual life of myth was inaccessible to much 'cook-book' Structuralism that followed Lévi-Strauss's lead. Of course, Lévi-Strauss did fitfully illuminate the other problem, because his texts are after all the brass-rubbings of the ethnographic experience of other ethnographers, of indigenous story-tellers, or of his own; for Lévi-Strauss is still an anthropologist, and *Tristes Tropiques*, for example, is one of the documents of his transmuted experience.

Nevertheless, we know what is meant when it is said that the failure of Structuralism was to generate a practice, or if you like a 'praxis' for social anthropology. It is necessary to add at once that we require something rather more thoroughgoing for a social anthropological practice than for, say, a literary praxis. In so far as he solved, or made trivial, the matter of text generating text, he did produce a praxis for text; and ultimately that is what has sped through literary circles. And why should it not? He himself refers to Dumezil and V. Propp, while the much neglected Czech (or really Slovak) school of folklore analysis had already been influenced by the semiology of Saussure and Structural Linguistics when Lévi-Strauss was an unknown. Listen to the very titles of Bogatyrev (1931): Prispevek k Strukturalniz-etnografii (*Slovenska miscellanea*, Bratislava), or (1935): Funkcno-Strukturalna metoda a metody etnografie a folkloristiky (*Slovenske Pohl'ady*). In addition there were other sources, discussed elsewhere.[11] Roland Barthes, for example, was an easier transmitter of Structuralism to the thinking masses than was Lévi-Strauss. The canonical bibliography of Structuralism (the body of sources Lévi-Strauss and others cited) was also read. Saussure, who is there named as the father of Structuralism, is as a result now often termed a Structuralist, not at all the same thing. Inevitably those who reject recent movements have turned on Saussure.[12] Piaget termed God a Structuralist: so much the worse, perhaps, in due course, for God. The bibliographies were (in any event) read and absorbed. Lévi-Strauss the anthropologist then disappears for practical purposes from Literary Structuralism.

Although in this way Lévi-Strauss repaid *to* literature what in an important sense he received *from* literature, it is not the case that Structuralism as transmitted to literature would have been the same if Lévi-Strauss had never lived. The 'praxis' for text-generation which illuminated criticism received genuine authority, even authenticity, from Lévi-Strauss's treatment of myth. That authority derived from peculiarities of texts that were still only one remove or so from absolute orality, and those 'fitful illuminations' from general anthropology were sufficient to give a kind of generative life to the dead literary texts lying about in library and study. Furthermore, his appropriation of the very term Structural for his anthropology, his particular selections from Prague linguistic Structuralism for his conception of binary oppositions, his generative terminology, combined with his tremendous *personal* vogue and through it the popularization of all related themes and tendencies, fully establish any claims made on his behalf for responsibility for the literary explosions, however muffled or distant. That vogue supported the simultaneous anthropological discovery of Althusser, Lacan, and Derrida. But by the middle 1970s in Social Anthropology, his home subject, the genuine failure of Structuralism had become the chief problem. Its collapse took with it the revisionist Marxism that was associated with it. The rubble buried most of the debate. That was the final collapse of Modernism in social anthropology.

Modernism

So let us retrace our steps. Can it really be that Modernism occupies an almost precisely datable span from 1920 to 1975, as far as social anthropology is concerned? Improbable though it seems, we *can* say that. Anthropological works and anthropological lives are very closely meshed, and are not impossibly numerous, bibliographically or demographically. Malinowski and his generation may have been potential converts to modernism before 1920, and Modernism may live on posthumously in plenty of living social anthropologists, but survival is, however, not as widespread as might be imagined. It is hard for social anthropologists to think against the grain of experience, and you can see ideas die among them, rather as if a light has been switched off. Other lights may be working, but the Modernist switch *is* off.

And who switched it on? Was it Malinowski? We can say that it was, because other possible actors were very thin on the ground. Although it is often important to look behind the man who received the credit to the man who really caused it all, there are not many candidates on the ground for the role of *eminence grise* for Malinowski – at least any in social anthropology. In his retrospective *Encyclopaedia Britannica* article (1926) Malinowski looked back to 1910 as the year of great changes, thereby tactfully dating the break to before his own fieldwork in the Trobriands (although in fact to the year of his own arrival at the London School of Economics). He singled out Seligman, his professor in London, as well as others, naming works published just before, during, and after 1910, such as: Frazer's *Totemism and Exogamy*, Seligman on the *Melanesians of British New Guinea*, Seligman's monograph with his wife on the Veddas, Van Gennep's *Rites de Passage*, Lévy-Bruhl and Boas on the mentality of primitive man, Rivers on Diffusionism and Evolutionism, and Thurnwald's various works; while Durkheim, in 1912, brought out *Elementary Forms of Religious Life*.

We now know a good deal more about the influences on Malinowski than we did. Durkheim played his role, no doubt. We have probably underestimated the quiet influence of Seligman in general. His interest in psychoanalysis, for example, has often been noted. Without Malinowski something might have started just the same. But surely the Seminar would not have come into existence – the concentration of anthropological talent in that way, time, and place? Many have regretted some aspects of the posthumous effect of Malinowski's ascendancy – myself among them (1971b: lx) – but a failure of Malinowski to appear on the scene would have redistributed our past in such personal ways that we cannot say *it* would have happened anyway. The *it* in question is, as usual in anthropology, not a school of abstract thought, but a particular way of interpreting experiences. The anthropologists *are* the thought of their discipline in a very direct way, that has an immediate bearing on Malinowski's role in founding Functionalism or, what in the present context I will now call Early Modernist Social Anthropology. Even today it is very difficult to make comments on the period without biography being brought into the issue by those who knew Malinowski. Leach, Gellner, and Jarvie (1966); Kuper (1973); and the early memorialists of the *Man and Culture* volume, valuably illustrate or discuss this feature. Yet in many ways it is all out of proportion, one feels. As Winston Churchill said of the great Midland King Offa: 'In studying [him] we are like geologists who instead of finding a fossil find only the hollow shape in which a creature of unusual strength and size undoubtedly resided' (Churchill 1956: 67). One cannot be happy with that void. Fortunately we can now see that prophetic situations express themselves in exactly that way. What was happening was what I have already called a rearrangement. One can describe the arrangement before the change began and the new arrangement when it was complete, but the rearranging itself stretches language to describe it (Ardener 1975b). The Seminar, we may independently conclude, really was as important as the memorialists all assert. Seminars can be created or imitated from each other, just as texts are. The Malinowski Seminar was (to appropriate our earlier terminology) evidently the Seminar as Life, not the Seminar as Genre.

The feeling of fulfilment lasted 20 years, or probably less. Malinowski went to the United States in 1938, never to return, but the magic space was held steady for long enough for us to see that it was the vessel whereby Modernism entered the subject. We shall not be surprised if anthropological Modernism took on a particular experiential shape as a result. I will accept the objection in advance that we do not know that it was 'Modernism' that entered, or (despite this paper) that there is something called 'Modernism' that could 'enter'. With an admirable provisionality I will speak only *as if* both these things are possible, giving grounds for so proceeding.

The condition that social anthropology passed through was analogous to that of other disciplines, some early, some late, in the last part of the nineteenth century and the first part of the twentieth century. Freud, Keynes, Einstein, Saussure, Picasso, Corbusier, effected obvious changes in psychiatry, economics, physics, linguistics, art, and architecture, while in English literature alone there came a row of famous figures – for example, Joyce, Eliot, D. H. Lawrence, the Bloomsburies. There is a *prima facie* case for linking together the phenomena that occurred with the appearance of these and other names. We shall not be surprised that there is overlap, and time-lag – such that for some fields the moment is earlier, for some others later. We shall be strongly tempted (as others have been) to place Marx in the sequence. He would be very early, and he may well have lasted longest.

The first point about Modernism is precisely its expropriation of modernity. No rivals were tolerated during its reign. Consider the paradox that as late as 1980, in almost all fields, the term 'Modern' was used of events and ideas whose beginning lay in the nineteenth century. Can you imagine 'Modern Art' being generally used in 1880 of the art of Ingres, or the 'Modern Novel' of the novels of Fielding? The nineteenth century was a truly modern age; the twentieth century was modern only 'as genre', and so (appropriately) 'Modernist'. Modern architecture (coyly called *moderne*) thus came to stalk the land for long after its naïve, Jaeger-clad, bicycle-riding, ocean-liner-obsessed founders had vanished. That image is a reminder that Functionalism was one of the *moderne* notions – common to the architect Corbusier and to Malinowski. It is hard for us nowadays to recall that 'functional' was then a resonant word – everywhere from engineering to biology to architecture to mathematics. *Isms* too are in themselves marks of the *moderne* – that is the declaring of *isms*. On the wilder shores of the *moderne* (as in *avant garde* art) the *isms* notoriously multiply and subdivide. We should already suspect on *a priori* grounds any conscious anthropological *ism* like Functionalism of expressing *modernitas*, while Malinowski's own contemporaries quite explicitly saw his role as equivalent to that of the great Modernists already listed. In 1938, the now exiled Freud recorded the visit of Malinowski to Belsize Park to present his respects.

A second feature of the Modern in the entry period in most areas of thought is that the initial innovation was seen as *technical*. This is very interesting in the light of later developments, but all the moderns have this in common: a *perceived* change of technique, however trivial. They pioneered the use of steel and concrete, or streams of consciousness, or psychoanalysis, or new geometries, or palette knives, or the dialectic, or the film documentary, or description, or synchronics, or context of situation, or ethnography, and so into the world of Malinowski's own anthropological contribution to the *moderne*.

Let us now summarize some of these features.

Malinowski's Modernism

1. THE APPROPRIATION OF THE MODERN

This goes without saying, from the tone of Malinowski's writings and that of his successors. 'Modern' Social Anthropology dates from him, still, sixty years on.

2. THE DECLARATION OF THE 'ISM'

This Modernistic feature has the effect of consciously placing the label before the event. This development was, in Modernism, parasitical on philosophies of historical progress, in which styles of the past in thought or taste received labels; the future received its labels in advance. The Modern is thus a kind of appropriated future. If it is required to select one central aspect of Modernism, this must be the one. The collapse of Modernism is inevitably perceived as the collapse of the future.

3. FUNCTIONALISM – THE LABEL

I will add here only the point that the term implied the definition of parts by wholes, rather than the reverse. Holism, and Gestalt Psychology were current at the time. Linguistics also introduced the idea in a specific way, through Saussure. His successors (contemporary with Malinowski and *his* successors) were of course known as Structural Linguists. Since we shall need to ask later whether Structuralism in anthropology is different from, or part of Modernism, it is important to note that Structuralism embodied very clearly, from the beginning, ideas that Functionalism (because of its idiosyncrasies) expressed only in strangely muffled ways.

4. THE TECHNICAL ADVANCE

(a) The method of participant observation was understood as the intervention of the social anthropologist at a point in time and a point in space (or a fixed time in a limited space), in which he or she behaved like an ideal metering device. This process raised the question of what was to be metered. The picture of the space-time process as a kind of flow was quite common among thinking people. The elements that flowed could be concretized as statistical parameters of notionally infinite kinds. The anthropologist cut these parameters in space and time at point S. The model resulting is the cruciform ('Christmas Card') one shown in *Figure 3.3*. Malinowski's observer thus stumbled on the notion of the synchronic system. The idea has strong parallels with the presentation of Saussure, who illustrates the idea of the transect very well. The links with Malinowski are indirect – through the *Moderne*. The interest in the synchronic is concretized in the artistic and literary movement through a rejection of a certain kind of history, and the discovery of holistic function in the present. *Joyce's 'Bloomsday' in 1904 is of the same substance, intellectually, as Malinowski's Trobriands.*

(b) *The units.* Malinowski did give names to the units in the flow of society: his 'institutions' – hypostatized reifications borrowed from the historicist predecessors. His early explanations of them as expressions of 'bodily needs', derives from the evolutionist nature of Malinowski's early thinking. The headings in his notebooks were not really the names of concrete 'institutions', but analytical classifications, and the success of the new fieldwork was a result of the examination of the conflict of classifications (actors' and observer's). The synchronic system was thus discovered (if you like) for the wrong reasons, with misplaced concreteness being attributed to the units. These hidden features were made explicit only much later by Structuralism and its congeners.

(c) *Representativeness ignored*. Functionalism never answered the question why representativeness was not apparently critical to the 'truth' of anthropology. This is the basic paradox of the subject. In Malinowski's time the problem could be avoided by the assumption that the 'distributions' in *Figure 3.3* were parallel in time and space. This would mean that in a primitive tribe neither a change in space nor a change in time would greatly affect the observing process – an astonishing assumption on the face of it. Yet it embodied quite widespread and tautological assumptions about what is now called the Third World. While every item of classification in the study of the 'First World' was delicately and finely cut, the tropics and other exotic areas were perceived in much broader and clumsier categories. They had 'climate' (stable, large-scale), while we had 'weather' (fine-grained, unpredictable). Spatial variables were seen as relatively massive in scale, so that variations over a territory (sampling in space) was not 'seen' as finely critical. As for representativeness in Time, the picture may be quickly blocked in. 'History' had shown that present-day primitives were broadly classifiable with ancient peoples, or peoples reported by the ancients. There was thus the possibility of several thousand years of broad stability. Why not, therefore, tens of thousands, or a hundred thousand years of stability? The gap between today and 100,000 years ago was not perceived as great. This was related to the general 'broadening' of categories where the Third World was concerned. All this stands out clearly in Malinowski's early views of the supposed Trobriand (and 'primitive') ignorance of physiological paternity. At the beginning, there seems to be no doubt that he really thought that there was a survival of 'primaeval' ignorance. Later he back-pedalled vigorously. Now, of course, we may have two million years of hominid 'symbolic' activity, and the timelessness of the primitive has no pseudo-historical support. Meanwhile the whole issue of 'knowledge' and 'ignorance' has been more carefully discussed – indeed in the 3rd edition of *The Sexual Life of Savages*, Malinowski himself already makes many of the relevant points.

(d) *Primitivism*. All of the preceding discussion can be contained in the fact that the 'primitive' was, when Malinowski received it, already a notion defined in the West by stability and wholeness. Here the links with the general ideas of the *moderne* are quite direct. The 'Negro Art' phase, and the obsession with the primitive of most of the figures of the Modern age is easily documented (consider only Picasso, D. H. Lawrence, Jacob Epstein, even E. M. Forster, and in other ways Freud and the psycho-analysts). Malinowski's work was just what was required – a modern primitivism for Modern people. We may note that the Primitive, for the *moderne*, was seen as unhypocritical, in touch with the natural, and at home with the erotic. It is no surprise therefore that, as Leach says (1966), *The Sexual Life of Savages* was the work by which Malinowski became most widely known among the lay adherents of the *moderne*.

(e) *Field fact.* It is as well to remind ourselves that anthropology is not primarily concerned to produce intellectual or artistic movements – or so its practitioners assume. Anthropology must be perceived in some sense to work. The idea of a method that would place the study at 'point S' at the centre of the universe would not have been enough if it had not apparently worked. The new Functionalist fieldwork was begun when the primitives themselves were politically and physically accessible. Classical fieldwork was

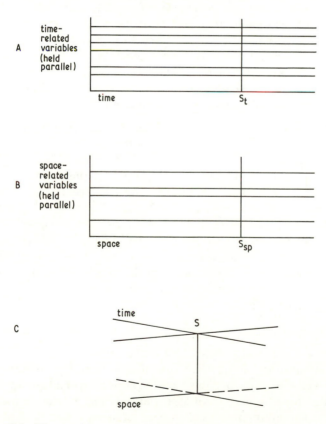

Figure 3.3   The participant anthropologist at point S. Ideal model

done under peculiar conditions that led the synchronic approach to appear to be a perfect fit to the facts. The societies studied were unnaturally peaceful. They were held in a ring, in which conflicts were minimized under colonial rule. If the anthropologists entered, the place was stable. In addition, administrators of the liberal as well as the illiberal kinds were Modern-Primitivists. They shared with their age the belief that primitives were changeless. Customs were codified, murders and violence were punished, conflicts arbitrated, anthropologists were permitted, and change was shunted off into the towns. The stability lasted for about twenty years. As we have seen, the assumptions about the anthropologist metering life at 'point S', were dependent on the hypothesized transsection cutting through distributions that were parallel. Lo! When anthropologists' studies were made, the distributions *were* parallel! Primitive stability, so long posited, was given concrete form in the colonial territories. Functionalism in its simplest form worked.

(f) *Unexpected results.* In sum, Malinowski's technical innovation was successful by a kind of Koestlerian sleep-walking. The idea of parts being informed by the whole really required a theory of opposition and system. The synchronic study of institutions required a theory of classifications. The timelessness of anthropological results derived from a theory of the synchronic yet to be appreciated. Misplaced concreteness reached its limits with the pseudo-timelessness of colonial, or colonialized, societies. In the post-war period the latter point occupied theorists as varied as Leach, Gluckman, and Worsley. By then the real world was on the move again.[13]

We see then that the technical advance that Functionalism represented, its conscious self-definition, and its appropriation of the future as well as of the past, make it a fairly typical example of the Early Modernist stream in the thought of the age. Characteristically, in anthropology this stream enters through a particular biographical experience and somewhat idiosyncratic procedures. A real novelty was however introduced, which resulted from the unexpected *kinds* of experience involved. In so far as there is, or will be, a post-*moderne*, it will be from that novelty that it will emerge. Fieldwork was, as it turned out, ontologically timeless: 'The Nuer', not 'The Nuer in 1936'. The discovery of a social time outside time was the paradoxical result of the apparently technical advance – one that ironically laid great stress on 'real time', in long periods of fieldwork.

The post-war period was Post-Functionalist in the sense that it was an 'unpacking' of the implications of Functionalism. The entry of large numbers of new practitioners of social anthropology gave the period a special quality.[14] It came to be called Structural-Functionalist, but it is the middle period of Modernism in social anthropology, called here Consensus Modernism. Its particular nature derived from the idiosyncrasy of Early Modernism, which had been incarnated, rather than argued, into existence. Malinowski had stamped it with a charismatic status that was felt by all his pupils. In a way, Structural-Functionalism was a retrospective re-theorizing, a dropping of the personal history of the Founder. It was unfortunate that this took time and involved the famous timelag.

By the time the 'charisma was routinized', anthropologists were looking back to ideas of the pre-war period in linguistics, science and philosophy. The result was a rapid ingesting of everything the subject had missed in the intervening years – a linking up of Anthropological Modernism with its more advanced versions in general thought. That is when the New Anthropologists came on the scene (Ardener 1971a; Kuper 1973). It seems clear to me now that their ideas (for example, those of Lévi-Strauss, Douglas, or Leach) represented the final recognition that the Malinowskian sychronicities were conceptual. It was recognized at the time, and since, that the non-French New Anthropologists were propounding something in some way 'like' the Structuralism of Lévi-Strauss, to which all were to some degree attracted.[15] As a result the whole period can be seen to be linked up with the fate of Structuralism – the theme with which I began this paper.

We have now confronted the question of whether Structuralism was the expected end of the *moderne* or merely its final efflorescence. It is easy to see how there have been conflicting conclusions. By 1960 the post-war Consensus (what we may call the conservative rethinking) in social anthropology was eroding rapidly. By 1970 there were no cogent defences for the many omissions of Structural-Functionalism. The fervour at the student and public level that the New Anthropology (what we may call the radical rethinking) produced had all the marks of a genuine change. Yet there were already surprising counter-indications. For example, Malinowski's Functionalism had succeeded in wiping out the old historicist anthropology, and had restocked the profession for 40 years, entirely within 10 or 15 years of activity. Lévi-Strauss's major work starts in the 1940s, yet Structuralism did not take off until the 1960s. It is in a significant sense over by 1975, to be followed by its heir, Structural Marxism, within a short time. As for restocking the profession, go to the ASA and *si monumentum requieris circumspice*! High Structuralism, then, came as 'a witness to the light but was not that light'.[16]

In brief, it was because Structuralism represented a consumption of anthropological texts, rather than a creation of them, that it can be shown to be an end rather than a beginning. Anthropology not as life, but as genre. Hence the (for some) alarming slither into literary trendiness, that eventually led the original New Anthropologists (even at times Lévi-Strauss himself) to begin that train of recantations that, by the end of the 1970s, merged with the queue of recantations from all the other branches of the *moderne*, in their kinds, and in their various garbs. The euphoria of the final period becomes more explicable as a phenomenon when one takes into account its incidence in time. In the intellectual archaeology of the *moderne*, in every field, at a point in the stratification, a line of ash occurs marking the 1960s like the traces of a wild consuming fire, just before the levels peter out. Each is a final effect of the substitution of genre for life in its own particular field. That must help to confirm the general conclusion that Structuralism in social anthropology was a part of Modernism not a 'Post-Modernism', and that it will turn out to be so in other fields (such as Literary Criticism) there can be no doubt. Meanwhile, social anthropology came of scientific age unnoticed by many in neighbouring disciplines, and indeed by many of its junior and senior practitioners, as a rather narrow but understandable concern with the career structure engaged their attention. But its period of 'de-modernization' has revealed that it was not only 'Modernism' that entered in 1920. The anthropological method is seen to be concerned with the life of structures, as we have heard from the beginning.

We have been discussing the decline of Modernism. That does not mean, let me emphasize with all energy, the decline of social anthropology. The fact is that to be a Modernist is now to be backward-looking. Its expropriation of the future has led only to a number of undesirable conditions in the present. Of late, various forms of Structuralism (even the misunderstood 'Post-Structuralism') have been belatedly announced as expressions of 'Post-Modernism' by various writers. My aim has been to suggest that that cannot be the case for social anthropology, which has some interest in these terms. The epistemological break that Structuralism represented compared with Functionalism, was for our subject (as we can now see) a subsidiary although important one. More controversially, I am of the opinion that Marxism, even in its various revisionist forms, is for social anthropology also a phase of Modernism. I should also make clear to non-anthropologists, especially, that my analysis of the colonial phase of Primitivism should not be taken to apply to the present state of social anthropological thought. Modernism, Early, Middle, or Late, is a set of ideas and concepts that derive from the folk-thought of the industrial countries in the era of the expanding world. A subject that is concerned with the world as experienced by all its inhabitants in their various cultural modalities will generate its own valid approaches. To that degree, social anthropology is already Post-Modernist – if it matters. But to demonstrate it would be another lecture. Meanwhile, we recognize the role of Malinowski, the extraordinary man who opened social anthropology to Modernism, while providing it ultimately with powerful tools for the criticism of Modernism itself – for a return, indeed, from genre to life.

Some responses to questions

I have been invited for the published version to expand upon certain positions sketched above. This is not a conventional history of social anthropology (for that we should look to the writings of scholars such as Stocking, or Urry). I should also like to retain some of its interest for a more general audience. I therefore make a few additional remarks here.

1. As far as Malinowski is concerned, I have since been present at a paper given by J. Jerschina at Krakow on 27 September 1984, entitled 'Polish Modernism and Malinowski's Personality'. For Jerschina, 'Polish Modernism' is a phase that extends from 1885 to 1914, and is associated with the 'Young Poland' movement. Malinowski, who took his doctorate at Krakow in 1906, was associated with thinkers of this group. Such a ready confirmation of the argument of this paper is not unwelcome, but it brings its own problems. For Polish 'Modernism' was a 'self-declared' literary grouping which was somewhat 'out of phase' with ideas contemporary with it in the West. It retained in particular strong Romantic leanings, looking back to Mickiewicz and others; it was (like all Polish movements) much concerned with the national consciousness. It exemplifies at the same time a constant symptom of Modernism: a pessimism about the (*really* modern) nineteenth-century civilization that it actually inherited. Nevertheless, a feature of Malinowski's work, which is in a way almost his hallmark – his mode of expression – seems strangely in tune with the 'neo-Romantic' shade that Jerschina demonstrates in Polish Modernism. The Modernism that I discuss is evidently a much broader phenomenon than the limited Polish literary Modernism. It is, nevertheless, somewhat paradoxical that Malinowski's characteristic trademark – his style and self-presentation – should probably derive from this 'smaller' Modernism, while I would credit him with the feat of introducing social anthropology into Modernism at large. This usefully illustrates the way that Modernism 'lifted all the boats', and provides a good example of the complex way that ideas and actions fit together (Ardener 1970).

Malinowski's achievement, I have continually argued, was effected in too short a time for it to have been entirely personal. It was a spark to the tinder. He did not come to London until 1910. He was out of England by 1914. On his return from the Trobriands he stayed in Tenerife until the publication of *Argonauts of the Western Pacific*. When appointed to his London post (after toying with returning to the Jagellonnian University at Krakow) he spent the vacations in the South Tyrol. He was on sabbatical at least once in the early 1930s, and he went to the United States in 1938. We may speculate why the Modernization of British social anthropology did not occur elsewhere in the country. Malinowski's very foreignness may have made him ready to attract (in the best sense) 'all and sundry', from all disciplines and from the newer countries of the world, without passing through the traditional British university establishments. The rather narrow intellectual range of Structural-Functionalism, which some later complained of, may have been a price paid for this.[17]

2. Did Structuralism mark the end of Modernism, or was it the beginning of

something new? In declaring that it was indeed an end, I need to point only to some predisposing features (apart from the general arguments already raised). One is that despite the flexible, and at times inchoate nature of Lévi-Strauss's theories, there has been a clear limit to the degree of development allowed in them by the master and his followers. Few clarifications have been accepted or revisions made. A second is the suspicious rapidity with which Structuralism has become naturalized in the study of text, including literary text. I have put it elsewhere in the form: 'Structuralism stumbled upon the homology between society and text, but developed no theory to account for it' (1977). Third (and connected with the last point), there was no evidence of any difference in fieldwork method that is primarily due to Structuralism. If there have been any changes they are not Structuralist. They lie in reflexive, 'personal anthropologies', or in various fields classed generally as Semantic (Crick 1976; Parkin 1982), or the like. The rediscovery of woman owes nothing to it. The improvement in the perception of the place of language perhaps owes more to the 'correctors' of Lévi-Strauss than to Structuralism as received. Structuralism did not therefore become an *anthropological* practice.

3. Structuralist-Marxism became a substitute for Structuralism for many in the 1970s for a number of reasons, among which the most satisfactory was its apparent provision of the missing 'praxis'. The material world was apparently placed in a causal relationship to the structural phenomena. The problem was that Structuralism 'idealized' Marxism, and not that Marxism 'materialized' Structuralism. Godelier is thus more interesting when elucidating the origins in geology of Marx's idea of a 'social formation', than he is when arguing the material bases of the social formation themselves. The 'arrows of materiality' were so redefined, 'modes of production' were so re-conceptualized, that we may say that materiality itself became 'text'.

4. The social space is inherently neither materialist nor idealist. Materiality is perceived by certain processes which themselves exhibit quasi-statistical features (Ardener 1982). The whole is a 'simultaneity'. In dividing up the simultaneity it is easy for theoreticians mistakenly to separate out an infinity of *conceptual* levels while leaving only one level for materiality. It is the nature of the simultaneity that (figuratively) if a tooth aches in one dimension it will ache in fifteen dimensions. Materiality does not gently fade or attenuate through the levels (so that ultimately only a sensitive princess would feel it like a pea hidden beneath the mattress). The converse is, of course, that *no level of materiality is free from conceptualization*. There are therefore no arrows of causation. Marxism can hardly be radical enough for us, therefore. It is surely enough to recognize its status as a part of Modernism. It bears all the stigmata of being the ultimate Modernism of Modernisms: its appropriation of all futures and all pasts, its technological or scientific aspirations, its definition of other modernisms and its absorption of them to itself, its ultimate irrealism in

the literal sense, together with the exaggerated synchronic equilibrium imposed upon the societies in which it is the defining philosophy – all these, combined with the historical period of its development, would suggest that we are in the presence of an archetype of Modernism. Politically the statement 'Marxism: the highest stage of Capitalism' is thus quite unparadoxical. Its continuous success in inspiring bureaucracies and élites to greater and more rigid technical control makes it the epitome of the transmutation of the life of politics into genre.

5. The 'epistemological break' in social anthropology that occurred with Structuralism is genuine enough (Ardener 1971a), but it did not *belong* to Structuralism. My analysis at the time of the New Anthropology noted most of the problematic features that I refer to in this paper. Perhaps it would be simpler to express the matter so: High Structuralism and its congeners were *expressions* of the break. Late Modernism is thus the disintegration of Modernism: that 'consuming fire' to which I refer in the paper itself. The situation after the break is still in process in the wide real world. For reasons I have already touched on, the fact that social anthropology was already transformed by the experience of multiplicity in the world has made it accidentally one of the branches of knowledge most prepared to experience the enormous conceptual changes that are involved.

6. In an earlier lecture (1975b) I referred in more detail to the 'stretching' of Western language by the rapid territorial expansion that took place in the age of discovery. It is a characteristic of our present situation that the 'deconstruction' of those 'stretched' (but still Western) concepts should be necessary to accommodate the hitherto unaccommodated cultural representations of the muted majority of the world. So the movements connected with language and relativism were therefore the true motors of the epistemological break in social anthropology. The proper expression of the principles involved has always been a grumbling controversy in social anthropology. The trajectory of that controversy points beyond Modernism.

7. The trajectory for Modernism in British social anthropology happens to be very clear, but it is part of other trajectories even in anthropology. Thus the line for American cultural anthropology shows fewer breaks, its theoretical horizons are broader; but this is not the place to multiply these diagrams. The representation of anthropology as text has also emerged there in distinguished forms, chiefly through Geertz. The main neglected issue is, of course, the theoretical source of the homology with text. Its neglect has led to the results that we see in the condition of European literary criticism, for which we (in our innocence) are partly responsible.

8. The omission of Radcliffe-Brown and other major figures from my account: this is because Radcliffe-Brown for me represents the course of British social anthropology if Malinowski had decided to accept the Krakow

appointment in 1922, and had not politically survived. Put in that way, it is no denigration of Radcliffe-Brown to say that whatever that unrealized future would have been like, it would have lacked certain positive features. We may on the other side hazard a guess that the long Structural-Functional consensus would not have occurred or would have broken up earlier.

9. A word on Ortega is necessary. He exemplifies the problem of the critic who writes during the period that he criticizes. The saddest feature is the initial optimism of such a critic. Ortega wished to supersede the nineteenth century, which he saw as complacently 'modern'. His critical account of his own age of mass man (1930, 1961) is in fact a penetrating attack on Modernism, but he wrongly thought that the age would be over more quickly than could possibly have happened, as if his perception would dissolve it. On the contrary, by 1955, the date of his death, the victory of its ideas was total and at its height. Ortega's initial perception of Modernism came through a demographic apprehension: of the sudden appearance of 'masses' of a new kind of people. This image has weakened the proper appreciation of his criticism, for he is describing an intellectual phenomenon, or better, a cultural representation, of tremendous power. The feeling of 'mass' is a by-product, not a cause. In fact, as we know, the individuals in the 'mass' have remained remarkably 'unmodernized'. The perception of peoples as 'mass' is (on the contrary) a key feature of Modernism. Ortega's recognition of this is thus ambiguously expressed, because he had no other language than that of Modernism in which to express his perception. Analogously, a critic of Modernism in the late 1960s might surely have hoped that a newer language was now available. But such critics were themselves overwhelmed by the appropriation of all forms of criticism itself by the hallucinating offspring of late Modernism. So once more the time-scale was extended. Yet cases like that of Ortega offer encouragement also. The underlying ambiguities of 1930 now appear to be the main statements, while his own historical period, instead of being more apparent, has become irrelevant. It *was* possible to see the invisible, after all. Ironically, Ortega's most apparently 'loony' idea, the unification of Europe, came to partial fruition in his time, although in totally Modernist form.

10. A final word on the apparent autonomy of ideas and their arbitrariness. We have been looking at a set of cultural predispositions which work themselves out at all levels. These predispositions are a class of phenomena that may be given various names ('templates', 'p-structures', are two that have been proposed). They are neither 'infrastructural' nor 'superstructural': their precise realizations are dependent on the contingencies of the time (Ardener 1970, 1978). Their autonomy is therefore an 'optical allusion'. Their arbitrariness of expression is the *result* of their lack of autonomy. Once again we are not in an 'idealist' space.

11. What of the current renewal of the debate on rationality? The rationality of human systems of thought was a topic of discussion in the 1960s associated with Winch, Jarvie, Beattie, and many others, in the period of the collapse of Structural-Functionalism. Yet again it emerged this year, in almost the same terms. Before that, in the dawn of Modernism, the Intellectualism of Tylor and Frazer had proposed the same issues. In the hiccup between Early and Middle Modernism in social anthropology, Bateson's *Naven* had raised similar questions. We may be tempted to say that this 'skirmish between the lines' (Ardener 1971a: 449) recurs at every 'epistemological break' in social anthropological thought. It may more mundanely express the unsolved question of how anthropology can ever be 'logically' possible within the vocabulary provided by the present age.

Notes

1 My thanks to, amongst others over the years, Jonathan Webber and Herminio Martins who invited me to speak on the theme of Modernism at a Seminar in early 1983. For 'intellectuals' many 'Structuralist' themes, and ideas like 'deconstruction', are being treated as 'Post-Modern' novelties. From social anthropology we can see that this is a misconception. They are, of course, in a sense novelties outside social anthropology, but I shall be saying in the end that the whole Structuralist movement is the fiery decline of Modernism itself. This paper is then on a small theme related to larger matters. Much of what I have said is an illustration of approaches in other papers.
2 My Malinowski Lecture (1971a) should be compared with the present exposition. There the 'New Anthropology' was shown to have suffered a failure of nerve, but it was hoped that Structuralism would develop out of its early phase. This did not happen.
3 See Kuper 1973; Harris 1969. The varied uses of the term 'Structuralism' form the most confusing element.
4 Romanticism reflected the Revolutions themselves. The image was of the Devil unchained (Blake, Byron, Brontë) in the form of the unpredictable individual, of almost cosmic scope and creative power. In those days it was not unfashionable to seek to attribute the industrial and social explosion to someone, rather than to a process. The Romantic hero, like the entrepreneur, is the individual embodying process. Modernism made *process* the hero. The only personal heroes recognized by Modernism were the founders of the Modernist movement. These founders became virtually immune from personal criticism, while the Romantic heroes were ruthlessly exposed as smaller than life, with 'feet of clay'. Yet, because the social and cultural development was slower in various countries, the Romantic expression co-existed chronologically with Modernism in different places. Despite the implacability of the dominant successor, it has shown power to survive it.
5 I may have improved the grammaticality of J. Kennedy. My citation of Ortega does not mean that he was a Modernist. Modernism redefined the past, and provided only one acceptable language for critics of the past. Ortega attempted to find a language 'between the lines'. (See further, 'Some responses to questions', below.)
6 The Special Foreword to the third edition of *The Sexual Life of Savages* (1932) was the source of these remarks. A typescript of the 1926 Contribution to the

68 Edwin Ardener

Encyclopaedia Britannica is lodged in the Library of the Institute of Social Anthropology, Oxford. There are many corrections in his own hand.

7 This discussion at times seemed to suggest that it was incorrect to criticize Malinowski only by his writings (e.g. Leach *et al.* 1966: 565).

8 My warm thanks to Dr Hodder, of Cambridge, Dr D. Miller of London University, Dr Henrietta Moore, and many others of the New Archaeologists, who allowed me to be present at their early symposia. I hope they do not disagree seriously with these words, and that they will recall that I had urged them to place their excellent sources figuratively in the hold, as 'Not wanted on the voyage', and to develop the New Archaeology from its own problems. As far as I know, that is what they are doing.

9 For some of these 'transformational' characteristics, see Ardener 1971b: lxi–lxviii. Transformational Generative Grammar (Chomsky 1957, 1965 and elsewhere) was the linguistic version of Late Modernism, and had the same or greater impact. It could not be called Structuralism because linguists already called their own period of 'Functionalism' (synchronic, descriptive) Structuralism! The linguistic movements were always less blurred, and more theoretically explicit than the anthropological ones. Nevertheless, it is always confusing when neighbouring disciplines borrow 'last year's clothing' from each other.

10 The same situation prevails in social anthropology now as it did then. The argument was that the language of 'structure' was exhausted. The post-Structural position was one which lacked any other specification than that it was non-Structuralist. It was argued that a new trajectory must already be in existence. Our bad experience of the premature expropriation of the term does not change the argument. It accounts, however, for why one does not wish to name any Post-Modernist possibilities in social anthropology, lest another 'nerveless [terminological] arrow miss its mark'!

11 There is no space to go over Central Europe's place in the terminological spectrum. We have here 'Functional-Structural' preceding 'Structural', before Malinowski was even dead. Were they 'mere' labels? At one level, yes, but ultimately nothing more expresses the unity of Modernist terminology than the appearance of these combinations all over our time-period.

12 To 'blame' Chomsky on Saussure as some now do, can raise eyebrows. Yet in linguistics the progression from 1916 has a certain unity.

13 By 'misplaced concreteness' I mean that the 'synchronic space' is timeless, not located in real space and time. Our residual Primitivism makes it possible for us to speak as if ethnographies represent 'really' synchronic unities.

14 One study (Ardener and Ardener 1965) shows that the tiny demography of the social anthropological profession in 1961 had nevertheless been greatly enlarged by the graduation classes of 1949–52.

15 It is possible in the mid-1980s for a graduate to ask in all innocence, 'who were the New Anthropologists?'. This suggests that many of their views are now quietly assimilated.

16 Imagine at any other time after 1920 being asked 'where is the *avant garde*?' and being unable to point to some recognizable person or tendency. Yet since 1975 or so, we would have to reply, 'They were with us when we set out but we have not seen any lately'. This vacuum occurs all over the humane disciplines (we may ignore the embarrassing party going on in Criticism around the corpses of Structuralism and its congeners). The notion of an *avant garde* is of course the very product of Modernists. They claimed to live in the expropriated future. The disappearance of the *avant garde* is one of the evidences of the end of Modernism, for without that future, where will it reside?

17 As a profession we have a propensity to lose touch with the common language of our

time. This, which is one source of our strength, is also the source of our failure to influence general thought, save at very rare intervals.

References

ARDENER, E. (1970) Witchcraft, Economics and the Continuity of Belief. In M. Douglas (ed.) *Witchcraft Confessions and Accusations*. London: Tavistock.
— (1971a) The New Anthropology and Its Critics. *Man* **6** (3): 449–67.
— (1971b) Introductory Essay. In E. Ardener (ed.) *Social Anthropology and Language* (ASA Mon. 10) pp. ix–cii. London: Tavistock.
— (1971c) Social Anthropology and the Historicity of Historical Linguistics. In E. Ardener (ed.) *Social Anthropology and Language* (ASA Mon. 10) pp. 209–41. London: Tavistock.
— (1975a) The 'Problem' Revisited. In Shirley Ardener (ed.) *Perceiving Women*. London: Dent; USA: Wiley.
— (1975b) The Voice of Prophecy: further problems in the analysis of events. The Munro Lecture. Publication forthcoming.
— (1977) Comprehending Others. Paper given to Wenner-Gren Symposium. Publication forthcoming.
— (1978/1980) Some Outstanding Problems in the Analysis of Events. In E. Schwimmer (ed.) (1978) *Yearbook of Symbolic Anthropology*. I: 103–21. London: Hurst. Reprinted in M. Foster and S. Brandeis (eds) (1980) *Symbol as Sense*. New York: Academic Press.
— (1979) Social Anthropology. In G. Duncan Mitchell (ed.) *A New Dictionary of Sociology*. London: Routledge & Kegan Paul.
— (1982) Social Anthropology, Language, and Reality. In Parkin (1982) (see below).
— (1984) Ethology and Language. In V. Reynolds and R. Harré (eds) (1984).
ARDENER, E. and ARDENER, S. (1965) A Directory Study of Social Anthropologists. *British Journal of Sociology* **14** (4): 294–314.
BATESON, G. (1936) *Naven*. Cambridge: Cambridge University Press.
BOAS, F. (1913) *The Mind of Primitive Man*. The Lowell Institute Lectures 1910–11. New York.
BOGATYREV, P. (1931) Prispevek k strukturalnizetnografii, *Slovenska Miscellanea*. Bratislava.
— (1935) Funkcno-Strukturalna metoda a metody etnografie a folkloristiky. *Slovenske Pohl'ady* **51**: 550–58.
CHOMSKY, N. (1957) *Syntactic Structures*. The Hague: Mouton.
— (1965) *Aspects of the Theory of Syntax*. Cambridge, Mass.: MIT Press.
CHURCHILL, W. S. (1956) *A History of the English-Speaking Peoples*, vol. 1. London: Cassell.
CRICK, M. (1973) Some Reflections on the ASA Decennial Conference. *Journal of the Anthropological Society of Oxford* **4** (3): 176–79.
— (1976) *Explorations in Language and Meaning: Towards a Semantic Anthropology*. London: Dent.
DOUGLAS, M. (1966) *Purity and Danger*. London: Routledge & Kegan Paul.
DURKHEIM, E. (1912) *Les Formes Elémentaires de la Vie Religieuse*. Paris.
FIRTH, R. (ed.) (1957) *Man and Culture, an Evaluation of the Work of Malinowski*. London: Routledge & Kegan Paul.
FRAZER, J. G. (1910) *Totemism and Exogamy* (4 vols). London: Macmillan.

HARRE, R. and REYNOLDS, V. (eds) (1984) *The Meaning of Primate Signals*. Cambridge: Cambridge University Press.

HARRIS, M. (1969) *The Rise of Anthropological Theory*. London: Routledge & Kegan Paul.

HASTRUP, K. (1978) The Post-Structuralist Position of Social Anthropology. In E. Schwimmer (ed.) *Yearbook of Symbolic Anthropology* I: 123–47. London: Hurst.

HASTRUP, K., OVERSEN, J., and RAMLØV, K. (1975) *Den Ny Antropologi*. Copenhagen: Borgen/Basus.

JARVIE, I. C. (1963) *The Revolution in Anthropology*. London: Routledge & Kegan Paul.

JERSCHINA, J. (1983) Polish Modernism and Malinowski's Personality. Unpublished Symposium Paper. Krakow, 27 September 1983.

KUPER, A. (1973) *Anthropologists and Anthropology: the British School 1922–72*. London: Allen Lane.

LEACH, E. (1957) The Epistemological Background to Malinowski's Empiricism. In Firth (1957): 119–37.

— (1961) *Rethinking Anthropology*. London: Athlone Press.

LEACH, E., JARVIE, I. C., GELLNER, E. *et al.* (1966) Frazer and Malinowski: on the Founding Fathers. *Current Anthropology* **7** (5): 560–76. (Earlier, in part, in *Encounter*, October, 1965.)

LÉVI-STRAUSS, C. (1955) *Tristes Tropiques*. Paris: Plon.

— (1958) *Anthropologie Structurale*. Paris: Plon.

— (1962) *La Pensée Sauvage*. Paris: Plon.

LÉVY-BRUHL, L. (1910) *Les Fonctions Mentales dans les Sociétés Inférieures*. Paris.

MALINOWSKI, B. (1926) Anthropology. *Encyclopaedia Britannica*. 13th edn. s.v.

— (1926) Anthropology. Typescript presented to E. Evans-Pritchard. Tylor Library: Oxford.

— (1932) Special Foreword. *The Sexual Life of Savages*. 3rd edn. London: Routledge & Kegan Paul.

ORTEGA Y GASSET, J. (1961) *The Revolt of the Masses*. London: Allen & Unwin. (Spanish edn 1930.)

PARKIN, D. (ed.) 1982 *Semantic Anthropology* (ASA Mon. 22). London: Academic Press.

PIAGET, J. (1971) *Structuralism*. London: Routledge & Kegan Paul.

POCOCK, D. (1973) The Idea of a Personal Anthropology. ASA Conference Paper (unpublished).

RIVERS, W. H. R. (1911) Address to the Portsmouth Meeting of the British Association.

SAUSSURE, F. de (1916) *Cours de Linguistique Generale*. Paris.

SELIGMAN, C. G. (1910) *The Melanesians of British New Guinea*. Cambridge: Cambridge University Press.

SELIGMAN, C. G. and SELIGMAN, B. Z. (1911) *The Vedas*. Cambridge: Cambridge University Press.

THURNWALD, R. (1912) *Forschungen auf den Salomon-Insel und dem Bismarck-Archipel*. Berlin.

VAN GENNEP, A. (1909) *Les Rites de Passages*. Paris.

Sybil Wolfram

4 Facts and theories: saying and believing

In 1916 Malinowski claimed, on the basis of fieldwork, that 'arguing by the law of logical contradiction is absolutely futile in the realm of belief, whether savage or civilised. Two beliefs, quite contradictory to each other on logical grounds, may co-exist, while a perfectly obvious inference from a firm tenet may be simply ignored. . . . The only safe way . . . is to investigate every detail of native belief' (Malinowski (1916) 1948: 194).

Malinowski was not passing a comment to the effect that different people in the same society may hold beliefs that contradict each other. He was attributing contradictory beliefs to the same people at the same time, and to people in other respects rational. 'Such beliefs', he said, 'do not arise from "pre-logical thinking" . . . The Native mind works according to the same rules as ours' (Malinowski (1916) 1948: 210). In any case, such beliefs may be found among the 'civilized' as well as the 'savage'.

There has been a vast amount of discussion of the points on which Malinowski supplied these observations. The idea that there may be contradictory beliefs common to a society is generally disputed. This is conspicuous in the recent collection of essays edited by M. Hollis and S. Lukes, *Rationality and Relativism* (1982).

Sometimes it is held, on theoretical grounds, that it is not possible for anyone to hold a contradictory belief, and hence that the ascription of such a belief to a society is always an error and must display misunderstanding of native beliefs on the part of the ethnographer. This view is often associated with Quine's name (especially Quine 1960: sec. 13). Sometimes the theoretical stance is not that self-contradiction or inconsistency is impossible but rather that it is irrational and anyone indulging in it is therefore also irrational. It is not fashionable to consider societies, whether our own, past, or other, as irrational, and those who treat the holding of contradictory beliefs as irrational rather than impossible have also tended to deny that societies can be said to have contradictory, and ergo irrational, beliefs.

The conclusion that societies are not irrational is occasionally reached by yet another route. This is to admit the existence of contradictory beliefs but to argue that those that exist are really rational. The most common explanation is that contradictory beliefs arise from insufficient 'monitoring' of the consistency of beliefs, that is, failure to observe their contradictory nature or else failure to respond to it by dismissing one or other of the inconsistent beliefs. This conduct may be presented as rational by an account of 'rationality' which includes the pursuit of self-interest or of specific objectives as 'rational', failure to do so as 'irrational'. And it has been argued that it would be irrational to spend the time necessary to ensure that no inconsistent beliefs are held (e.g. Hollis 1982: 72; Horton 1982: 242–60).

Lately there has been another ingenious suggestion, viz. that in some cases what is believed is not a specific fact or theory but is rather of a fuzzy nature to the effect that favoured sentences are true on some construction (Sperber 1982). Belief that 'man is rational', the exact meaning of which is unclear, might be cited as a case in point. It is claimed that all the apparently irrational beliefs reported in societies are really of this sort, there being (it is held) no genuine historical or ethnographic evidence of actual contradictory beliefs of a factual nature (Sperber 1982: 175). It is also suggested that it is rational for members of a society not to question such beliefs in order not to fall out with their society (Sperber 1982: 177, n. 43).

When a similar conclusion is reached by a profusion of different arguments, it sometimes proves to have been mistaken. A famous case in moral philosophy is that of the so-called naturalistic fallacy, for fifty years 'the one thing proved in moral philosophy'. It came to be questioned, decided by many to have been no fallacy, and the various arguments considered to be so poor as to make it amazing that they were ever accepted.[1] The case in hand bears some resemblance to this case in that by now it is not clear exactly what the claim is when it is denied – contra Malinowski – that societies' beliefs can be irrational, nor which, if any, of the not altogether compatible arguments for the conclusion is the clinching one.

I want to begin by focusing on a question which, perhaps because of an initially trivial appearance, has received relatively little discussion. This is the question of *saying*, as opposed to believing, something contradictory or inconsistent. The topic of contradictory assertions or utterances is more intricate and of more intrinsic interest than appears at first sight and it also helps to disentangle and throw light on the more popular and more complex question of the existence or otherwise of irrational beliefs. A distinction is often drawn between what people say and what they believe in as much as it is acknowledged that they may say – or write – what they do not believe and remain silent about many things which they do believe. But while a distinction is admitted to exist between what is said and what is believed, this is not much explored and it is often lost sight of as discussion proceeds.

Logicians commonly distinguish between contradiction and inconsistency.

In formal terms p and q are contradictory if they must be of opposite truth values, that is, q must be true if p is false and false if p is true. 'It is the case that X' and 'It is not the case that X' generally satisfy this requirement. P and q are 'inconsistent' if they satisfy the less stringent requirement that they cannot both be true. Thus it cannot be the case that there were both 317 divorces and under 250 divorces in England before 1858. The claim that there were 317 (*Encyclopaedia Britannica* 1967, vol. 7: 514) and the claim that there were under 250 (Graveson 1957: 5) are inconsistent rather than strictly speaking contradictory: both cannot be correct but both can be – and indeed are – incorrect.[2] However, for ease of exposition I shall use the terms 'inconsistent' and 'contradictory' interchangeably in what follows, except where something hangs by it, to cover both contradictions and inconsistencies.

Another common distinction is between what I shall call 'blatant' and non-blatant contradiction. What I am terming a 'blatant' contradiction is approximately what was distinguished by Locke nearly three centuries ago (Locke 1690: Bk 4) as 'self-evident' or 'trifling' in the slightly different setting of tautology. As spelt out by Locke, we have a self-evident truth if it is the case that anyone understanding the meaning of the individual words used must know that what the sentence they compose says is true as in 'A triangle hath three sides' or 'Oyster is oyster' (Locke 1690: Bk 4, especially chapters 7 and 8).[3] Likewise we have a self-evident or blatant contradiction if anyone understanding the meaning of the words in a sentence must know that what the sentence says is not true. Non-self-evident contradictions, or what I shall call 'non-blatant' ones, are those where, although the meaning of the words is actually such that what they say cannot be true, the necessarily false nature of what is said could escape notice even by someone understanding the meaning of the individual terms. Obvious cases are where the contradiction does not occur within a single uttered sentence or, if it does, the sentence enjoys a complexity or mode of expression such that someone could be said to understand the words in it without knowing that what is said must be false. 'Some circles are not circles' or perhaps 'Some circles are square' are in this sense blatantly contradictory. But 'If a man marries his mother's brother's daughter, then his father-in-law is not his uncle' though contradictory is not blatantly so. It is possible to know the meaning of all the individual words without thereby necessarily knowing that what is said is false. The distinction between blatant and non-blatant contradictions is not absolutely clearcut. One might well wish to argue for degrees of blatancy, and speak, as I shall sometimes do, of e.g. 'fairly' or 'not so blatant' contradiction.

Two more sets of distinctions are important to what follows. Both are between different senses that can be given to 'X said so and so'. 'So and so' can refer to the sentence he uttered in quotation marks, say 'J'ai froid'. It can refer to what has a given meaning as when we translate the words he spoke 'J'ai froid' and explain that what he said was 'I'm cold'. 'So and so' in 'He said so and so' can also equally correctly refer to what he stated to be the case, in this instance that he was cold.[4] To add to the confusion, 'He said so and so' is ambiguous between what is sometimes called affirming or asserting so and so and just uttering it. To affirm or assert is, roughly, to put forward as true that so and so. In English and many other European languages saying the pertinent words (words that may express that so and so) in the right tone of voice or writing them down with the appropriate punctuation is the way to assert something. In English the sentence form used is shared with questions, sometimes with expressions of hope or with commands ('There will be light'), sometimes even with denying that so and so, as when I say sarcastically 'How fascinating this is'. And clearly one language may differ from another in the way it marks off so-called affirming and asserting from other uses to which words can be put, such as asking questions, issuing commands, and so on.

Armed with these distinctions, it seems evident that there could be no impossibility about *uttering* words of contradictory form. For one thing, they can occur in compound sentences e.g. following 'it is not (or cannot be) the case that', or be offered as examples of contradictions. For another, the format of a contradiction can be used to put forward what, given the meaning of the words as employed on that occasion, is not a contradiction at all.

Tautologous form can be used to make statements not rating as tautologies as in 'boys will be boys' or 'cats are not dogs'; similarly the format of contradiction is in common use in English for asserting what are not generally taken to be contradictions but rather e.g. qualifications as in 'Well, he was and he wasn't' in reply to 'Was he polite?' or 'He is and he isn't' to 'Is he a gentleman?'. It would probably rightly be said that neither are instances of 'affirming' or 'asserting' contradictions, in the first cases because no affirming or asserting of the contradiction is going on, in the second because it is not contradictions which are being asserted or affirmed. What is claimed is usually not that no contradictions can be uttered but rather that none can be *asserted*.

The examples chosen to demonstrate this point are normally blatant contradictions or what is represented as 'p and not-p'. The argument is that because what is stated could not be true, and, moreover, must be known by the speaker not possibly to be true, therefore what he says cannot be a genuine *assertion* and/or that if he utters the sentence in question in the normal assertive mode he must be irrational. Thus Taylor in *Rationality and Relativism*: 'We call someone irrational who affirms both *p* and not-*p*' (Taylor 1982: 87), or Newton-Smith, concerning the invented natives, the Herns: 'It would be difficult to maintain that they were even asserting' (Newton-Smith 1982: 109). If 'rationality' is taken to include the procuring of some objective, as in Taylor and others it is, then it seems far from clear that what, for want of a better word, I shall be obliged to call 'asserting' a contradiction must be irrational. A wide variety of purposes can be served by the utterance or assertion of contradictions.

With many we are familiar in our own society. Thus the chairman of a session or meeting might summarize the results of a discussion as p and not-p as a courtesy or a joke, agreeing with both parties, evident though it may be that both cannot be right. Or his object may be to avoid quarrelling with either of two opposing groups, or to be in a position to say he was right whichever of two contradictory views proves correct. Someone may utter both p and not-p in the hope that believers in p will think he believes p, believers in not-p that it is not-p that he supports. Thus a politician in search of votes, or an administration to placate a divided populace. Again, p and not-p may be uttered by the same mouth or different ones in collusion to induce confusion in the enemy or irritation in an opponent, or to provoke a response injurious to the hearer (he is stunned into silence or loses his temper) and advantageous to the speaker (who gains face or wins the vote).

In the context of, for example, contemporary Anglo-American philosophical discussion it is not generally thought legitimate to enunciate contradictions and it is considered acceptable to assert that what has been uttered is a contradiction – to promote the truth. No charge can lie against me if I argue, for instance, that Taylor is not quite right when he writes 'We call someone irrational who affirms both p and not-p' and, moreover, is contradicting himself when he goes on to add 'By extension, someone who acts flagrantly in violation of his own interests, or of his own avowed objectives, can be considered irrational' (Taylor 1982: 87). It would be perfectly acceptable for me to point out that there are cases where it would be flagrantly in violation of someone's pursuit of his avowed ends if he did not affirm both p and not-p. But in other contexts the affirming of contradictions is partly or fully licensed while pointing out the contradiction is not. To say that someone has contradicted himself could be taken 'personally' and in ill part even in some academic discussions, as tantamount to an accusation of either lying or irrationality. It may be considered offensive, disrespectful, foolish, not A's place, etc. It is easy to conjure up cases. Professor Y's institution is hoping for funds from X. X is uttering blatant contradictions. Y points this out and loses the funds for his institution. He could also lose them by denying p, which X has said or believes.[5] Perhaps more interesting are more generally licensed utterances of contradictions. The affirmation of blatant contradictions is, for instance, a stock-in-trade of comedy and comedians, and slightly differently of oracles. Newton-Smith speaks of assertions of 'p and not p' as arising, uninterestingly, from stupidity or confusion (Newton-Smith 1982: 109). Here it would be pointing out the contradiction that displayed these qualities. Licence to utter contradictions may also be a prerogative of other sections or roles in a society. The Church is commonly quoted, among others by Malinowski (Malinowski (1916) 1948: 320, notes 75 and 76). One might add doctors to patients or, more generally, those in roles of or with de facto power over others – the boss, an administration, the rulers of a society or sub-society.[6]

Two, or at least two, questions arise. One is the similarity or otherwise of the assertion of contradictions to that of statements which are not actually contradictory but are false. Another is the relation between contradictory or false assertions and contradictory or false *beliefs*.

In giving examples of common uses of contradictions I have not distinguished between the more and less blatant. In some cases it may not much matter. However, a certain implausibility attaches to uttering very blatant contradictions by mistake, that is, without realizing that they are contradictions, and this is not so with regard to unobvious contradictions. Certain of the purposes that may be served by the assertion of what the speaker knows to be contradictory statements are more likely to be achieved if the contradiction is blatant, others if they are not too blatant. Blatant contradiction may be the more effective expression of power, but the politician in pursuit of the votes of believers in p and believers in not-p or the administration placating a divided populace by telling one section one thing and the other the opposite probably succeeds better if the contradictory nature of the utterances made is not too evident, and thus the contradiction might be veiled by the use of different vocabulary, or some separation in time or space between the affirmation of p and the affirmation of not-p or the use of different mouths for the assertion of the one and that of the other. Similar distinctions can be made in the utterance of what is not as such contradictory but merely false.

We speak not only of inconsistent and contradictory statements but also of statements inconsistent with or contradicted by facts. These are not usually regarded as irrational in the same way as contradictions and inconsistencies. Yet the difference can be made to appear very slight, both in the realm of utterance and in that of belief.

A false statement may be blatantly false, the facts being obvious or well known or its improbability great, or it may be less blatantly so. When someone makes a false statement he may do so knowing it to be false or unwittingly, in the same way that someone may assert contradictory statements with or without realizing it. The assertion of false statements may occur for purposes not dissimilar to those of contradiction: someone may assert p, which is false, as a kindness, a courtesy, a joke, to avoid a quarrel, to win a vote, to get a proposal accepted, to insult, provoke, bewilder, mislead, and so on. Similarly, with the social acceptability or otherwise of disputing p. It may be as discourteous, offensive, disrespectful, foolish, infra dig to utter a denial of p as it is to point out a contradiction. Again, it may be socially more acceptable to make a false statement than to say that the statement is false, whether because of the content of what is said (p being generally accepted, the right kind of thing to say, a comfort to X, the truth is a state secret or a professional confidence) or because of the relative positions of the speakers (p is asserted by a superior) or because to deny p is to accuse an asserter of p of lying, carelessness, ignorance. There are societies, of which our own is probably an instance, where lying (or careless error) is disapproved of but accusations of lying (or careless error) are worse.

So much for the similarities between assertions of contradictions and falsities. The reason why theoretical discussions so often treat self-contradiction as irrational and falsities not is probably partly that the self-contradictions concentrated on are those I have called blatant, while the falsities are thought of as not blatant. But it almost certainly also arises partly from the common failure to keep the domains of assertion and belief properly apart.

I have made the point that someone may assert a statement he does not believe to be true or not assert a statement he does believe to be true. But the difference between assertions and beliefs is not exhausted by the fact that the one can occur without the other. We speak of reasons for asserting something and of reasons for believing something. But the use of the term 'reasons' is rather different in the two cases.

'Reasons' to say or not say something are normally objectives. 'Reasons' to believe or not believe something generally consist of evidence as to its truth or falsity. 'He said that the gentleman was kind in order to please him' or 'he did not say p in order not to offend X' is a correct form of speech. 'He believed (or did not believe) that so and so in order to such and such' is not. For instance, someone may utter p, believing or not believing it, in order to induce others to believe or utter it, but he cannot believe something in order to induce beliefs and utterances. Conversely, 'He believed that the gentleman was kind on the evidence of the gift he gave' is intelligible in a way that 'he said so and so on the evidence of such and such' is normally not. Good, or rational, and bad, or irrational, reasons differ accordingly. Thus, it may be rational/irrational to *say* p because the saying of p has good/ill effects but it is, at the least, a straining of the language to suggest that it is rational/irrational to believe p because believing p would bring about good/bad results. On the other hand, while the rationality or irrationality of saying that p need not depend on whether evidence for its truth is ample or lacking, strength of known evidence is the criterion for the rationality or irrationality of *believing* that p.[7]

This difference between assertions and beliefs has obvious consequences. What someone asserts is often evidence of what he believes, but it is not foolproof evidence since there are many objectives other than imparting his beliefs for which he may say something, and among the things he says there may be ones as to whose truth or falsity he has no opinion or which he believes to be false.[8] If there are false or contradictory beliefs in societies, that which brings them about will be of a different nature from that which brings about false or contradictory assertions: causes of assertions must be sought in the realm of objectives, but that of beliefs in the treatment of evidence.

In 1982 Lukes urged against Taylor (Taylor 1982: 94 ff.) that the Church was rational to refuse to countenance Galileo's discoveries, but to do so he shifted the discussion from the irrationality of the Church's refusal to *believe* Galileo's discoveries to the rationality of the Church's *saying* that they were false (Lukes 1982: 292–97). He may, of course, have been right that the Church's interest was in what to say, but if we wish to arrive at conclusions about the rationality or otherwise of societies' beliefs, then we need to concentrate on causes or grounds for beliefs, and not entangle this with the causes or purposes of assertions.

Among the reasons (causes or grounds) for which people may believe p is of course that someone else has said that p is true. People differ widely in their trust in what is said or written. This may arise from circumstance, how generally what they hear or read is true, how reliable they find some particular source, whether they also hear p disputed. Or it may be due to the nature of the persons. In *Methods of Ethics* (1874), Sidgwick remarked that human nature being what it is, people go on believing what they are told even if they are told what is not true frequently or in particular settings (Sidgwick 1874: Bk 3, Ch. 27). However, it is obvious that individuals, eras, societies may differ in the sources they trust. Some for instance may be prone to believe the Church, others scientists, governments, the printed word, gossip, yet others may believe no one. Individuals or groups may also be differently affected by the same number of lies or errors they are told so far as belief in the next statement is concerned.

'Seeing is believing', and direct observation is often a source of belief that something is the case. However, 'seeing' is equally not always reliable. It does well with sticks and stones and colours but 'seeing' that A has measles, B is dying, that C is lying or D is miserable requires interpretation of what is actually seen and heard, which rests on inductive generalization, that is, on past observations that where there is X there is Y (when someone has spots of this or that nature, he has a particular virus, when he averts his eyes, he is saying what he knows is not true, etc.). And a standard point about 'Whenever X, then Y' is that no amount of observation can ensure that there will never be an X which is not Y. Incorrect generalizations and fallacious inferences may be more or less common. 'Observation' may, rightly or wrongly, be more or less trusted.

It would generally be acknowledged that the different sources which may lead people to believe that p can well induce them to believe many things that are false, and equally that some may believe that p and others that not-p. What is disputed is usually only whether the same person can both believe that p is true and believe that p is not true, or more particularly whether a society can hold beliefs which are inconsistent with each other. Sometimes the possibility is legislated away.

Quine, for example, in arguing for the 'referential opacity of belief contexts' simply assigned the truth value false to all instances where 'He believes that . . .' is followed by a blatant, or less blatant, contradiction as in 'He believes that the capital of Honduras is in Nicaragua' or 'He believes that the man in the brown hat is a spy and that Ortcutt is not a spy' where the man in the brown hat and Ortcutt are the same person (Quine 1953, 1956, and 1960: secs 30–1, 44).[9]

In *Rationality and Relativism* Hollis, although allowing that there may be 'false and irrational beliefs' (Hollis 1982: 75), that 'much of what is believed is surely false or suspect' (Hollis 1982: 72), even that 'Mankind could hardly survive without beliefs which are incoherent, unlikely, disconnected or daft' (Hollis 1982: 72), gives an account of how beliefs are ascribed which precludes the possibility of ascribing inconsistent beliefs to the same person: 'Formally speaking, to know on evidence *e* that S believes *p* involves knowing that, on evidence *e*, it is more likely that S believes *p than that S believes anything inconsistent with p*, and that *e* can be relied on' (my italics) (Hollis 1982: 73). In other words, should S appear 'on evidence e' to believe p and to believe not-p, we attribute to him only one or the other, that which on evidence e it appears likelier that he holds.

However, if we turn to 'evidence e', it is clearly a complex affair, and not, at least evidently, such that S can never be said to believe both of two incon-sistent statements to be true. That S is prone to assert p is, as we have seen, by no means conclusive evidence that he believes p. If it were, then the fact that contradictory assertions occur would itself be sufficient to dispose of the theory that contradictory beliefs are impossible. That S asserts p is not in itself proof that he believes p, and conversely not being given to asserting p is no proof, nor often evidence, that he does not believe p. There are beliefs so taken for granted that they are rarely, if ever, voiced: such for example is the English belief that a person is equally related to the kin on each side. Or they can be so secret that to divulge them would be e.g. treason. Other common candidates for 'evidence e' are that S has grounds for p (evidence that p is true) or acts as if p. Either is compatible with the possibility of holding contradictory beliefs. S may have grounds for believing p and grounds for believing that not p. He is often told both. Or some of his observations suggest that p is true, others that not p is the case. In some such instances, we may speak of his beliefs as changing from one time to another, in others that he believes neither p nor not-p, in yet others (with Hollis) that it is really, on balance, p he believes and not not-p. But in some cases we normally speak of conflicting or inconsistent beliefs.

The probable reason for which some have tried to expunge these is that evidence of belief in p includes reactions to 'not-p' being asserted, argued for, acted upon, etc., and it does appear, at least at first sight, as if someone who asserts, has grounds for, acts as if p and similarly for not-p, must discontinue one or the other if he is brought face to face with what he is doing. For while a non-blatant contradiction may go unnoticed, a blatant contradiction cannot. However, it is a fact that the perception of a contradiction does not always cause the perceiver to re-examine the evidence, alter his conduct, cease from asserting both p and not-p, any more than being offered evidence that some particular statement is true or false always induces or removes a belief in its truth.

It is generally conceded that a false belief need not be an irrational one. This is because the evidence available to someone may point the wrong way.

An irrational belief that p is a belief that p is true when there is not much evidence available that it is or when the evidence is conflicting or suggests that it is false. I have claimed that someone can be said to believe two contradictory or inconsistent things and that he may even continue in these beliefs when the contradiction is made evident to him. It does, however, seem that his beliefs must here be more or less irrational. One reason for this is that the evidence which induces belief in not-p is so much evidence against p, and vice versa. This is so whether or not he realizes that he holds beliefs inconsistent with each other. If he does realize this and continues in his beliefs, this is more irrational because he knows very well that one or other belief must be false, even if he does not know which.

Resistance to the idea that someone, and, in particular, societies, may have irrational beliefs seems to stem from three principal sources, one rational, two less so. One reason for the resistance is undoubtedly the somewhat foolish idea that if someone holds an irrational belief, then he must *be* irrational, and *mutatis mutandis* for societies. One swallow does not make a summer, and it takes a good many irrational acts and beliefs for a person or society to rate as irrational. After all, he or it may exhibit much rationality also. A second, partly consequential, not very good reason for denying the existence of irrational beliefs is irrational egalitarianism: if there can be irrational acts and beliefs, then one person or society can have more than another, just as if there can be evil or inefficiency there can be more in one place than another. In fact, such comparisons are often hard to make because not only are rationality and irrationality, good and evil, efficiency and inefficiency matters of degree, but also individuals, institutions, societies can differ in the respects or areas in which they exhibit them. It does indeed follow that an individual, institution, or society can be very irrational, or very evil, or very inefficient. Malinowski, who regarded the Trobriand Islanders' disbelief in physical paternity as erroneous and probably irrational, was at pains to point out that the Trobriand Islanders were not in general irrational, merely through lack of interest or some initial error or the nature of the evidence before them, wrong on this, to us, seemingly simple matter. He did not exhibit a similar tolerance of some of the Nazis' beliefs or acts. The 'whole doctrine of Aryan superiority of race . . . is essentially mystical' he said in his posthumous work *Freedom and Civilisation* (Malinowski 1947: 213); he went on to speak of 'Nazi magic preached at the end of a machine gun' (Malinowski 1947: 309), and denounced totalitarianism as a 'denial of man's natural birthright' (Malinowski 1947: 151, 317). The acts of individuals or of groups that may be or seem 'rational' in the sense of promoting their own self-interest without regard to others' interests may of course be very damaging to others, and an institution or society in which e.g. falsehood or the promulgation of self-contradictions thereby becomes very common is at the least unattractive.

The other reason for denying the existence of irrational beliefs is very much more respectable. In the past, beliefs – and acts – were written off as false or

irrational when they were nothing of the kind. No one concerned to understand a society or era will wish to make this mistake. But it does not follow that
all acts and beliefs are rational, nor need they be to be explicable. I shall finish
with some examples, taken from England, and one or two caveats and general
comments.

In 1853 a Royal Commission on divorce gave a number of incorrect figures
for nineteenth-century divorces, *inter alia* putting the total number at 110
instead of 175 (Royal Commission 1853: 10), and presented divorce, then
done by private act of Parliament, as expensive, cumbersome, and slow. The
divorce rate had in fact risen, and divorce was not expensive but lucrative for
the complainant due to damages he received (not mentioned); it was also
rapid unless there were problems about the evidence of adultery (the sole
grounds). Whether the misrepresentations were deliberate or not, what the
Commission said can be seen as rational: it successfully promoted the end of
altering the procedure for divorce. The findings of this Commission have been
believed ever since,[10] again not very irrationally, for Royal Commissions are
expected to be reliable in their findings. At the time, there was an incentive
for members of Parliament promoting reform to repeat them: it induced the
belief that the measure would open to the poor what was open to the rich, in
England a much used and ever persuasive platform for changes. It is improbable that the reasons given were the real ones or what was said believed, and
until the real reasons and actual beliefs are discovered, one could not pronounce on their rationality or otherwise. There is no doubt of a general feeling
among many that divorce reform was due, and this (whether rational or not)
would create a predisposition to irrational belief of points in its favour.

My other example is again from kinship. It is an old English belief that
'in-breeding' results in below-grade and especially idiot children. Since at
least the late eighteenth century, aided by experiment with animals, extensive
studies of cousin marriage and genetic theory, it has also been believed that if
the original stock is good, in-breeding improves it. This has not, however,
dislodged the original belief that in-breeding produces idiot children. These
were once regarded as God's punishment for the wrong of in-breeding; now
the belief is sanctified by 'scientists' findings'.[11] This seems a good example of
inconsistent beliefs of – contra Sperber (Sperber 1982: 175) – a factual nature.
We might be able to explain, for example, the persistence of the old belief by
the desire to have a suitable justification for forbidding sexual unions between
blood relations. But, just as seeing the Trobriand Islanders' denial of physical
paternity in terms of, for example, the matrilineal nature of the society might
explain that, it cannot render the reasoning rational. It only shows why people
might be inclined to irrational beliefs in this area, viz. that they have customs
or wishes that have no obvious base.

The beliefs and assertions that I have considered here are of a fairly specific
and straightforwardly testable nature. 'Classificatory' beliefs (that there are
five colours, that kinship is of two kinds) and theories of great generality (God

guides the world, every event has a cause), where notions of strength of evidence, correctness, and consistency are less clearly applicable, have been left on one side.[12] It seems after all that Malinowski was right to hold that ill-founded, false, even blatantly inconsistent beliefs may be found at the level with which I have been concerned, and that the prevailing fashion of trying to treat them as 'really rational' is unhelpful. However, it has emerged that not all false or contradictory assertion indicates mistaken or irrational belief. The ethnographer intent on investigating native beliefs has to find his way through courtesies, deception, mystification, displays of superiority, tall stories, Lewis Carroll humour and the many other possible uses besides that of imparting beliefs to which assertions may be put.

Assertions, then, are a less direct route to beliefs than might sometimes seem convenient. But the brief examination conducted here in connection with contradictions and falsities suggests that, for that very reason, conventions of talking and writing could prove as rich in ethnographic interest as those of sex or eating.

Notes

I am grateful to Professor T. E. Downing for much stimulating discussion of points in this paper and to Dr B. M. Levick for helpful criticism of the final version.
1 For detail see Wolfram 1982: 262–74.
2 The figure of 317 was given in a return for the House of Commons, May, 1857 (House of Commons 1857: 117), that of 'under 250' probably derives from a Royal Commission on divorce 1853 (*Royal Commission* 1853: 10). The figure was actually approximately 325. See also above, p. 81 and note 10.
3 For detailed discussion see Wolfram 1978: 27–53 and Wolfram 1980: 89–99.
4 These distinctions were first made in Strawson 1950.
5 If p is part of a genuine contradiction Y would then also be agreeing with X by asserting not-p but this may not be so if 'p' and 'not-p' are only inconsistent. See above pp. 72–3.
6 They may be imitated by those who do not have but wish to look as if they have the roles – rather as the Duke of Omnium (Trollope 1858: Ch. 19) fails to greet his dinner guests – a prerogative of, if anyone, royalty or foreign potentates. One of the guests, Frank Gresham, is unimpressed, and indeed leaves the house.
7 Someone's saying that p is not usually a reason for his believing that p, unless he is filled with a megalomania whereby he believes that anything he has uttered must *ipso facto* be true – though it is a common enough English saying that liars come to believe their lies.
8 The honest man does not normally pursue objectives at the cost of saying what he does not believe but not all men are honest and some lies are white lies.
9 Quine often interchanges 'assents to' or 'sincerely denies' with 'believes' and 'believes that not'. (Related criticisms of Quine may be found in Wolfram 1975: 230–46.)
10 *Inter alia* by subsequent Royal Commissions on divorce 1912–13. (*Royal Commission* 1912–13 vol. 3: 11) and 1956 (*Royal Commission* 1956: 4 para. 18). The 1967 *Encyclopaedia Britannica* figure for divorces is an honourable exception; like

all other sources it repeats the story that divorce was open only to the wealthy (*Encyclopaedia Britannica* 1967 vol. 7 'Divorce': 515). In fact, one of the first divorces, in 1701, was by a London grocer (Box: 12 & 13 W 3, *c18*), and the poor or lowly continued to obtain them. There were butchers and bakers, and provision for procuring a divorce *in forma pauperis* – exercised by one Chippindall, Gentleman, in 1850 (13 & 14 Vic, *c22*), and reported in *The Times* (May 16, 1850, p. 7, col. d). For detail see Wolfram 1985.

11 For detail see Wolfram 1983: 308–16.

12 I have expressed views about these in Wolfram 1973: 357–74.

References

BRITISH PARLIAMENTARY PAPERS (1969–1971) 3 vols. Irish University Press.

ENCYCLOPAEDIA BRITANNICA (1967) Divorce by W. La, vol. 7.

GRAVESON, R. H. (1957) The Background of the Century. In R. H. Graveson and F. R. Crane (eds) *A Century of Family Law*. London: Sweet & Maxwell.

HOLLIS, M. (1982) The Social Destruction of Reality. In M. Hollis and S. Lukes (eds) *Rationality and Relativism*. Oxford: Basil Blackwell.

HOLLIS, M. and LUKES, S. (eds) (1982) *Rationality and Relativism*. Oxford: Basil Blackwell.

HORTON, R. (1982) Tradition and Modernity revisited. In M. Hollis and S. Lukes (eds) *Rationality and Relativism*. Oxford: Basil Blackwell.

HOUSE OF COMMONS (1857) 'Divorce Acts'-123-sess 2, reprinted in *British Parliamentary Papers* vol. 3 (1971), 117.

LOCKE, J. (1690) *An Essay Concerning Human Understanding*. Revised editions 1694, 1695, 1700 and the 5th edn. publ. posth. 1706. Currently preferred edition P. H. Nidditch (ed.) (1975). Oxford: The Clarendon Press, based on the 4th edition (1700).

LUKES, S. (1982) Relataivism in Its Place. In M. Hollis and S. Lukes (eds) *Rationality and Relativism*. Oxford: Basil Blackwell.

MALINOWSKI, B. (1916) Baloma; The Spirits of the Dead in the Trobriand Islands. *Journal of the Royal Anthropological Institute* 1916. Reprinted in B. Malinowski, *Magic, Science and Religion and Other Essays*.

—— (1947) *Freedom and Civilisation*. London: Allen & Unwin (edited by P. Kaberry after Malinowski's death in 1942).

—— (1948) *Magic, Science and Religion and Other Essays*. Glencoe, Illinois: Free Press.

NEWTON-SMITH, W. (1982) Relativism and the Possibility of Interpretation. In M. Hollis and S. Lukes (eds) *Rationality and Relativism*. Oxford: Basil Blackwell.

QUINE, W. V. (1953) Reference and Modality. In W. V. Quine *From a Logical Point of View*. Cambridge, Mass.: Harvard University Press.

—— (1956) Quantifiers and Propositional Attitudes. *Journal of Philosophy* 1956, Reprinted in W. V. Quine *The Ways of Paradox*.

—— (1960) *Word and Object*. Cambridge, Mass.: MIT Press.

—— (1966) *The Ways of Paradox and Other Essays*. New York: Random House.

ROYAL COMMISSIONS (1853) *First Report of the Commissioners appointed by her Majesty to enquire into the law of divorce and more particularly into the mode of obtaining divorces a vinculo*. Reprinted in *British Parliamentary Papers* vol. 1 (1969).

—— (1912–13) *Royal Commission on Divorce and Matrimonial Causes* 3 vols. London: HMSO. Cmd 6478.

—— (1956) *Royal Commission of Marriage and Divorce*. London: HMSO. Cmd 9678.

SIDGWICK, H. (1874) *Methods of Ethics*. 7th edn 1963. London: Macmillan.
SPERBER, D. (1982) Apparently Irrational Beliefs. In M. Hollis and S. Lukes (eds) *Rationality and Relativism*. Oxford: Basil Blackwell.
STRAWSON, P. F. (1950) On Referring. *Mind* 1950. Reprinted in P. F. Strawson *Logico-Linguistic Papers* (1971). London: Methuen.
TAYLOR, C. (1982) Rationality. In M. Hollis and S. Lukes (eds) *Rationality and Relativism*. Oxford: Basil Blackwell.
TROLLOPE, A. (1858) *Doctor Thorne*. London: Chapman & Hall.
WOLFRAM, S. (1973) Basic Differences of Thought. In R. Horton and R. Finnegan (eds) *Modes of Thought*. London: Faber & Faber.
— (1975) Quine, Statements, and 'Necessarily True'. *Philosophical Quarterly* **25** (100).
— (1978) On the Mistake of Identifying Locke's Trifling-Instructive Distinction with the Analytic-Synthetic Distinction. *The Locke Newsletter* **9**: 27–53.
— (1980) Locke's Trifling-Instructive Distinction – a reply. *The Locke Newsletter* **11**: 89–99.
— (1982) Anthropology and Morality. *Journal of the Anthropological Society of Oxford* **13** (3).
— (1983) Eugenics and the Punishment of Incest Act 1908 [1983] *The Criminal Law Review*: 308–16.
— (1985) Divorce in England 1700–1857. *Oxford Journal of Legal Studies* **5** (2): 155–86.

Paul Hirst

5 Is it rational to reject relativism?

The debate on rationality and relativism seems set to become interminable and insoluble. 'Debate' is a misnomer; rather it is all too often a contest that takes place from fixed positions and in which both sides draw sustenance from the intellectual weaknesses of their opponents. The problem is: can this 'debate' ever get us anywhere? Relativism *is* pernicious if its most extreme consequences are enthusiastically embraced, but the effective antidote is neither to postulate a general human 'rationality' nor to suppose that we have independent means of demonstrating that the methods of modern science are of universal validity. Instead, we need strategies for *coping* with the consequences of relativism, accepting that our knowledges lack foundations in independent criteria of validity but without falling into a perspectivism that treats all views as equally valid. Such strategies need to be of another order from the meretricious demonstration of the logical inconsistency of systematic relativism or a pointing to the evident 'success' of Western science and technology. For all the critical scorn poured on them, relativist views have not gone away. They continue to be adopted and defended by able people in the social sciences.

In order to present my case I shall first consider Barry Barnes's and David Bloor's 'Relativism, Rationalism and the Sociology of Knowledge' (1982), in which they defend the productivity of a thoroughgoing relativism in the sociology of knowledge.[1] I shall argue that their claim that the sociology of knowledge can set aside questions of the validity of a knowledge, and concern itself with how knowledge, irrespective of its truth, acquires credibility, leads to unacceptable consequences. Second, I shall consider an example which raises the question of the difference between validity and credibility in an acute form: the rise and decline of witch-hunting in early modern Europe. I shall argue that the decline in witch-hunting is neither a function of the declining credibility of the belief in witches *per se*, nor a function of the rise of a new type of scientific rationality in the seventeenth century which provided the intellectual resources to challenge the truth of the belief in witches. To anticipate, I shall claim that the decline in large-scale witch-hunting is in part a loss of confidence in the legal process of the hunts, and this loss of confidence takes the form of a concern about the *validity* of the evidence thus gathered by witch-hunting tribunals.

Before doing this I shall spell out what seem to be the issues in the complex debates on rationality and relativism. The first issue is the question of 'anthropological' relativism – to put it in its most extreme form, whether there exist other cultures that are so different from ours that they are inexplicable in our terms, ultimately incomprehensible to us because we cannot translate them into our own terms, and whose terms have a value equal to our own. Many sociologists and anthropologists answer in the affirmative, that there is no basic human 'rationality' and no scheme of explanation that can be legitimately and objectively applied from its source in one culture to account for beliefs and practices in another. The best we can do is to recognize another culture's account of itself, to the extent that the problems of translatability and the limits to commensurability permit. To this the anti-relativists tend to reply with an emphatic negative and insist on the existence of an underlying common human rationality. Our common cognitive equipment and existential situation impose certain minimum conditions for inter-communicability. Underneath our cultural differences we share a common potential for rationality. Hence we are justified in pursuing the objective of a group of sciences that will apply to all humanity.

The second issue is the question of 'epistemological' relativism – that is, whether or not there are culture-independent standards of truth that cannot be reduced to local considerations of belief or to the non-demonstrable assumptions of a particular explanatory scheme. The answers here tend to be more complicated – varying from at one extreme straightforward defences of the universality of truth criteria and the cultural neutrality of objective scientific knowledge to relativist views that seek to make the validity of knowledge nothing more than a matter of local consensus, an agreement to agree, at the other extreme. It is possible that one could subscribe without inconsistency to the second kind of relativism without accepting the full consequences of the first, but that the opposite is more difficult, if not impossible.

The problem is that both these questions are overloaded to the point of collapse if one's supposition is that the way to resolve them is a definite answer pro or contra. To tackle the first question is often taken to demand some relatively defensible position on the existence or non-existence of our 'common human nature' – involving an account of our common cognitive capacities and the nature of the processes of our language acquisition and use. Such a question, apparently empirical and determinate, is actually complex and ambiguous. The anti-relativist faces a tall order given the state of our knowledge in psychology and linguistics, but, for the same reason, the relativist is equally hard-pressed (unless one is willing to rely on mere scepticism and the ultimate conditionality of the answer).

In fact were we able to specify a 'common human nature' this would not settle the question. The anti-relativist needs to explain *how* our common human nature underlies and is not subverted by the very real cultural differences that do exist, how it is that a common make-up really does enable us to surmount the problems of cultural differences in explaining other people's beliefs.[2]

To tackle the second question demands some means of putting an end to the irreconcilable proliferation of positions in modern epistemology. This question is bogged down by its formulation in terms of legislative epistemology, by its demand for a culture-neutral 'guarantee' which independently underwrites the validity of scientific knowledge. Our problem is not a lack of epistemological guarantees, but a surfeit of incompatible ones offered by very different and violently opposed philosophical doctrines. There seems little chance of this war of competing truth standards ceasing if we accept the classical epistemological premises from which it begins.[3]

In one sense a challenge to the naïve hyper-relativism and ultra-culturalism one finds in a good deal of modern sociology and social anthropology is to be welcomed. There can be no doubt that extreme relativism generally leads to an undesirable downgrading of the influence of biological and psychological factors on human capacity and conduct. Even worse is the fact that the most extreme perspectivism and relativism would make sociology and social anthropology pointless – to each culture and sub-culture its own equally valid and incommensurable world view. The problem is that the challenge to relativism of this kind is all too often made by a form of rationalism that is dogmatically convinced of the possibility of independent criteria of valid knowledge, believes that these criteria are possessed by the modern natural sciences, and holds that, in general, Western science and technology have contributed to progress and the betterment of humanity. Each of these convictions is problematic and can be challenged by intelligent relativist arguments. For example, Barnes and Bloor base much of their case for adopting a relativist stance on the weakness of arguments for independent criteria of valid knowledge which are of universal applicability, challenging both empiricist and rationalist versions. Unfortunately, the one view tends to breed the other, each feeding off the other's shortcomings.

Barnes's and Bloor's relativism

Barnes's and Bloor's (1982) paper represents a succinct statement of an extreme relativism that combines the anthropological and epistemological poles. It has the subtle difference that questions of the ultimate truth or falsity of knowledge or belief are bracketed for purposes of sociological analysis. To accept formally that all ideas are equally true involves logical contradictions, and so they make relativism a methodological device in a certain strategy of sociological investigation. For such a sociology ultimately there is no defensible difference between validity and credibility; truth or adequate evidence are merely the products of local, socially conditioned agreements to agree. It should be noted that this bracketing is accompanied by strong philosophical arguments against effective general standards of validity. Barnes and Bloor clearly do not think they are forgoing anything of substance in their bracketing, merely avoiding a logical contradiction. For them what are called 'truth' and 'validity' by social agents are conventional and variable standards that are socially determined. Such terms are like our uses of 'good' and 'bad', essentially normative and dependent on the effects of socialization, the social support of justified conviction and the pressures of social control.[4]

This epistemological relativism, validity as socially sustained and conventional, leads to an anthropological relativism, that such standards vary between cultures and that there is no culture-independent justification for them. Thus, they argue against the views of Hollis (1967) and Lukes (1967) and contend that there is no 'common core' of human abilities to perceive and judge which makes a 'bridgehead' between cultures and which makes translation and communication possible. Translation is at best merely a practical and local convention – it can never be perfect. Barnes and Bloor contend: 'The bridgehead argument is a plea for a single pure observation language' (Barnes and Bloor 1982: 4). Without this we cannot establish 'natural kinds' such as would enable us to compare rigorously human beliefs about an orientation to the world in a way that we could assess their rationality or irrationality *tout court*.

Whilst the issue of 'bridgeheads' is secondary to this paper it is necessary to make some remarks on this claim. An argument about the possibility of 'bridgeheads' need involve the postulate of an observation language if, and only if, its purpose is to establish a culture-neutral reference point, the function of which is to provide an objective means of deciding about the truth and rationality of beliefs. If by 'observation language' we mean a theory-neutral organization of sense data, such that theoretical languages or beliefs can be measured relative to an objective 'common core' of human experience, then it is clear that it is a non-starter. Barnes and Bloor have argued against this with some force and cite a number of powerful challenges to the concept of an observation language in this sense.[5] It is a powerful challenge to a position hardly anybody holds – not even Hollis (1967).

The point of most 'bridgehead' arguments is more pragmatic, it is that despite all the theoretical arguments about translation and cultural relativity we *really can* communicate with other peoples and that there are good biological and cultural reasons for this. There is no reason to push this pragmatic claim further, into making it an argument for a culture-neutral standard for judging beliefs based on our species-specific common cognitive equipment and our common situation in the world. The absence of such a standard does not stop actual 'bridgeheads' being constructed or stop the knowledge thus gained being defensible as an anthropological account. To claim 'bridgeheads' are possible, that we are not trapped within the points of view of incommensurable cultures, does not depend on postulating an observation language. Furthermore, the possibility of building 'bridgeheads' may not stem from our having the same attributes and experiences, such contacts may arise in spite of very decided asymmetries in experience and cognitive development on the part of those involved. Bridgeheads do not presuppose a strong 'common core', indeed they may arise from fascination with difference. What is required is the conviction that interaction is possible and that we can learn from it. Radical relativist arguments if taken seriously would undermine this conviction. Not all 'bridgehead' arguments are good ones, certainly we need not suppose a common 'human nature'.

Barnes and Bloor are sociologists of knowledge and they seek to defend the view that the validity of a knowledge, in the sense of its acceptance and credibility, is dependent on its social context. Valid or true knowledge is what is normatized as valid in a social context, is given assent to as such, and conforms to certain cultural expectations about the world. This leads them to conflate validity with credibility as sociological phenomena. But it is difficult to see how, despite their arguments, their radical methodological relativism does not lead to the problematization and undercutting of the sociology of knowledge as a defensible discipline. To say we lack a satisfying account of a supra-contextual standard of validity is *not* to make beliefs or standards no more than a function of the support or credence they derive from their social context. That is a non-sequiter. Standards of what is to count as knowledge clearly orignate *somewhere* and would not operate as they do without certain social conditions, but they need not be confined in their applicability or validity to the social conditions of their origin. Validation and evidentialization are social processes, but that in itself does not relativize or negate the products of those processes, judgements about knowledge claims. We can judge and compare standards of validity and knowledge claims even if we lack the supra-contextual archimedian point of a universal standard of truth. The fact of possessing such a universal standard would be, as Barnes and Bloor recognize, sociologically largely irrelevant, its epistemological power would not guarantee its acceptance even if we postulate 'rational' agents at whom we direct the claim that such a standard exists – unless we also postulate those agents have a common interest in giving assent to such a claim.

Whatever the fate of epistemological doctrines a determinist sociology of knowledge must make strong claims for the multi-contextual objectivity of its own process of knowing. For its procedures to work, that is, to situate knowledges in their social contexts and to explain how they are distinctively the products of their contexts, a sociology of knowledge must be able to say what both the knowledges and their social situations *are*. As a discipline it must have supra-contextual means of access to what it studies. To make deterministic claims the procedures of the sociology of knowledge must be both multi-contextual and generally defensible. Otherwise, if such claims to defensible objectivity are forsworn, then there is no reason to regard the sociology of knowledge as more than a purely context-specific game of reductionism which indefensibly claims to explain the origin of other beliefs and knowledges. Without strong claims to its own objectivity and the defensibility of its procedures we have no reason to believe that such a sociology has got either a given knowledge or its purported context right, let alone the relation between them. If the sociology of knowledge can place esoteric disciplines and bodies of thought in relation to social contexts very different from our own, say seventeenth-century Europe, then Barnes and Bloor's objections to the analysis of 'other cultures' fall.

Barnes and Bloor regard truth and falsity in their social use as terms like good and bad. Truth is what we give credence to and feel justified in so doing. The danger here is that in stressing the *social* nature of standards of validity, they tend to reduce validity to a social convention, to what happens to be given credence in a particular context.

It *is* possible to distinguish between credibility and validity without assuming validity to be a universal standard independent of the particular means of demonstration used by definite knowledges. Barnes and Bloor in effect equate validity with a truth that is independent of the definite means in some particular body of knowledge which we have to use to argue for it – with correspondence to a neutral observation language or with the proofs of a universal reason. Their radical conflation of validity with credibility makes all means of demonstration and evidentialization at par. The lack of satisfactory meta-arguments for our criteria of validity, arguments that are independent of substantive knowledge claims and that independently ground the means used in making these claims, does put limits on our ability to justify claims to validity. It does mean that in the absence of an autonomous epistemological 'foundation' to the distinct knowledges we use and value we are compelled to rely on what those knowledges use as their own standards of the adequacy of arguments and evidence. But Barnes and Bloor have in effect accepted the strong rationalist and empiricist claims to identify supra-contextual standards of validity with epistemological grounding. To lack such a grounding is *not* to be unable to claim that some kinds of argument or evidence are superior to others and are capable of judging these others.

To reduce claims that a certain explanation or account is 'better' than another to nothing more than socially generated agreement that this is so is self-defeating. Arguments and evidence do convince that one case is better than another, by *arguing* and *showing*. Arguing and showing cannot be done or justified except by doing them – they cannot be grounded or guaranteed – but, without guarantees, it *is* possible to advance justifiable claims for better and worse. These claims can operate multi-contextually and can change others' standards of what is a credible and justifiable belief. These claims can be held to stand even if some people do not agree. For example, the fact of Creationist dissent does not mean that Genesis and neo-Darwinian evolutionary theory are at par as knowledges. The sociology of knowledge can help us to understand the conflict between evolutionary biology and modern Creationism, but not if it starts by regarding them at par in terms of the validity of their arguments and evidence. To do so would be to misread both the social and the intellectual character of the struggle. To recognize the indefensible nature of Creationist claims is a condition of understanding their style of argument and method of campaigning, in particular their shift from the 1920s attempt at the simple prohibition of the teaching of evolutionary biology to the demand for 'equal time' for Creationist teaching.

Barnes and Bloor say:

'Our equivalence postulate is that all beliefs are at par with one another with respect to the causes of their credibility. It is not that all beliefs are equally true or equally false, but that regardless of truth and falsity the fact of their credibility is to be seen as equally problematic. . . . This means that regardless of whether the sociologist evaluates a belief as true or rational, or as false and irrational, he must search for the causes of its credibility.' (Barnes and Bloor 1982: 23)

They go on to claim this 'places all beliefs on a par with one another *for the purposes of explanation*' (Barnes and Bloor 1982: 25, my emphasis). But it does more, for in effect it simply places all beliefs on a par with one another. This can have disastrous effects on sociological explanation.

A certain kind of relativism about epistemology, that is, to accept that there is no viable meta-theory or epistemological grounding of knowledges, leads to exactly the opposite of what Barnes and Bloor claim. They are led to their position because their relativism extends not merely to epistemological doctrines but to each and every knowledge claim. If we reject this hyper-relativism then we must recognize that we cannot be satisfied with the bracketing of validity and with concentrating on the question of how a belief or knowledge becomes credible. It is no use saying this is for methodological purposes, for such a bracketing undercuts the sociology of knowledge both in terms of its ability to study certain problems and its ability to justify the results of its study. Without some defensible standard of validity there is no certainty whatever in the notion that something is credible. Even if we are solely concerned with establishing how a belief acquires 'credibility', how do we know that people indeed agree to agree or that they actually *do* hold something to be credible? If validity and credibility are collapsed *nothing* is credible, even our belief that we know others agree to agree. To know something is credible to a certain group is to be able to argue and show it to be actually held as such. Further, if one attempts to distinguish between credibility and credulity – to claim that there are genuinely justified grounds for one belief and not for another – then we are already distinguishing between forms of assent to knowledge to a degree that warrants the reintroduction of the term validity. If we do not do this then we are hopelessly trapped; not only can we not say reliably whether a belief *is* credible to people – we are condemned to be credulous about the question – but we can also not argue that their belief is what it is and that it is credulous. We must either believe or remain silent.

Barnes and Bloor might well retort that my validity is little better than credibility, indeed, identical to it. In arguing against claims for universally valid and context-independent standards of knowledge, they attack certain rationalist and empiricist epistemological doctrines, but they confuse all arguments for validity with these doctrines' conceptions of it and in consequence ignore possible positions which do seek to defend forms of validity without guarantees or foundations. At points they appear to agree with the possibility of assessing the validity of knowledge claims, arguing that whilst knowledges are not all equally true this is irrelevant to their socially constructed credibility. However, truth and falsity are conceived as themselves socially relative: '"True" like "good" is an institutionalized label used in sifting belief or action according to socially established criteria' (Barnes 1974: 22). To say as they seem to do at one point in their 1982 paper that the sociology of knowledge is a positive discipline, which explains *how* knowledges arise, on a par with cognitive psychology, would be a modest claim against the grandiose pretensions of legislative epistemology were it not for the fact that the *way* they argue seems to undercut any possibility of the defence of such a discipline at all.

Hacking's (1982) paper argues persuasively that the truth and falsehood of propositions depend on the styles of reasoning appropriate to those propositions. He argues that although the truth of propositions in a particular style of reasoning may depend on data, the style itself does not. Styles arise in historical contexts and therefore depend for their existence on contingent events.

Hacking insists that 'propositions of the sort that necessarily require reasoning to be substantiated have a positivity, a being true or false, only in consequence of the styles of reasoning in which they occur' (Hacking 1982: 64).[6] Such a conception of the historicity of knowledge is radically different from Barnes's and Bloor's 'sociology of knowledge'. For relativity to a conceptual scheme does not mean that we are unable in practice to distinguish between validity and credibility. Clear criteria of validity are available in different schemes and knowledges, what we do not have is a meta-conceptual justification for the forms of validity such schemes propose. Hacking has no general difficulties about the objectivity of knowledges – once it is recognized such objectivity exists within a conceptual scheme for which there are no guarantees. Hacking's position challenges legislative and foundationalist epistemology without also collapsing whatever specific force demonstrations and evidence have. Hacking offers a defensible half-way position between the vertigo of perspectivism – and its reduction of all the components of knowledge to a context – and the ultimately impossible project of a guarantee of knowledge which is non-contextual. In this way we can begin to see how we may be able to avoid the related disorders of a single syndrome – legislative epistemology and ultra-relativist anti-epistemology.

Validity, credibility and witch-hunting[7]

The decline in witch-hunting had little to do with a waning of belief in the entity 'witch'. The displacement of such entities as 'witch' or 'Devil' furthermore has seldom taken the form of set-piece debates among intellectuals about their existence or non-existence. In Western Europe, witch-hunting declined dramatically after 1660, but at that time most of the members of the élites responsible for the persecutions 'believed' such beings existed. It was not a withdrawal of credence in the existence of witches that ended the trials, probably more like the reverse.

For modern science and common sense to accept that there are 'witches' in the sense of the European popular tradition – persons capable of doing harm by occult means and of flying through the air at night to do evil in the company of their fellows – is a prime example of a *credulous* belief. Its adoption and sanction by the learned would appear a prime example of superstition and irrationality, a hangover from the Middle Ages into the era of Galileo and Newton. Yet the dominant view held by the Church from the tenth to the fourteenth centuries was that belief in witches was a credulous and pagan popular superstition that should be stamped out and punished. The *Canon Episcopi* treats *belief* in the existence and occult power of witches as heretical. Belief in witches is illusionary and those who believe themselves to be witches are deluded by Satan. In the early fifteenth century this position is reversed – it is held that witchcraft practice really does exist and it is now the practice of witchcraft rather than the unjustified and credulous belief in it which is culpable and heretical. Learned opinion changes and goes so far as to adopt popular beliefs about night-witches and flying, previously condemned as credulous. The reasons for this reversal are complex but, as Cohn (1975) and Kieckhefer (1976) show, it is closely connected with the suppression of heretical movements.

The doctrinal basis for large-scale hunting developed virtually contemporaneously with the Renaissance and was no hangover from Medieval 'superstition'; Cohn remarks:

'until late in the fourteenth century the educated in general, and the higher clergy in particular, were quite clear that these nocturnal journeyings of women . . . were purely imaginary happenings. But in the sixteenth century and still more in the seventeenth century, this was no longer the case. And that is what made the great witch-hunt possible: witch-hunting reached massive proportions only where and when the authorities themselves accepted the reality of nocturnal journeyings. For without such journeyings, no witches sabbats.' (Cohn 1975: 224)

Without sabbats there was no basis for the naming by the accused of large numbers of other witches during the inquisitorial procedure and, therefore, no basis for large-scale hunts. In the absence of such belief in the reality of sabbats by the learned, accusations of witchcraft would depend largely on charges of *maleficium* by those injured or aggrieved, whereas the inquisitors' belief in the sabbat and the procedure of accepting denunciations enabled and required them to obtain an account of the names of all those recognized by the accused who were present at the sabbat.

Learned belief embraced as credible what tenth-century bishops had been instructed to regard as credulous. This goes against our entrenched post-Enlightenment views of the dialectic whereby rational argument and the critical use of empirical evidence triumphed over credulous and unjustified belief. Alasdair MacIntyre (1967), arguing against the relativism of Peter Winch, expresses this dialectic very clearly:

'In seventeenth-century Scotland, for example, the question could not but be raised, "But are there witches?" If Winch asks, from within what way of life, under what system of belief was this question asked, the only answer is that it was asked by men who confronted alternative systems and were able to draw out of what confronted them independent criteria of judgement.' (MacIntyre 1967: 129)

MacIntyre supposes a rationality emerging from the clash of alternative systems of belief; independent criteria of judgement are developed by men seeking the truth about the differing views on the reality of witchcraft. Unfortunately, this is not what seems to have happened in Scotland. The existence of witches was affirmed by a massive consensus of learned and popular opinion. It was not the existence of witches but the utility and justice of the methods of bringing them to trial that became a matter of dispute. Larner (1980) shows this very well: the Lord Advocate in the crucial period, Sir George Mackensie, was certainly sceptical about the process of detection and trial of witches, but his manner of defending the accused was to concentrate on defects in evidence and procedure as any good lawyer would. This left the wider context of belief in witches and the general legitimacy of witchcraft trials untouched.

Throughout Europe the question 'But are there witches?' – although posed by sceptics – was not and could not be consequential in the context of the witch trials. The opponents of witch-hunting such as Weyer, Scot, and Spee, were not effective in ending witch trials largely because learned belief in witches was *not* credulous and because the inquisitorial process, far from being an ancient abomination, was part of the relatively recent *rationalization* of judicial procedure. Indeed, the opponents of witch-hunting in the first half of the seventeenth century were beaten in open argument by the supporters of forensic demonology. The leading advocates of this ghastly discipline were not the stereotypical fanatical, credulous, and sexually repressed monks, but included men of first rate and critical intellects like the lawyer and political theorist Jean Bodin.

Contra MacIntyre the intellectual defenders of witch-hunting could sustain their belief with some confidence *because* they were convinced it was rational and supported by evidence. MacIntyre asserts that our own criteria of know-ledge *are* rational, relative to other beliefs such as those of the Azande or seventeenth-century witch-hunters. He is right. The problem is that the forensic demonologist could have asserted the same in the seventeenth century, and with the same certainty that he was right. This is not to say that given what we know they *are* right or that their view is of equivalent validity to our own today; it is not. The damaging point is that for a crucial period in the witch-hunting the forensic demonologists won, not by eliminating their opponents by physical force, but by the intellectual force of arguing and showing. They did so by defending a relatively new view among the learned about the reality of witches and a relatively new legal procedure against opponents whose positions often resemble those of the *Canon Episcopi*. They were defending doctrinal and procedural innovations by, in many cases, rigorous argument and reference to evidence, not by maintaining ancient and credulous belief by authoritarian force.

If we say that the forensic demonologists exhibit rationality in the way they present and defend their case, that neither are they merely credulous nor does their argument depend on mere credibility, but can sustain propositions previously regarded as incredible and that were seriously challenged as such at the time, then we face a more serious problem than the cosy relativism of agreements to agree, or the less cosy effects of social control. Arguing and showing *do* work, but all arguments, however 'rational', depend on premises and those premises derive from what is perceived as legitimate as a point of departure. Rationality cannot be separated from styles of reasoning. In other words, premises involve suppositions about both forms of procedure in argu-ment and the existence of entities necessary to the argument, and those latter are deemed to be a sufficiently secure context for the argument. Take a classic of forensic demonology like Sprenger's and Kramer's *Malleus Maleficarum*. Far from being credulous assertion it bristles with theological and other arguments against objections to the belief in witches and the proposed pro-cedure for finding them. Take a typical passage:

'those err who say that there is no such thing as witchcraft, but that it is purely imaginary, even though they do not believe that devils exist except in the imagination of the ignorant and vulgar, and the natural accidents which happen to a man he wrongly attributes to some supposed devil. For the imagination of some men is so vivid that they think they see actual figures and appearances which are but the reflection of their thought and then these are believed to be the apparitions of evil spirits or even the spectres of witches. *But this is contrary to true faith*, which teaches us that certain angels fell from heaven and are now devils, and we are bound to acknowledge that by their very nature they can do many wonderful things which we cannot do. And those who try to induce others to perform such evil wonders are called witches.' (1436: 35, my emphasis)

Sprenger and Kramer argue what can be argued and at a certain point confine themselves to demonstrating the consequences of certain beliefs. To claim 'But this is contrary to true faith' is *not* irrational. Rather it is the reverse which is irrational: to suppose that the existence of God or Satan can be settled by argument or earthly evidence. The two monks are clear as to what are matters of faith and what are not. Well into the eighteenth century, entities specified by faith are generally accepted as a starting-point for legitimate arguments. The opponents of demonology suffered from the difficulty that few of them were willing to question such premises, and were caught on the logic of the consequences.

Even if the powers of the Devil are a premise given by faith, the observation and classification of human actions were not. Forensic demonology as used in the inquisitorial process did not lead to all and any behaviours reported to it being classified as witchcraft. Mental illness, epilepsy, demoniacal possession, etc., were known by observational signs and differentiated from witchcraft. Lawyers and inquisitors were not making a category mistake and classifying signs of mental disorder as witchcraft as some historians of psychiatry like Zilboorg (1935) have supposed. We are not dealing with a circular or self-confirming belief but with a procedure of investigation which sought by observational means among others to identify a specific class of culpable beliefs and practices. Forensic demonology is no more irrational than failed observational sciences like phrenology or the cranial measurement of criminals.

The Spanish and Italian inquisitors were notoriously sceptical about witchcraft accusations and confessions and were relatively leisurely and 'lenient' in their pursuit of and sentencing of cases. This did not mean that inquisitors were publicly or privately sceptical about the existence of witches in the abstract or that they rejected the demonological stereotypes based on the sabbat, merely that they were securely in control of heresy and therefore in a position to avoid paranoid persecutions and to judge the relatively few cases that came before them on their individual merits.[8]

Witchcraft trials in their classic form appear to modern appraisal to be self-evidently self-confirming because the defendants appear as a result of denunciation; their guilt is proven by their confession extracted through torture and the accused are required as part of their confession to denounce in turn their associates at the sabbat. Indeed, it is this very logic of confession and accusation which fuels the hunts, which makes them so socially destructive and uncontrollable and on which procedural criticisms came to centre. It is worth while pointing out, however, the reasons why this form of process could persist for a long time without appearing absurd. The first point to notice is that the inquisitorial procedure used in the Continental hunts but not in England was common to both witchcraft trials and serious criminal trials. Second, that both processes employed judicial torture as a means to prove guilt by confession. Third, that the inquisitorial form of process was a legal innovation, introduced for proceedings against clerics from the twelfth century onward, gradually introduced as the method of proceeding against all heretics and institutionalized, and also introduced by the secular authorities for criminal cases, being in widespread use by the early fifteenth century.[9]

In the sixteenth century it was still being developed and reformed for both witchcraft and criminal cases as shown by the *Constitutio Criminalis Carolina* (1532), for example.[10] Torture was, therefore, a generally accepted method of judicial examination and confession was the normal standard of full proof. The inquisitorial procedure was regarded as and was more rational, certain, and reliable than the accusatory procedure and it placed greater weight on the role of judges and lawyers in the assessment of evidence and in the determination of guilt. Neither torture as a means of eliciting evidence nor confession as a standard of proof were therefore unusual or exceptional in the context of the sixteenth- and seventeenth-century trial practice.

What *was* exceptional was that the safeguards normal in criminal procedure were abrogated in witchcraft trials; witchcraft was the *crimen exceptum*. The procedural differences were essentially three. First, that in the normal criminal procedure *partial* proof was a condition for the application of torture, and the accused would typically have either strong circumstantial evidence or the testimony of one witness as partial proof of guilt, whereas in the exceptional procedure denunciation was sufficient. Second, that evidence or denunciations were not subject to the status constraints of the normal criminal procedure, that is convicted felons, excommunicants and so on were banned from giving evidence as the sole basis for conviction in criminal trials whereas a convicted witch's testimony could count as evidence in a witch trial. Third, that whilst leading questions were supposed to be forbidden in criminal investigations under torture and the periods and manner of torture supposed to be strictly regulated this was either ignored or standards relaxed in witchcraft trials. Such criticisms were raised by jurists like Godelman in the sixteenth century well before the decline of large-scale hunting. They were dismissed because of the extent of the threat as evidenced by the use of the procedure itself. The exceptions to the normal standards of justice appeared to be justified by the nature of the crime and the magnitude of the perceived threat – much as modern states use exceptional legislation in periods of war and political crisis. We should not be surprised by a category like *crimen exceptum* when we recall twentieth-century British legislation like DORA or the Prevention of Terrorism Act.

It is in the exceptional nature of the procedure in witchcraft cases that the main source of the decline in witch-hunting is to be found. It is not that inquisitors, judges and lawyers doubted that there *were* witches, nor that they had general objections to seeking them out and burning them, nor that they doubted the value of torture and confession given proper safeguards. As Midelfort (1972, 1979) and Larner (1980) have argued for Southwestern Germany and Scotland respectively, the large-scale hunts and trials exposed the problematic nature of the procedure for those who were willing to see it. Such hunts became self-generating and, as they did so, they passed beyond the marginals and misfits who tended to be the subjects of the initial denunciations to include more and more persons of conventionally good character, even including town councillors, petty nobility, and minor court officials. Perhaps if old and marginal women had denounced only old and marginal women the procedural crisis would not have become so apparent. People did doubt, however, because unrestricted torture *was* exceptional and they had other procedural standards against which to measure it. The arguments against the exceptional procedure were forensic and not primarily about the ontological status of witches. They were about the validity of the procedures as a means of *finding* witches, and centred on the *quality* of evidence produced by the procedure. In the general ontological argument the demonologists tended to beat their critics, while in the dispute about the forensic value of the inquisitorial process quite different questions of validity came to be posed. Here sceptics of a rather different stamp prevailed in practice. In many cases hunting just stopped rather than being stopped by any explicit decision of the judical authorities.

It should not be thought that the simple fact that confessions were elicited by torture was decisive. Although contemporary critics did repeatedly point out that unrestrained torture and leading questions did tend to worthless confessions being made and in words suggested by the examining judge or inquisitor simply to end the pain. In England judicial torture proper was not used and witches still confessed. Moreover, not all confessions have the stereotyped air of a twentieth-century show trial. Some were made with relatively little coercion and with a wealth of circumstantial detail. Popular belief – as stereotyped in learned demonology – was available without prompting and in the seventeenth century new standards of confession were being enforced by the Catholic Church and the examination of conscience was a discipline practised in various Protestant congregations. Ordinary people in the mid-seventeenth century were schooled *how* to confess more thoroughly than they had been but a century before. Inquisitors and judges could often feel they were eliciting spontaneous testimony that provided evidence for their worst fears. The criticism of the exceptional procedure did not therefore need to doubt the truth of *all* confessions merely some of them, any more than the critics of police corruption and the fabrication of evidence need to doubt the guilt of all those convicted in criminal trials today. It was not that the procedure could not find witches, it was that it was not reliable enough to find only them or to send to the fires only a tolerably small portion of the innocent. God would indeed know the innocent but unrestrained hunting had evident social costs that undermined authority and faith for those not fortunate enough to have passed before the greatest Judge. Unrestrained hunting led to a situation where nobody was safe from denunciation save the very highest ecclesiastical and civil authorities. As a method of policing the faithful and casting out the enemies of God it bred suspicion and reserve. It created an atmosphere which favoured the witches since it could lead to a doubting of earthly justice and through it despair in Divine Justice. Ultimately, it would undermine the ties between the religious and between them and their priests and pastors necessary to maintain faith and religious discipline.

It should be noted that at the very point when hunting dies out the means had become available to combat religious deviation in general and, therefore, to supervise flocks such that the temptations of witchcraft can be countered through religious police rather than the fire. It is now widely argued that the sixteenth–seventeenth centuries saw the full Christianization of the peasantry and lower orders in Europe and that the Reformation and Counter-Reformation led to new standards of preaching and pastoral care. Protestants and Catholics both struggled to impose new standards of belief and conduct on their congregations, to have an effective pastoral presence in the villages of the common people. Delumeau (1977) and Larner (1980) among others devote attention to this process. As Larner points out for Calvinist Scotland, the very aim of creating a Godly People led to a drawing of boundaries between those within and obedient to, and those without the Law; witch-hunting was one central means of defeating the Enemies of God. Education, preaching, and pastoral supervision were ultimately the most effective means since they installed religious discipline in the interstices of village society and stamped out error and evil at root.

In order for such religious discipline to take full hold it required stable political authority and the suppression of organized opposition. After the mid-seventeenth century a relatively stable religious territorialization of Europe is enforced by the Peace of Westphalia 1648 and the virtual suppression of Protestantism in France consequent on the revocation of the Edict of Nantes (1685). Under such conditions the hunts could rapidly cease, as they did. Without close pastoral control and without the stabilization of religious territories, such that organized heresy is reduced to limits manageable by ordinary religious police measures, the pressure to use the exceptional procedure would doubtless have become overwhelming. It is the defects in the procedure rather than any change in belief that led to *effective* criticism of the hunts; it is the stabilization of religious authority and the containment of heresy that made that criticism effective and lasting. Later, most members of the political and legal élites came to doubt the existence of witches – how much later is a matter of conjecture and varies from country to country. But nowhere was it well established before the large-scale hunting stopped.

I hope this example goes some way to illustrate *why* we need to distinguish between validity and credibility in respect of belief and claims to knowledge. To do so is not to erect some universal and independently grounded standard of truth, nor is it to deny the value of sociological contributions to explaining the rise and fall of bodies of knowledge. Standards of validity and styles of reasoning do have a history. This neither invalidates their use in assessing other styles nor renders them inherently contextural. Our modern methods of arguing, showing, and investigating in the natural and social sciences are not of a piece; they may be at odds with one another in some cases, but as such, and given what we know, they do allow us both to assess and account for previous knowledges like forensic demonology. Montague Summers notwithstanding, that discipline would not stand five minutes in open argument today and *not* merely because the consequences of our agreement to agree. In the seventeenth century that discipline could defeat its opponents in open argument and without simply depending on the confirmation and authority of the background popular beliefs. Ultimately, the issue reduces to premises for arguments and the value of styles of reasoning. We have no grounding independent of our premises for our distrust of the premises of forensic demonology, but good reasons for so doing *within* our premises.

The danger of Barnes's and Bloor's claim for the sociology of knowledge in their paper is that in defining valid knowledges as those that become credible they appear to reduce the process by which that happens to the production of a consensus or to a 'belief system'. We have seen how far the rise of forensic demonology depended on argument and evidence – both to reverse previous learned incredulity and to defeat intellectual opponents who did not find it credible. Forensic demonology was not credulous; it adopted popular beliefs but *not* their basis for credence among the ordinary people. The learned demonologists used the resources of theological and legal reasoning, also empirical evidence and classificatory diagnostics for sifting out different sources of behaviour like madness and witchcraft.

In a society that accorded great weight to theological, legal and empirical-scientific reasoning and to the use of evidence, such as one finds among the learned in sixteenth- and seventeenth-century Europe, the construction of the credibility of a knowledge cannot be a matter of agreeing to agree, of 'holding' beliefs. As a *social* process it must include an element of genuine intellectual struggle using resources of argument and demonstration whose outcome is not pre-given. It is a *bad* sociology of knowledge that ignores the construction of social relations in which standards of validity – historical no doubt and to be supplanted perhaps – and the intellectual processes by which standards are hammered out are accorded some genuine autonomy. Barnes's and Bloor's *de facto* conflation of validity and credibility in their (1982) paper seems to me to ignore this sociological fact.

But if such standards can function autonomously it does not follow that, *post eventum*, judgements on the basis of different standards will concur. The forensic demonologists had a more consistent and effective case than their opponents about the reality of witches, and witch-hunting was displaced for reasons other than a general decline in the belief in the existence of witches. It would be difficult to call the demonologists irrational *tout court*. The category of 'rationality' cannot get us far if we accept that some forms in the belief in witches are not irrational relative to prevailing premises and styles of reasoning. It is difficult to prove these premises irrational *per se*, although such premises have almost no force today and we can say why. We can say that true faith is not the centre of our prevailing knowledges and we can argue persuasively why we reject faith as a point of departure for any valid knowledge claim. We judge forensic demonology to be inferior to our explanatory schemes. But, ultimately, premises are *premises* and arguments have what demonstrative force they do in a conceptual scheme. Rationality is a matter of judgement when it concerns the relative merits of very different ways of arguing and showing. It seems to me that we lose little by accepting that relative to the suppositions and standards of its time forensic demonology – rigorously pursued – was 'rational'. If standards of validity and styles of reasoning change, so what? It does not make my given argument or knowledge claim today or yesterday any the stronger or weaker, only a good case pro or contra can do that.

The fact of *shifting* standards of validity is no reason either to embrace Barnes's and Bloor's form of hyper-relativism nor to seek bogus, supra-contextual 'foundations' and 'guarantees' for our knowledges. Relativism is pernicious to the degree that it makes the fact of shifting standards an argument against the resources of the knowledges we deem to be valuable and relatively correct. A category like 'rationality' appears to be a poor defence against this perniciousness, not because as some relativists would appear to claim there are no knowledges which are candidates for the status but far too many. There *are* irrational beliefs, but knowledges which rationalize their premises, argue rigorously from them, allow a place to evidence, and know where empirical claims stop, are not among them. Regrettably, repulsive and ghastly disciplines like forensic demonology – and some contemporary candidates – can be argued to be 'rational' in most modern meanings of the term. People may be rational without being right or good, according to our standards. Adding that latter phrase does not undermine or diminish the value of judgements according to those standards. We have to use and justify them. It is up to us to do so and not to abandon judgement.

If our example is of illustrative value it is also of value in showing that the rise and fall of beliefs about entities must be assessed in relation to the full complexity of the practices in which they serve as background support, or means of demonstration. Demonology's decline was highly consequential upon the fact that it was *forensic*. The defects of the inquisitorial procedure for the *crimen exceptum* in the large-scale hunts are evident to us, but in the seventeenth century they were gradually and painfully discovered. The forensic value of demonology did not alter because the belief in witches declined and ceased to offer the procedure support. Rather, the defects in the procedure for *finding* witches led to a situation in which lawyers and inquisitors ceased to hunt them; in the long run the decline in hunting helped to sustain a decline in belief.

This sociological point is in no sense helped by the conflation of validity and credibility. Intellectuals and persons in authority were secure in sound reasons for believing in witches. Given that security and given the knowledge of God's omnipotent judgement they could argue about the procedural defects of hunting. If hunting had been the only source of the credibility of the belief, confirming it like a ritual and reinforcing consensus, the decline of the practice would have been much more difficult. Legal procedure was widely viewed as a domain of technique; as something to be assessed, reformed, and improved. This makes a great difference. The sociological argument about the decline of witch-hunting is actually *aided* by recognizing an élite which accords autonomous functions to standards of validity, to arguing and showing, in areas like theology, law, and empirical science. Validity and credibility cannot be conflated on pain of a sociology that is all too willing to be credulous about belief.

Notes

1 Barnes and Bloor have written extensively on these issues, see for example Barnes (1974) and Bloor (1976). An earlier and briefer version of my criticism of Barnes's and Bloor's relativism is to be found in Hirst (1984).
2 Hacking: (1982: 61) makes this point clearly and forcefully.
3 For a discussion of the problematic nature of the classical epistemological doctrines of empiricism and rationalism see Hindess and Hirst (1977), Ch. 1.
4 See Barnes (1974) Chs 1 and 2.
5 See Barnes (1974) Ch. 1 and Hesse (1980) Chs 2 and 3.
6 See Foucault (1972) for an important source of Hacking's argument.
7 I have discussed witchcraft at greater length in Hirst and Woolley (1982), Pt 3.
8 See Ginzburg (1983) and Monter (1983) Ch. 4.
9 See Langbein (1977) and Ruthven (1978).
10 See Langbein (1974).

References

BARNES, B. (1974) *Scientific Knowledge and Sociological Theory*. London: Routledge & Kegan Paul.
BARNES, B. and BLOOR, D. (1982) Relativism, Rationalism and the Sociology of Knowledge. In Hollis and Lukes (1982): 21–47.

BLOOR, D. (1976) *Knowledge and Social Imagery*. London: Routledge & Kegan Paul.
COHN, N. (1975) *Europe's Inner Demons*. St Albans: Paladin.
DELUMEAU, J. (1977) *Catholicism between Luther and Voltaire*. London: Burns & Oates.
FOUCAULT, M. (1972) *The Archaeology of Knowledge*. London: Tavistock.
GINZBURG, C. (1983) *The Night Battles*. London: Routledge & Kegan Paul.
HACKING, I. (1982) Language, Truth and Reason. In Hollis and Lukes (1982).
HESSE, M. (1980) *Revolutions and Reconstructions in the Philosophy of Science*. Brighton: Harvester.
HINDESS, B. and HIRST, P. (1977) *Mode of Production and Social Formation*. London: Macmillan.
HIRST, P. (1984) Witches, Relativism and Magic. *Sociological Review* **32** (3).
HIRST, P. and WOOLLEY, P. (1982) *Social Relations and Human Attributes*. London: Tavistock.
HOLLIS, M. (1967) The Limits to Irrationality. *European Journal of Sociology* **7**: 265–71.
HOLLIS, M. and LUKES, S. (1982) *Rationality and Relativism*. Oxford: Basil Blackwell.
KIECKHEFER, R. (1976) *European Witch Trials*. London: Routledge & Kegan Paul.
LANGBEIN, J. H. (1974) *Prosecuting Crime in the Renaissance*. Cambridge, Mass.: Harvard University Press.
— (1977) *Torture and the Law of Proof*. Chicago: Chicago University Press.
LARNER, C. (1980) *Enemies of God: The Witch Hunt in Scotland*. London: Chatto & Windus.
LUKES, S. (1967) Some Problems about Rationality. *European Journal of Sociology* **7**: 247–64.
MACINTYRE, A. (1967) The Idea of a Social Science. Reprinted in Wilson (1970).
MIDELFORT, H. C. ERIK (1972) *Witch-Hunting in Southwestern Germany 1562–1684*. California: Stanford University Press.
— (1979) Witch-Hunting and the Domino Theory. In Obelkevich (ed.) (1979).
MONTER, W. (1983) *Ritual Myth and Magic in Early Modern Europe*. Brighton: Harvester.
OBELKEVICH, J. (ed.) *Religion and the People 800–1700*. Chapel Hill: Carolina University Press.
RUTHVEN, M. (1978) *Torture: the Grand Conspiracy*. London: Weidenfeld & Nicolson.
SPRENGER, J. and KRAMER, H. (1971) *Malleus Maleficarum (1486)*, translated by M. Summers. London: Arrow.
WILSON, B. (ed.) (1970) *Rationality*. Oxford: Basil Blackwell.
ZILBOORG (1935) *The Medical Man and the Witch During the Renaissance*. New York: Cooper Square (1969).

Mark Hobart

6 Anthropos through the looking-glass:
or how to teach the Balinese to bark

So much has been said to so little avail about rationality that to add to it would be pretty pointless. However a curious document has come my way which suggests that disquisitions on rationality reveal more about their authors than about what they claim to speak. I quote briefly.

'Sometimes the Tsew really appear backward. Their utter conviction in their superiority can be very straining on an outsider; for they use every opportunity to compare others unflatteringly with themselves. While they display a shrewd mercantile flair, no small technical ingenuity and awesome military might, it is the manner by which they justify their prowess which mystifies one not born with their assumptions and mode of reasoning. Nretsew peoples are thought to excel in the finest human attribute, being *laniotar*, or *Ar* in common parlance. This quality above all they asseverate to be the cause of their success. According to the learned elders *Ar* is so important in Nretsew life that they define humanity by its possession and animality by its absence. I suspect my dilatory and uncertain grasp of this concept has given them ground to doubt whether I am indeed truly human. For unless one is *Ar*, it transpires one cannot understand what it is.

Today was most depressing. As the Tsew constantly invoke *Ar* to account for every institution from agricultural practice to moral injunctions, I returned to trying to understand it. The priests to whom I spoke quite failed to see how contradictory I found their ideas about *Ar*. For humans are defined by *Ar*, but some are more so than others. Not being *Ar* enough opens one to ridicule; and tens of thousands of Tsew have been incarcerated by their fellows, often until death, on the charge of lacking *Ar*. The quality of *Ar* is inferred from speech and action by the priests, but while these persons epitomize this highest of virtues, the same priests are widely treated with contempt by many. Traditionally the truth about *Ar* was revealed by the two great Culture Heroes, Otalp and Eltotsira, who it seems agreed on little else. Texts in esoteric language abound and sects proliferate, each professing the true interpretation and using it to refute the others. Foolishly I remarked that, as every sect's criteria were different, they might argue at cross-purposes for ever, only to be told scornfully that this showed I did not understand *Ar*. Surely it is inconsistent for each priest to boast an idiolect and disagree with all others, but unite to insist there to be only one true *Ar*.

Squabbles break out constantly. For instance, in the Order of Srenildrah, a young apostate, Sekul, was caught coping with the ambiguities of *Ar,* by preaching that it was of two kinds, *Arwan* and *Artu*. The magnitude of the heresy was brought to light by the arch-priest Silloh who reaffirmed the doctrine that there could be only one true *Ar*, because this was the necessary condition of thought itself. This peroration was though promptly criticized by another, Htims Notwen, who opined that the necessity of *Ar* derived from it being the condition of effective action.

When challenged, however, Nretsew priests often resort to arguments of a quite different order. They affirm categorically that the world could not make sense without *Ar*; or point to the material superiority of the Tsew as proof of *Ar*; the very flexibility of their argumentation itself being further proof that. . . '

At this juncture the text, which appears to be a kind of ethnographic diary, gradually becomes unintelligible. Later entries suggest that the anonymous author succumbed to drink, a fate one gathers popular in that culture.[1]

We hold these truths to be self-evident

Recent work on rationality is not unlike a hall of mirrors: it is a dazzling display of possibility – and improbability. Each reflection is so life-like and incontrovertible, and comes framed in its own style of erudition. The trouble is there are so many versions, each right, that one is faced with a surfeit of certitudes, each different. The profusion can hardly be explained away as a matter of interpretation of perspective; for each account claims to state the true and necessary way things are. If there be, as is mooted, a universal 'common core' of rationality and shared perceptions, which vary only according to the 'logic of situation' (Horton 1982: 257), the diversity of views suggests there are as many situations, or logics, as there are authors. The predicament, read carefully, is that of the Tsew. For how, so to speak, is one sure that what one sees is windows on the world not oneself in mirrors? To continue the metaphor, the only way of knowing is to try to smash through the mirrors to whatever lies beyond. To dally may be to meet the fate of that famous armchair introvert who

'. . . weaves by night and day
A magic web with colours gay.
She has heard a whisper say,
A curse is on her if she stay
    To look down on Camelot.'

REASON AND ITS DISCONTENTS

My recourse to metaphor might seem out of place in discussing rationality. Talk of mirrors is not a mere conceit though. For abstract notions, like reason, tend to be portrayed figuratively through metaphors that are hidden, or are far from as dead as they seem. I wish to explore here some of the presuppositions behind the imagery and consider how far assertions about the universality of rationality are a matter of fashion and cultural style. The point may be made by comparing received wisdom on reason and logic with Balinese ideas and use. The result is intended to be a critical ethnography in the sense that, rather than judge Balinese usage against the 'objective' yardsticks of particular academic traditions, I shall try critically to reflect on each discourse by contrast with the other.

Briefly my argument is as follows. The claims by proponents of a universal rationality, whom I shall label 'universalists', are mutually inconsistent enough to vitiate their claims to be self-evidently true, let alone offer a coherent set of criteria by which to evelute other cultures.[2] Part of the inconsistency stems from the sheer range of uses of terms like 'reason'; part from the degree to which such ambiguous notions disguise the play of metaphor and presupposition.

We easily assume our epistemological categories to be necessary, self-evident, or even natural. For instance the link of logic and language with the world tends to be represented visually as one of reflection. Strict universalists are prone to argue that what is mirrored must be *essentially* the same everywhere and be perceived by identically organized minds. I shall question whether it is realistic to assume such universal essences or to regard human nature or 'mind' as if it were some kind of essentially definable object or process.

Given this shared view of the world, activities we can understand are therefore labelled 'rational' and those we cannot 'symbolic' (See Barley 1983: 10–11). Such categories, however, presuppose ideas about the consistency of utterances and their coherence with a notional 'order' in the world. For each category is assumed to be homogeneous and to hold good not only for the collective representations in any one society, but across cultures as well, despite the abundant evidence to the contrary. The issue is not whose presuppositions are right, but whether it is possible to represent what is going on accurately enough in any instance even to begin serious discussion. Appeal to reason, in preference to other ways of interpreting statements and actions, involves selection and power. If we stretch others on the rack of reason, we run the danger of reducing them to incoherent screams, and ultimately silence.

Rationality and reason are, anyway, peculiarly difficult notions to review critically because they have so many, and frequently incompatible, senses. They have played the role of key, or constitutive, concepts in much Western discourse since the pre-Socratic philosophers (or better, our retrospective reading of their fragmentary texts). Worse still, reason and other equally ambiguous notions – like thought, truth, nature law, and reality – are usually mutually inter-defined. This makes the application of such ideas to other cultures difficult and, arguably, impossible. If it be the hallmark of symbols to be polysemic, then the key concepts of proponents of universal rationality seem to be highly symbolic.

Appeal to the generality of reason has other serious shortcomings. Much of the argument seems to beg the question. The case for the necessity, or inevitability, of a common universal rationality often relies on the use of just that rationality to argue the point. The position steers dangerously close to *petitio principii*. While philosophers are trained in ways of side-stepping such impasses, the innocent anthropologist may be reminded of another simple man's expostulaton:

'for these fellows of infinite tongue, that can rhyme themselves into ladies' favours, they do always reason themselves out again.' (*Henry V*, Act v, ii)

In the recent excited mating of philosophy and anthropology, it is easy to overlook a potential incompatibility. Philosophers are concerned to establish generalities and guidelines, such as how we ought properly to think, or must needs regard rationality, if we are to make the world coherent; anthropologists by contrast are interested in what cultural representations are about and how people use them, not with how they ought to. The more reflective and fungus-infested ethnographers, grappling with the idiosyncrasies of someone else's culture, are often struck by quite how far our own assumptions permeate attempts to 'make sense' of others'.

These remarks might seem obvious, but 'the entry of the philosophers' (in Gellner's phrase (1973)), into the business of telling anthropologists what they should be doing and what their data mean, requires us to reflect on whether reason is, as is claimed, the panacea for all cultural confusions or whether it is merely latter-day epistemological colonization. It is remarkable that the model of scientific rationality should be thrust upon others at the time that its presuppositions are under devastating attack from many of its own luminaries (Quine 1953; Kuhn 1962, 1977; Feyerabend 1975; R. Rorty 1980). One wonders if the two are unconnected? Be that as it may, anthropologists are being made to dance a lobster quadrille to a rationalist tune, being cast off into the ethnographic sea only to be rejected when we swim back with disconcerting news.

The rationalist case may be presented as a paradox inherent in the 'relativism' imputed to its opponents. It is that: 'the best evidence against relativism is, ultimately, the very activity of anthropologists, while the best evidence for relativism seems to be in the writings of anthropologists' (Sperber: 1982).

In fact, it is advocates of a universal rationality who put themselves in a self-referential bind. (Why Sperber's paradox need not apply to anthropologists will be reviewed later.) For rationalists of almost any hue must refuse 'to divorce reasons from objective truth' and insist that 'it has to be objectively true that one thing is good reason for another' (Hollis and Lukes 1982: 10, 11). If this be so, it is hard to see how rationalists can then disagree among themselves so sharply as to the good reasons for their own arguments (on which see Hollis and Lukes 1982: 12–20). The criticisms are not *ad hominem*. If there are so many good reasons for asserting incompatible truths, by the rationalists' own criteria of valid argument, either there is a good deal of slippage between reason and truth, or reason alone cannot provide good reasons, or truth has many facets, or some such difficulty. Whichever is so, reason is not quite what it is claimed to be. Sperber's paradox may be turned back on him simply by substituting 'rationality' for 'relativism' and 'rationalists' for 'anthropologists'.

An equally thorny patch for rationalists is what they mean by 'reason' and 'rationality'. They are remarkably loth to define them; and when they do they usually disagree. This is not surprising, as the great champions of reason from Descartes to Leibniz or Kant differed so deeply over what reason was and could do. As power theorists tend to fall back on force as the *deus ex machina*, so do rationalists in the last resort to logic. It is to pretty palaeolithic ideas of logic, though, like the laws of thought' or a simple logic of propositions, to which they turn. The hesitancy in pinning their epistemological flags to the mast even here may be because the going gets treacherous long before reaching the murky waters of a logic of classes, predicate calculus, or non-standard logics aimed at coping with some of the more massive leaks in the ship of reason.

Logic is not then so simple or safe. The complexities of the truth-conditions even of elementary 'if . . . then' constructions, which worry semanticists (Kempson 1975; Wilson 1975; Lyons 1977: 138–229), have exercised some of the finest philosophical minds (e.g. Russell 1905; Strawson 1950, 1964). If logic is so troublesome why assume it to underwrite the universal efficacy of reason? For such 'deductive logic is but a poor thing, being merely a tool for achieving consistency. Rationality *requires more than* consistency' (Newton-Smith 1982: 110, my emphasis). At best it seems we need more than logic. What this surplus is varies between philosophers. So does whether the resulting rational brew is an *a priori* condition of intelligibility (Hollis 1982), or an *a posteriori* test of practical, let alone interpretive, success (Newton-Smith 1982; Horton 1979, 1982; Taylor 1982).[3]. The further one inquires, the more of the universalist plight mirrors that of the monocular Tsew in a three-dimensional world.

IMAGES OF KNOWLEDGE

Rationality is more than just consistency. Not only is 'our concept of rationality *richer*', but permits 'a *higher* – or in some sense superior – *view* of reality (Taylor 1982: 88, 89, my emphasis). Is it not curious that a rationalist has recourse to metaphor to explain an idea deeply inimical to the whole notion of metaphor? For rationalists traditionally eschew the figurative. The truth against which reason measures itself is the world, mirrored in language. Tropes have no place in formal logic or empirical truth (see Quine 1979: 159–60); and a deep distrust of rhetoric can be traced as far back as the great Greek systematizers.

This putative ancestry throws light on the claims, and the blind spots, of much rationalism. For, it is argued, logic was devised to counter the persuasive oratory used in public debate in Greek city states (e.g. Lloyd 1979: 59–125; Todorov 1982: 60–83). It sets out to be more persuasive still than rhetoric, by grounding its appeal in 'necessity' or 'reality'. It is conveniently forgotten that both rhetoric and logic involve, as we shall see, relations of power.

A more amusing way in which rationalists use figurative language is in depicting their opponents. Critics of the supremacy of reason are labelled 'soft' relativists. These unfortunate, woolly-minded romantics are unable to 'rise above' their feelings and prejudices; whereas rationalists are hard-headed, with a higher, clear view of things. The image of intellectual he-men, grappling with a tough reality, comes out in their imagery of building 'bridge-heads' (e.g. Hollis 1970: 215) and surviving in a harsh world of 'material-objects' (Horton 1979). Meanwhile your poor relativist is condemned, like the poet Bunthorne, to 'walk down Piccadilly with a poppy or a lily, in your medieval hand' (*Patience*, Act 1; away, one trusts, from the London School of Economics!). The more or less loony relativism that universalists ascribe to everyone else presupposes a dichotomy focused upon reason, which skews the potential coherence of everything else. This nicely makes the point that taxonomies of rationality are not neutral and involve power. Unfortunatly the (*autre-disant*) relativists often go along with this ascription and merely read 'hard' as 'rigid', and 'soft' as 'flexible'. My worry about universalism, however, is exactly the opposite. It is not 'hard' enough: it allows in too many questionable assumptions about the nature of the world, human beings, language, knowledge, and order. Deny it as they do, rationalists live in a very 'soft' world, comfortably furnished with the latest concepts and meanings (woolly 'mental' suppositions and 'obscure intermediary entities' (Quine 1953: 22)) which, to a sceptical eye, look just as quaint and ethnocentric as do the Tsew.[4]

Apart from striking spatial and tactile images, rationalist argument is often shot through with a visual metaphor of language and logic as a 'mirror of nature'.[5]

'It is pictures rather than propositions, metaphors rather than statements, which determine most of our philosophical convictions. The picture which holds traditional philosophy captive is that of the mind as a great mirror, containing various representations – some accurate, some not – and capable of being studied by pure, non-empirical methods. Without the notion of the mind as mirror, the notion of knowledge as accuracy of representation would not have suggested itself. Without this latter notion, the strategy common to Descartes and Kant – getting more accurate representations by inspecting, repairing and polishing the mirror, so to speak – would not have made sense.' (R. Rorty 1980: 12)

To the extent that anthropologists are concerned less with how the world ultimately is than with the forms collective representations take empirically, such presuppositions become a matter for study in ourselves and in others. If rationalism is 'the story of the domination of the mind of the West by ocular metaphors, within a social perspective' (R. Rorty 1980: 13), one might ask what models, if any, are found in other cultures?

Visual metaphors of knowledge seem so obvious as to rule out would-be contenders. Other mammals, however, make more use of sound, smell, and touch, than we. How, for example, might the world appear were senses other than sight primary? For olfactory beings (some breeds of dog come to mind) presence would presumably not be a sharp there-or-not matter, but a fairly sudden proximity and a gradual weakening of stimuli (see Jonas and Jonas (1976) for some amusing possibilities). It would be an analog world of subtle degrees, not of clear digital distinctions (see Wilden 1972: 155–201). Logic, of course, is the stereotype of unambiguous division; and attempts to adapt it to to the world of uncertainty and shades of meaning in which we live are still in their infancy.

Such reflection is not just barren speculation on the doings of brutes. For Balinese popular ideas about the grounds of knowledge are different from ours, and quite subtle. The visual metaphor of knowledge is pretty explicit. Terms for knowing are mostly linked to sight.[6] The Balinese also recognize a hierarchy of senses. Sight is widely held to be the most reliable guide to the material world, but it cannot deal with the past, the future and what is not visible. Hearing occupies an ambiguous role. Balinese often stress language's capacity to shape and transmit information, but it is recognized that language is polysemic, and double-edged to boot; for it is moulded by the purposes, perceptions, and interests of speakers and listeners. So speech may be used to lie as easily as to say what someone thinks to be the case. As Goethe once remarked, 'If I make a mistake, anyone can see it, but not if I lie'.

Balinese epistemology seems not simply to be a folk model. For it is closely parallel to, and historically may well derive from, Indian Nyāya philosophy which recognizes four ways (*pramāb̩a*) of obtaining valid knowledge.[7] this is not to imply that the issue can be ignored if a culture does not have a literate philosophical tradition, as the chapters by Overing and Salmond make abundantly clear. Before trying to bury the corpse of possible alternative rationalities, we might inquire what others do, not just what we think they ought to do.

IDEAS OF TRUTH

Ideas of truth, like Byzantine contracts, admit of many readings. The view implicit in most universalist arguments is a version of a classical account, again traced traditionally to Aristotle, which runs crudely as follows. Language 'contains' meaning in the form of propositions, by referring to reality through some form of correspondence. As a theory of signs, the connexion is by virtue of imitation (resemblance), natural association (causation, or motivation) or convention (a cake which may be cut many ways, see Todorov 1982: 15–99). This 'Correspondence Theory' of truth and meaning also offers a common-sense account of translation. For the equivalence of sentences in different languages is guaranteed in so far as the propositions they embody describe a single reality.

One of the most thorough-going attempts to restate and defend this traditional (intellectualist) position is by Sperber (1975, 1982). In his view, proper knowledge of the world is represented linguistically in propositions, all other uses of language being tidied away into a class of 'semi-propositional representations' (1982: 169), which are referentially defective, and therefore ambiguous and suspect. At best speakers may express their attitude to what is said and listeners choose the most relevant, or appealing, interpretation. Such spastic propositions include not only poetry and 'symbolic' utterances but also, *mirabile dictu*, most culturally transmitted statements of belief and even the arguments of what he chooses to class as his 'relativist' opponents.

What assumptions does such a view of truth make? First, the link of language and truth is expressed in at least two incompatible metaphors. Language is seen here as 'containing' meaning, or truth: a 'conduit metaphor', which simplifies and distorts the ways language actually works (Reddy 1979). somehow language also 'represents' reality, which assumes a 'mimetic' or 'copy' metaphor (Goodman 1981). So true knowledge is often represented visually (for instance in terms of spatial metaphors, as a 'theoretical landscape', Salmond 1982). Second, introducing reality as the means of equating propositions in different languages merely creates yet another step in translation.[8]

In its extreme form 'Correspondence Theory' works by simply shrugging off most kinds of statement that puzzle and interest anthropologists and non-verbal communication (see Goodman 1978, 1981) as emotional 'attitudes' (See A. Rorty 1980). Even if a more eclectic view is taken, such theories are part of a particular historical tradition and ignore the question of how other cultures represent the world, or indeed how they hold language or knowledge to work. Correspondence Theory is like a dog with one leg – in bad need of support from a contextual, performative, or pragmatic theory of truth and meaning as a prosthesis.

Balinese ideas about truth embody subtly different presuppositions. Yet their views show great consistency and sensitivity to the grounds, and limits, of empirical knowledge, without straining metaphor. They are fashionably up to date in denying anyone, except conceivably Divinity, a privileged access to reality and have a theory of human nature which is not essentially founded on rationality (unlike Aristotle's definition of Man as a 'rational biped').

Let usd start with terminology. Several words may be provisionally glossed as 'true' in one sense or other. For instance, *patut* (*beneh* in low Balinese, cognate with Malay *benar*) implies being coherent, fitting, or appropriate in a given context. The closest term to our notion of empirically true seems to be *wiakti* (in high Balinese, *saja* in low), 'manifest', or *sayuwakti*, evident.[9] What is at stake becomes clearer in the light of the critical distinction between *sekala*, visible, embodied, and *niskala*, invisible, unmanifest. For what is *sekala* may be known far more fully to human beings than what is *niskala*.[10]

The differences between what I take as the Balinese and universalist presuppositions are delicate but crucial. They pose the Balinese problems too. For the distinction between manifest and unmanifest is equivalent neither to the dichotomy between present and absent, nor true and false. The states are not dichotomous, but overlapping. The unmanifest may be invisible; it may be visible but not present; it may be present as an aspect of, or hidden within, what is visible. There is an ontological and epistemological gulf between *sekala* and *niskala*, from the point of view of humans (who straddle the gap in life, between being visible and engaging in behaviour; and thinking and feeling, activities that are unmanifest in others). As we shall see, the Balinese are cautious about making statements that confuse their two categories, a sensibility which, to my mind, keeps them out of a lot of trouble.

Sekala admits of at least two readings. Narrowly, it is what is visible; broadly, what the senses can perceive. The difference adds to the complexity of Balinese judgements. Knowing about the unmanifest, in its various senses, is as important as it is fraught with uncertainty.[11] The care Balinese villagers show in distinguishing the two realms curtails the dubious use of metaphor to represent the unknown through the known. For example, as time is *niskala*, it cannot be described catachretically by analogy with space, which is *sekala*.

The failure to inquire into Balinese epistemological categories means that the debate about the nature of time in Bali, which is claimed really to be cyclical, linear, durational, or punctuational, is largely irrelevant (see Geertz 1966; Bloch 1977; Bourdillon 1978; Howe 1981).

The part played by the various senses in establishing truth is interesting. To know empirically that something is so, *wiakti*, normally requires visual confirmation. As most cultural knowledge is obviously acquired from others through speech, its accuracy is open to question and so needs careful qualification. Therefore the Balinese are wont, with commendable restraint, to prefix unverified statements with qualifiers like *wènten orti*, 'it is said' (literally: there is news), or *kalumbrah*, 'it is widely held'. Otherwise where their experience is inadequate to generalize or say for sure they may introduce modal terms such as *minab* or *mirib* (probably, possibly; expressible, perhaps for my benefit, as percentages!). To dismiss such compound statements, as does Sperber, as 'semi-propositional', is to fail to grasp that the Balinese in daily life are often more punctilious than we, not less.

While the Balinese stress sight as a means of knowing, it does not follow that they draw a dichotomy between phenomena and noumena, nor between appearance and essence. The unmanifest, in whatever sense, is not the essential. Nor is the Balinese Chain of Being simply correlated with the ability to grasp the unmanifest. Dogs, for example, whose place is far humbler than their English fellows, can see, hear and smell what humans cannot including invisible spirits and gods. So their knowledge of the unmanifest is, in many ways, greater. *Sekala* so circumscribes what people can know for sure that any individual's knowledge is inevitably partial (a sensitivity to differences in aptitudes, interests, and emotions, let alone the context of utterances, further the Balinese disinclination to take statements at face value). Balinese ideas of what is manifestly so or not so cannot comfortably be grafted onto our model of propositions being true or false. Scepticism over human abilities sets the Balinese sharply apart from Hellenic, and later, traditions of the omnipotence of reason. Be that as it may, they display a healthy empiricism which deserves study, not *a priori* dismissal.

So far I have described the most certain means of knowing about what is manifest. The remainder deal with the unmanifest. At this stage it is useful to consider the parallels and differences between the Balinese and the traditional Nyāya doctrine of the four ways of knowing. These are summarized in *Table 6.1*, which gives, as well as the Nyāya terms, the Balinese equivalents, which derive from Sanskrit and Old Javanese. One might note that ideas about direct perception have much in common. Whereas the priestly sources I know (which is only a small sample from a vast, and largely unexplored, textual tradition) stress *Anumāna*, inference from observation, popular thinking tends to run this together with *Upama*, the use of example in comparison (*Upamāna* in Nyāya). Most villagers regard both as providing some clue to what has not been witnessed directly; the former, which rely on

Table 6.1 *Indian and Balinese forms of knowledge*

Nyāya term	means of knowing	Balinese term*	means of knowing	popular ideas
Pratyaksa	perception	*Pratyaksa*	direct observation	same
Anumāna	inference	*Anumana* (*Anumata*)	or perception inference from observations	both inference from evidence and comparison treated as examples (*upama*) of various kinds
Upamāna *Śabda*	comparison verbal knowledge	(*Upama*) *Agama*	teaching of religious men	any verbal (*sabda*) or written (*tutur*/*tattwa*) source, especially historical or religious texts

*Terms found in Brahmanical texts or in general use among ordinary village Balinese.

past observed connexions (what we might term 'inductive reasoning'), are held to be more precise than the latter, which depend on comparing (*nyaihang*) entities that are by definition not the same.

THE QUESTION OF LOGIC

The Balinese use of a kind of inferential reasoning (*Anumāna*) is critical to an understanding of how they construct and interpret arguments, including those recalcitrant assertions we tend to label 'symbolic'. As the volume is about rationality, I shall concentrate on inference here. This is not to suggest that other forms of knowledge are marginal. On the contrary, inference is only one of many ways of interpreting texts, theatre and ritual. So I shall suggest later the potential importance of the others.

Knowledge acquired from others puts most Balinese in something of a dilemma. On the one hand, it is how one learns culturally transmitted knowledge and much else besides; on the other, its accuracy cannot be checked. Texts may also contradict one another, or offer incompatible accounts. Here the tendency is to adopt the version most fitting to the circumstances. In other words, consistency, or coherence, is treated as at least as important as any correspondence to unverifiable past events.

The possibility that something like the Nyāya mode of reasoning, or 'syllogistic', might be used in Bali is interesting enough to look at it more carefully. To understand what is involved, it is useful to return to the contrast between Balinese and Greek (or later) ideas of logic. For the rationality debate, at least as far back as Lévy-Bruhl, rests on the purported failure of people in other cultures to observe 'the laws of thought'.

What are these laws then? They are 'the law of identity' (A is A; every subject is its own predicate); 'the law of non-contradiction' (A is not not-A; contradictory judgments cannot both be true); and 'the law of excluded middle' (everything is either A or not-A; no middle judgment can be true, while the falsity of one follows from the truth of the other).

The question is, though: quite what status do these laws have? Unfortunately, they have been interpreted in different ways by their own proponents, being taken as, roughly, either descriptive, prescriptive, or formal. Aristotle is often viewed as regarding the laws as primarily descriptive of 'being as such', rather than as describing the activity of thinking. Prescriptively they have been understood, however, as stating either absolute or conventional standards of reasoning (Keynes 1884 and Ayer 1936 respectively). Again they have been treated as formal propositions which are true in virtue of their form and independently of any content whatsoever (Leibniz and, in a different way, Kant). The problem for rationalists is which of the readings to take. If they are prescriptive or formal laws, how do they have immediate bearing on the issue of ethnographic variation? If they are descriptive, who is to say before empirical investigation what form they might take? Rationalism shows its colours here in fusing two senses of law. And one might ask *'sed quis custodiet ipsos Custodes?'*

More is at stake here than is often realized. On one reading, Aristotle's law of non-contradiction is a defence of the metaphysical principle of identity in face of Heraclitus who is reputed to have maintained it to be possible for the same thing to be and not be, because things were 'becoming' rather than 'being'. The law of identity also raises questions about the status of the copula (see Derrida 1979). Does it express equality or identity? Or is it a relation of subject and predicate? If the latter, what does it imply about the subject's existence? Obviously one interpretation of the laws of thought would make nonsense, as the Tsew so avidly did, of other interpretations. Despite the fervent wishes of its supporters, at some point logic involves metaphysical presuppositions (as Hollis has lately conceded (1982: 84)). Which of these interpretations should be the yardstick of rationality is partly responsible for the confusion which engulfs the topic.

Even if we overlook these serious drawbacks, how suitable are the laws of thought for evaluating culture? For a start, such laws by design apply best to, and have been derived from, not art or ritual, but language – usually *in vitreo*. On sceptical grounds, rather than assume a transcendent realm of propositions, it is wise to look at how the laws of thought apply to what people say, or presuppose in speaking and acting. For instance, unless speech is very elaborated, speakers tend to assume a measure of common knowledge with their audiences, the nature of which needs study. This raises questions about both the possible contexts and the standards to which speakers conform (see Grice (1975, 1978) on a pragmatic theory of 'conversational implicature'). For rationalists, the catch is that contexts and standards are a pragmatic, and so ethnographic, issue. If so they cannot be circumscribed easily, or *a priori*, by a semantic logic. This is a nasty problem for 'practical reason' which is an empty notion if there are no circumstances for reason to be practical in! Oscar Wilde may have been right when he remarked, 'I can stand brute force, but brute reason is quite unbearable. There is something unfair about its use. It is hitting below the intellect.'

It is hardly surprising, therefore, that an attempt has been made to claw back context and standards of co-operation into a formal model, amenable to the laws of thought (Sperber and Wilson 1982). The aim is to show that such standards are a necessary condition of communication (I suspect this may beg the question) and that *relevant* context is logically implied by the utterances themselves. Besides such technical questions as whether a logic of implication or entailment is better suited to this task (Kempson 1977: 139–56), relevance has proved hard to pin down. The simplest utterances presuppose far more than is allowed and imply a range of quite different possible circumstances (Moore 1982). The whole exercise is academic anyway, because it assumes a prescriptive view of logic, the universality of which has yet to be demonstrated. Now, if the standards accepted in the culture in question differ, it is not much use telling people that they are wrong because they failed to adopt Sperber's and Wilson's criteria!

BALINESE USES OF INFERENCE

It is one thing to argue that yardsticks, hallowed by years of scholarly port-drinking, like the laws of thought may be inadequate to explain how people in other cultures reason. It is another to put something in their place. One starting-point is the styles of reasoning that people in a culture use and recognize as legitimate. For if statements are made and judged according to invoked canons of reasoning, and presupposition, such canons are empirically part of the ethnography.

So let us turn to the Balinese. If, as we saw, logic involves metaphysical presuppositions, how do they affect Balinese styles of reasoning? The postulate of an unmanifest implies that, however probable an argument, the unmanifest is never subject to empirical verification. *Niskala* enters Balinese representations in another way.[12] In popular Balinese thinking there are three elements: water, fire, and air, from which all visible form is composed. Each element moves (typically, water downwards, fire upwards, air laterally or freely) or indeed may change nature. The corollary of this mutability is that composite forms are also continuously transforming (*metemahan*). Villagers were delighted when I protested this did not fit hard objects like steel axes or mountains. They remarked that the hardest metal wears with time, mountains erode, and, in Bali, are even volcanic.

The implication for the law of identity is that the Balinese view of the world as transforming, becoming something else, is remarkably close to Heraclitus's supposed position. Further, as the unmanifest is empirically unverifiable, this requires the law of excluded middle to be modified in practice, because a third possibility might always hold. Lastly, the law of non-contradiction is deliberately breached in order to express kinds of uncertainty (see the chapter by Wolfram), or the play of political power. Even if one allows the laws of thought as the formal preconditions of intelligibility, they still need applying to the world to which utterances refer.

I mentioned that the Balinese recognize a form of inferential reasoning closely resembling Nyāya syllogistic, which has five stages:

1. This mountain is fire-possessing.	– *pratijnā*	(hypothesis)
2. Because it is smoke-possessing.	– *hetu*	(reason)
3. Whatever is smoke-possessing is fire-possessing, like kitchen, unlike lake.	– *udāharaṇa*	(example/general principle)

4. This mountain, since it possesses smoke, possesses fire.	– *upanaya*	(application)
5. This mountain is fire-possessing.	– *nigamana*	(conclusion)

(from Potter 1977: 180–81)

The Balinese may actually use this example, when speaking of volcanoes (where reasoning is supplemented by periodic, and often catastrophic, observation).

Balinese inference differs from Nyāya in stressing the first three stages and in allowing flexibility in the order of citing the reason and the example. If someone fails to understand the first three, however, something like stages four and five may be added, as an afterthought. A conversation in a coffee-stall should illustrate Balinese usage.

1. Farmers in Sukawati (a village in the South) use ploughs on their ricefields.	– *nerangang kewèntenan*	(describing the situation)
2. Because the earth is very hard to work.	– *kerana*	(the cause ?)
3. It is like the ricefields of Jèro Mangku Dalem (naming the owner of the hardest fields in the area).	– *praimba*	(the example, but not visible to the listener)

Or a father giving a *salak*, a fruit with a skin like a snake's, to a small boy spoke as follows:

1. One can eat *salaks*.	– *katerangan*	(description)
2. They are like oranges.	– *nyaihang*	(comparing)
(3. Because they contain *merta* (roughly: nourishment) not *wisiya* (poison).)	– *mawinan*	(the reason ?)

In the latter case, the example was given immediately and the reason added only when the child seemed uncertain. Unless one is speaking to the young or with formal authority, it is considered arrogant to hold forth, and one waits for suitable interjections from listeners, or for them to draw false conclusions, before suggesting one's own. The preference for dialogue (*saling mesaut*; *megatik*; *timbal*) makes much use of the audience's knowledge. So it stresses the pragmatic aspects of this kind of inference.

Speaking of Balinese reasoning as syllogistic may, in fact, be misleading. It has little in common with the Aristotelian syllogism with its stress on consistency between propositions and analytical as against synthetic knowledge. As Charles Lamb summed it up, such 'logic is nothing more than a knowledge of words'. By contrast, the Balinese are closer to the kind of inductive reasoning, or 'inference', proposed by John Stuart Mill. As Potter argued, exponents of Nyāya 'view inference as consisting of judgements whose referents are existing things, not, as we in the West are prone to do, as relating to words or concepts' (1977: 182). Rather than spend time arguing whether, or in what sense, Balinese have formal logic, it might be more profitable to consider how they make use of what they do have.[13]

Several features are worth note. The first stage of argument rests firmly on observation, but commonly has a contextual limit (not all mountains are volcanic, not all farmers use ploughs). This is quite different from the universalist tendencies of syllogisms of the form: 'All x are y'. In the second stage, why something should be so (the *explanans*) is spoken of as either *kerana* or *mawinan*. Whether these can be translated as 'cause' and 'reason' is a moot point in a culture the metaphysics of which does not draw a contrast between the physical, and mental, in a Cartesian fashion.

We can also see the singular status of the unmanifest and how inference and comparison are conflated. When the example cited is visible (or otherwise perceptible) at the time to the listener, it is described as a *conto* (Old Javanese, sample). When it is not, it is referred to as a *pra(tiw)imba* (Sanskrit, image, model, shadow), a term as widely used as it is hard to pin down. It is used of absent examples as well as analogies; but it always seems to carry the implication of being an imperfect instance, because something has to be taken on trust, or because the connexion is indirect or spurious but useful. Balinese reasoning can as easily be used to compare unlike things (*salak* and oranges) as to draw strict inferences. For instance, one old man recalled how he had explained what a plough looked like to his grandchild (ploughs were not used in my village) with the *praimba* of the weapon carried by Sang Baladewa, a character in the shadow play version of the Mahabarata. Care in specifying the sense of example or comparison is a means of stating precisely the nature of the connexion between subject and illustration, and so indicates how reliable the argument is as a whole. Would that most writers on rationality were so fastidious.

APPARENTLY ILLOGICAL STATEMENTS

To what extent does Balinese reasoning offer a way of understanding seemingly flagrant breaches of the laws of thought? Below I give examples of how Balinese use inference to interpret cultural statements. For they find many collective representations as puzzling as we do. The point is not to show how rational, or otherwise, the Balinese are in someone else's terms, but to illustrate how villagers set about coping with such representations when they need to explicate them, not just leave them as matters for priests (whose knowledge, as opposed to authority, often adds little to the interpretation).

Many odd statements come about through bad translation. An example is:

1. *Carik-carik urip.* = ricefields are alive.

The problem is not so much circumscribing 'ricefields' as misrendering the contrast set *urip: padem*. What is predicated of *urip* is a subject with a capacity for action (*laksana*; see Zoetmulder 1982: 958), or for organized movement or resistance (e.g. large trees). *Padem* is used of things that normally lack such capacities (like stone, metal and non-volcanic mountains). Now anyone who has sat watching a ricefield knows it is a highly mobile micro-environment. The statement sounds odd largely because of a lack of correspondence between the range of terms in different languages.

The difficulties begin, however, when *urip* is predicated of objects as various as buildings, cars or metallophone orchestras, after rites have been performed over them. On one interpretation buildings, for instance, are 'animated' by the use of 'life-substances' (*pangurip*, Howe 1983: 154–55). This translation, however, arguably ignores Balinese ideas about the nature of being, as *urip* may be predicated of any system of energy (*bayu*; cf. Old Javanese, and Sanskrit, *vāyu*). For cars move, metallophones turn movement into sound, buildings react in resisting wind and earthquakes. Without claiming this solves all the problems, study of presuppositions is a sensible preamble to translation.

Statements of belief need handling with care. We need to know something of Balinese metaphysics and their views on well-formed utterances. For instance, in various contexts it is quite possible to hear the following statement:

2. *Pantun kehyangin antuk Batari Sri.*
Which it is tempting to translate as:
The Goddess Sri is incarnated (present mystically) in rice.

Kehyangin is one of several terms the Balinese use to express the problematic relationship of the unmanifest to the manifest. It would be easy to dismiss this as a classic example of pre-logical thought; but this hardly does justice to the complexity and subtlety of the relation of *sekala* and *niskala*.[14]

The Balinese are careful in speaking about deities and tend to avoid, especially if they are speaking formally, expressions like:

2a. *Tiang* $\frac{memanah}{pracaya}$ *wènten Batara.* =

I $\begin{matrix} \text{think} \\ \text{believe(1)} \end{matrix}$ God(s) exist(s).

but allow

2b. *Tiang ngega wènten Batara.* =
    I believe(2) God(s) exist(s).

Instead they tend to use some expression like:

2c. *Ring* $\frac{mánah(an)}{kepracayaan}$ *tiangé, wènten Batara.* =

   In my $\frac{\text{thought}}{\text{belief}}$ God(s) exist(s).

   The issue of belief is too complicated to exhaust here, but the following comments were often made. The first expression is *solèh*, something akin to a category mistake. For Gods are *niskala*, but believing or thinking is an act, or state, of which the subject (but not others) is aware, and so is *sekala*. The sentence therefore confuses categories. The third expression avoids the problem because thought and belief are abstract, *niskala*. This also makes the sentence provisional, as *niskala* cannot be verified and so does not require the evidence with which assertions about *sekala* should be backed.
   Thought and belief are also held to be mediated by desire. This suggests one explanation for there being two words for our 'belief'. The first, *pracaya*, is a difficult word (Sanskrit, *pratyaya*, and Old Javanese, *pracaya*, to trust, to be sure, convinced). For the Balinese it has the connotation of not knowing, but wishing, or expressing trust. The second, *ngega*, is to know something to be the case and also to desire it, or express commitment to it. Statements using *ngega* are most commonly made by priests on the basis of tangible evidence of the presence of Gods (a sudden chill on a hot day; a wind no one else notices). So *ngega* is properly used as a verb because the belief and Gods are both *sekala* in this case. *Manah* is more recondite still. It comes from Sanskrit *manas*, mental powers, and is treated in Nyāya doctrine as a sixth organ of sense and, in the Buddhist Abhidharma as 'the subjective disposition that receives the sense stimuli and comprises them, giving them the peculiar subjective admixture that is never absent in either perception or cognition' (Guenther 1976: 16–17). The Balinese, whose heritage is Hindu-Buddhist, may use *manah* in either sense. Crude ascription of 'irrational beliefs' to the Balinese not only misses the subtleties of use, but also relies on the crassest correspondence approach to translation.
   More complex examples bring out villagers' use of inference and also possible readings of the law of identity to boot. When faced with collective representations which defy observable proof, the Balinese may argue as I heard them do over the following statement:

3. *Batara-Batari meraga angin.* =
     take the form of
Gods   wind.
     have the body of

Following the stages of argument discussed above, this is read as:

1. Gods are like air, which is unbounded and invisible.
2. This is because gods are *niskala*, but are apparently capable of action or bringing about effects.
3. Wind is unbounded and invisible, but is capable of action or bringing about effects.

The argument is by analogy and so is inexact (gods are not wind), but the comparison is held to be fitting in other respects.

A more difficult example is one which derives from ritual invocations (*mantra*) and the symbolic classification of compass points with deities, colours, elements and so forth. At first sight this mixes categories of the manifest (e.g. elements) and unmanifest (gods). The point, however, is that *descriptions* of gods are manifest and based on imagery or analogy (as in paintings depicting deities). For instance, the Hindu God Viṣṇu (Wisnu in Bali) is associated with North, black or dark blue, water, and other features. It is tempting to render the connexions as predicative. Even in the simple utterances of villagers the grounds for so doing are far from clear, as in

4. *Ida Batara Wisnu Ida* $\begin{matrix} selem. \\ toya. \end{matrix}$ =

Lord Wisnu – $\begin{matrix} black. \\ water. \end{matrix}$

(In the absence of a copula sign in Bali, I use a dash to avoid prejudging the issue.)

It does not follow from this that black or water can be simply predicated of Wisnu ('Wisnu is black' is a different kind of attribution from 'Wisnu is water'). At various times I have heard inferences using one of the following comparisons (in stage 3 of reasoning):

a. As a person's thoughts (*manah*), or intentions (*tetujon* which translates equally as 'direction' or 'goal') move the body, so does water move by the intentions or thoughts of Wisnu.
b. As kings are said to control (*megambel*) their subjects, so does Wisnu control water.
c. As food contains nourishment (*merta*), so does water contain Wisnu.
d. As the headman of this village is called such-and-such, so water is called Wisnu.

The last is clearly an equative, rather than a predicative, sentence (on the significance of the difference, see Lyons (1977: 185)). All the inferences are, however, treated as speculative by virtue of the distance between the nature of the subject and the comparisons.

Deliberate contradiction is also used to indicate uncertainty. If someone is asked, for instance, whether they are tired, it is not uncommon to reply:

5. *Yèn (ngeraos) lesu, lesu;*
yèn (ngeraos) ten lesu, ten lesu.
If (one says) one is tired, one is tired;
If (one says) one is not tired, one is not tired.

It was usually agreed this cryptic remark should be read as follows. If one is working and is asked if one is tired, one might not be but might become so later, or vice versa. Then one is embarrassed by telling what turns out to be a falsehood. So it is better deliberately to equivocate (*ngèmpèlin*) over what is still unsure.

The example may help to clear up another curious construction. The expression runs:

5a. *Yèning Batara kebaos alit, alit pisan;*
yèning Batara kebaos ageng, ageng pisan.
If God is said to be small, He is very (too) small;
if God is said to be big, He is very (too) big.

This was usually explained in terms of the nature of *manah*. Gods are unmanifest; therefore they have no size or form, and can as well be said to be infinitely large or infinitely small. If one says they are big, they are too big to see; if one says they are small, they are too small to see. To speak of gods (a manifest activity) is due to one's *manah*, one's desire or disposition to picture them a certain way. The agent's thoughts or feelings are seen as an active part of knowledge, speculation, and speech – a point which suggests that the relationship of representations, or texts, and the audience is quite different from the neutral role we tend to impute to recipients of culture.

There are other circumstances under which deliberate contradiction may be used, as in the following example where a prince was speaking about a very powerful neighbour.

5b. *Yèning Cokorda derika ngandika putih selem miwah selem putih,*
bènjang putih dados selem, selem dados putih ring panjak-panjakidané.
If the Cokorda (the prince's caste title) there says white is black and black white, the next day for the populace (literally: his slaves) white becomes black and black white.

Subsequent explanation made it clear that the prince had in mind his neighbour's power to order convention at will, not to change colours. Contradiction is used to signal an authoritative utterance, here one that is counter-factual or, better, in defiance of general Balinese usage. Among other things, this example indicates the Balinese sensitivity to the role of power in determining convention; and the potential weaknesses of the fourth path to knowledge, speech (*sabda*).

PRACTICAL REASON

What bearing do Balinese ideas of inference have on the practical use of reason? If *manah* shapes perception and cognition, it is hard to generalize about the relation of means to ends, separate from individual interests in specific contexts. Like many peoples, including ourselves in day-to-day life, the Balinese seem to stress situational logic, in a broad sense, not seeking timeless and dubious universals.[15]

Discussion of practical reasons often overlooks the degree to which models vary culturally and historically in assumptions about the nature of humans and society. This affects the definition of ends, what means are legitimate or efficient, and even what self-interest is (both 'self' and 'interest' being notoriously hard to define). If one allows too much into context, anything can be made rational or logical (see Gellner 1970: 26). A simple-minded utilitarianism is still fashionable, despite the serious weaknesses of models of humans as 'maximizing', 'minimizing' or 'satisficing' (see Ryan 1978).

> '*Il y a une infinité de conduites qui paroissent ridicules et dont les raisons cachées sont très sage et très solides.*' (La Rochefoucauld, *Maximes*: CLXIII)

One way round these difficulties is to argue that there *must* be some universal 'material-object language', in terms of which humans everywhere approach 'reality', because in practice humans are so adept at adapting means to ends (Horton, 1979). On close inspection, however, all this says is that those who still survive have adjusted to their environment enough to have not yet died. To infer from this the existence of a universal practical reason is far-fetched. It assumes, for a start, that people necessarily do the same things for the same reasons. Worse, it implies that reason is the sufficient condition of action, a curiously idealist assumption for what claims to be a common-sensical stance. After all, it is one thing to trace the rationale behind action *ex post facto*, it is quite another to state that reasons are the causes of action (see Hollis 1977: 185, who is commendably cautious here). Is such adjustment desirable anyway? For 'the reasonable man adapts himself to the world: the unreasonable one persists in trying to adapt the world to himself. Therefore all progress depends on the unreasonable man' (Shaw, *Maxims for Revolutionists*: 238).

Returning to the Balinese, talk about rational means to ends without referring to the situation and to the actor is held to be *gabeng*, ill-formed and incomplete (the word is used of empty ears of rice). In place of a dichotomy of means and ends, the Balinese commonly recognize a triad, by adding the agent with his, or her, tastes, perceptions, emotions and interests. Rather than typify some 'essential' person ('the reasonable man' – but never woman – see Herbert 1935), the Balinese I know tended to stress the differences between people, even among family and friends. If we assume homogeneity, the Balinese come closer to assuming diversity.

For Balinese villagers even apparently basic collective representations, from laws to ritual, are liable to be revised situationally in the light of *désa*, *kala*, *patra*, place, occasion and circumstance, according to the interests, or perspectives, of those involved. Given their presuppositions about the un-manifest, relevant context is likely to include *niskala*, however unverifiable its effects. So what we might dismiss as 'ritual' should be seen as linked to the uncertainty that action in the world – say in rice cultivation, at which the Balinese are most technically proficient – is adequate in itself.

Arguably the Balinese are at least as consistent as we. Rationality is, after all, hardly a clear concept and, like the Tsew, we invoke it more often to express a commitment to its cultural importance than to say what it is. Far from rationality always being opposed to ritual, we ourselves revel in rituals of rationality: the genre of gangland films portrays excessive or narrow practical reason; exotic tourism is less often an encounter with the Other than a confirmation of superiority; politics is often the dramatic display – or replay – of class or cultural predilections as rational interest, as perhaps are seminars and books on rationality. 'Rational' is ultimately always what we are, or I am; 'irrational' is what others, or you, are. To paraphrase von Clausewitz, 'Reason is nothing more than the continuation of prejudice by other means'.

Now the Balinese start from an intriguingly different set of presuppositions about human nature, which imply the diversity, rather than unity, of human beings. The human psyche has three constituents, familiar to Indologists, the *triguna*: *sattwa*, knowledge or purity, *raja(h)*, emotion or passion, and *tamas*, desire or ignorance. These are linked to three goals of human life, the *triwarga*: *darma*, the disposition to do good, *art(h)a*, the pursuit of wealth or prestige, and *kama*, the enjoyment of sensual pleasures. The Balinese Chain of Being is founded upon three processes also: *bayu*, energy, *sabda*, speech, and *idep*, thought (see Hobart 1985). Plants are energy systems only; animals have both energy and the capacity for simple sounds; humans possess thoughts as well; while Gods shade off into pure thought.

So potential conflict between aspects of personality is built in, as is their conjunction. For the Balinese, knowledge, like logic, is empty and boring without emotion to provide interest (see de Sousa (1980: 128) on the link of rationality and emotion in salience. The implications for practical reasons are interesting. As Taylor remarks, for the Greeks, 'to say that man is a rational animal is to say that this is his telos, the goal he implicitly is directed towards by nature. To achieve it is to attain happiness and well-being' (1982: 95). In contrast to the *summum bonum* of happiness reached by reason working on the world, the Balinese have to balance different goals, different faculties, and different drives. Their world is more complex and, to my mind, psychologically more percipient, than one where humans strive monomaniacally, towards a single universally admired *telos*.

The idea noted above that human nature is the same everywhere rests upon a questionable distinction of the 'individual *versus* society' (which led Durkheim among others into a dubious ontology (Lukes 1973b: 3)). For it makes little sense to account for variation socially, while holding human nature constant, unless the two are held to be distinct. Arguably individuals and societies are not reified entities but relationships, in which cultural conceptions of one affect the other, or better both are mutually constructed (see Bhaskar (1979: 39–47) on a naturalist attempt to retain the dichotomy). The impact of hypostatizing the distinction has been to create endless confusion as to whether rationality is to be predicated of collective representations, individual humans or whatever. It does not solve the problem of rationality, it merely clouds the issue.

The weakness for dichotomies in Western academic discourse has actually created much of the rationality debate. For not only must propositions be true or false, but statements analytical or synthetic, truths necessary or contingent, assertions literal or metaphorical, representations accurate or inaccurate, reason practical or pure, actions rational or irrational, and people objective or subjective. Oddly, dualism is often held to be the attribute of 'primitive societies', not of ourselves – an example of the tendency to displace onto 'the Other' what is uncomfortable or unspeakable in our own categories.

One can, of course, happily reduce other cultures to a homogeneous pabulum to be fed into a universalist mill by suitable selection and translation (as, despite his protests, does Horton (1982)). Unfortunately, this begs most of the interesting questions and is inimical to empirical ethnography, which might establish whether it has any ground or not. An anthropologist who adopts the homogeneity axiom is liable to find he has slit his own throat on Occam's razor.

The presupposition of homogeneity has another aspect. It leads easily to assuming the possibility, desirability, or inevitability of consistency of thought, a coherence between thought and the state of the world, and order in that world. This passionate defence of systematicity is the more remarkable in the face of an argument by Gödel, which draws upon these very presuppositions, to the effect that such systematicity is impossible. The concept of order in Western thought is problematic at the best of times (see Bohm 1980; Kuntz 1968; Talbot 1981). So it is worrying when order is presupposed in analyses of other cultures and not considered as a proper topic for investigation. We have to date precious little idea of how people in other cultures conceive of, represent, or assume order.

Radical translation anyway is never a one-off business. It is a dialectic in which assumptions are modified as knowledge builds up. This will presumably differ for each culture, or its preferred interpretational schemes. So the idea of critical ethnography suggests an empirical way out of the translational trap without destroying 'the Other' with imported taxonomies. The metaphor of mirror equivalences gives way to gradually accumulated knowledge. We might have to start with a view of language and logic as mirroring the world somehow, but we land in trouble if we stop there and do not pass through the looking-glass. If we stay put, we may find 'the mirror cracked from side to side'. And we know what happened to that unfortunate mirror-gazer.

There is a well-known story told by old Balinese hands. In the version I know best, two Dutch scholars, Grader and Hooykaas, were sitting with Miguel Covarrubias, a Mexican cartoonist and ironically author of the best-known book on Bali, and talking to a Balinese priest. At one point Grader interrupted to correct the priest's language, according to prevailing Dutch grammatical ideas about Balinese. A few minutes later a dog in the compound began to bark and Covarrubias turned to Grader and asked him why he did not teach the dog to bark properly! The danger of wearing the blinkers of reason is that one ends up teaching the Balinese how to bark.

Appendix

Contraries of 'rational' and 'reason', or their synonyms in common English usage

1. RATIONALITY

intellectuality	v	affectivity
humanity	v	animality
culture	v	nature
objectivity	v	subjectivity
universality	v	particularity
generality	v	specificity
rational	v	empirical
necessity	v	contingency
science	v	arts

2. REASON

reason	v	emotion
–	v	folly
–	v	madness

–	v	intuition
–	v	mysticism
–	v	fantasy
–	v	imagination
–	v	romance
–	v	magic
–	v	superstition
–	v	experience
–	v	instinct
–	v	understanding (Kant)
–	v	cause
–	v	action
–	v	instinct
–	v	biological drives
–	v	violence
cosmos	v	chaos

3. LOGIC

logic	v	fact
logical	v	empirical
necessary	v	arbitrary
sense	v	nonsense
meaningful	v	meaningless
reflective	v	unreflective
Zweckrational	v	*Wertrational*

Notes

1 I am indebted to Miner (1950) for drawing my attention to the possible existence of the Tsew. This chapter is a shortened version of the original work, which will appear in full in due course. In particular the final sections have been drastically shortened.

2 Clearly terms like 'rationalism' and 'universalism' are sufficiently broad, if not downright ambiguous, to allow birds of many a theoretical feather under their wing. Consistently, I hope, with my concern about the dangers of essentializing, I use such terms as loose labels, preferably drawing upon authors' self-description of their works. Where relevant I indicate whose argument is at issue.

Similar caveats about essentialism obviously apply to my use of terms like 'culture' and 'the Balinese'. I do not wish to suggest there is any essential Balinese culture. There are only the myriad statements and actions that people living on the island of Bali, and calling themselves Balinese, engage in. Much of my information comes from the settlement in North Gianyar where I did research, but the results have been checked as broadly as possible. In referring to the Balinese I include high and low castes unless otherwise stated.

3 It is often unclear whether the claim is that we must assume a common rationality for the purposes of translation, or whether it is some ontological commitment to rationality as a human universal. The going gets rough when one asks of what 'rational' is predicated. Is it of collective representations, of persons, of thought, of action, or of criteria of verification? If it be thought, are we speaking of propositions, utterances, semiotic regularities, or semantic rules? If it be action, what relation do these have to the actor (for instance, are they causes of action)? A problem here is settling what is rationality and what a rationale. The closer the argument gets to postulating rationality as *a priori*, the more it is open to criticisms of the kind levelled against Chomsky for suggesting so much can be bracketed away in a theory of 'innate abilities'.

4 As Hacking has pointed out, the rationalist model tends to assume a complex relationship between four postulated entities. These are a knowing subject (or mind), speech (or ideas), an external reality (note the spatial metaphor), and experience (unmediated by culture and conveniently universal) of that reality available to the knowing subject (1975: 157–87). Each of these entities and the relation between them have come to raise increasingly serious problems. For instance the primacy of the knowing subject is under challenge (conservatively by Strawson (1959), more radically by Althusser (1972) and Foucault (1972, 1984a, 1984b)). The relation between language, experience and reality, let alone the status of each, has been shown to be very problematic (e.g. Wittgenstein 1958; Quine 1960; Kuhn 1962; Goodman 1978). It seems unwise in the light of these difficulties to try to apply the model to other cultures without careful reflection on what it presupposes.

5 The image which pervades this model of knowledge is the mind as an internal eye. Knowledge was a showing 'to the eye, the only eye, the inward eye. That which was shown was the principle: namely the origin, the source. The source was the *essence*, that which made the object what it is' (Hacking 1975: 162, my emphasis). What finally upset this view was the recognition that 'knowledge is public, and is not merely a mode of existence of "human nature", "understanding", or "reason" ' (1975: 166). The links between knowing as seeing, reason, human nature, and essence will be discussed in due course.

6 *Nawang*, and *uning*, the words I gloss as 'knowing' in low and high Balinese respectively, are linked to the root *tawang*, and near homonym, *ening*. Both signify 'clear', 'transparent'. Another important term, *meturah-turahan*, 'guessing', is literally working out what something is in very poor light.

7 The common Balinese version is discussed below and varies in several interesting features. Only one form of knowledge rests mainly on observation, while two make much use of language. This leaves the Balinese in something of a quandary over their reliability, as we shall see.

8 Gellner offers a succinct critique of this approach (1970: 24–5). Tarski (1956), whose theory of 'truth-conditional semantics' provides the most elegant version of 'Correspondence Theory', argued cogently that it would not work for natural languages anyway.

9 The words are found in Old Javanese, the language of Balinese texts and priestly knowledge, as *wyakti*, evidence, clarification, and *sawyakti*, clear, universally known (Zoetmulder 1982: 2347), the last making the point that such knowledge is public. In Sanskrit *vyakti* refers to manifestation, visible appearance (Gonda 1952: 176).

10 Compare Sanskrit *sakala*, consisting of parts, complete; also Old Javanese, in visible or material form, pertaining to the world perceptible by the senses (Zoetmulder 1982: 1603). Also Sanskrit *niṣkala*, without parts, undivided (see Gonda 1952: 363); in Old Javanese, immaterial, invisible. I do not intend to go here

into the issue of the ontological status of the two terms, as they raise complex questions concerning Balinese ideas about substance or matter, and the existence of particulars and universals (on why this is important, see R. Rorty (1980: 33–45)).

11 The disjuncture between the manifest and unmanifest suggests a more consistent explanation than most for the Balinese interest in trance, revelation (*wahyu*, compare Sanskrit *bāhya* (being) outwardly visible) and the existence of an extensive vocabulary for kinds of manifestation on the one hand; and for the practical problems of inferring intentions and feelings in legal and interpersonal contexts on the other.

12 Each constituent may be perceptible, invisible or, at least, transparent. So any sensible combination of elements also embodies *niskala*. Old Javanese texts refer to there being five perceptible elements (from the Sanskrit *pañcamahābhūta*; cf. *pañcatanmātra*, the five immaterial elements from which the former are produced). The Balinese reduce these to three by treating the remaining two, ether and earth, as spatial domains.

13 Again I have no space to discuss Balinese uses of propositional logic of the 'if . . . then' kind, although as Example 5 suggests, this exists. One reason behind this omission is that there are awkward problems in trying simply to translate Balinese *yèn* or *yèning* (low and high Balinese respectively) as 'if'. Apart from it not always being clear when the 'then' clause follows, it is not uncommon to produce a statement with two parts *both* prefixed by *yèn*, (not as in Example 5, where one can reasonably infer the consequent). So the effect in crude translation reads like a sentence with 'if . . . if'. The use of *yèn* is made more problematic by it being used of present and future action, whereas what is past is spoken of widely using *wisdin*, normally translated as 'although' and used in a manner identical to *yèn*. The term therefore appears to be closer to a signal that what follows is provisional or conditional in a broad sense which would differ from the antecedent-consequent relationship implied in 'if . . . then'. The problem requires a closer analysis of tapes of Balinese language use than I have been able to complete to date.

14 Two of the most commonly found expressions are *kehyangin*, from *hyang*, god, spirit, plus the passive verb form, and *kedulurin*, the active form of which *nulurin* implies 'to participate in', as in work activities or a festivity – an amusing parallel with Lévy-Bruhl's notion of 'mystic participation'. In passing, my analysis of language usage suggests that priests and villagers when speaking carefully are more likely to use what is usually called the passive voice, indicated by *ke. . . in*, than the active in these situations. This raises interesting questions of whether Western grammatical categories are really appropriate here, or whether something else is being implied.

15 There is no room to discuss every aspect of so vast a subject as rationality here. Omissions include Weber's distinction of *Zweckrationalität* and *Wertrationalität*, partly because of the degree to which they rest upon an increasingly questionable distinction between fact and value (see Putnam 1981). Of more interest is the stress placed by the Frankfurt School of Critical Theory on the notion that knowledge (and therefore the kind of 'rational' procedures appropriate to its exploitation) depends on the purposes to which it is directed – a view with which the Balinese would heartily concur. Habermas, for example, distinguishes three such purposes: technical interests served by empirical-analytical sciences, practical interests using historical-hermeneutic methods, and an emancipatory cognitive interest requiring a critical approach (1978: 302–17). The dangers of confusing these levels and also of mixing rationality and rationales are neatly spelled out.

'From everyday experience we know that ideas serve often enough to furnish our actions with justifying motives in place of the real ones. What is called rationalization at this level is called ideology at the level of collective action. In both cases the manifest content of statements is falsified by 'consciousness' unreflected tie to interests, despite its illusion of autonomy.' (1978: 311)

My slight concern here is how easy it is to establish real interests, while reference to levels and consciousness suggests a lingering essentialism at work.

References

ALTHUSSER, L. (1972) Marx's Relation to Hegel. In *Politics and History: Montesquieu, Rousseau, Hegel and Marx.* London: New Left Books.

ARMSTRONG, A. H. (1947) *An Introduction to Ancient Philosophy.* London: Methuen.

AYER, A. J. (1936) *Language, Truth and Logic.* London: Gollancz.

BARLEY, N. F. (1983) *Symbolic Structures: An Exploration of the Culture of the Dowayos.* Cambridge: Cambridge University Press.

BENOIST, J.-M. (1978) *The Structural Revolution.* London: Weidenfeld.

BHASKAR, R. (1979) *The Possibility of Naturalism: A Philosophical Critique of the Contemporary Human Sciences.* Brighton: Harvester.

BLOCH, M. (1977) The Past and the Present in the Present. *Man* NS **12** (2): 278–92.

BOHM, D. (1980) *Wholeness and the Implicate Order.* London: Routledge & Kegan Paul.

BOURDILLON, M. F. C. (1978) Knowing the World or Hiding it: A Response to Maurice Bloch. *Man* NS **13** (4): 591–99.

COLLINGWOOD, R. G. (1940) *An Essay on Metaphysics.* Oxford: Clarendon Press.

— (1946) *The Idea of History.* Oxford: Clarendon Press.

DAVIDSON, D. (1974) Belief and the Basis of Meaning. *Synthese* **27** *(3 and 4).*

— (1975) Thought and Talk. In *Mind and Language.* London: Oxford University Press.

DERRIDA, J. (1979) The Supplement of Copula: Philosophy Before Linguistics. In J. Harari (ed.) *Textual Strategies.* London: Methuen.

de SOUSA, R. (1980) The Rationality of Emotions. In A. Rorty (ed.) *Explaining Emotions.* Berkeley: California University Press.

DUMONT, L. (1977) *From Mandeville to Marx.* London: University of Chicago Press.

FEYERABEND, P. (1975) *Against Method.* London: Verso.

FOUCAULT, M. (1972) *The Archaeology of Knowledge.* Translated by A. M. Sheridan. London: Tavistock Publications.

— 1981. The Order of Discourse. In R. Young (ed.) *Untying the Text.* London: Routledge & Kegan Paul.

— (1984a) *Histoire de la Sexualité. Vol. II. L'Usage des Plaisirs.* Paris: Gallimard.

— (1984b) *Histoire de la Sexualité. Vol. III. Le Souci de Soi.* Paris: Gallimard.

GARFINKEL, H. (1967) *Studies in Ethnomethodology.* New Jersey: Englewood Cliffs.

GEERTZ, C. (1966) *Person, Time and Conduct in Bali: An Essay in Cultural Analysis.* Yale Southeast Asia Program, Cultural Report Series 14.

GELLNER, E. (1970) Concepts and Society. In B. Wilson (ed.) *Rationality.* Oxford: Basil Blackwell.

— (1973) The Entry of the Philosophers. In *Cause and Meaning in the Social Sciences.* London: Routledge & Kegan Paul.

GOMBRICH, E. (1963) Meditations on a Hobby Horse, or the Roots of Artistic Form. In *Meditations on a Hobby Horse and Other Essays on the Theory of Art.* London: Phaidon.

— (1979) *The Sense of Order.* London: Phaidon.

GONDA, J. (1952) *Sanskrit in Indonesia*. Naghpur: International Academy of Indian Culture.

GOODMAN, N. (1971) Symposium on Innate Ideas: (c) The Epistemological Argument. In J. Searle (ed.) *The Philosophy of Language*. Oxford: Oxford University Press.

— (1978) *Ways of Worldmaking*. Brighton: Harvester.

— (1981) *Languages of Art*. Brighton: Harvester.

GRANDY, R. (1973) Reference, Meaning and Belief. *The Journal of Philosophy* **70**: 439–52.

GRICE, H. P. (1975) Logic and Conversation. In P. Cole and J. Morgan (eds) *Syntax and Semantics: Speech Acts. vol. 3*. London: Academic Press.

— (1978) Further Notes on Logic and Conversation. In P. Cole (ed.) *Syntax and Semantics 9: Pragmatics*. London: Academic Press.

GUENTHER, H. V. (1976) *Philosophy and Psychology in the Abhidharma*. London: Shambhala.

HABERMAS, J. (1978) *Knowledge and Human Interests*. 2nd edn. London: Heinemann.

HACKING, I. (1975) *Why Does Language Matter to Philosophy?* Cambridge: Cambridge University Press.

HERBERT, A. P. (1935) The Reasonable Man. In *Uncommon Law*. London: Methuen.

HOBART, M. (1985) Thinker, Thespian, Soldier, Slave: Assumptions about Human Nature in the Study of Balinese Society. In M. Hobart and R. Taylor (eds) *Context and Meaning in South East Asia*. Ithaca, NY: Cornell University Press.

HOLLIS, M. (1970) The Limits of Irrationality. In B. Wilson (ed.) *Rationality*. Oxford: Basil Blackwell.

— (1977) *Models of Man*. Cambridge: Cambridge University Press.

— (1982) The Social Destruction of Reality. In M. Hollis and S. Lukes (eds) *Rationality and Relativism*. Oxford: Basil Blackwell.

HOLLIS, M. and LUKES, S. (eds) (1982) *Rationality and Relativism*. Oxford: Basil Blackwell.

HORTON, R. (1979) Material-Object Language and Theoretical Language. In S. C. Brown (ed.) *Philosophical Disputes in the Social Sciences*. Brighton: Harvester.

— (1982) Tradition and Modernity Revisited. In M. Hollis and S. Lukes (eds) *Rationality and Relativism*. Oxford: Basil Blackwell.

HOWE, L. E. A. (1981) The Social Determination of Knowledge: Maurice Bloch and Balinese Time. *Man* NS **16** (2): 220–34.

— (1983) An Introduction to the Cultural Study of Traditional Balinese Architecture. *Archipel* **25**: 137–58.

IONS, E. (1977) *Against Behaviouralism*. Oxford: Basil Blackwell.

JAKOBSON, R. (1960) Concluding Statement: Linguistics and Poetics. In T. Sebeok (ed.) *Style in Language*. Cambridge, Mass.: MIT Press.

JONAS, D. and JONAS, D. (1976) *Other Senses, Other Worlds*. London: Cassell.

KEMPSON, R. (1975) *Presupposition and the Delimitation of Semantics*. Cambridge: Cambridge University Press.

— (1977) *Semantic Theory*. Cambridge: Cambridge University Press.

KEYNES, J. N. (1884) *Studies and Exercises in Formal Logic*. London: Macmillan.

KRIPKE, S. (1977) Identity and Necessity. In S. P. Schwartz (ed.) *Naming, Necessity, and Natural Kinds*. London: Cornell University Press.

KUHN, T. S. (1962) *The Structure of Scientific Revolutions*. 2nd edn enlarged 1970. London: University of Chicago Press.

— (1977) *The Essential Tension*. London: University of Chicago Press.

KUNTZ, P. G. (ed.) (1968) *The Concept of Order*. London: University of Washington Press.

LLOYD, G. E. R. (1966) *Polarity and Analogy: Two Types of Argumentation in Early Greek Thought*. Cambridge: Cambridge University Press.

— (1979) *Magic, Reason and Experience: Studies in the Origin and Development of Greek Science*. Cambridge: Cambridge University Press.

LUKES, S. (1967) Alienation and Anomie. In P. Laslett and S. Runciman (eds) *Philosophy, Politics and Society 3*. Oxford: Basil Blackwell.

— (1970) Some Problems about Rationality. In B. Wilson (ed.) *Rationality*. Oxford: Basil Blackwell.

— (1973a) *Individualism*. Oxford: Basil Blackwell.

— (1973b) *Emile Durkheim: His Life and Work*. Harmondsworth: Allen Lane.

LYONS, J. (1977) *Semantics*. 2 volumes. Cambridge: Cambridge University Press.

MARRIOTT, M. (1976) Hindu Transactions: Diversity Without Dualism. In B. Kapferer (ed.) *Transaction and Meaning*. Philadelphia: Institute for the Study of Human Issues.

MINER, H. (1956) Body Ritual among the Nacirema. *American Anthropologist* **58**: 503–7.

MOORE, T. (1982) Comments on Sperber's and Wilson's Paper. In N. V. Smith (ed.) *Mutual Knowledge*. London: Academic Press.

NEEDHAM, R. (1975) Polythetic Classification: Convergence and Consequences. *Man* NS **10** (3): 349–69.

NEWTON-SMITH, W. (1982) Relativism and the Possibility of Interpretation. In M. Hollis and S. Lukes (eds) *Rationality and Relativism*. Oxford: Basil Blackwell.

OLSON, M. (1965) *The Logic of Collective Action*. Cambridge, Mass.: Harvard University Press.

POLE, D. (1975) The Concept of Reason. In R. F. Dearden, P. H. Hirst, and R. S. Peters (eds) *Reason: Part 2 of Education and the Development of Reason*. London: Routledge & Kegan Paul.

POTTER, K. (1977) *Indian Metaphysics and Epistemology*. Princeton: Princeton University Press.

PUTNAM, H. (1971) Symposium on Innate Ideas: (b) The 'Innateness Hypothesis' and Explanatory Models in Linguistics. In J. Searle (ed.) *The Philosophy of Language*. Oxford: Oxford University Press.

— (1981) *Reason, Truth and History*. Cambridge: Cambridge University Press.

QUINE, W. V. O. (1953) Two Dogmas of Empiricism. In *From a Logical Point of View*. London: Harvard University Press.

— (1960) *Word and Object*. Cambridge, Mass.: Harvard University Press.

— (1970) *Philosophy of Logic*. New Jersey: Prentice-Hall.

— (1979) A Postscript on Metaphor. In S. Sachs (ed.) *On Metaphor*. Chicago: University of Chicago Press.

REDDY, M. (1979) The Conduit Metaphor. In A. Ortony (ed.) *Metaphor and Thought*. Cambridge: Cambridge University Press.

RORTY, A. (1976) A Literary Postscript. In A. Rorty (ed.) *The Identities of Persons*. Berkeley: California University Press.

— (1980) Introduction. In A. Rorty (ed.) *Explaining Emotions*. Berkeley: California University Press.

RORTY, R. (1980) *Philosophy and the Mirror of Nature*. Oxford: Basil Blackwell.

RUSSELL, B. (1905) On Denoting. *Mind* **14**: 479–93.

RYAN, A. (1978) Maximizing, Moralizing and Dramatizing. In C. Hookway and P. Pettit (eds) *Action and Interpretation*. Cambridge: Cambridge University Press.

SALMOND, A. (1982) *Theoretical Landscapes: On Cross-Cultural Conceptions of Knowledge*. In D. Parkin (ed.) *Semantic Anthropology* (ASA Monographs 22). London: Academic Press.

SPERBER, D. (1975) *Rethinking Symbolism*. Cambridge: Cambridge University Press.

— (1982) Apparently Irrational Beliefs. In M. Hollis and S. Lukes (eds) *Rationality and Relativism*. Oxford: Basil Blackwell.

134   Mark Hobart

SPERBER, D. and WILSON, D. (1982) Mutual Knowledge and Relevance in Theories of Comprehension. In N. V. Smith (ed.) *Mutual Knowledge*. London: Academic Press.

STRAWSON, P. (1950) On Referring. *Mind* **59**: 320–44.

— (1959) *Individuals: An Essay in Descriptive Metaphysics*. London: Methuen.

— (1964) Intention and Convention in Speech Acts. *Philosophical Review* **73**: 439–60.

TALBOT, M. (1981) *Mysticism and the New Physics*. London: Routledge & Kegan Paul.

TARSKSI, A. (1956) The Semantic Conception of Truth. In *Logic, Semantics, and Metamathematics*. Oxford: Oxford University Press.

TAYLOR, C. (1982) Rationality. In M. Hollis and S. Lukes (eds) *Rationality and Relativism*. Oxford: Basil Blackwell.

TODOROV, T. (1982) *Theories of the Symbol*. Oxford: Basil Blackwell.

WALLACE, A. F. C. (1961) *Culture and Personality*. New York: Random House.

WILDEN, A. (1972) Analog and Digital Communication. In *System and Structure: Essays in Communication and Exchange*. London: Tavistock.

WILSON, D. (1975) *Presuppositions and Non-Truth-Conditional Semantics*. London: Academic Press.

WITTGENSTEIN, L. (1958) *Philosophical Investigations*, translated by G. E. M. Anscombe. Revised 2nd edn. Oxford: Basil Blackwell.

ZOETMULDER, P. J. (1982) *Old Javanese–English Dictionary*. 2 vols. The Hague: Nijhoff.

David Parkin

7 Reason, emotion, and the embodiment of power

Dualisms as triadisms

The various dichotomies framing debates on rationality are revealing. Relativism may be opposed to rationality, but may also be opposed to universalism. The latter slides over into objectivity and so is contrasted with subjectivity. Subjectivity subsumes emotionalism, which itself is set up against reason. Thus, from rationality and relativism we move to reason and sentiment. Three issues arise from this muddle. One is the attempt to disentangle such apparent confusion. We can subdivide kinds of rationality into, for instance, cognitive and strategic (de Sousa 1980: 129), or we can distinguish arch-rationalism from anarcho-rationalism (Hacking 1982: 51–66), recognizing that in all such cases a notion of objective truth is in some way implied and, with it, a potential universalism (for example, even if a society does not have a particular version of reality, it remains a possible option to be taken up from among those available to humanity (Gellner 1982: 187–88)). We can also subdivide types of relativism, such as conceptual, perceptual, moral, cognitive, and those of truth and reason (Hollis and Lukes 1982: 6–20), and no doubt many more. I do not wish to add to this aspect of the debate, but rather to ask why it has arisen at all.

A second issue is the extraordinary resilience in our own ordinary English language of the tendency to contrast emotion with reason and then to draw further parallels. Thus, emotions are subjective states that are the responsibility of the individual and so, at the particular moment of their expression, relate to him or her alone. Reason is the property of reasonable persons who are held to be in the majority and who would, if all problems of the world could be solved, exist everywhere.

But how far are such lofty ideals put into practice? Television anthropology may temporarily convert liberal middle-class business executives to the idea that other peoples' reasonings may legitimately be different from theirs. But when dealing in their offices next day with Third World import and export deliveries, they may easily revert to less charitable explanations in terms of 'different mentalities'. Nor are the beleaguered businessmen alone.

That the one- and many-mind distinction in ordinary English language is unlikely ever to be altered by academic debate need not surprise us. It is a variation of the distinction between human and less-than-human which seems to be employed in different ways by peoples the world over and is a frequent topic of anthropological concern (Southall 1976; Arens 1979). What is interesting is the way in which this contrast becomes re-cast as that of reasoning selves and emotionally irrational others. The contrast has a scholarly pedigree, too, as Chapman shows in the portrayals of Celts over the centuries (1982).

Third, then, it is not the seemingly unsuspecting ordinary English speaker alone who uses the opposition of reason to emotion as the basis of further argument. When they are not reflecting on its epistemological inappropriateness, academics use it too, the most recent example being a model of political language proposed by F. G. Bailey, who distinguishes between hortatory and cerebral rhetoric, the former depending on the evocation of sentiment and the latter on rational argument. A third mode is called pseudo-cerebral. It is speech which poses as rational but uses specious argumentation. For an English-speaking readership Bailey's account is convincing (1981). As he also shows (1983) the strategic use of emotional display may be the most appropriate and so, in the circumstances, most rational means of persuasion. But could such alternating rhetorical devices work in a culture that did not distinguish clearly or at all between reason and emotion? Indeed are there such cultures?

I mention Bailey's work because, figuratively, to distinguish the heart and head as the separate loci respectively of sentiment and intellect, irrationality and logic, or emotion and reason, is a part of our Cartesian heritage that has surely shaped the questions raised by the debate on rationality. If we ourselves did not think in terms of heart versus mind it is unlikely that we would have moved on to ask whether other peoples are equally rational, and, if not, in what ways they differ from us. In other words, out of our own heart-versus-mind dichotomy we have developed that of relativism and rationality. The grand academic debate is itself epistemologically couched in folk usage.

I have been deliberately glib in speaking thus of a Cartesian heritage, for that is how we have popularized Descartes' views on mind and body. In fact, of course, there is more to the distinction than that. It is relevant to ask briefly why theoretical popularization has reduced Descartes' complex argument to a simple duality.

It is perfectly acceptable to say that Descartes' distinction between mental phenomena (mind) and physical phenomena (body) is dualistic. Within each of these the dualisms continue: mind is composed of intellect (which refers to ideas outside the mind, e.g. God) and of will (consisting of attitudes to these intellectual ideas, e.g. God exists or does not exist). Physical body consists of matter and of motion. Confining ourselves to mind, we find a further intriguing duality in the distinction within the will between two types of attitude towards ideas of the intellect. One is desire-aversion and the other assertion-denial. The former leads into a concern with volition, including the emotions of love and hatred. The latter, assertion-denial, is the basis of judgement. As long as these dualities and sub-dualities are regarded as parts of an overall scheme, then we can continue to think in terms of an encompassing dichotomy of mind and body.

But two factors dislodge the simplicity of this dichotomy. The first is the difficulty of controlling, so to speak, a concept like volition or emotion. In the English language we often speak of desires and hatreds overwhelming judgements calculated on the basis of factual assertions and denials. Emotion, that is to say, frequently subordinates reason. It assumes inordinate significance. In doing so, volition or emotion may seem to stifle not only judgement but intellect itself, in so far as it shapes our ideas of the things supposedly existing outside our minds. The second discomforting factor is the tendency among philosophers, including Descartes, to add to the dualism a third, independent agency (not always regarded as such, however). Thus, Socrates sees *thumos* as mediating and monitoring thought and 'appetite'. Plato does propose a dualism of the soul and the body-senses, from which a soul must escape in order to achieve clarity of thought as well as immortality. But his soul is tied in one direction to mental functions and in the other to the eternal Ideas through *eros* or transcendental love: soul thus looks to emotion, a third agency, as a route to intellect. Aristotle specifically suggests a trinary characterization: there is nutritive soul designed for ingestion and procreation; animal soul for perceiving, remembering, and imagining; and rational soul by which humans alone are endowed with the capacity for thought. For Descartes himself, his early idea of mind as an independent homunculus inside the body becomes incompatible with his later dualism of mind-soul and body. Thus, on the one hand he sees mind as receiving sense impressions from the brain, a part of the body, and of acting upon matter including the body. On the other hand, in identifying mind with soul, he describes the latter as able to exist independently of the body, capable indeed of leading a disembodied life (Rée 1974: 91–117). Putting the point very simply, mind can only operate on and through matter, including the body, while soul can exist independently of matter. Yet mind is supposed to be identical to soul. The dualism of mind and body comes across rather as an unacknowledged triad of mind, soul, and body.[1]

Such triads arise because a place has to be found in the scheme for a transcendental link with God; soul provides this link. Soul as part of mind can judge (or err), while soul as part of God can love (or hate). But even when, in the post-Enlightenment period, a link with God is no longer thought necessary, a triadic scheme persists. Thus, while Tönnies distinguishes natural will (our emotions and general volition) from rational will,[2] he adds a third, social will, which is concerned with what he calls three great systems, order, law, and morality. In other words, instead of God providing the necessity for a third independent agent or will, we have society itself. Tönnies did not consciously seek to substitute society for God in his triad of wills, but this is in effect what happened, as with other post-Enlightenment scholars. Indeed, the substitution anticipates Durkheim's observation that, as a definition of a social fact, God is society.

I find it difficult to know when these triadisms gave way to the dualisms of which we now speak in modern times. It may have stemmed from Durkheim's own opposition of society and individual. The primacy of society over individual was his attempt to crush the explanation of social institutions through psychology. Psychological explanations of the individual, including his volition and emotions, were rendered irrelevant. Saussure, basing his opposition of *langue* to *parole* on that of society and individual, also privileged *langue* and regarded *parole* as the analytically irrelevant utterances of individuals. What mattered was *langue*, the generative powerhouse of utterances, a dualism which was later given a firm Cartesian pedigree by Chomsky. So, Cartesian dualism became Chomskian dualism. Somehow, the triadisms, not always clear or acknowledged, got lost.

Feelings and power as rationality

The shift from ambiguous triadism to firm dualism has brought two other developments. First, the dualism is not simply that of opposed but equal concepts. Rather, as with *langue* over and against *parole*, the concepts are ranked. Second, though it is individuals who create the unique utterances we call *paroles* or performance, they are depicted as doing so without emotion (to use the term in the conventional sense). Competence or *langue* is the knowledge of rules or grammar, while *paroles* are the rule-governed creations which individuals, however innovative they may be, refer rationally to the collective reason enshrined in *langue*.

In recent years some anthropologists have reacted against this reliance on intellect in structuralist explanations of culture, arguing that ratiocination is sustained more by intuition, aesthetics, and emotional factors than by a neutral calculation of logically possible alternatives (Milner 1969 (after Bergson 1975); Lewis 1980; Tonkin 1982; Parkin 1982; Rosaldo 1980). The argument is that people may strive to achieve the latter, but whether or not they are aware of it, their thinking remains framed by personal values and inner states. They may evaluate a decision differently in the light of its apparent consequences and of their changing moods and dispositions.

Although it is a modern reaction against structuralism in anthropology, this second view shares affinities with Hume's dictum that passions do and should rule reason, and that reason should be the slave of passion (Baier 1980).

Whereas dualists, including structuralists, privilege rationality (via rules) over sentiment, Hume reverses this priority.

Baier notes that Hume classifies passions in a number of ways: direct and indirect, violent and calm, agreeable and uneasy, regular and irregular (reciprocated and unreciprocated), instinctive and acquired, activating and passive, and so on (Baier 1980: 404). She focuses on the force of passions in their struggle to master reason. Parallels are made with the distinctions of Spinoza between free active passions and unfree sovereign ones, of Nietzsche between sovereign-free sentiments and those that are slavish and reactive, and of Hume himself between self-sustaining pure and other-directed impure passions. Note the vocabulary of hierarchy and conflict. 'Pride' is taken as an emotion that embodies this battle. For Hume, if pride is properly socialized by the collective moral sentiment then it will not become self-conceit but will applaud virtue: 'I am proud of my nation's achievements but not chauvinistic'. It will insist on 'morally proper' reasons for decisions: 'My society's values should be respected but not arbitrarily imposed on others'. I think that these metaphors of force, control, and struggle in depicting the interplay of emotions with each other and in the domination of reason, are significant. For they are part of the language used by proponents who compete to have their versions of 'reason' or of 'emotion' accepted, thus revealing the inevitable power and political dimension of such imposed definitions.

There is, however, a third view which, as far as ordinary language will allow, merges reason and emotion. Taking an example of this 'coherence' view from Wilson (1972: 182–89), we can say that what makes a human different from a highly intelligent robot is that a person makes sense of a decision one has made not only in terms of whether it will secure the goal one has set oneself, but in terms also of whether it fits one's feelings and attitudes towards the object of the decision. Certain kinds of 'transactional' anthropologists might counter with the view that, in taking decisions, people do balance the emotional and pragmatic costs of a goal. But this comes close to tautology if the argument is that all acts are utilitarian because, whatever we do, it is part of a means to an end. Wilson's point is that, unlike robots, people seek a coherence of feeling and attitude in the things they (decide to) do, and that this makes nonsense of the dichotomy between reason and emotion. In other words, no reason can be given for an act or decision that does not also involve the actor's emotions, however weak or strong. There is no conflict between reason and emotion.

Interestingly, the three views map out some of the ways in which we ourselves justify actions. Our English idioms reveal this. 'He is hot-headed', meaning that he should train his reason to curb his passions. 'He is a cold fish', meaning that more sentiment and less calculation are needed. But, 'He dedicated himself to the task with a passion', meaning that he balanced reason with emotion quite well. Many other phrases indicate one or other priority or preference. They reflect the persistent difficulties underlying the dualistic attempt to think only in terms of reasoning mind and body and excluding sentiment. A dualistic hierarchy may appear more 'scientific' (though modern scientists rarely associate themselves with them any more), but depart seriously from folk views. The ambiguous triadism in such concepts as mind, soul, and body, or reason, passion, and body, more accurately reflects the way ordinary people approach, explain, and justify situations and their involvement in them.

Again, as a paradigm of three views of society, they denote fixed hierarchy (as in reason, *langue*, competence, and society, being over and against emotion, *parole*, performance, and the individual); permanent struggle to gain or retain mastery (as in Hume's assertion that passions must rule reason); and harmony and equality (as in the mutual embeddedness of reason and feeling). A history of ideas thus turns out to be an analogue of social possibilities as well as the way people may map their individual actions.[3]

Moreover, the views define the conditions of rationality. First, rationality intimates a capacity to repair disturbed hierarchies of values, to reconcile conflicts of opinions and interests, and to bring them into supposed order and harmony with each other. Second, rationality entails decision-making and choices and therefore conflicts, contradiction, struggle, force, power, and control. Third, however, rationality as coherence presupposes that reason and emotion are not in conflict but are shaped by each other and convince more through an apparent rightness of 'feel' and 'fit' than by any demonstrable proof. For example, the awe of a man gazing at an indescribably beautiful scene may, for those moments, make the idea of the non-existence of God irrational and unacceptable to him. Let me now illustrate these views ethnographically.

Some previous definitions of rationality have stressed efficiency in the relationship of means to ends. But this raises the Weberian question of whose interpretation of means and ends is accepted as the most efficient: peoples themselves may disagree and so the outside analyst steps in authoritatively with his interpretation. We can instead start with interpretative disagreements recognized by the people whom we study: some may not see a conflict, while others do; but this in itself constitutes a conflict in their interpretations. The concept of rationality, then, simultaneously presupposes disagreement and the possibility of consensus. It therefore concerns the politics of personal rivalries, loyalties, interests, and identities. At stake is not only who gets the most land or property, but also how much of one's selfhood is left of whoever loses the fight to have one's interpretation accepted. Among the Giriama of Kenya, this primacy of selfhood for some, though not all of them, makes sense of their habit of bankrupting themselves by selling land and trees to pay for lavish mortuary rituals concerning one of their members.

Two reasons may be given, or be apparent for this habit. First, the shame in losing personal esteem through being judged ungenerous is greater than the shame of bankruptcy. Another reason for expensive ceremonies is that they have been called at the request of an ancestor or must be held in honour of one, not necessarily the member of the homestead who has just died. Certain Giriama may publicly acknowledge these as just reasons. Through careful planning a few of them stage lavish rites but keep enough of their property 'hidden' to re-establish themselves. Such successful farmers do systematically relate means to ends in what they see as the most efficient manner. But they do so through an interpretation of ceremonial obligation which conflicts with that of other farmers. Those other farmers claim that a sponsor should be unstinting even to the point of bankruptcy either because to do otherwise is shameful to self, family, and clan, or because one or more ancestors will be offended and will punish the family. However, entrepreneurial farmers reason privately among those they can trust that provided a sponsor is *seen* to be generous then both ancestors and personal and communal honour will be satisfied (Parkin 1972).

If this were all there is to the situation, we would say that these simply represent alternative rationalities, each of which characterizes a particular category of persons. But the situation is inconstant. The role of emotions enters into it through the opinions and expressed feelings of other people and of the ancestors which shape the interpretations of what has been or might be done. To offend those who hold other opinions is to incur their displeasure, anger, and even vengeance. Taking the 'right' decision is not only a question of reaching a particular end, but may be an attempt to avoid personal fear and guilt, as well as the wrath or mere ridicule of others. Moreover, avoiding the effects of others' as well as one's own sentiments, or seeking approval through them, may become more important than preserving one's property. We often redefine our aims which have already been reshaped through our changing emotions. Thus it is that the once successful entrepreneurial farmer visibly loses his grip and joins the ranks of the poor. He (or a member of his family) had become sick and, fearing ancestral vengeance or the witchcraft of jealous neighbours, no longer made a secret of his property holdings and so soon lost them through the obligation to fund ceremonies and proffer gifts and help. In Giriama society, as elsewhere in Africa, there are many examples of rapid fluctuations in family fortunes within a single generation as well as between them, for which the standard economic explanation of insufficient liquidity is not the only one and itself only scratches the surface.

A reason can, then, always be found for acting in a particular way, and more than one reason may be held. Ceremonial generosity may be the means to avoid shame, the effects of others' envy, or ancestral displeasure, or to satisfy communal expectations and so seek support in a subsequent endeavour. If it is convincing, any reason will stick. Even madness may be interpreted as a rational attempt to escape the impossibility of meeting the otherwise rational demands of everyday life. A personal or cultural flow chart of alternative reasons for decisions would not indicate a fixed number of logical possibilities but, given people's imaginative creativity, an expanding list in which preferences and priorities would constantly be changing, and in which deletions and substitutions would also occur.

Here, it is important to stress that this imagination is not simply the play of an innovative intellect which refuses to recognize logical bounds. Such a view would reduce interpretative creativity to the infinite articulation of different possible judgements. I am arguing instead that emotions are non-judgemental shapers of decisions. That is to say, emotions act autonomously, or at least appear to do so, in giving sense to an interpretation, not through comparison with other possible decisions but by making *that* particular interpretation seem fitting. Emotions thus make for aesthetic as well as functional appropriateness. For example, homoeopathic magic makes sense not necessarily because it is seen to work but because it presents a pleasing and persuasive picture, image, or metaphor of feasibility. Many such pleasing images involve the use of people's bodies. Thus, magicians often heighten the drama of their performance through stylistic movements and gestures. Bodily drama and emotion here draw on each other and at the same time result in acts, decisions, and suggestions that are regarded as reasonable as well as pleasing. Among the Giriama, the stalk of a certain herb oozes a white sap when broken. The stalk is stroked gently by the herbalist and is offered into a prepared liquid which is then drunk by a mother having difficulties breast-feeding her child, each phase being given stylistic emphasis and accompanied by ancestral and other incantations. The breaking, oozing, stroking, offering up, and recitation evidently arouse a range of feelings, a number of which are obvious and appear to be commonly held.

A moving together

We would be missing much of the sense of the occasion simply to call this therapy. I suggest that it is an instance of aesthetic appropriateness and has to be thought of as a moving-together of reason, emotion, and body. The ideas of both Sartre (1958) and Merleau-Ponty (1962) are relevant here, as well as those of a number of anthropologists who have looked ethnographically at the bodily loci of reasoning emotions (e.g. Blacking 1977; Lienhardt 1980; Rosaldo 1980; Heelas 1981; Harris 1978; Lewis 1980).

I start, however, with some standard observations on the various ways in which the body and its parts are associated with social power and authority. Familiar examples are the grid:group dichotomy proposed by Mary Douglas (1970), by which different bodily postures correspond socially with either individualism or conformity; the hierarchy of head and loins among the Fipa described by Willis (1967, 1980) which underwrites centralized political legitimacy; and the association of right- and left-handedness with authority and submission respectively (Needham 1973).

Other ethnographers will generally accept these kinds of correspondences between the human and social body. But if I understand the ways in which they were elicited, they are intellectual classifications. That is to say, people in the society concerned will explain to the ethnographer or to uninformed fellow-members what is socially represented by the dichotomy of head and loins, or of right and left, or of loose as against stiff bodily posture. Sometimes, further associations are accounted for by the ethnographer himself, but the initial dualism can generally be explained by some members of the society.

This being so, those same members of the society will comment on the correctness or appropriateness of bodily usage. Thus, on the rare occasions when a Giriama woman is allowed to drink alcoholic liquor, she must do so holding the gourd from which she drinks in her left hand. Since the occasions are so rare, she may have to be reminded of this obligation. Similarly, there are appropriate burial positions for ordinary men and women and for special men who are members of a secret society. Sometimes there is dispute as to the direction in which the deceased's head must face. But that there are rules concerning this is not disputed.

In all such cases, and there are many, people have to be told what to do. Usually they accept this without question as an authoritative statement from someone in a legitimate position to make it: elder to young man, man to woman, adult to child. Sometimes people are also told what dire effects will ensue if the custom is not carried out. This is the realm of command and explanation. It is an area of discourse which places reason in control of body.

But there is another area of discourse which reverses this. Spirit possession, madness, hysteria (the three are distinguished), witchcraft, and persistent violence, drunkenness, and thieving, must be explained by a diviner. Such behaviour is explained as the result of what we might loosely call imbalances in human nature. I call them imbalances because the Giriama do not believe that a person can be intrinsically or irredeemably evil: at some stage, usually remarkably quickly, he will be brought back into the fold, even if he subsequently leaves it again. A large number of terms, roughly translatable as greed, lust, envy, jealousy, malice, resentment, anger, are used to refer to these imbalances of character and the accompanying behaviour. In English we would say that emotions are seen as controlling the body and its actions.

However, to describe such behaviour as due to imbalances of character presupposes that the Giriama regard the morally proper person as balanced and others as deviating from this. But this is a Western imposition. The Giriama view such alternations of virtue and vice as that which makes up a human being: a purely virtuous or a purely wicked person does not exist, so why bother to set these up as polar models? Thus, while there are rules governing the use of the body (e.g. right or left hand) which appear to privilege reason, there are other kinds of bodily behaviour (spirit possession, causing illness through witchcraft, theft, violence) which appear to be caused by such emotions as desire, greed, envy, and malice.

This wording however, once again, puts us into a trap set by Western thinking. Key terms for the sources of these emotions themselves refer to parts of the body. Moreover, the same key terms may refer, ambivalently, to reason. In other words, the same terms may refer to what we call body, reason, and emotion. For us to argue then that for the Giriama reason controls body in the field of ritual prohibitions, but that emotions govern body where there is destructive behaviour, is to distinguish analytical categories that distort the more packed-in, polysemic discourse of the Giriama themselves.

The key terms in Giriama that show this polysemy, as probably in most Bantu languages, refer directly to heart, liver, kidney, eye, and possibly head, each with derived terms and meanings:

moyo = physical heart, life, selfhood, reason, mind, determination, but also feelings, innermost sentiment, hope, willingness, will, and desire, and thence to

choyo = (lit. little heart) = greed, selfishness, envy, but also palpitating spot in veins, blood, and also *m'fundo moyo* or *fundo ra moyo* (lit. knotted heart) = malice, envy. The idea of innermost feelings is also found as one of the meanings of the word for liver, thus

ini = physical liver, core emotion (usually negative, like *ifu* kidney), and thence to

kiini = (lit. little liver) = innermost part, kernel of nut, stone of fruit, yolk of egg, heart of tree, and core of meaning or argument

dzitso = physical eye *and* spring of water, but also greed, envy, more usually in the form of

kidzitso = (lit, little eye) = envy, covetousness, and directly associated with witchcraft. The plural form is

matso = physical eyes, but, unless qualified (e.g. *matso mai* bad eyes = a kind of witchcraft), lacks the sinister, emotional connotations of the singular. Instead, as in expressions such as *matso mafu* (open eyes) or *kukala matso* (to be awake) there is the sense of being alert and in a stable, reasoning frame of mind.

kitswa = physical head, top or higher part, that which leads, authority, but also pride, arrogance, including

dzitswa-ro = (lit. that large head) = stupid person

My inclusion of the word for head reveals a Western bias. As will be seen it only marginally touches on all three aspects of reason, emotion, and body. It is certainly part of the body, but, except that to be an authority requires wisdom, and that leaders tend to be proud, the co-associations are weak. The greatest sources of feelings and thought are the heart, liver, and kidney, and, to a lesser extent, the eye and eyes. All three, including eye with its secondary meaning of spring of water, refer to internal origins, the innermost being those of heart and liver. This accords with Lienhardt's findings among some non-Bantu African peoples, the Nilotic Dinka and Luo of Eastern Africa (1980). Outside Africa, as in Shakespearian England, the heart 'thinks' as well as 'feels', and the liver is the seat of passions (*Much Ado About Nothing* III. ii.13, cited by Gregory 1984).

Other bodily terms are important among Giriama. *Milatso* is blood and can, when used in aphorisms, stress the reasonableness of marriage and affinity ('blood follows cattle', i.e., that cattle exchanges make marriages which make children). It can also refer to 'natural skills', e.g. *ana mulatso wa kufuga ng'ombe*, he knows how to keep cattle. In its adverbial form *kilatso*, the term refers to blood guiltiness (i.e., spilling blood in battle or in sacrifice) and to bad fate. Blood is contrasted with flesh, for which the word is *nyama*, which also means meat, live animal, and spirits which possess people and so denotes a general principle of animation.

Other bodily terms are also used metaphorically and show their potential for indicating existential dilemmas, e.g., *ku-nyerezeza mukono* is to offer one's hand gently in respect, while *ku-kala na mukono* is to 'stay with the hand', i.e., have a tendency to pilfer. The hand is for giving as well as for taking. However, none of these other terms goes as far in this respect as heart, liver, kidney, eye, head, blood, and flesh.

On the one hand, then, the heart, liver, kidney, and eye are the seat of conjoined reason and emotions in general. On the other hand, particular kinds of reasoning and emotional behaviour are identified by terms that have nothing directly to do with the body, though etymologically they may originate in practical, bodily actions. With regard to the latter, what is impressive is, (a) the large number of terms for what we might translate as emotions and reasoning faculties; and (b) how possible it is to distinguish these as such. In other words, while the Giriama see the origins of reason and emotion in particular parts of the body, they nevertheless distinguish reasoning from emotion in specific references to actual cases of behaviour.

There are terms denoting grief, loneliness, longing, love, lust, greed, envy, jealousy, malice, anger, fear, doubt, despair, disgust, shame, pride, trust, hope, determination, and others. Many such translations into English miss the different ways in which emotions may be linked among the Giriama. Thus, to take just one example, *utsungu* means poison, bitterness, resentment, and anger, on the one hand, but also grief on the other. It is the feeling experienced at a funeral of a loved or respected relative or friend. A man or woman is grieved at the loss but also bitter that it has happened at all, and angry with the witch who caused the death. Since the witch will be made to pay, the sentiment carries within it both the consequences of the loss of a dear one and the intention to avenge his or her death.

Intentionality is thus built into descriptions of emotional states, and yet a completely separate vocabulary exists to describe acts of thinking, pondering, intending, comparing, explaining, understanding, remembering, reminding, and deciding. Two underlying notions figure prominently: making clean, clear, or bright, and aiming or pointing in a particular direction. Cleaning, clearing, lighting (the way), and directing are practical, purposive activities. They are premised on intentionality, as we would call it, just as are the descriptions of emotions.

Thus, to take some examples, *ku-ng'alira* means to shine upon (moon, sun, or fire), while the passive form, *ku-ng'alirwa*, is to understand, i.e. have made clear to one. Similarly, *ku-aza* can be translated as to reflect or consider possibilities, and is etymologically related to *ku-aka*, to burn brightly. Derived forms are *ku-azuka*, to reach a decision after thinking about it, and *ku-azya*, to cause someone to think about something. 'To make the way clear' becomes linked to ideas of direction. Thus *ku-era* means to be or become clean or clear, and the derived form *ku-erekeza* has the sense of to aim at and thence to intend. The act of pointing a way opposes destination to departure and so the word has an additional sense of to be opposed and therefore to compare. The causative *ku-erekezanya* means to explain to one another or come to an agreement, while the static form, *ku-erekezeka*, is to be capable of settlement and of explanation, and therefore to be thinkable. The many forms of inflection in Bantu verb stems allow for a wide range of increasingly abstract ideas to be developed out of a basic term for a practical act.

The case of divination

While the specific terms for emotions presuppose intentional acts, the terms for thinking are etymologically rooted in them. But both can be seen as making up a complementarity. The intentionality behind terms for emotions is always to return a fragmented part of the self back to its core, or to avenge its fragmentation by another. A diviner's diagnosis travels, so to speak, over different parts of the patient's body, indicating different emotions as symptoms and causes of the patient's affliction or misfortune. He finishes his diagnosis by fixing on a particular part of the body as the one which is out of order. He then suggests therapy, to be carried out by another doctor, which will re-establish bodily-emotional harmony. In acting autonomously, bodily emotions wander or split off from the core of innermost self. The diviner indicates both the source of the trouble and a means of bringing back together the wayward parts (Parkin 1979). The diviners' intentionality, embodied in the idioms of pointing and explaining, complements the intending grief, love, hatred, anger, or malice of the patient or his attacker. The result will be to return them to heart and liver, the innermost loci of what we call reason and emotion.

Divination has a powerful performative aspect. Its apparent empirical success depends on the persuasive artistry of the diviner. His knowledge of local social ties and enmities may sometimes be a necessary condition of accurate predictions, but his dramatic skills make them convincing and credible. I have been much impressed by the way in which Giriama diviners, and sometimes other ritual experts, bring their own bodies into the perform-ance. They may sing, move in a rhythmic manner, alter their voices when possessed, go into trances, jump out of them, and assume dramatic airs. They bring together not only their own bodily parts, but also their judgements and feelings into an aesthetic whole. This aesthetic moving-together is what gives sense to the divination. It reduces conflict between judgement, emotion, and the body and so presents them as an appropriate response to disorder.

Thus far, we can see how this Giriama co-ordination of body, reason, and emotion might seem to conform to Merleau-Ponty's phenomenology of per-ception (1962, 1945). That is to say, the diviner achieves his own unity of body, mind, and feelings through interaction with that of his patient. Indeed, he creates his own unity at the same time as he creates that of the patient. He dissolves the distinction between himself as subject and the patient as object, making them both an inter-subjectivity, to use Merleau-Ponty's concept. Neither reason, nor emotion, nor body, prevails one over the other. Nor does the diviner's unity prevail over that of the patient, nor that of the patient over the diviner's. The simultaneity or, as I would prefer, the moving-together, extends over the complete range of perception and interaction. It materially expresses the polysemy of heart, liver, kidney, and eye.

Where in this, however, are the powers and forces that I earlier said characterized our own Western ideas of emotions as being potentially out of control and in conflict with each other, with the body, and with reason? The view from Merleau-Ponty establishes their harmony. Sartre, with whose work that of Merleau-Ponty is associated, suggests a radical extension to this view (1958, 1943).

For Merleau-Ponty the uniqueness of each individual, i.e. of myself, which you can see but I cannot, and of yourself, which I can see but which you cannot, creates an ambiguity which leads us into further understanding of the world. The possibility of reflecting on this unseeable aspect of ourselves expands our horizons. But for Sartre this capacity of the other to see myself as I cannot (e.g. by catching me looking through a keyhole and causing me to feel shame), alienates myself from that other (1958: 259–63). Alienation may be unfortunate but it is what is basic to human relationships and makes up our being in the world. Thus, though through my body I act upon the world, as a subject acting upon an object, I am ultimately an object for the other who can always catch me in *flagrante delicto*. He has the upper hand over me and so alienates my body from me. I do the same for him, but unfortunately that helps neither of us. For Merleau-Ponty our body optimistically reveals possi-bilities, while for Sartre it entails alienation before revelation (Rabil 1970: 30–31).

Where does this leave the Giriama? The Giriama diviner's ideas concerning illness and misfortune are understood by him to be held by no higher authority than himself or some other diviner. He may privately concede that other diviners are better (though rarely if ever), or that all diviners rely on spirits. But all are part of the same Giriama authority. However, with the advent first of Arabic and later of Western medicine, this has for a long time and perhaps always been a fiction. New ideas compete with old and clients seek them. This obliges a diviner to incorporate them. But he can only do so by making concessions to the world-order or episteme of which the new ideas are part.

Thus, at an earlier time in Giriama society diviners had to compete with the growing power of Arabic Islam which diagnosed and prescribed through the use of numbers, astrology, and the Koran, as well as through herbal remedies. Two kinds of diviners emerged, non-Muslim Giriama and Muslim Swahili. The latter were, and still are, regarded as more efficacious. They are also more expensive. With the advent of European missions and British colonialism in the nineteenth century, Western medicine offered new competition. Its metaphysics of diagnosis and prognosis insist on still further specialization: a doctor must have education, training, and facilities, which are way beyond that available to Giriama diviners, who can only imitate them at best.

In the first case, the Islamic concept of *dini* (religion) confronted the pre-Islamic one of *uganga* (traditional medicine). In the second case, Western medicine acted through Christian schools and hospitals and opposed both traditional and Muslim divination, strongly resisting synthesization. The political power underlying its introduction was that much greater. In the case of both Muslim and Western medicine, the Giriama diviner was, so to speak, caught at the keyhole by the other. He could, however, move into Islam without too much difficulty, and gain mastery of Muslim divination. A common feature of both Muslim and non-Muslim divination facilitating this is the reciprocal roles of diviner and client in helping each other reach a mutually satisfactory diagnosis and cure through the use of vocal, facial, and other bodily cues. With Merleau-Ponty we can say here that the reciprocal revelation widens horizons of understanding.

However, while a Giriama diviner might become Christian (though I know of none), he could not move into Western medicine. The epistemological boundary between himself and Islam was that of religion, which he could cross. But the barrier placed against him by Western medicine was a specialized concept of reason, to which access could only be had through training which, given its scarcity, was inevitably privileged: a chief's son, residents of localities with mission schools, those living near roads, shops, and 'European' towns, and, more recently, the children of successful farmers and professional workers, were the ones most likely to have this privilege. It is a barrier which divides those shamed by their inadequacies from those proud of their achievements. It matches the alienation of allegedly ignorant patient from his allegedly omniscient, Western-trained doctor, and accords more with Sartre's observation. The patient can never 'know' that part of him which the doctor diagnoses as symptom and disease for he lacks precise scientific medical understanding of cause and effect. But nor does the doctor 'know' that his supposed omniscience is false and that he, too, depends on his patients' cues and co-operation in reaching diagnoses. They are further alienated from each other in that, while a herbalist's or diviner's apprentice is first his client and friend or relative, a patient can hardly ever assume the status of his 'Western' doctor, who in turn may lose the capacity to empathize with those he treats.

Whereas the traditional diviner might be little more than an ordinary elder of a small neighbourhood, perhaps one day becoming more famous, the modern, Western-trained doctor is from the beginning marked out in a number of distinct ways. Not only does he have access to knowledge and equipment that no local elder could attain, he is also distinguished physically. He dresses differently, has fixed premises which are set apart from the village, and is subject to recall and redeployment to other areas, rarely his natal one. His physical isolation and separateness contrast with the manner in which the diviner and his practice merge with and operate through his surroundings. Moreover, the 'Western' doctor stands over, so to speak, the patient who is rendered passive and not held to play a rhythmic, reciprocal role in the interaction. The doctor diagnoses and prescribes authoritatively as one body acting not through but upon another. He literally here embodies the power of an imposed Western rationality. The patient, for his part, is required to remain mute, any expression of pain, distress, or concern becoming easily labelled as emotionalism, neurosis, or some such.

Some Giriama are beginning to adopt this popular Western distinction, with its echoes of so-called Cartesian dualism, between reason as most fully expressed through education, and emotion as ideally under reason's control. This view co-exists with beliefs in the efficacy of traditional diviners and herbalists, who often do not so much reach curative decisions as exchange roles with their patients in a drama out of which come mutually acceptable suggestions. We may say that this latter is a rationality whose sense derives from a coherence of mind, body, and emotion. The 'new' alternative is a rationality evincing the non-reciprocal power of modern, 'Western-style' specialists most of whom normally live and were trained outside the society of their Giriama patients.

Notes

1 Curiously, in the same passage that he claims *not* to distinguish between mind and soul, as distinct from body, Descartes nevertheless refers to mind and soul by the different French terms (*ésprit* and *âme*) (cited in Rée 1974: 117).
2 'I distinguish between the will which includes the thinking (the natural will) and the thinking which encompasses the will (the rational will) . . .' (1955: 119, my bracketed inclusions).

3 We are reminded that Socrates' three parts making up the human soul (thought-reason, *thumos* or 'regulatory spirit', and the appetitive and impulsive) paralleled the three classes of educated governors or kings, soldiers-police, and lower classes, making up his Ideal State.

References

ARENS, W. (1979) *The Man-Eating Myth*. New York: Oxford University Press.

BAIER, A. (1980) Master Passions. In A. Rorty (ed.) *Explaining Emotions*. Berkeley: University of California Press.

BAILEY, F. G. (1981) Dimensions of Rhetoric in Conditions of Uncertainty. In R. Paine (ed.) *Politically Speaking*. Newfoundland Institute for Social and Economic Research. Philadelphia: ISHI.

— (1983) *The Tactical Uses of Passion*. Ithaca and London: Cornell University Press.

BERGSON, H. (1975) *The Creative Mind*. Totowa, NJ: Littlefield, Adam.

BLACKING, J. (ed.) (1977) *The Anthropology of the Body* (ASA Monographs 15). London: Academic Press.

CHAPMAN, M. (1982) 'Semantics' and the 'Celt'. In D. Parkin (ed.) *Semantic Anthropology* (ASA Monographs 22). London: Academic Press.

DEED, F. (n.d.) *Giryama-English Dictionary*. Nairobi: Church Missionary Society.

GELLNER, E. (1982) Relativism and Universals. In M. Hollis and S. Lukes (eds) *Rationality and Relativism*. Oxford: Basil Blackwell.

GREGORY, A. (1984) Slander Accusations and Social Control in Late 16th- and Early 17th-Century England. D. Phil. Thesis, University of Sussex.

HACKING, I. (1982) Language, Truth and Reason. In M. Hollis and S. Lukes (eds) *Rationality and Relativism*. Oxford: Basil Blackwell.

HARRIS, G. (1978) *Casting out Anger*. Cambridge: Cambridge University Press.

HEELAS, P. and A. LOCK (eds) (1981) *Indigenous Psychologies*. London: Academic Press.

HOLLIS, M. and S. LUKES (eds) (1982) *Rationality and Relativism*. Oxford: Basil Blackwell.

LEWIS, G. (1980) *Day of Shining Red*. Cambridge: Cambridge University Press.

LIENHARDT, G. (1980) Self: Public and Private. Some African Representations. *Journal of the Anthropological Society of Oxford* 11: 69–82.

MERLEAU-PONTY, M. (1962) (1945) *The Phenomenology of Perception*. London: Routledge & Kegan Paul.

MILNER, G. (1969) Siamese Twins, Birds and the Double Helix. *Man* (NS) 4: 5–23.

NEEDHAM, R. (ed.) (1973) *Right and Left*. Chicago: Chicago University Press.

PARKIN, D. (1972) *Palms, Wine and Witnesses*. San Francisco: Chandler.

— (1979) Straightening the Paths from Wilderness. *JASO* 10: 147–60.

— (1982) Introduction to his (ed.) *Semantic Anthropology*. London: Academic Press.

RABIL, A. JR (1967) *Merleau-Ponty*. New York: Columbia University Press.

RÉE, J. (1974) *Descartes*. London: Allen Lane.

RORTY, A. (ed.) (1980) *Explaining Emotions*. Berkeley: University of California Press.

ROSALDO, M. (1980) *Knowledge and Passion*. London: Cambridge University Press.

SARTRE, J.-P. (1958) (1943) *Being and Nothingness*. London: Methuen.

de SOUSA, R. (1980) The Rationality of Emotions. In A. Rorty (ed.) *Explaining Emotions*. Berkeley: University of California Press.

SOUTHALL, A. W. (1976) Nuer and Dinka Are People: Ecology, Ethnicity and Logical Possibility. *Man* (NS) 11: 463–91.

TONKIN, E. (1982) Language vs the World: Notes on Meaning for Anthropologists. In D. Parkin (ed.) *Semantic Anthropology*. London: Academic Press.
de TÖNNIES, F. (1955) (1857) *Community and Association*. London: Routledge & Kegan Paul.
WILLIS, R. (1967) The Head and the Loins. *Man* (NS) **2**: 519–34.
— (1980) *State in the Making*. Bloomington: Indiana University Press.
WILSON, J. R. S. (1972) *Emotion and Object*. Cambridge: Cambridge University Press.

Joanna Overing

8 Today I shall call him 'Mummy': multiple worlds and classificatory confusion[1]

In the world of anthropology we are always faced with the worry of how to handle 'chaos' in our data. In our fieldnotes there inevitably lurks a certain amount of material that we perceive as 'disorderly', 'illogical', and 'contradictory'. We ponder over such data, feel guilty about their presence; and in the end must make a decision about how we are going to deal with them. Many, in bafflement, ignore the delinquent items and treat them much as problem children who come from other neighbourhoods; others turn, in hope, to the arena of figurative language to demonstrate not delinquency, but the presence of a favoured child, the poetic one. As a South Americanist, I would be quite foolish to underestimate the power of analogic thought and its frequent use by Amerindians in their ordering of the overwhelmingly transformational universe in which they describe themselves as taking part. Nevertheless, my main argument in this paper will be that we often wiggle out of facing certain implications about the chaos in our data by resorting too quickly to such labels as 'metaphor', 'metonymy', and 'analogic' or 'figurative' thought: we say that our informants are rational, but because we do not truly understand their statements we construe their rationality as tropic creativity.[2]

We often protect ourselves from handling 'alien' truths that are disturbing to us by turning to the more 'solid' ground of tropes. I do not mean more 'solid' in the analytical sense; rather, I am speaking of an emotional response. It is easier for us to accept the poetic informant than to accept (even intellectually) a person who claims to believe what is totally crazy, untrue, and irrational according to our own empirically based truth conditions and formal rules of logic.

I agree with Lévi-Strauss that one of the most crucial problems in anthropology is to understand how the 'other' classifies what is for us his extraordinary world. How, for instance, do we interpret such statements from the Piaroa, the Venezuelan Indians with whom I did fieldwork: 'The tapir is our grandfather' and 'the supreme god, the tapir/anaconda who is a male chimerical being, is "mother of plants"'? Lévi-Strauss gives one answer; I shall explore another.

The metaphoric safety net

In *Totemism* (1963), Lévi-Strauss evades what would be an emotional problem for himself by defining totemism out of the realm of religious thought and by showing that classification is the aim of the 'savage', not belief or truths about actual relationships between the human world and the world of nature: the aborigine is speaking not literal truth, but truth that is indirect and metaphorical. Lévi-Strauss concludes *Totemism* by remarking (1963: 104) that he has reduced the reality of totemism 'to that of a particular illustration of certain modes of thought', and 'the alleged totemism pertains to the understanding [that is] . . . primarily of an intellectual kind'. Lévi-Strauss does unfold a salient aspect of tribal classificatory logic, that of analogy, where in his words (1963: 77) 'it is not the resemblances, but the differences, which resemble each other' that counts, e.g., crow is to eaglehawk as clan A is to clan B. The 'primitive' is claiming neither mystical nor blood relatedness to his totem and therefore does not believe the similarity that he might be thought to believe when he calls his neighbour a parrot or crow.

Forthcoming from the Lévi-Straussian understanding of metaphor is the evasion of an analysis of similarity (the relation between my neighbour and a parrot) which, after all, as much as difference and analogy, is crucial to the understanding of metaphoric statements (see Sapir (1977: 5–12, 22–8) on this distinction; also see Searle 1979; Paivio 1979; Black 1979). In contrast to the position Lévi-Strauss takes on metaphor where similarity is given short shrift, Ricoeur in *The Rule of Metaphor* observes that to metaphorize well is to see resemblance (1978: 23), and to see similarity is the genius stroke of metaphor (1978: 27). In Girard's more colourful language, 'the all-purpose differentiating machine is beginning to look like a played-out toy, a primitive noise-maker', and the 'metaphysical dualism [of, say, *langue* and *parole*] is disintegrating. . .' (1978: 174).[3] It is relevant to note that much of the more recent interest in the role of similarity in metaphoric construction is linked to an emphasis upon the creative power of metaphor in unfolding new dimensions of reality, whether in science or in literature (see, for example, the edited volume by Ortony (1979)).[4]

It is the evasion by anthropologists, and by structuralists in particular, of the issues of similarity, knowledge, and belief that I shall be discussing below. As structuralists, we take peculiar utterances out of the realm of 'religious' knowledge by claiming that most strange identifications are part of a system of analogic classification and, as such, are illustrations of a universal and rational thought process (albeit an unconscious one) in which man as intellectual always engages.[5] In making such claims, and *only* such claims about 'totemic thought' or mythic thought', structuralists not only bypass the problem of belief but, even more importantly, preclude the possibility of understanding the 'possible' alternative worlds of others. The evidence that Lévi-Strauss, himself, tended to shy away from this possibility is his throw-away line in *The Savage Mind* on religion, where he remarks (1966: 95) that 'the poverty of religious thought can never be overestimated'! 'Rational man' becomes enshrined to the neglect of 'man as believer' or man as 'one who knows'.

Ironically, then, as structuralists, we can also underestimate the sophistication of our informants in the construction of their worlds: we obscure its content, form, and richness by reducing their own – literal – descriptions to a cognitive process with which we ourselves can cope, that of analogic thought made manifest through metaphor. Culler notes (1981: 189–202) that the recent emphasis on the cognitive respectability of metaphor in its linkage with *la langue* and rationality has privileged metaphor as a sort of metaphor of figurality, as a king of tropes. I argue that it is time for us to withdraw the metaphoric safety net which lies beneath us. Instead, we should view literal statements about the world as such, no matter how strange their content, rather than treat them as merely another example of the differentiating structure of the mind at work – or merely 'as a code which makes it possible to pass from one system to the next' (Lévi-Strauss 1963: 96): from the natural to the social, or the social to the astrological for example. The line between the metaphoric and the literal utterance is at any rate a fine one (see Searle 1979; Black 1979: 41), a possibility that most anthropologists have chosen to ignore.

I also wish to argue that the implication of withdrawing such a net does not involve the issue of one or another type of cognitive process:[6] to withdraw it is rather a matter of accepting the reality of alien truths for the alien. As I have already suggested, we often label statements as metaphorical because to us they are obscure, ambiguous, or not logical, as well as outrageous (compare Sperber (1975) on the topic of 'symbol'): we do not wish to call the 'other' irrational; we wish to emphasize the unity of the human mind. However, the problem lies not with the logicality of the alien (or, dare I say it, his rationality), but with our own misunderstanding of, or lack of attention to, ordinary language usage and the pragmatics of ordinary speech acts which are common to both us and the 'other'. There still remains too much within our own analyses of the hidden force of both philosophical realism and logical positivism that conditions our own ideas about the proper relation of language to the world. As I shall suggest below, we are expecting from the 'tribal' a use of language that even our scientists do not always use and about which they disagree (see Feyerabend (1975: Chapter 17) for the liveliest discussion of this debate). In construing strange utterances e.g., 'the primordial penis of the father of the animals will impregnate my wife if I do not chant tonight', we should be looking at language use and its relation, not to the world as we believe it to be, but to the knowledgeable alien's understanding of the world. Whether a statement is metaphoric or not – at least for the purposes of this paper if one should wish to argue that all utterances are metaphoric – is a matter of the acceptance or non-acceptance by another of the truth of a 'peculiar' set of statements about the world or a universe of worlds. On the whole, it is our own metaphysical prejudices which prevent us from learning enough about the worlds of others to disclose the sensibility of their understanding of such worlds.

In the next sections I shall illustrate the dangers of the metaphoric safety net when used for security in analyses of the domain of kinship. The holes in the net are much too large to provide the safety sought. I hope to show that the kinship terms of others may well be a good deal more alien than we imagined them to be. Piaroa kinship terms, as highly abstract categories, are comprised of complex relational properties which link them to various aspects of what to us is a very strange ontology.[7] This strange ontology and the kinship terms are part and parcel of the same system.

As a bow to the recently edited volume by Hollis and Lukes, *Rationality and Relativism*, I would like to point out that the ethnographic example with which I am dealing has relevance to various issues that were focused upon by its authors. For example, the questions raised by Hacking's discussion (1982: 49–51, 58–61) of the incommensurability of 'styles of reasoning' and by Barnes's and Bloor's (1982: 39) of 'arrays and judgements' and the argument by all three authors with Hollis and Lukes and their notion (Hollis 1982; Hollis and Lukes 1982) of a 'bridgehead' (a terrible term for the anthropologists, given its military derivation)[8] are to a large extent answerable only through ethnographic evidence. The philosophers can judge for themselves the philosophical implications of any particular description. As an ethnographer, I personally tend to find the relativists of the volume more convincing than the hard-line anti-relativists as I recently argued in a paper[9] where I expressed my own suspicions of any attempt in anthropology to develop an 'objective' unified language of observation: our problem in anthropology is not the attainment of proper definitions nor even that of translation; rather it is that of learning, attaining the knowledge and understanding of, a framework of thought and action based upon an entirely different set of universal principles (see Feyerabend 1975: 269–85)[10] than any previously known by us. The next stage of investigation, I argued, is the creative use of our own language to express such a system and thereby to communicate incommensurability. Having said this, I must admit that Hollis's assumption of a 'bridgehead' filled with universals (e.g. material object perception beliefs and the law of contradiction) that allows us to enter the cultures of others is a luring one. I simply do not know which universals to place in the box, and I think that probably such linkages between 'us' and 'them' vary in a surprising way from culture to culture: thus, its content cannot be assumed *a priori*. (Also see Newton-Smith, a hard-line anti-relativist, who seems to agree (1982: 115) with me on this point, if probably for different reasons than my own.)

Chaos and disorder in kinship classification

To illustrate my points ethnographically, I shall use a selection of chaotic data that I collected during fieldwork with the Piaroa, Amerindians of the Venezuelan rain forest. The domain within which this chaotic data falls, as mentioned above, is that of kinship, the very area about which I am supposed to be relatively well informed and the area about which anthropologists feel most competent and sophisticated in their ability to handle technicalities in an orderly manner. However, the kinship relationships with which I am now dealing are not those of 'normal' social life, but rather those among beings in Piaroa mythic history. To a large extent this is specialist knowledge, the intricacies of which form part of the wizard's knowledge. I have been interested to discover if there is an order, a 'proper' set of principles or a logic, underlying the manner in which wizards posit kin and affine relationships among the gods, the animals, the fish, the birds, and the plants of Piaroa mythic time. Although the positing of such relationships appears chaotic, the terms that the wizards use are identical to those of everyday Piaroa life: the terminology is Dravidian in type, where the distinction of kin and affine relationships is made in the three medial generations (see Overing Kaplan 1972, 1973, 1975).

At first glance an endeavour to seek such order is a quixotic venture. As everyone knows, a mythic world is a chaotic universe, filled with beings busily transforming themselves into one creature or another: indeterminacy in the ordering of mythic relationships is perhaps the hallmark of an Amerindian mythic past as a social system, where sisters become wives, fathers become brothers, lovers become sons, fathers become fathers-in-law, husbands become fathers, and so on.

Indeterminacy, however, also marks the ordering of social relationships within the Piaroa this-worldly land. And this is sufficiently so that I began to question the depth of my understanding of how the Piaroa thought about their use of kinship terms in the ordering of their social relationships. There, too, outside the range of first cousin collaterality, those at one time classified as father may become re-classified as brother, those as sister become re-classified as wife, or as son-in-law become son: one's classificatory decisions are not viewed as absolute. Genealogical relationships, even when known, are frequently ignored in the classification process (Overing Kaplan 1975). In short, the Piaroa application of kinship terms is highly unpredictable. Each person may choose, make one's own decision about, the quality of relationship one wishes to have with others; for one's kinship to others is not absolutely 'given' to one by parents. One can ignore one's father's reckoning, or mother's, and reckon relationships through a spouse if one so desires. One may suspend judgement about another altogether for a period, leaving the other in a classificatory vacuum until finally a decision is made –

about the possibility of future marriages or power alliances, or simply about the character of the other.

I originally analysed the Piaroa kinship terminology purely in social terms, as categories used in classifying others as kin or affine. My emphasis then was upon the Piaroa use of their terminology: their use, I decided, would lead me to its meaning (Overing Kaplan 1975). I still believe this to be proper procedure, but I was using only partial data in my analysis. When listening to the way in which the Piaroa made decisions about their application of terms, I saw that such decisions were filled with talk of their fear of anacondas and jaguars, as well as talk of love, friendship, marriage, and political alliance. To classify another as 'in-law' in Piaroa society can be very dangerous: 'in-laws' can use sorcery against you, transform themselves into anaconda, jaguar, or a thunderbolt to attack you. In contrast, those classified as 'kin' do none of these things: they protect you, work with you, and live with you if possible.

From even a cursory reading of Piaroa cosmology as it relates to social structure, I saw expressed overtly an ontological principle that associates society with difference and danger, and non-social existence with identity and safety (Overing Kaplan 1981, 1984). The general attitude of the Piaroa towards the universe is that contact, interaction, and the mixing of things that are dissimilar, *although necessary* for survival and to social life, lead to danger, that is, the association of affines, humans with animals, women with men, is dangerous but necessary for social existence. Thus, we can understand their ideal marriage being the endogamous one, the marriage with someone as like you as prescriptive rule allows. Heaven, for the Piaroa, is a place with no affines: in asocial safety one dwells after life in one's place of creation with those like you 'in kind' (*tu itso'tu*, 'a plurality of beings similar to self').[11] Social life, the interaction of dissimilar beings, also entails death. All immortal beings in the Piaroa cosmos live alone, have a solitary existence.

To understand better the Piaroa notions of similarity and difference, I decided to look at the relation between Piaroa everyday use of their terminology and their understanding of the world of anacondas and jaguars as expressed through their cosmogony and through the exegesis of wizards. I thought that the attempt to analyse the bizarre kinship relationships of mythic time might lead to principles at work in ordinary social life that I had missed precisely because I was treating it as 'ordinary'. This was obviously the case. Kinship relationships when contextualized within mythic history places them within the more theoretical world of explanation, where fundamental questions about existence in this world, whether for humans or animals, gods or demons, are explored. Very briefly for now, kinship and affinity as social states, when placed within the context of cosmogony, become subsumed under broader metaphysical principles, such as the nature of similarity and difference, and take on ontological dimensions that go far beyond the distinction of kin and affine as we might understand such a distinction within a

'normal' social context. The fact that we can classify the relationship terminology as Dravidian is of much less significance than the metaphysical loading
the terms receive when informed by cosmogonic principles. The ontological
principles affecting the use and meaning of Piaroa kinship terms that will be
discussed below are (1) the nature of being of a kind and being different, (2) a
multiple world cosmology where neither time nor space absolutely separates
the worlds, and (3) as a corollary of the second principle, the social world is
not a privileged one: there is no bedrock of social identity or reality over and
against which the individual can be opposed.

Metaphoric extension, semantic analysis and the fantastic

When I describe below the kinship relationships of mythic time, I am not
speaking of a metaphoric use of kinship terms. The Piaroa state them to be
true, factual, and not metaphorical. The Piaroa often use metaphor, and their
own term for a metaphoric statement is *dak'a*. As they explain the term, it is
calling something what it is not; it is an analogy: it postulates relationships
between domains which are not true. Creativity in language use is highly
valued among the Piaroa in everyday talk, where skill in inventing aes-
thetically pleasing *dak'atu* (metaphors) is always a source of amusement in
verbal play. Through shrewd use of affixes a man can become a mountain, a
tree, an animal, a lake, or ambiguously any of these things.

The linguistic process that provides creative richness to everyday talk is
identical to that used by wizards in their nightly chanting, but the construal of
everyday language play and language 'play' of the wizard is absolutely
opposed.[12] Everyday play is false, while a wizard who states the kinship
relations among mythic beings, that monkeys are affines to fish, or states that
the father of a child is a wild pig, is making literal statements. The father of the
child is not metaphorically, but literally, the primordial father of the wild pig
who crossed worlds, came from his home beneath the earth, to commit a
carnal act. In short, the Piaroa definition of metaphor, which for them
depends upon the falsity of the statement, is identical to our normal judgement of whether or not a statement is figurative or literal.[13] When a Piaroa
assents to the truth of the statement that 'the tapir is their grandfather', a
statement that to us sounds bizarre, we are nevertheless dealing with a literal
statement about truths in the world as he knows them.

On the topic of understanding metaphors, Searle stresses (1979: 96, 103,
113, 120) the importance of background factual information to their comprehension. Before we can distinguish a metaphoric from a literal statement
we must share with the speaker the relevant understanding and knowledge
about the world. We must know all the predicates of being F and of *not* being
F (also see Kuhn on this topic, 1979: 412) – according to the speaker. Thus,
the decoding of an utterance as literal or figurative must be at the level of the

speaker's intentionality, and not at the level of the sentence itself (also see Lyons 1981: 108).[14] To interpret intentionality, the hearer must share with the speaker a similar set of principles and knowledge about the world. With metaphor there is an intentional incompatibility between the utterance and truths about the world,[15] however such truths may be understood by the speaker. With a literal statement there is no such incompatibility. In the case of mythic statements, the knowledge is specialist knowledge that is only partially shared among members of a community. However, as Boyd notes (1979: 31; also see Putnam 1977b: 120, 132), deference to the knowledgeable expert (as a Piaroa would defer to the wizard) is a general principle of rationality,[16] and most linguistic competence is not at any rate acquired by the use of language but rather by social and intellectual skills.

I am leading up to two related points which should be obvious. First, to understand Piaroa kinship terminology one must learn enough about both the knowledge they share and expert knowledge and understanding of the universe before one can understand the predicates of being labelled 'mother', 'father-in-law' and 'father' in Piaroa language usage. To do otherwise would lead the anthropologist to construe their ontological statements as meta-phorical ones; while what in fact is the case is that their ontology is metaphor for us. Second, formal semantic analysis of kinship domains is in its method and its assumptions about the world an impediment to the outsider's com-prehension of Piaroa use of their kinship terms: its methods and assumptions preclude the possibility of learning the metaphysics of others.[17]

As Lyons observes (1981: 66), the empiricist tradition has been immensely important to the development of modern formal semantic analysis where priority has always been given to the phenomenal attributes of entities in the discussion of denotation (e.g. F, FB, that is, those related to ego in a particular, consanguineally defined way). Scheffler, the strongest advocate of the method in kinship studies, treats kinship terms as a set of lexemes which denote *natural kinds*, as is made evident in his insistence (1978: 4, 5, 13, 525–27) that kin terms can only refer in literal use *to genealogical (con-sanguineal) relationships established through human reproductive processes*. The traditional theory of natural kinds (see Lyons 1981: 69–72; Putnam 1977a: 110–11, 1977b: 120) assumes that the external world is made up of entities whose existence is independent of mind and language; natural kind classes share the same essences. It was also assumed that to know the meaning of any expression that denotes a natural kind is to know its intention, or its defining property, the necessary and sufficient conditions that must be satisfied for any entity or stuff to fall within the extension of the lexeme (e.g. father) in question. The quest in kinship analysis for the 'primary meaning', the 'logical priority' of one particular meaning is predicated upon the under-standing that the components of the natural kind in question are *universal* across languages (see Lyons 1981: 82; Scheffler 1978: XI).[18] However, as Goodman remarks (1978: 12), nothing is primitive or derivational prior to anything apart from the constructional system at hand; natural kinds are *relevant* kinds, those important for a particular analysis and a particular theory (Goodman 1978: 101; also see Putnam 1977a: 101). The assumption by Scheffler that he is dealing with natural kind terms led him to the position of excluding all social and cultural data from his analysis (see Scheffler 1978: 30–33, 85): to get at 'structurally prior' meaning (1978: 26, 30–31), the terms must be treated as a set of words closed to any cultural or social consideration. By his own method and the assumptions upon which they are premissed, Scheffler must define 'structurally prior' in consanguineal terms.

Another problem with natural kind theory is that one society's 'natural kinds' are 'cultural kinds' for the next and for the observer of that society.[19] Natural kinds in the traditional (scientific) sense are in fact combined and divided by languages arbitrarily for culturally explicable reasons, not 'natural' ones (Lyons 1981: 72). The point is that to use *our* understanding of natural kinds (or, rather, the 'cultural kinds' of the anthropologist) as the basis for understanding the meaning of another society's classifications is to impose our own metaphysical prejudices upon our analyses of them. For instance in *Australian Kin Classification* (1978: 524) Scheffler labels all kin-class statuses that the aborigines establish among dreamtime beings, and between themselves and these beings, as metaphoric extensions, as not true kinship relationships. Scheffler's reasoning (1978: 524–25) is that dreamtime beings cannot be related to the aborigines through human reproductive processes; they therefore cannot be related through kinship ties – as *he* defines them.

The Piaroa, on the other hand, *say explicitly* that mythic kinship relationships are true kinship relationships (their classifications of them are true), as too are their own relationships with mythic beings. That gods and animals are in kinship relationship to one another disturbs our own classification of animate beings into species, and it is perhaps also a problem for our category of 'humankind'. From our point of view, we can either say that the Piaroa are naïve or that kinship for the Piaroa is not 'primarily' about human reproductive processes, or even about the relation of social roles to such processes. That the latter is the more fruitful course to follow is what I shall illustrate below.

The problem of formal semantic analysis and its assumption of natural kinds can be shifted to another level: it is assumed by our own metaphysics that mythic beings and dreamtime beings are not in the class of natural kinds. Therefore, by definition relationships with them should be excluded from a formal analysis of 'kinship' terms. Our own metaphysics is that mythical beings and dreamtime beings belong to the realm of the 'fantastic'.[20] However, the 'fantastic' can only be understood by someone who sets what is 'real' (capable of explanation through natural law) against that which is imaginary or supernatural. It can only exist in a society which articulates its own experience in terms of that simple dichotomy: the fantastic as a genre is a product of the nineteenth century (Todorov 1970), and the dichotomy of the real as against the fantastic does not have a place in Piaroa pre-suppositions about the world. In Piaroa theory, mythic time and space and now-a-day time and space are not mutually exclusive: they partake of one another and 'everyday' life is no less 'fantastic' than life in mythic time.[21] Thus, the Piaroa do not decode myths in the same mode as we do.[22] Also, as a footnote, most mythic beings in at least one of their transformations are human in form; but their kinship relationships do not hinge on this fact.

As one last comment for this section, I am not saying that it would be impossible to do a formal semantic analysis of Piaroa kinship terms. A complicated and contrived componential analysis or a set of transformational rules might indeed be possible on a *post hoc* basis, where any particular labelling is understandable in the context of a particular argument. However, those that interpret such classificatory possibilities, whether wizard or lay-man, are not guided by any compelling clear and simple underlying classi-ficatory or definitional logical priorities. They do *play* with possibilities.[23] Thus, our *post hoc* 'model' of classificatory logic would be precariously 'based' upon the layman's and the wizard's genius, creativity, and capacity for interpretation. 'Ours' and 'their' views would be conflated. What is more, from any way of looking at such constructions, the Piaroa multiple world cosmology would play havoc on their predictive value.

Mythic kinship relationships among the gods, animals, fish, and plants[24]

In Piaroa cosmogony, before the creation of this-worldly space, the world beneath the earth was populated by Sun gods, Thunder gods, the 'parents' of animals and fish, and the chimerical Tapir/Anaconda gods. Members of each such category of being dwelt in their own homes deep within the earth, where also were housed the powers that they owned. As these subterranean powers became slowly unleashed on earth it was their force that was responsible for the creation of all elements and beings of the surface level and for the knowledge and the capabilities that allowed for existence there. Most of the powers responsible for the form and the life of the earth's surface came from the subterranean home of Ofo Daa, one of the chimerical tapir/anacondas. It was through the means of two great gods, Kuemoi and Wahari, whose births were his deed and whose powers he gave them that most of the elements of the world of the Piaroa were created. As a fractionalization on earth of the powers of the supreme tapir/anaconda deity, the powers of the two great creator gods were distinct and opposed in their nature and their result.[25] Kuemoi, born in water and master of that domain, created all cultural artifacts, all plant food, and the means to use the earth's resources (the knowledge and capabilities for acquiring and processing food). Wahari, who was born beneath the earth and who became master of the jungle, created all the natural elements of the world, its topography. He also created the Piaroa and all branch animals and birds of the jungle.

Mythic time was one of violent disorder, a world of reciprocal violence, where the two creator gods fought continual battles with one another for the control of resources and powers over which each was respectively master: Kuemoi stalked beings of the jungle for food; Wahari stole cultural artifacts from Kuemoi. In the meantime, as creations and battles over their control took their course, kinship relationships among the participants of mythic time were established. For example, the two creator gods became affines of one another: Wahari married Maize, the daughter of Kuemoi.

The continuous world of mythic space, where all beings on the earth's surface daily interacted as kin or affine to one another, was converted at the end of mythic time into a world of discontinuity or, rather, a universe comprised of multiple worlds. The forces of power that allowed for the knowledge and the capabilities for using the earth's resources – culture – proved to be too dangerous to exist free for the taking within the social world on the surface of the earth. They were thus taken out of this world to be housed in celestial space to be contained there in crystal boxes within the abodes of present-day gods. They also still exist beneath the earth where they remain in their primordial untamed wildness. The process that dispersed the destructive forces of creation on earth was one that led to the compart-mentalization into distinct abodes, separated by layers of space and skies, of each category of being who in earlier days dwelt on one spatial plane.[26] Speciation also took place and beings who once could mate no longer can (usually) do so. When 'animals' received their animal form they left their jungle home and returned to their homes of creation beneath the earth to populate the jungle through the sorcery of the Piaroa wizard. While Kuemoi and Wahari remained on earth reincarnated respectively as anaconda and tapir, many of Wahari's relatives left their terrestrial homes to dwell as gods in celestial space.

An analysis of the classification by wizards of kinship relationships among mythic beings revealed that (1) wizards used the terms polysemically: each term has multiple meanings or a cluster of predicates; (2) the application by a wizard of a term in any given instance was determined by the predicates or cluster of qualities they wished to stress or ignore in the labelling of the relationship between particular beings within a specific set of mythic events; and (3) the wizards used the labels both as egocentric and as class terms. Any particular classification can be seen as sensible only when placed within the context of the above three factors. The classification of one mythic being to another in kinship terms is determined by the unpredictable combinations of the following predicates.

1. EVENT

All relationships have a past and a future. (See *Figure 8.1.*) Beings began their residence on the surface of the earth in certain relationships with one another,

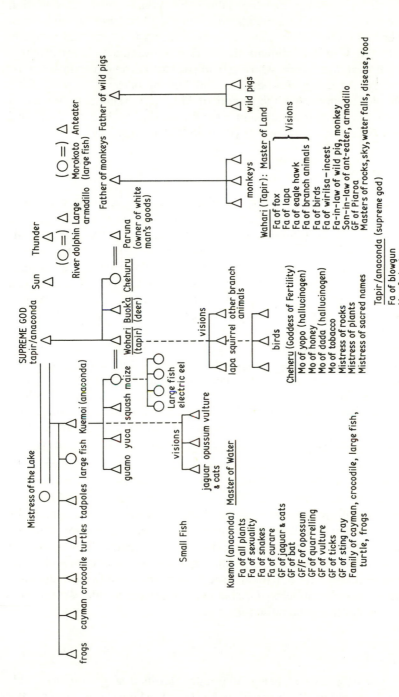

Figure 8.1 Kinship relationships among mythic beings

and as social relationships developed through marriages, births, competition, and so on, kinship ties accommodated to events. Most large fish began their life on earth as wives of large land animals. Later, when large fish competed over resources with large animals, the relationship was one between brothers-in-law. The fish, Morokoto, who began life on earth as daughter-in-law to the older being, Anteater, married him and thereby became his wife. River dolphin, depending upon the period of history, is related to Wahari as son-in-law (as competitor), daughter (as the child of Wahari's wife through his father-in-law's sorcery) or wife (through Wahari's sorcery).

2. RELATIVE AGE

See *Figure 8.2*. In the evolution of beings on earth, the oldest came from beneath the earth, from within earth or water homes. The first to emerge were the armadillos, the large anteaters, and the tadpole, and all are 'grandparents' of most other beings. Kuemoi and large fish were the next to emerge, and are often labelled as of the same generation as the oldest beings: as brother, brother-in-law, or as wife, actual or classificatory to them. The next generation to emerge was comprised of Wahari, his siblings, and his brothers-in-law. Wahari was then responsible for the creation of the Piaroa, the branch animals and, youngest of all, the birds of the jungle.

Although at least five to six generations can be distinguished in the evolutionary scheme, the terminology used covers no more distance than that between grandparent and grandchild. Anteater is grandfather of both monkeys and the creator god, Wahari, who 'created' monkeys. It should be noted that relative age can override the principle of consanguineal relationship, e.g., Opossum, the result of an incestuous relationship between Kuemoi and his daughter, is classified as Kuemoi's grandchild, and not as his son.

3. GENDER

Gender is not always a stable criterion. Tapir/Anaconda, the supreme deity, is mother of plants; his force led to their creation through his son, Kuemoi, who is classified as father of plants. Fish are in a particularly ambiguous gender state, as discussed above. Their gender can be determined by the predicate of relative age or habitat association, or by event (a marriage) or by a quality of power relationship (see below). Large toad, a male, is classified as grandmother of frogs and poisonous snakes.

4. SIZE

The largest of a class of beings is usually classified as grandfather, elder brother, or parent of all others within the class. The largest species of monkey

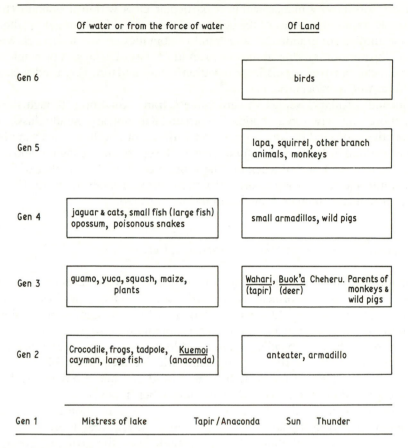

Figure 8.2   Evolution of mythic beings

is grandfather of all other species, who are in turn in the relationship, depending on size, of elder/younger brother to one another.

5. HABITAT ASSOCIATION (living together)

The association with the domain of land or the domain of water is critical to determining whether the relationship is 'kin' or 'affine' and, as such, creatures essentially of a kind or different from one another, as were Kuemoi and Wahari, the one born in water and the other beneath the earth. Monkeys are 'kin' to most land animals, but in an affinal relationship to fish. The large fish are wives or brothers-in-law of large land animals. One wife of Wahari who is master of land is the large fish, Morokoto, while another wife is Maize, the daughter of Kuemoi, the master of water.

First corollary. Animals within a particular class within a domain (for example, types of monkey of the domain of land) are elder/younger brothers of one another, or grandfather and grandson; but they are treated as a class as 'son', 'brother-in-law', or 'grandson' to another class of beings. A principle of synecdoche can override distinctions within a class, and terms are used as class terms as well as egocentric ones.

Second corollary. Beings who are 'forces', transformations, 'thoughts', or 'creations' of the two creator gods, Wahari and Kuemoi, are usually classified respectively of land or water and thereby affines of another. For example, birds, created by Wahari, are affines of fish. The opossum, the jaguar, and the vulture are 'creations' of Kuemoi. These three creatures are neither of land nor water. However being associated with the force of water, they are classed as affines of land animals, if any relationship is posited.

6. SPECIFIC CONSANGUINEAL OR MARITAL RELATIONSHIP

Specific 'consanguineal' or marriage relationships can override a classification based upon class, the principle of synecdoche, or domain – and vice versa. The eldest armadillo is husband to the two fish, Morokoto and River Dolphin, who both in turn address the two younger armadillos as 'sons'. They thereby conform to their husband's terms of address, instead of classifying the younger armadillos as affines in accordance with a principle of habitat association. Wahari lived in the same habitat as wild pigs and monkeys, and he created the latter; but he is classified as their father-in-law.

It should be noted that the category 'consanguineal relationship' must be taken in the broadest possible sense: in mythic time, sexual intercourse was only one of several methods of reproduction, or of the giving of life and creating. We must similarly treat the notion of 'giving life to' with caution. The Piaroa have an elaborate and rich vocabulary for speaking of selfhood, its powers, and its life, and the receiving of such powers (see Overing 1985). They consider the receiving of life as a *process* that continues throughout one's life. In the first instance, they distinguish between the 'life of the senses' (*kàkwà*) and the 'life of thought' (*ta'kwarü*), both of which are separate from one's form. Processual aspects of acquiring life, unfortunately, are not always considered in analyses of kinship.

Other than through sexual intercourse, other means through which life was conferred in mythic time were as follows, not all of which are mutually exclusive:

(i) To create through visions or through one's thoughts. There is a rich language through which such creations are expressed: to divine (*bok'okwinü*), to think of (*amukwadinü*), to create through hallucinogenic vision (*k'adü*), to create through imagination or sorcery (*máriyá*). Any such creation can be referred to as the creator's 'thoughts', his *a'kwa*.

(ii) To create through the dough of drugs within one's stomach.

(iii) To create oneself or to give oneself one's form.

(iv) To create through the force of the deity, the tapir/anaconda.

(v) To create through the food the created one will eat.

(vi) To give form to from plants.

(vii) To give knowledge to.

(viii) To create through the withdrawal of the spirit of the eye.

(ix) To create by transforming into.[27]

Any of the above types of creation, including that through sexual intercourse, *may or may not confer the label of parenthood.*

7. PREDICATES OF ACTION (e.g. betraying, aiding, competing, stealing from): or Morality and the Quality of Relationship

Each relationship is associated with a cluster of predicates of action. I shall concentrate, as example, on the connexion of codes of power with the creator/created class of relationships. There is variation in the way in which the Piaroa classify the relationship between the creator and the created, between Wahari and Kuemoi and those that they created. Three different kinship relationships are posited: father/child, father-in-law/son-in-law, and grandfather/grandchild. In these cases, the criteria of domain, age, and even creation can be overriden by another component, that of the specific quality of a power relationship as manifested in a dramatic event or condition, and as such entailing goodwill, hostility, or a specific type of control over alter's powers. These classifications also entail assessments of identity and difference, as also do classifications based upon the predicate of habitat association.

Wahari, the master of the jungle, is either father, father-in-law, or grand-father to his creations, and these distinctions are highly significant to an understanding of the quality of his relationship to these creations. Wahari created through sorcery most branch animals and most birds. Each such species for which he was responsible is categorized by the Piaroa as 'Wahari' *henü*, a 'thing of Wahari', and as such, their father. He created certain of these species through a vision: these are 'Wahari *a'kwa*', his 'thoughts'. (In everyday life, a Piaroa will refer to his child as *cha'kwa* – 'my thought'.) Once these animals were created, he transformed himself into their image to accomplish spectacular acts of wizardry. The hummingbird, the eagle hawk, the lapa, the most important symbols of Wahari's power, are his trans-formations, his thoughts, and as such his sons. His relationship to these creations is a benevolent one, and in so far as they are so frequently the image with which he clothes himself, they clearly share with him a common identity: Wahari is 'of a kind' with those creations he classifies as 'son'. Most birds are classified by the Piaroa as 'jungle animals', and thus they are of the same habitat domain as Wahari.

There exists another set of jungle animals whose relationship to Wahari is that of children-in-law, and he is their father-in-law. Included in this category are all species of peccaries, monkeys, tamandu, and younger anteaters. This is a puzzle, for they are of the same habitat as Wahari, and, indeed, he was the 'master of their house'. He also 'created' them; but the role he played in their creation is totally different from that of the animals he classifies as children. He created his children from scratch: he thought them into existence, and then gave them form by using various plants of the jungle. Monkey, peccary, the armadillos, and the anteaters already existed when Wahari was born: they came to earth from their homes beneath the earth without the help of Wahari. Although they have a common identity with Wahari through domain and house, Wahari's relationship to them was ultimately a malevolent one, of the nature expected of one essentially different in kind, a competitor and an in-law. At the end of mythic time he transformed them into animals, gave them their animal form, and at the same time stole ritual from them. He presented their sacred musical instruments and their songs to his sister, Cheheru, who now in turn gives them to the Piaroa. Thus, the relationship between Wahari and these land animals from whom he stole culture is equivalent to that between Wahari and Kuemoi, who spent most of mythic time stealing from each other's domain. The acts of stealing and transforming humans into animals, and taking away their 'life of thought' (ritual), take priority over domain association in the classification of the relationship of Wahari to peccary and monkey.

Kuemoi, master of water, also achieved a considerable number of creations during mythic time. He, in contrast to Wahari, is often classified as grandfather to the beings he brought into existence, both those to whom he is actual father, such as opossum and electric eel, and those whom he created through vision and fashioning by hand, jaguar and all other cats, ticks, and biting insects, the sting ray, and other creatures nasty to jungle animals. He, as Wahari, also transforms himself at will into his own creations, especially into jaguar and poisonous snakes. The question is, why is he grandfather and not father to these creations?

As one of the older creatures of the universe, he may be classified as grandfather by merely positing the age criterion. However, there are other possibilities. Grandfather is frequently used in Piaroa classification to express a relationship of guardianship, and more specifically the guardianship and control over another's malevolent force or powers. For instance, each disease has its own grandfather: the tapir/anaconda supreme god is grandfather to gonorrhoea; white-lipped peccary is the grandfather of childbirth disease; the nightjar is grandfather of 'go round, fall down' or dizziness disease; Kuemoi is grandfather of boils. In each case, the grandfather controls the disease of the animals who give disease in retaliation for the ritual stolen from them, and orders them to send it (Overing 1982). All Kuemoi's creations have powers that are highly dangerous to 'beings of the jungle', and, as such, are lumped together as 'Kuemoi's thoughts'. It is, in general, believed that he controls them today and is still responsible for the evils and dangers of his creations.

The reason for the Piaroa claiming that tapir is their grandfather can now be explicated. The tapir is the reincarnation of Wahari, a transformation which occurred at the end of mythic time. He created the Piaroa, but is labelled as their grandfather because he gave them the ritual and the thoughts that he had stolen from the animals. The Piaroa benefit further from Wahari's malevolent act because they can now eat the animals in the form into which Wahari transformed them. The Piaroa, themselves, view this eating as a malevolent act on their own part (see Overing 1985), and take the edge off their malevolence by transforming before the meal all animal flesh into vegetable. The Piaroa claim they are in no kinship relationship to edible animals because, as they say, they eat them. As fellow beings of the jungle, they should be in a kin relationship (as beings of a kind) with them; while plants, as children of Kuemoi, should be affines to them. Affines might eat one another; kin never do. In transforming animal flesh to vegetable they are reclassifying animal food into a category which would be 'possible' to be eaten. The ambiguity nevertheless remains for, even worse, the animals live in primordial human form beneath the earth. The Piaroa therefore posit no kinship relationship with edible animals, preferring to leave them in a state of classificatory suspension of nullity.

8. WORLD INHABITED. A multiple world cosmology and the creativity of the wizard

This item should in fact be a sub-section of the first listed predication, that of 'event'. However, it is more comprehensible listed last and separately.

Sequencing has little ontological value for the Piaroa. They recognize the existence of a number of real worlds separated from one another in both time and space, but which are today in constant interaction: elements from one world, from the present or the past, are continually entering, becoming a part of, and leaving another (Overing 1982). The 'Grandfathers of Disease', who I have discussed above, are personages who in their past state of being during a period of mythic history enter the Piaroa world of nowaday time to order the animals to send the Piaroa disease. Most worlds, social or otherwise, for the Piaroa are highly indeterminate. Thus, to speak of an 'aspect' of the world or of one of its domains as if it has a set existence would be erroneous. Identity, what something or someone is, depends not upon sequential links, as is the case for us, but upon identity with respect to what that something is within that world as it is organized at a particular point in time.[28] The separation of time and space has no significance to this ordering. What someone is at *any* one point in time becomes a product of the possibilities of his relationships in the past, the present, and the future.[29] A person is always intermeshed in many worlds, and the composition of self is thereby in a constant state of flux. Even cultural capabilities come from outside the terrestrial social world of the Piaroa; they come to the person at his will and with the aid of the wizard from the celestial abode of the gods (Overing 1982, 1985). The metaphysical and the everyday are intertwined: forces of power enter Piaroa land from several worlds, and it is these forces that give life, death, and disease to the present-day world of the Piaroa (Overing 1982).

The chore of the wizard is to control these forces so that life is advanced and disease and death are kept at bay. Much of the world as a social world is the wizard's own creation, one in constant transformation as he daily brings elements in from other worlds, as he chases forces out of the social world, as he brings past worlds into the present, and unites present worlds with the past. The comprehension of other worlds and the creation of new ones go on together.[30] The ability of the wizard to conjoin worlds, delete elements, transport forces of the past into the present, and vice versa, poses neither an ontological nor epistemological problem (nor a logical one) for the Piaroa. Through his powers of sorcery, the wizard is able to visit all worlds, including all periods of the mythic past; he *sees* them and walks there and knows their reality.[31] He can see that which has been and that which is, and also that which has been *as* that which is. Elements from all worlds, past and present, have equal, unsequenced, ontological status for the wizard.[32] The Piaroa are not ahistorical; but, for them, to know identity one must know a context, and not a history.

The ontological principle that takes little note of chronological ordering applies to the wizard's classifications of mythic beings in his telling of mythic events. When sequencing is ignored, genealogies by definition are chaotic. The wizard in telling of an early event in mythic time may dress some of the actors in the story with an identity that they assumed late in mythic history. The Waikwoni are a case in point. The Waikwoni in mythic time were lovers of Cheheru, the sister of the creator god, Wahari. In the transformations at the end of mythic time, when Cheheru was transformed into the ethereal Goddess of fertility, the Waikwoni became her children. The wizard, in focusing upon certain elements, and not others, of the relationship between Wahari and either Cheheru or the Waikwoni in early mythic history may well depict the Waikwoni as 'sons-in-law' (ZCh) of Wahari, and not as 'brother-in-law (ZH).

The wizard, in focusing upon particular *moral qualities* of relationship in his classifications, makes creative play with the possibilities open to him from the past, the present, and the future of the relationship in question.[33] He also plays with the strands of relationships that tie any one individual to a number of significant others, which further jumbles the principle of sequencing. How Wahari is related to the fish, Morokoto, varies depending upon whether he relates to him/her through Anteater or through his own wife. This is the same process that goes on in everyday use of kinship terms. Thus, the principle of creative play must be incorporated as a sort of 'free-floating' predication, a highly unpredictable element in the application of terms, whether by the wizard or in ordinary everyday use. It is a principle that plays havoc with any notion of 'logically prior' meaning.

In summary, it is impossible to establish the specifications of necessary and sufficient conditions for the use of any kinship terms as it is applied in the classification of relationships of mythic time: the criteria of membership within the class 'father', for instance, cannot be fixed by definitional convention, for example in accordance with any one of the specific predicates listed above. Nor can the criteria of membership within specific classes, with the exception of ego's marital partner and his/her relations to first cousin collaterality, be fixed by definitional convention for *this-worldly social* relationships. We can, however, *understand the predication* of fatherhood, if we grant the flexibility in the use of labels as just discussed.

The predication of 'father' as used in the mythic past is as follows: (1) is of the same habitat domain, (2) lives with one (in Piaroa theory, the process of living together leads over time to the sharing of the same physical essences), (3) eats the same food, (4) shares resources, (5) is a benevolent user of power *vis-à-vis* ego, (6) uses the same power forces as ego, (7) gives one life force, (8) is male, (9) is of the first ascending generation – in one world, or the other. The predication of father-in-law in mythic time is the obverse excepting predicates eight and nine. The Piaroa are clearly using concepts of kinship and affinity to distinguish relationships of similarity and difference, and vice versa. To be classified as kin or affine, 'of a kind' or 'different' implies not merely being of the same or different domain, of the same or different physical essence, but also the sharing or not sharing of sets or bundles of social and moral qualities. With many relationships the sets of social qualities overlap (sometimes due to different world or time contexts), or the physical associations are in conflict with their social and moral correlates. The relationship then is an ambiguous one, and a choice of *salient* predication must be made. We have seen in Wahari's relationship with jungle beings that 'to give life force to' and habitat association can be less salient predicates of 'father' than the quality of power relationship that holds between ego and alter: treachery overrides all other predication.

Finally, it is clear that through our understanding of the predication of kinship terms in the mythic past and the cosmogony and associated ontology within which it is set, we can then (and only then) understand the use of kinship terms to express the connexion between beings of different worlds, and the positing of kinship relationships between beings who in present-day time are of different species. That the Piaroa claim 'the tapir to be their grandfather' no longer sounds strange, for we have the *knowledge* to understand the utterance. To explain it, we do not need to resort to either the notion that the Piaroa feel, believe, themselves to be in a 'mystical' relationship to the tapir or to the notion that the Piaroa are speaking metaphorically. It is not the possible relationship of humans to animals that we need to explore, but rather the predication of the term *grandfather* and the multiple world cosmology of the Piaroa. The tapir is the reincarnation of Wahari, the god who created the Piaroa: he is not classified as father to them because he is in an ambiguous relationship to them according to the Piaroa understanding of the predicates of power coding. He gave them a power that in its use is malevolent vis-à-vis those 'of a kind' with them in an earlier world. Through his gift, they transform humans ('jungle beings', as the Piaroa are also classified) into animals,[34] they eat them, and use the ritual stolen from them by Wahari. Therefore, in accordance with the highly salient power code predication, tapir is properly classed as 'grandfather' to the Piaroa.

Personal kind terms

It has become increasingly the case for philosophers to state their doubt over the possibility that analytic definitions (that is, specifications of necessary and sufficient conditions) can ever be found in the case of philosophically important concepts, such as 'natural kinds' (see, for example, Wittgenstein 1953; Putnam 1977a: 110–11; Kuhn 1979; Boyd 1979: 379). Because these concepts often consist of complex relational properties, they require non-definitional reference fixing. According to Kuhn (1979: 412; see also Putnam 1977b), it is through knowledge of ostensive reference fixing (pointing out) that 'natural kind' terms (as birds, heat, electricity) in the natural sciences are comprehended. Kuhn is mainly concerned with terms that play a role in causal relationships in the universe, where comprehension demands, not definition, but a number of acts of knowledgeable ostension. His point is that laws and theories enter into the establishment of reference where 'natural kind' terms are at issue. Their complexity is such, and their referents sufficiently ambiguous, he argues, that a choice of a specific defining description would be an arbitrary one.[35]

Horton (1979) has noted that Africans within tribal culture have opted for a *personal idiom* in their abstract theoretical constructions that deal with cause and effect in the world. For the tribal, his area of sophistication is the domain of human social relations, an area which in comparison is rather poverty stricken for the Westerner, who feels more secure in his control over the non-personal 'world of nature'. It is not the 'natural' world our informants wish to control; rather, to control the personal is for them to control the world(s). In agreement with Horton's stress upon the theoretical importance of personal idiom for the 'tribal',[36] I suggest that in the realm of kinship theory we are dealing with what we can call *'personal kind' terms* that are, like concepts of 'natural kinds',[37] highly abstract, philosophically important concepts, which defy definition,[38] and which share the openendedness and inexplicitness typical of all theoretical terms that refer to 'kinds' comprised of complex relational properties and networks of similarities and differences, rather than of particular internal constitutional properties (see Boyd 1979: 358).

We should look more closely at the personal idiom through which the 'tribal' builds up his theoretical statements about the universe. What is this idiom, but what we have labelled 'kinship terms'? The Piaroa have no other classifications, except the terms 'master' and 'mistress', through which to think about and to label relationships. Despite our own elaborate techniques for analysing terminologies, we have not sufficiently recognized our inform- ants' sophistication in using relationship terms and the significance of these terminologies in indigenous theory constructions. In so-called 'kinship-based' societies the terms take on a very heavy metaphysical loading that yet must be explored by anthropologists. Our own anthropological language is much too sloppy (see my own glosses of terms in this paper!) and too sparse to account for the theoretical complexity of our informants' use of 'kinship' terms. Our questioning begins to appear to be the equivalent of using their labels of 'natural' (or 'personal') forces, and understanding of them, to describe our theories of atomic energy, or to use medieval witchcraft theory as the cos- mology through which to explain modern-day biochemistry. We reduce tribal usage and theory of personal relationships to our own very weak language of kinship, a language that speaks of 'genealogical relationships', 'social cate- gory', 'amity', and marriage alliance. We then think we have explained the use of kinship terminologies within our informants' societies. We glibly speak of 'the morality of kinship'; but if we try to define such an idea beyond the vague notion of 'amity', we see that we understand little. What does 'amity' mean? If we are dealing with highly abstract, and culturally specific theor- etical languages through which relationships between elements in the world are understood, that which is the 'morality of kinship' in one society will not be congruent with what we might call the 'morality of kinship' in the next.

My main point is that I think it is probably a mistake, and a bad one, to reduce tribal kinship terminologies to kinship and affinity, or to social cate- gories, or to consanguineal relations. They do, of course, usually refer to such things, as we understand them to be; but they may well have more important predicates, the soliciting of which takes us into an alien world of explanation and modes of understanding the relationship among items in the universe – whether between humans, animals, gods, forces of power, or inanimate objects.

Piaroa 'kinship terms', or rather, as renamed, *personal kind' terms*, are used by the wizards to explain the relationships among beings in their cos- mological history. Such 'personal kind' terms are used at the most basic as well as at the most abstract level to provide explanations of differences and similarity among beings and the implications of being the same and being different. Such understandings then play a large conceptual role in the playing out of political and social life in everyday society. Part and parcel of the Piaroa

theoretical construction of 'personal kind' concepts, and the associated knowledge of the personal that such construction demands, is a highly sophisticated
political philosophy, one that is deeply suspicious of coercive power, of power
over the labour of others and its products, of power greedy in expression (see
Overing 1984, 1985). There is no room, of course, in this paper to spin out the
relationship to everyday social and political life of their 'personal kind'
theory. However, what I can say is that when I stress the importance of
looking at indigenous ontologies and cosmologies for an explication of their
'kinship' classifications, I am not presenting an idealist, poetic line: I am
talking about the bread and butter of the anthropological endeavour, where
our concern is to understand the everyday world of politics and economics, of
social and moral relations, in societies that are very different from our own.

Literary metaphor

I shall conclude by making a suggestion which in the light of my previous
argument will appear to be rather maverick. When we are faced with very
peculiar statements that our informants insist are literal, are true according to
their truths about the universe, we perhaps should treat such statements
methodologically as we would literary metaphors in our own culture. Searle
(1979: 103, 105) and others (Rumelhart 1979; Black 1979; Sadock 1979)
believe that construing a metaphor is, after all, only a natural extension of
ordinary thought: they refuse an absolute distinction between figurative and
'proper' thought. According to Searle (1979: 96, 105; and see Kuhn 1979:
415–16), with both the literal and the figurative we are dealing with networks
of similarities (and differences) in determining the way in which language
attaches to the world[39] or is used in the world. Our problem in understanding
the literal peculiar statement is that we have insufficient knowledge of the
truths about the alien worlds with which we are dealing. Metaphor, in
general, allows us cognitively to pass from the familiar to the unfamiliar; it is a
mechanism for changing our mode of representing the world in both thought
and language (on the creative strength of metaphor, see Petrie 1979: 447;
Black 1962; 1979: 39,41; Ricoeur 1978: 236, 239; and Crocker 1977). To attain
access to what are for us non-epistemic truths, the most basic of anthropological chores, the strategy of metaphoric construal of such truths would
help to provide the creativity we need to do so. Just as Levin suggests (1979:
131) for the construal of a literary metaphor, our construal of a peculiar
utterance given to us by an informant requires us to construe the world so as to
make sense of the utterance: what gives is the world, not the word (see Levin
1979: 131, 134), the reverse of what occurs when we mistakenly treat literal
statements as metaphor. The poet is creating an 'impossible' possible world,
or a possible 'impossible world', as you will: a world where mountains sit on
an eternal stool, or a thunderbolt is your next-door neighbour.

In construing the poetic metaphor and in construing the peculiar statement of an informant, it is creativity and a suspension of disbelief that we need, not a reinterpretation of language. If we can agree with philosophers such as Searle (1979: 103, 105) and Kuhn (1979) that the recognition of similarity is a comprehension strategy, a matter of knowledge, it is shared notions of similarity that we must comprehend. Thus, while we know perfectly well that we are not dealing with metaphor, to treat the peculiar statement as literary metaphor is a good strategy, a way of directing us in the knowledge quest of understanding why our informants are saying something is the same or different, of understanding their notions of similarity, and the strategies used to make such decisions. I am merely saying that if we recognize the creative aspect of metaphoric thought, to treat a literal statement *as if* metaphor may allow us to be more creative in discovering the system of relations recognized by our informants in their claims that their utterances are true ones.

Notes

1 A draft of this paper was presented at the London Intercollegiate Seminar (1982), at the School of Oriental and African Studies. I wish to thank members of the seminar for their spirited discussion. I am also grateful for the interest and the aid given me by Mark Hobart, Ernest Gellner, David Parkin, and Mischa Penn which helped me immensely to clarify some of the issues raised in the paper. I hasten to add that they may well not agree with me on these issues. I also wish to thank the SSRC for the Research Grant (HHP 6753) which allowed me the time to analyse much of the field data upon which this paper is based. My warm thanks go to Nora Dudwick for drafting the two figures within the text.

2 The pun is not mine, but was created by Parkin (1982: xxv) and used by him as a topic in the Introduction to his edited volume, *Semantic Anthropology*.

3 Girard also remarks (1978: 163) that because Lévi-Strauss equates differentiation in the symbolism of myths with the process of 'human thinking', he does injustice to the conjunctive elements in his own symbolic network. Sapir (1977) makes the interesting distinction between 'internal' and 'external' metaphor. The stress in the first instance is upon similarity, e.g. what does George share with a lion? While in the second the emphasis is upon an analogical relationship which is Lévi-Strauss's understanding of metaphor.

4 Also see Ricoeur in *Rule of Metaphor* (1978), where he develops a theory of metaphor that conjoins poetics and ontology.

5 Girard argues (1978: 158) that through structuralism Lévi-Strauss has purged anthropology of a large number of interesting questions having to do with religion, belief, and morality. I tend to agree with Girard on this matter (see Overing 1985; also see Goody 1977: 25).

6 We are also rescued from many of the insidious problems associated with what 'the metaphor' is in fact doing, where each answer gives a particular interpretation that implies or directly talks about either the logic or the mysticism of 'tribal' thought itself. For instance, is metaphor creating resemblances (e.g. talking about the mystical participation of elements or does it entail a philosophy of universals) or is it stressing the differences of domains which resemble each other, and as such is an example of analogic thought (Overing 1982)?

7 Here and throughout the paper I mean by ontology assumptions about existence underlying any conceptual scheme.

8 See the OED (1971: 275) which defines 'bridgehead' as a fortification covering or protecting the end of a bridge nearest the enemy.

9 'Translation as a Creative process: The Power of the Name'. Paper presented at the SSRC symposium at the University of St Andrews on the Comparative Method in Social Anthropology, 1983.

10 Feyerabend in this context means by 'universal principles' the presuppositions about the world upon which a given theory is based. Such principles, he argues, are relative to the theory at hand (see Feyerabend 1975: 269–85).

11 The concept of the afterlife as a world with no affines is a familiar theme in South American lowland ethnography. See, for example, Maybury-Lewis on the Akwē-Shavante (1967), Crocker on the Bororo (1979), and C. Hugh-Jones on the North West Amazon (1979).

12 See Overing 1982.

13 Aristotle in *Poetics* states that a metaphor consists of giving the thing a name that belongs to something else (see Ricoeur 1978: 14–15).

14 In this discussion on utterance meaning, Lyons (1981: 108–09) distinguishes between verification theory and the 'use theory' of meaning, the latter being a reaction on the part of Wittgenstein, Austin, and others against the former. Also see Culler on intentionality (1981: 203) where he speaks of one way of locating a metaphor as in the space between what is meant and what is said.

15 Many philosophers on metaphor, such as Searle (1979), are talking about the relation between the utterance and the 'truth conditions' of the world, i.e. the world as a *fixed* world that is knowable through scientific investigations. Also see Putnam in the article cited below (1977b).

16 This discussion lies outside another interesting question about metaphor, that of *its* truth value. Black (1979: 41) states that it is a violation of philosophical grammar to assign truth or falsity to strong metaphors, in so far as they do generate insight about 'how things are'. In more colourful language on the subject, N. Goodman comments (1968: 73) that metaphor 'might be regarded as a calculated category-mistake – or rather as a happy and revitalising, even if bigamous, second marriage'.

17 See Overing (1983) where I dwell on the problem of definition in ethnosemantics and kinship analysis.

18 Another problem of assuming the 'logical priority' of meaning, much less the 'psychological validity' of ethnosemantics (e.g. see Scheffler and Lounsbury 1971: 137; Goodenough 1956), is that, as Lyons remarks (1981: 82), 'there is no reason to believe that what is basic in the sense of being maximally general is also basic in the day-to-day thinking of most users of a language'.

19 See Lyons (1981: 72–3) on the difficulty in general of differentiating between 'natural' and what he labels 'cultural' kinds.

20 This discussion on the 'fantastic' questions even further the formal semanticist's aim to unfold what is 'psychological reality' for his informants, an unconscious reality that only the ethnographer through his methods can learn.

21 See Culler (1975: 136) on the culture-bound nature of literary genres.

22 Fairly early on in my fieldwork with the Piaroa I asked a wizard through his son who knew some Spanish for another 'cuento' (story) about creation. Neither understood the word; and I elaborated, mentioning that stories do not need to be true. This was a complicated mistake that took a couple of weeks to rectify.

23 See the interesting criticism of Chomsky by Hymes (1971: 54–6) where he discusses creativity and aspects of linguistic ability that do not rely on an *underlying* 'competence' of the speaker, as Chomsky defines it.

24 I have written elsewhere detailed descriptions of Piaroa myths and the knowledge of the wizard (Overing 1982, 1985).

25 *Time* magazine (29 October, 1984, p. 47), in an article on Nobel Prize winners, comments on science's attempt to prove the so-called unified field theory which would link the four forces of nature in a single set of equations. To quote *Time*, 'scientists believe all four forces are manifestations of one fundamental superforce, which split into different forms after the birth of the universe'. I cite this passage to point out that 'bridgeheads' into foreign cultures can crop up in most unexpected (and abstract) form.

26 See Overing (1982) for further details on this process.

27 In the Piaroa language, one verb covers both 'to make' and 'to transform into'; thus, Wahari *adikwinü* signifies both a creation by and a transformation of Wahari.

28 See the philosopher Nelson Goodman (1978), a nominalist and empiricist, on the relation between scientific theory and a multiplicity of worlds. He argues in a clear and interesting manner for the view that scientific theories (and art) are best understood as so many ways of world making and creating.

29 See Overing 1982 for an elaboration on the specifics of these different worlds.

30 See Nelson Goodman (1978: 22) who argues that in science comprehension and creativity go hand in hand; he comments that 'knowing is as much remaking as reporting'.

31 Through hallucinogenic visions, the wizard sees himself walking in these other worlds where he sees, as well, their contents. The Piaroa privilege the verity of sight over other senses.

32 I do not think that philosophers have considered the possibility of cultures for whom hallucinogens have epistemological value. In such cases, there is an absence of an epistemological bedrock, i.e. one objective world – 'this one'.

33 See Parkin (1982: xxvi–xxxiii) who stresses in general the importance to anthropological analysis of recognizing 'play' and 'creativity' within performative language.

34 The great ceremonial feast of the Piaroa is a re-enactment of the last feast given by Wahari when he transformed 'animals' into animal form and took from them their ritual (see Overing 1985).

35 Boyd (1979: 379) gives as example the problem of choosing a defining description for 'electric charge', for which the actual establishing of a referent requires a good deal of knowledge and exposure to varied members of that 'kind'.

36 I disagree, however, with Horton's acceptance of the Strawsonian hypothesis of the universality of an everyday material-object language from which all secondary theoretical elaborations are constructed, through the 'stretching' of this everyday language (see Horton 1979).

37 I am referring to 'natural kinds' *only* as discussed by such philosophers of science as Kuhn (1979), Wittgenstein (1953), Boyd (1979). Also see Lyons (1981).

38 Boyd states (1979: 363, 374) that the insight that reference fixing mechanisms are typically non-definitional is one of the most important achievements of recent analytical philosophy. He speaks then of the importance to scientific creativity of 'theory-constituted metaphors', ones that posit the high possibility of similarity.

39 Many philosophers of science, but not all (see Goodman 1978; Feyerabend 1975) assume one real objectively fixed world. As Levin remarks (1979: 131), 'implicit in Searle's account of metaphor. . . is the assumption that given an incompatibility between the utterance and conditions in the world, the conditions are to be taken as fixed, and it is the utterance that must be construed. Now this is not a logically necessary position.'

References

BARNES, B. and BLOOR, D. (1982) Relativism, Rationalism and the Sociology of Knowledge. In M. Hollis and S. Lukes (eds) *Rationality and Relativism*. Oxford: Basil Blackwell.

BLACK, M. (1962) *Models and Metaphors*. Ithaca: Cornell University Press.

— (1979) More about Metaphor. In A. Ortony (ed.) *Metaphor and Thought*. Cambridge: Cambridge University Press.

BOYD, R. (1979) Metaphor and Theory Change: What is 'Metaphor' a Metaphor for? In A. Ortony (ed.) *Metaphor and Thought*. Cambridge: Cambridge University Press.

CROCKER, J. C. (1977) The Social Functions of Rhetorical Forms. In D. Sapir and J. C. Crocker (eds) *The Social Use of Metaphor*. University of Pennsylvania Press.

— (1979) Selves and Alters among the Eastern Bororo. In D. Maybury-Lewis (ed.) *Dialectical Societies*. Cambridge, Mass.: Harvard University Press.

CULLER, J. (1975) *Structuralist Poetics*. London: Routledge & Kegan Paul.

— (1981) *The Pursuit of Signs*. London: Routledge & Kegan Paul.

FEYERABEND, P. (1975) *Against Method*. London: New Left Books.

GIRARD, R. (1978) *'To Double Business Bound': Essays on Literature, Mimesis, and Anthropology*. Baltimore: Johns Hopkins University Press.

GOODENOUGH, W. H. (1956) Componential Analysis and the Study of Meaning. *Language* **32**: 195–216.

GOODMAN, N. (1968) *Languages of Art*. Indianapolis: Bobbs-Merrill.

— (1978) *Ways of Worldmaking*. Brighton: The Harvester Press.

GOODY, J. (1977) *The Domestication of the Savage Mind*. Cambridge: Cambridge University Press.

HACKING, I. (1982) *Language, Truth and Reason*. In M. Hollis and S. Lukes (eds) *Rationality and Relativism*. Oxford: Basil Blackwell.

HOLLIS, M. (1982) The Social Destruction of Reality. In M. Hollis and S. Lukes (eds) *Rationality and Relativism*. Oxford: Basil Blackwell.

HOLLIS, M. and LUKES, S. (eds) (1982) Introduction. In M. Hollis and S. Lukes (eds) *Rationality and Relativism*. Oxford: Basil Blackwell.

HORTON, R. (1979) Material-Object Language and Theoretical Language: Towards a Strawsonian Sociology of Thought. In S. C. Brown (ed.) *Philosophical Disputes in the Social Sciences*. Brighton, Sussex: Harvester Press.

HUGH-JONES, C. (1979) *From the Milk River*. Cambridge: Cambridge University Press.

HYMES, D. (1971) Sociolinguistics and the Ethnography of Speaking. In E. Ardener (ed.) *Social Anthropology and Language*. (ASA Monographs 10). London: Tavistock Publications.

KUHN, T. (1979) Metaphor in Science. In A. Ortony (ed.) *Metaphor and Thought*. Cambridge: Cambridge University Press.

LÉVI-STRAUSS, C. (1963) *Totemism*. Boston: Beacon Press.

— (1966) *The Savage Mind*. Chicago: University of Chicago Press.

LEVIN, S. (1979) Standard Approaches to Metaphor and a Proposal for Literary Metaphor. In A. Ortony (ed.) *Metaphor and Thought*. Cambridge: Cambridge University Press.

LYONS, J. (1981) *Language, Meaning, and Context*. London: Fontana.

MAYBURY-LEWIS, D. (1967) *Akwẽ-Shavante Society*. Oxford: Clarendon Press.

MILLER, G. (1979) Images and Models, Similes and Metaphors. In A. Ortony (ed.) *Metaphor and Thought*. Cambridge: Cambridge University Press.

NEWTON-SMITH, W. (1982) Relativism and the Possibility of Interpretation. In M. Hollis and S. Lukes (eds) *Rationality and Relativism*. Oxford: Basil Blackwell.

ORTONY, A. (ed.) (1979) *Metaphor and Thought*. Cambridge: Cambridge University Press.

OVERING KAPLAN, J. (1972) Cognition, Endogamy and Teknonymy: The Piaroa example. *SWJA* **28**: 282–97.
— (1973) Endogamy and the Marriage Alliance, *Man* (NS) **8** (4): 555–70.
— (1975) *The Piaroa: a People of the Orinoco Basin: a Study in Kinship and Marriage.* Oxford: Clarendon Press.
— (1981) Review article: Amazonian Anthropology. *Journal of Latin American Studies* **13** (1): 151–64.
— (1984) Dualisms as an Expression of Difference and Danger: Marriage Exchange and Reciprocity among the Piaroa of Venezuela. In K. Kensinger (ed.) *Marriage Practices in Lowland South American Societies.* Urbana: University of Illinois Press.
OVERING, J. (1982) The Paths of Sacred Words: Shamanism and the Domestication of the Asocial in Piaroa Society. Presented in symposium on Shamanism in Lowland South American Societies: 44th International Congress of Americanists, Manchester.
— (1983) Translation as a Creative Process: The Power of a Name. Presented at the SSRC symposium at the University of St Andrews on the Comparative Method in Social Anthropology. December 1983. Also in L. Holy (ed.) *Comparative Method in Social Anthropology.* London: Athlone Press.
— (1985) There is no End of Evil: The Guilty Innocents and their Fallible God. In D. Parkin (ed.) *The Anthropology of Evil.* Oxford: Basil Blackwell.
PAIVIO, A. (1979) Psychological Processes in the Comprehension of Metaphor. In A. Ortony (ed.) *Metaphor and Thought.* Cambridge: Cambridge University Press.
PARKIN, D. (1982) Introduction. In D. Parkin (ed.) *Semantic Anthropology.* London: Academic Press.
PETRIE, H. (1979) Metaphor and Learning. In A. Ortony (ed.) *Metaphor and Thought.* Cambridge: Cambridge University Press.
PUTNAM, H. (1977a) Is Semantics Possible? In S. Schwartz (ed.) *Naming, Necessity and Natural Kinds.* Ithaca: Cornell University Press.
— (1977b) Meaning and Reference (as in above-mentioned).
RICOEUR, P. (1978) *The Rule of Metaphor.* London: Routledge & Kegan Paul.
RUMELHART, D. (1979) Some Problems with the Notion of Literal Meaning. In A. Ortony (ed.) *Metaphor and Thought.* Cambridge: Cambridge University Press.
SADOCK, J. (1979) Figurative Speech and Linguistics. In A. Ortony (ed.) *Metaphor and Thought.* Cambridge: Cambridge University Press.
SAPIR, D. (1977) The Anatomy of Metaphor. In D. Sapir and C. Crocker (eds) *The Social Use of Metaphor.* University of Pennsylvania Press.
SCHEFFLER, H. (1978) *Australian Kin Classification.* Cambridge: Cambridge University Press.
SCHEFFLER, H. and LOUNSBURY, F. (1971) *A Study in Structural Semantics: The Siriono System of Kinship.* Englewood Cliffs, NJ: Prentice-Hall.
SEARLE, J. (1979) Metaphor. In A. Ortony (ed.) *Metaphor and Thought.* Cambridge: Cambridge University Press.
SPERBER, D. (1975) *Rethinking Symbolism.* Cambridge: Cambridge University Press.
TODOROV, T. (1970) The Fantastic in Fiction (translated by Vivienne Mylne). In *Twentieth Century Studies* **3**. (May 1970): 76–92.
WITTGENSTEIN, L. (1953) *Philosophical Investigations* (translated by G. E. M. Anscombe). New York: Macmillan.

Ladislav Holy

9 Fire, meat, and children:
the Berti myth, male dominance, and female power

When Malinowski is praised as an excellent ethnographer, it is always his technique of participant observation and his working through the native language that are emphasized. What deserves equal appreciation are the epistemological aspects of his research methods. Although he always assumed the natives' rationality, he also realized that they cannot formulate 'definite, precise and abstract' statements about the 'fundamental assumptions' underlying their belief (Malinowski 1922: 396). These, however, have to be grasped by the ethnographer, for it is only in relation to them that the notion of the natives' rationality has any meaning. Malinowski has overcome the problem by assuming that the native professes the reality of belief he faces not only 'with his tongue, but lives through partly in imagination and partly in actual experience' (1922: 397). The 'fundamental assumptions' that make the belief or conduct rational have thus to be formulated by the ethnographer him- or herself. In this respect, 'the objective items of culture, into which belief has crystallized in the form of tradition, myth, spell and rite are the most important sources of knowledge' (ibid.). In formulating it, the ethnographer's work is a creative one in that it 'brings to light phenomena of human nature which, in their entirety, had remained hidden even from those in whom they happened' (ibid.).

The significance of all the existing forms of expression, the assumption of the rationality of the belief and conduct and the creativity of the ethnographer's work have thus all been related in Malinowski's methodology and since his time, any discussion of the epistemological problems of the anthropological method of research has dealt in one way or another with this package of notions. In fact, the whole development of our methodological sophistication can be seen as a growing awareness of the implications of these interrelated notions.

When we started to realize that social facts are not givens but constructions endowed with meaning, the creativity of the ethnographer's work acquired a much deeper significance than that recognized by Malinowski; for if the ethnographer participates in the lives of his subjects when doing his fieldwork, he also participates in the construction of meaning and by implication in the construction of the very facts which he then sets to analyse and explain (Rabinow 1977: 152). Our recently increased awareness of the ethnographer's own experience as the source of his knowledge stems directly from this realization.

Our awareness that the native knows more than he puts into words has increased and acquired new significance with the development of symbolic analysis, which Malinowski had not fully appreciated as relevant for his purposes. In spite of his awareness that not everything that can be presumed to be known by the natives is expressed in verbal form, the natives' utterances still remained for him the main source of his understanding of their world, and the limitations of his understanding can be seen as deriving from his over-reliance on what the informants said (Weiner 1976: 10).

When the analysis concentrates on symbolic practices as the source of information about the knowledge of the society's members, it not only assumes that more is said in any given culture than is actually uttered in words (as Malinowski did) but it also ascribes equal significance to verbal and non-verbal modes of expression (as Malinowski did not). In line with these assumptions Ardener (1972) has brought to our attention alternative models of society from those traditionally formulated by ethnographers on the basis of folk models derived from the 'articulate' male segment of the population, and has suggested that the alternative female models can be arrived at through the analysis of symbolic thought and action. He showed that the fact that men freely articulate their views to one another and to the ethnographer while women are 'muted' (Ardener 1975) is a rational response to their different cultural experience.

In this paper, which is specifically concerned with some aspects of the multiplicity of Berti's own models of their society,[1] I take up the problem of talk and silence as rational response to the actors' cultural experience. Ardener has formulated his views in the context of the 'problem of women', i.e. in the context of technical and analytical difficulties in dealing ethnographically with a 'human group that forms about half of any population and is even in majority at certain ages' (Ardener 1972: 135). I likewise consider the multiplicity of Berti models within the 'problem of women'. Unlike Ardener, however, I will not be concerned with models that differ in the placing of the boundary between society and nature, i.e. with models that picture men and women differently in relation to society on the one hand and nature on the other, but rather with models of gender relations that picture men and women differently in relation to one another. I also pursue a different line of analysis from that which he took. While his concern was to show that different models are expressed through different modes of discourse, my main concern is to show that the actors' models may as well be seen as determining their discourse. In particular, I want to show to what extent these models determine what is and what is not the subject of verbal expression.

Berti women articulate as clearly as men do their own model of gender relations, although they do not express it as forcibly and as often as men express theirs. Each model of the world is ultimately the result of the experience of the world. As women's experience is different from that of men for obvious reasons of their physiological difference as well as of the division of tasks among them, it is only to be expected that male and female models will differ. Apart from the verbally expressed male and female models, a different model of gender relations is expressed in Berti symbolism and ritual action. This model is fully shared by men and women and it depicts the sexes as complementary; this complementarity is also expressed in the theory of procreation to which again both men and women subscribe.

As it is obviously impossible to deal with the complexity of gender relations in the space of one paper, I limit myself to the discussion of some of the aspects of the two models verbally expressed. My main purpose is not only to throw some light on the rationale behind the fact that men and women talk about different aspects of gender relations when they articulate their respective models, but also on the rationale behind their collusion of silence about certain symbols through which the relations between the sexes are expressed.

Male and female models of gender relations

The model explicitly expressed by Berti men is that of male dominance and female subordination. The relations between the sexes are expressed metaphorically in the often heard saying *rājil giddām, mara warra* ('the man is in front, the women behind'). This saying expresses what is seen as the appropriate form of women's deference towards men as well as the leadership role of men; it is often quoted to explain and justify the fact that men make all major economic and all political decisions and that they are charged with responsibility for the conduct and morality of women in their roles as fathers, brothers, and husbands.

The explicitly asserted notions of the greater importance of men and lesser importance of women are corroborated by certain aspects of gender symbolism. Berti lateral symbolism exhibits in its own cultural idiom a general contrast of values in that the right is clearly the auspicious and left the inauspicious side (Holy 1983). When left and right are used as symbolic vehicles for expressing the relations between men and women, men are associated with the right and women with the left, as when the afterbirth is buried inside the yard to the right side of the entrance to the hut if the baby is a boy and to the left side if it is a girl.

But it is bones and flesh that are the main symbolic vehicles for expressing the preeminence of men and the subordinate position of women. The association between bones and masculinity and flesh and feminity derives directly from the theory of procreation according to which the bones and sinews of the child are created from the sperm and the child's flesh from the women's blood. The sperm and menstrual blood get mixed into a clot inside the womb which grows bigger and bigger after each subsequent intercourse. After about two months sinews first appear inside the hitherto undifferentiated clot and thereafter bones gradually develop within the sinews. Only after that does the flesh of the child begin to grow around the bones and sinews.

The sinews and bones do not only provide support for the outer flesh. They are seen as active part and the flesh as a passive part of the body: the movement of the body emanates from sinews; the sinew moves the bone and the flesh follows the movement of the bone to which it is attached. This notion is supported by common experience. A person with a flesh wound can still move around, but anybody who has broken a bone can no longer move his arm or leg.

This theory of the mechanics of the body is projected into the image of the social order through the mediation of the symbolic association of men and women with bones and flesh respectively. That a man is in front and a woman behind, or a man leads and a woman follows becomes then much more than a particular social convention: it is natural and it cannot be otherwise because men are bones and women are flesh (*rujāl udam, awīn laham*).

Although women accept the leadership role of men explicitly asserted in the men's model and fully subscribe to the symbols of maleness and femaleness which legitimize it, they nevertheless, explicitly assert a different model of gender relations, particularly when they are among themselves and when they are, as they often do, either critical of men's actions or laugh at their expense. It is a model which depicts men as dependent on women. This model is not only explicitly expressed by women; it is also made clearly manifest to both men and women through the division of labour among them.

There are tasks which can be, or customarily are, performed by only one sex. Only men slaughter animals, and attend to camels and sheep at pasture, and only men spin cotton, sew, make leather bags, ropes, and wooden utensils. Most of the tasks that are customarily performed by women can be performed by men if no woman is available. Thus only women harvest, but a man can do so if there is no female labour available in the household: he cuts the millet stalks with an ordinary knife instead of the special harvesting knife which is an implement handled solely by women. Only women winnow the threshed grain; again a man can do that in emergency. It is, however, always shameful for him if he has to resort to winnowing and he takes special care not to be seen by others when doing it. Only women husk millet in wooden stamps, grind flour, cook meals, and brew beer.

There are thus tasks for whose performance women depend on men and tasks for whose performance men depend on women. The mutual dependence of the sexes is, however, not symmetrical and it is this asymmetry which the women's model emphasizes. When portraying men as dependent on them, women invariably stress that a woman can easily live on her own, as indeed many do, either temporarily when her husband is away from the village, or permanently if she is divorced or a widow. If there are only women present in the household when they want to kill a chicken, they either ask a neighbour or any passing-by men to do it for them. Fresh meat is rarely eaten by the Berti and the slaughtering of animals is rare. Furthermore, meat can always be purchased from the butchers in the market without resort to one's own slaughtering. The dependence of women on men is thus only occasionally made manifest in the existing division of labour; moreover, it can be easily alleviated through the culturally recognized alternatives. When a woman who lives on her own needs a leather bag, a rope, or a utensil which only men manufacture, she can again buy it in the market. If she has camels or sheep which have to be grazed outside the village, she is certainly wealthy enough to be able to hire a herder.

Unlike a woman, a man cannot live on his own. Although he could harvest his own field and thresh and winnow the grain all by himself, he cannot cook his own food and brew his own beer. At most he occasionally brews tea if he is anxious to control not only the direct expenditure on this commodity but also its consumption.

Apart from occasionally brewing tea, men cook only meat of sacrificial animals for communal ritual consumption. They must of course resort to cooking when they are temporarily without women either on pasture with sheep or camels or when travelling. In the latter case, they are always particular to camp outside a settlement where they would cook for themselves without being seen by others.

It is unthinkable for a man to do everyday cooking. It would be a clear indication that he failed to maintain a woman who would care for him as a woman should for a man. As food and beer have to be prepared daily, the men's dependence on women for the performance of these tasks is made manifest continually and more directly than the women's dependence on men. Moreover, there are no culturally accepted alternatives to the preparation of food in the household: although beer can be obtained from the market, cooked food cannot.

The asymmetry in the mutual interdependence of the sexes that the women's model of gender relations emphasizes, manifests itself in yet another important way that the women are always ready to point out. The man's status as an elder who has a right to take part in settling disputes, i.e. his status in the public domain, depends on his being *rājil be bētu* (man with a house), i.e. on being head of his own household, in which his daily sustenance is provided for him by his wife.

It is the man's role in the public domain and the general domestic orientation of women that are being emphasized in the men's model: men dominate because women hold no position of authority in the public domain. Only men travel far afield while the women stay at home all the time. The overall passivity of women, which accounts for their subordinate position, is expressed by saying that a woman does not fight (*al-mara mā 'indu 'aza*) or does not carry out litigation (*al-mara mā 'indu gadīya*); even if she is involved in a dispute or the case concerns her directly, she is represented by a man, either her father or husband, under whose protection she is.

The women's model clearly privileges the domestic domain; women have power over men not only directly because of their monopoly over the processing of food but also indirectly in that it is the man's status within the domestic domain that is the basis for the ascription of his status in the public domain. For this reason women can see themselves as making the men what they are. A man without a wife has no status in the public domain. He acquires it only after he has married and established his own house. If he subsequently gets divorced, he does not lose his status as an elder but his prestige does become significantly impaired. It has been pointed out that the source of the woman's power is her monopoly over the processing of food. A woman acquires this power, and thus becomes a fully adult member of her sex, only after she has been associated through marriage with a particular man and through this association has acquired her own domestic fire which is the symbol of her independent existence. Until her marriage she was not a woman (*mara*) but a girl (*binei*). An adult unmarried man is not referred to as a boy (*walad*) but as a bachelor (*'āzib*). As such, he is not yet a full man; he becomes one only when he has his own house. As a woman acquires her power only through her association with a particular man, a man acquires his authority only through his association with a particular woman. Women thus depend for their power on men and men for their authority on women.[2] But this relationship is again not symmetrical. The status of a woman as mistress of her own fire, which enables her to lead an independent existence, is not affected by her subsequent divorce; after her divorce she does not revert to the status of a *binei* fully subject to the authority of her father. She becomes *'azaba* (divorcee) who can maintain her own independent household (as most divorcees do) virtually for the rest of her life and who controls all her economic transactions as well as all her subsequent relations with men, either as lovers or future husbands. If she remarries, and even if her new husband has never been married before, her new house (if the husband does not simply move in to live with her in her house) will not be built in a ritual way as her first house was, nor will her new hearth. Unlike a woman, a man after divorce reverts to what he was before his marriage – an *'āzib* (bachelor) with a concomitant loss of prestige awarded to proper elders, i.e. *rujāl be bētum* (pl. of *rājil be bētu*). Whereas a woman only needs to be married once to be forever a fully adult member of her sex, and in fact as a divorcee gains a considerable degree of economic autonomy which a married woman does not enjoy, a man has to be perpetually married to qualify as an adult member of his sex. If he does not have his own house, he can regain his full status in the public domain only with advanced age, when the fact that he is an elder of a group of his own descendants (even if he lives as a dependant in a household of one of his children) is more important than the fact that he has no house of his own; and when his status as a *shāib* (an old man) becomes more significant than that he is technically an *'āzib*.

The existence of female power in male-dominated societies has been recognized and given due attention in numerous studies of gender relations. Analytically, it has mostly been presented as part of women's strategy to subvert all-pervasive male dominance or as their defence mechanism against it (see Cronin 1977; Ullrich 1977). More generally, women's refusal to cook or sexually to cohabit with their husbands has been pointed out as a usual strategy to which women resort to gain their way in the face of men's dominance or as a sanction against men's actions or conduct which they consider inappropriate (Paulme 1963; Cohen 1971; Strathern 1972; 27, 45–6; Rosaldo 1974: 37; Lamphere 1974: 99). The Berti women too exploit their power. The woman's favourite stratagem in the case of a dispute with her husband or when she feels that she has been maltreated by him is to refuse him sexual access and to refuse to cook for him. Her latter act is of course publicly much more telling than the former one for sexual intercourse is an act properly carried out only in the privacy of one's own house whereas men from neighbouring houses often eat together either in the guest shelter of one of the houses or in the open space outside the homestead's fence. This communal meal starts after the dishes have been brought from all the respective households either by the men's wives or by the boys who already take their meals with other men. Although it is not polite to comment on it openly, the fact that a dish has not arrived from a particular house is noted by all and the situation becomes more humiliating to the man concerned the longer it persists. His situation is not immediately obvious if he takes his meals with other male members of his household inside his own house. But he cannot, of course, go on without food forever and a man who is eventually forced to seek his nourishment away from his own house also displays his dependence on a woman by publicly manifesting his defeat by her.

When a woman refuses to cook for her husband, she does more than merely inconvenience him: she challenges or indeed effectively defies the authority that he holds over her. Their control of the processing of food thus provides Berti women with more than a convenient strategy through which they can keep male dominance within bearable limits. They clearly construe it as giving them power over men, and seizing upon this notion they construct their own model of gender relations: men may be strong, they may be in front, and they may hold authority over women but it is only through their ultimate dependence on women that they are what they are. Women may not be free agents, but neither are the men: they have to operate within the limitations set up by women's control over the processing of food.

Both men and women are aware of one another's models and they are thus faced with the problem of accommodating the alternative model within the terms of their own in order to maintain the latter's credibility. One of the possible ways of solving this problem is to deny the credibility of the alternative model by seeing it as a fiction not sustained by the known facts. Rogers (1975) has analysed this solution to the perceived discrepancy between men's and women's models of gender relations in peasant societies where, she argues, women explain away the men's model of male supremacy as a 'myth' which it is just simply convenient for them to subscribe to openly so that they can maintain their 'real' power. The problem with this analysis is that the analyst has to take sides in the actor's dispute and concur with either the women's or men's view as the 'true' one. It would be possible to arbitrate in this way on the validity of the views expressed by Berti men and women and to follow the strategy of most analyses of gender relations, in which their quality has been evaluated in terms of men's and women's respective control over strategic resources (Friedl 1975; Rosaldo 1974; Sanday 1974) or in terms of their exercise of political or ritual power. To see the control over resources or the exercise of political or ritual power as determined directly on the basis of sex would be, however, too simplistic in case of the Berti. Only the right to make political decisions is ascribed to a person directly on the basis of sex in the sense that this right is not granted to women and that only a man can be an elder. But here again it is not merely the elder's sex that is decisive but also his status as the household head.

The control of strategic economic resources is not ascribed on the basis of a person's sex. It accrues to the household head who need not necessarily be a man; when a woman is a head of her own household, her control over the household's resources is equal to that of her male counterpart. The woman, however, assumes the position of a household head only when there is no male to occupy it. Even then she can never assume the role of a village elder which automatically accrues to any male household head. Although the Berti women can thus assume certain typically male roles, in direct comparison to men, the possibilities open to them are still greatly circumscribed. In this respect the relationship between the sexes could be seen as distinctly asymmetrical. But I see the weakness of such conclusion as deriving from the necessity to introduce into the analysis some measure of objective significance of certain facts that goes beyond the Berti's own perception of their significance.

That a different perception is involved in the Berti's own view of the situation is suggested by the fact that if not verbally, then certainly in their behavioural practice both men and women fully admit the validity of the other's model. Women accept their subordinate position and through doing so admit and reaffirm the dominant role of men; they do not deny men their authority over them. Equally, men recognize and accept their dependence on women and through so doing admit and reaffirm women's power. In their practical attitude, both sexes thus subscribe to a different model of gender relations than the one which they assert verbally. The credibility of the verbally asserted models, which is perpetually undermined by this practical attitude, is maintained through the imposition of specific meaning on the myth that deals explicitly with the origin of gender relations.

It tells that long time ago, there were people called Farkh al Ganān (or Abunganān) who lived up on a hill. They were all women and their children were all female.[3] They were tall, big and strong, their bodies covered in hair. They hunted wild animals in the plain below the hill by chasing them, and lived on their meat which they ate raw as they had no fire.

One day they saw a strange light glittering in the plain below the hill. They were frightened and ran up the hill to hide themselves. Next day, the light was there again. Farkh al Ganān were curious about it and went to investigate it. They came upon a group of riders; they were all men and their horses were all male.

The light which so frightened the Farkh al Ganān was a fire. The men were sitting around it cooking their food on it. They gave Farkh al Ganān some to eat. It tasted much better than the raw meat and Farkh al Ganān asked the men for the fire so that they could use it too for cooking their food. The men said that they would give Farkh al Ganān the fire if they would give them their daughters for wives who would bear them children. Farkh al Ganān agreed and so they exchanged their daughters for fire with the men.

The myth is a short, simple, and straightforward story. It has not the elaborate, repetitive structure which, according to Lévi-Strauss, is typical of myths. Even so, it exhibits the scheme of 'oppositions governing its organization behind the mythical "discourse" ' (Lévi-Strauss 1966: 136): above/below (the women on the hill, the men in the plain), nature/culture (animal existence of the hairy women without fire, the cultural existence of the fully human men with fire), wild/domesticated (women hunting wild animals, men riding domesticated horses), raw/cooked (women eating raw meat, men eating cooked food), asexual/sexual reproduction (the women bear children on their own, the men need women to bear them children), etc. I do not intend, however, to analyse the 'syntax' of the myth (Lévi-Strauss 1970: 7–8) and to unravel the ultimately unverifiable hidden meaning of the myth encoded in the interrelations among the elements of its underlying structure of binary oppositions. I propose instead to concentrate on its 'message', i.e. its subject matter (Lévi-Strauss 1970: 199) or what Willis called ' "conceptual-affective structure", itself formed from the basic "bricks" of mythological thought – sets of binary discriminations' (Willis 1967: 521).

Probably the most important message of the myth is that the source of female power does not lie in women's nature and does not stem from anything that is inherently or naturally feminine and over which neither women nor men exercise control. It is socially constituted and rests on women's control of specific cultural resources and not of the forces of nature. This control, in its turn, is the result of the original transaction that occurred when men and women were brought together for the first time.

While both men and women agree on the source and nature of the female power, they substantiate their respective models by imposing different meaning on the transaction described in the myth.

In the following discussion, I consider the myth first from the male and then from the female point of view.

Female power and the male model of gender relations

Men can be fully aware of the women's power and feel no need to deny it because the myth clearly implies to them that it was men who gave women their power in the first place. It shows that the fire, which makes possible the female monopoly of the processing of food on which their power rests, was given to them by the men. The myth not only establishes men as the original masters of fire; it also puts across the message that they surrendered their control over it to women voluntarily. Hence everything the women are today is due to men. In this respect, the myth clearly attempts to explain away the contradiction between the model of gender relations according to which men dominate women and the model according to which they are dependent on them. It suggests that men have been dominant all the time and that even those aspects of gender relations which seem to indicate that women have some power over men are really understandable only within the context of the all-pervasive dominance of men over women. Any power the women may hold over men, they hold because the men ceded it to them.

The women, however, did not obtain the fire for nothing; in exchange for their access to it, they gave themselves to men. This exchange ended the independent existence of the sexes and the apparent ability of women to reproduce themselves without men: the women lived on the hill with their children who were also all female; the myth does not tell anything about the men's children but it clearly implies that they had none before they met the women, and could have none, otherwise there would be nothing they needed the women for. From now on, the complementarity of sexes in the repro-duction has been established. This too can be seen as the result of the men's wishes: the women received fire in exchange for surrendering for ever their apparent ability at self-reproduction and by making themselves dependent on men in the discharge of their reproductive power.

Even though female power may be seen as confirming the ever existing male dominance and superiority, for it exists only because men agreed to it in the first place, such power nevertheless perpetually challenges the asserted men's dominance which can be maintained only if men succeed in controlling it, i.e. if they succeed in doing what they had successfully done in the mythological past. To control female power is at once the men's main problem and the price they have to pay for having acquired their children through their transaction with women. In practice it means that they can sustain as credible the model of their dominance only in so far as particular men continually succeed in controlling the power of particular women.

In the existing analyses of female power in male-dominated societies, this dominance (unless perceived as a 'myth') has been conceptualized as something taken for granted and accepted by both men and women; it has been conceptualized as basically non-negotiable and women have been seen as mobilizing their power, or resorting to it, merely in defence against the dominance of men.

This is certainly not how the Berti conceptualize the relationship between men and women. For Berti men particularly, male dominance is an ideal that exists in actuality only in so far as it has been successfully negotiated; it is as if the Berti men were saying that a man *should* be in front and *is* in front if he successfully manages to be in front against the ever present opposition of female power. It is rather that female power is taken for granted and accepted by both men and women as an ever-present, non-negotiable force and men dominate only in so far as they successfully manage to curb or control it. This makes sense, of course, once we realize that power is probably the only attribute whose possession cannot be successfully pretended; it exists only as long as it is real. On the other hand, men's authority over women, as any other authority for that matter, has to be perpetually claimed and exists only in so far as it has successfully been claimed by some and recognized by others. I would suggest that this is also the reason why the men's model is more often and more loudly asserted than the women's model. The Berti men speak and the Berti women for most part do not, not because the men dominate and the women are subordinate, or because men are articulate and women inarticulate, or even less because it is in their nature to do so. The men speak because they cannot afford not to if they want to sustain the notion of their dominance; women do not speak, or at least not as often as men do, because they do not need to (see Weiner 1976: 233).

Within the context of the women's model of power relations between the sexes and the male model of authority relations it also makes sense that polygyny and great number of children are seen as the signs of a man's prestige for they are at the same time the signs of his successful management of his relationship to a particular woman or women made possible through his effective control of female power.

Although the manifestations of women's power are limited, the means by which a man is able to cope with a woman who refuses to yield her power are even more restricted. He has no monopoly of control over anything a woman cannot obtain without his co-operation. He can, of course, withhold sex as a woman can, but then he is harming himself and not the woman for he is refusing himself his children. If everything fails, he can divorce his wife. The asymmetry of the divorce right which accrues only to the husband but not to the wife, has again been seen by a number of analysts as a manifestation of male dominance. Such a meaning of divorce is construed on the basis of specific cultural experience according to which divorce leaves the woman destitute, and on the unwarranted presupposition of its universality. The Berti cultural experience is distinctly different. For them divorce is the ultimate sign of the man's failure to control his wife. It is the sign of the victory of her power over his authority. He has lost and he also suffers most. While a divorced woman can go on living on her own, a divorced man has to attach himself to his mother or sister, at least for his sustenance, if not in terms of his actual residence in her household. He can manage to obtain his sustenance from his own household only if there is an adult daughter in it who can cook and brew beer for him. Whatever the case, divorce for him means changing his dependence on one particular woman for a dependence on another; it makes the validity of the female model blatantly obvious.

I mentioned before that female power is conceptualized not as deriving from women's nature but as socially constituted. The myth suggests that women hold it because it was granted to them by men in course of the transaction which took place between them. As it is power that has been relegated, its exercise involves responsibility and its abuse by women to get their own way is seen by men as irresponsible behaviour. As men experience women's power when, in their view, women have abused it, they tend to see women as generally irresponsible; *awĩn mā lēhum gharat kabĩr* ('women do not care much'), the men say. In its turn, this irresponsibility of women provides the rationale for the men's control over them. That women hold power is thus on the one hand the outcome of men's dominance and superiority while on the other hand, women's power makes the male dominance a necessity.

Male dominance and the female model of gender relations

Just as men are fully aware of the women's power and do not try to deny it, the women do not try – even privately – to deny men's superiority; they recognize and accept it. To be able to do so, they have to reconcile their views that they hold power over men with their other view that men are superior to them and they have somehow to answer for themselves the obvious question of why they accept the dominant position of men when at the same time they claim to hold power over them.

It is again the myth about the origin of gender relations that provides the women with an answer to this question. As I mentioned before, the myth clearly establishes that the source of women's power is not their nature but their monopoly over the control of fire established in the course of the original transaction between the sexes. While the myth reassures the men that they have not lost their control over fire as a result of the women's cunning but handed it over to them in an exchange from which they came out as winners for they gained through it their ability to have children, it reassures the women that the original exchange was not forced on them by the men either. The myth clearly implies that the women themselves longed for the cultural existence of men and in this it reminds them that it was their wish to abandon their animal-like existence and through acquiring the fire to become fully human beings as the men were. They acquired the fire from the men not simply because men gave it to them of their own accord and hence can take it again from them should they so wish but in exchange for their procreative power. By agreeing to bear men their children, the women paid for it. From the time of the mythical transaction between the sexes, the children have belonged to men and their patrilineal affiliation is the cultural expression of this fact.

That the children belong to their father and not to their mother, as the Berti usually express it themselves, is on the one hand the result of the mythical transaction, and on the other hand the source of men's dominance over women and of the senior men's dominance over junior men. Thus, the father dominates his sons and daughters, and the husband dominates his wife because his rights in her were transferred to him by her father. The Berti express the asymmetry of the conjugal relationship by saying that it is the man who marries a woman and not a woman who marries a man. Like female power, male dominance too is perceived not as natural but as socially constituted; in this context it is logical that the brother–sister relationship is the most egalitarian of all cross-sex relationships.

The women existed independently of men before the mythical transaction took place but they lived without culture in an animal-like state. Through this transaction they acquired their control of fire which enables them to exist independently of men in a fully cultural and human way; men lost the possibility of their independent existence in the exchange. Through surrendering their control of fire to the women in exchange for the possibility of having children, the men became dependent on women both for their sustenance and for procreation. By making men dependent on them, women acquired their power over them. But even nowadays women can lead an independent existence only after they have been associated through marriage with a particular man and through this association each one acquired individually her own domestic fire and hence the means of her independent existence. In this respect, each marriage re-enacts for each individual couple the original mythical transaction between the sexes. The contemporary practice thus reinforces the message of the mythological story that the power over men which women enjoy results from a specific transaction between men and women and is part of the reciprocity between them. Women gained power in the mythological past and have power now only through their dependence on men; they have to recognize male dominance because it is only through their dependence on particular men that they gained monopoly of food processing which is the source of their power. Typically, a woman gains this power only through marriage, i.e. through individually entering into a relationship with a particular man that was part of the original exchange between the sexes described in the myth.

In accepting the dominant position of men women do nothing more than accept the myth as a dogma (Robinson 1968: 123), for the myth tells that women became fully human beings through striking a bargain with men. It is part of their human morality to honour the conditions of this bargain. The men certainly see it in this light: they consider a woman who abuses her power and openly defies her subordinate position not only as an irresponsible but also as an immoral creature. The women's view of men's morality is the same. They too consider men's authority as being conditional on their fulfilment of the obligations which were part of the original bargain between the sexes. They see men's obligation towards and responsibility for their children as the counterpart of their right in them.

Produce not intended for direct domestic consumption is controlled and sold in the market by the male head of the family. His behaviour is seen as responsible as long as he uses the money to buy the clothes for the family members, to pay the legitimate expenses like poll tax, damages, and his sons' bridewealths, or to reinvest it in livestock from which his children will benefit and which will devolve on them through inheritance after his death. His behaviour is seen as irresponsible when he uses the money for buying things for his own personal use (like a horse, a gun, or a sword, for example), or when he uses it to pay his own bridewealth for an additional wife. It is typically in situations like these that a woman will exercise her power and refuse to cook for her husband who, in her opinion, has behaved in an irresponsible way.

In the same way in which the man's authority over his wife or daughters guarantees that they will behave in a responsible manner, each man's dependence on a particular woman guarantees that he too will behave responsibly.

The symbols of the interdependence of the sexes

By asserting their own model of gender relations while admitting the validity of that asserted by the other sex, both men and women tacitly acknowledge that the sexes are mutually dependent on one another.

When women explicitly assert the men's dependence on them, they point out that it arises from the fact that only women process food. Because they do the everyday cooking, women also regularly handle and control fire, including the collecting of firewood which is the women's task: men help only occasionally when the logs are too big for a woman to split with an axe. Embers are perpetually kept alive in the hearth on which cooking is done. If the fire goes out, it is hardly ever relit with a match. Instead, glowing embers will be

obtained from the neighbouring house and every evening, before the main
meal of the day is prepared, women and children going around with broken
potsherds to ask for the embers from a neighbour are a common sight in every
Berti village.

Regularly to attend to fire is a job of women and a man who does it is like a
man who cooks: he is despicable. This, I would suggest, is the reason why the
Berti despise blacksmiths and why hardly any Berti men earn their living by
making and repairing iron tools. Berti men of course need to and can use fire
occasionally. A man has a fire in his own hut to keep him warm during the
winter nights. Men use fire when cooking meat of the sacrificial animal in the
village mosque, when they extract the melon-seed oil which they use for
treating leather bags, when they are burning the old straw in the field before
sowing, or when they are burning down the nests of birds in the fields. Any
time the men need to light their fire, they start it with embers which a woman
gives them from the hearth in her hut. This makes it clearly manifest to both
men and women that it is women who control fire and at the same time it
makes fire a powerful symbol of men's dependence on them.

Beer also symbolizes men's dependence on women, although not as vividly,
for men can obtain it from the market, whereas for cooked food they depend
solely on their wives, daughters, and sisters. That beer, nevertheless, has
symbolic significance in the context of gender relations and the sexual division
of labour through which they are sustained, is attested by the fact that women
who sell beer in the market are despised. A beer-seller subverts women's
power by making beer available to men for cash. Because through her actions
she undermines female solidarity *vis-à-vis* men, her conduct is seen as
immoral and it makes sense that she is considered a prostitute: sex and food
(including beer) is what other women give to men free. As a woman can also
refuse to grant them to a man, they are the signs of her power over him. In this
context, it is logical that a woman who sells one of them is seen in the same
light as the one who sells the other. This interpretation is supported by the fact
that it is women who more readily express their condemnation of those who
sell beer for cash. On the whole, men do not see anything wrong with women
selling beer, unless they are their kin. That beer-sellers are mostly women
who live on their own correlates with the fact that it is often their only source
of income as well as with the fact that they are less subject to the control of
other men and women.

The objects for which women depend on men also have their symbolic
significance. As mentioned before, the women depend on men for meat and
wooden utensils but they can again obtain both these commodities from the
market. From the male point of view, butchers and woodcarvers are
analogous to the women selling beer; they too are despised. The Berti
consider both the killing of animals and the cutting of trees as taking life. Both
activities are morally justified and seen as necessary as long as they are
performed to satisfy personal needs; they become despicable acts when

carried out for profit. I would argue, however, that butchers and woodcarvers are despised not because of the profit that motivates them but again because they undermine the men's relationship with women by making available to them commodities for the supply of which they would otherwise be dependent on men. This interpretation is again suggested by the fact that it is men, rather than women, who express their contempt for butchers and woodcarvers.

As it is fire which clearly and vividly symbolizes men's dependence on women, which the women explicitly assert and of which the men are made often acutely aware, it is only logical that the mythological story which explains how men and women came into contact for the first time, also explains the origin or discovery of fire.

In a manner typical of myths (Lévi-Strauss 1967), the Berti myth too contradicts the ethnographic reality to which it is supposed to refer. In the myth it is men who use fire to cook and women who procure meat; at least, the myth is silent about the men hunting while specifically mentioning it as the women's occupation. It is obvious that in the same way in which the men transferred their control over fire to women, the women must have transferred their control over the provision of meat to men so that the division of labour existing in the mythological past could transform into the present-day one.

Control over three different resources could be seen as object of the transaction between men and women described in the myth: children, fire, and meat. Control over all three of them is significant in shaping the existing relations between men and women. But while the myth is all about the transfer of control over children and fire, it is completely silent about the transfer of the control over meat. At best it implies, but does not spell out, that the killing of animals, and hence the ultimate control over the distribution of meat, was ceded by women to the men following the coming together of the sexes. It also leaves it unclear whether anything like that happened at all; maybe the food men cooked on their fire was meat and in the mythological past both sexes hunted.

There is thus a clear asymmetry in the explicit attention that the myth gives to control of fire (the symbol of men's dependence on women) and to the right over children (the symbol of men's dominance) on the one hand, and in the explicit attention to fire and meat (the symbol of women's dependence on men) on the other hand. This asymmetry reflects, of course, the present-day relative significance of fire and meat as symbols of gender relations. But considering that meat has, nevertheless, its symbolic significance in the context of these relations, it appears reasonable to assume that there may be more profound reasons behind the deliberate vagueness about the role of meat in the mythical transaction between the sexes.

In the asymmetrical structure of its narrative, the myth seems to justify the relations between the sexes as portrayed in the men's model. By refusing to acknowledge explicitly that women might have conceded their control of meat voluntarily to the men in the same way in which men ceded their mastery of fire to the women, the myth dismisses from consideration the possibility that present-day gender relations may be the result of the wishes of both sexes, not just the men. In this respect, it can be read as a 'sociological charter' (Malinowski 1948: 120) of male supremacy and seen as a 'male' story, putting across the men's view of gender relations which does not have to be fully shared by women themselves.

Given, however, that the myth is perpetuated by women,[4] it seems to be more accurate to see it as the charter of women's power and as a 'female' story which puts across the women's view of gender relations. If the women made explicit that this control passed from them to men after the sexes had come together for the first time, the original exchange between men and women would cease to balance. It would be one in which the women clearly lost, because in exchange for their gain of control over fire, they ceded to men not only control over children but also control over the distribution of meat. If control over meat were seen as part of the original transaction, women would have lost, for they would have yielded more to the men than they received from them in return.

It is ultimately not really important whether we understand the myth as a 'male' or as a 'female' story. What it tells about the transaction between the sexes makes good sense both to the women who tell it and to the men who listen to it. The silence about meat entering into the original transaction between the sexes suits them both, for only if control over meat is not made into an issue can female power and male dominance be seen as balancing out and the notion of sexes as interdependent, which is shared by both men and women, be sustained as credible. By the same token, the symbols which are the object of explicit verbal discourse are also truly 'collective representations'. The crucial point is, however, that anything is potentially capable of being used as a symbol but not everything is. When attention focuses not on the analysis of the symbolic structure as such but on the process of its production, i.e. when the question asked is not how are the symbols logically related but what is the logic of symbolic practices, it is no longer sufficient to see the symbolic structure as a 'body of representations seeming to be the production, emanation or reflection of an undifferentiated society or culture', for 'at least in their being employed and uttered, symbolic relations vary as a function of the identity and position of those who use them and of those to whom they are applied' (Augé 1982; 60).

As Augé rightly pointed out, 'one cannot give an exhaustive account of mytho-logics if one simply reads myths' (Augé 1982: 60). The logic of symbolic practices embodied in the mythological story can only be grasped when the myth is understood for what it is to those who tell it and who listen to it, i.e. when it is comprehended as a 'charter' in Malinowski's sense. In following Malinowski's sociological insight, we can go, however, beyond his axiomatic assumption of the rationality of the natives' belief and conduct and to *show* that the various forms of expression of belief are themselves a rational response to their experience. In making the natives' rationality explicit in this way, the creativity of the ethnographer's own work then acquires its full significance.

Notes

1 The Berti are sedentary cultivators living in the Northern Darfur Province of the Republic of the Sudan; they are Muslims and speak their own dialect of Arabic. Material for this paper was collected during several field trips sponsored by the Czechoslovak Academy of Sciences, the International African Institute, the Queen's University of Belfast, and the Social Science Research Council. Generous financial assistance of these bodies is gratefully acknowledged.

The original version of this paper was read to the anthropology seminar at Hull and Manchester; I am indebted to their participants for offering helpful comments. The final version of the paper also benefited greatly from comments by Dr K. Milton, Professor J. Blacking, and Dr J. Overing.

2 I use the term authority in the sense of 'the right to take certain decisions' and power as the 'ability to affect or secure such decisions as one wishes, although these decisions are either not allocated as rights, or are the rights of other persons' (Smith 1960: 19).

3 The female sex of the original inhabitants of the hill is not only explicitly stated in the story; it is also clearly implied in their name (Farkh al Ganān), which is the name of whitish pigeons living in the mountains. When mating, they make a sound which reminds the Berti of women wailing after the death. The Berti believe that these birds were originally women who went on lamenting the death of their husbands long after the funeral instead of accepting it as God's will. God was angry with them and punished them by transforming them into birds. There exists also a vague notion that the birds are descendants of the people who originally inhabited the tops and slopes of the hills. This is also the reason why the Berti do not eat them.

The word *ganān* has no meaning in itself but *farkh*, although used for both sexes in its sense of 'children' (*farkh al jidād* – domestic chickens; *farkh al hamām* – young pigeons) has a clear connotation of femininity like *awlād* (lit. sons), although also used for both sexes in its sense of 'children', has, nevertheless, clear connotations of masculinity. *Farkha* is also a female slave.

4 It is perpetuated by women and always told alongside other mythological stories, fairy tales, and humorous narratives of amusing events which happened to fictitious contemporaries.

Story-telling usually takes place in the late evening. Older boys and girls often meet at a specific place in the village to play riddles in the evening, and particularly on moonlit nights children play various games in the open space in the village, often watched by a group of women sitting in front of one of the houses, and often younger men who joined the women to joke with the younger of them. When boys and girls have exhausted their supply of riddles or when the children grow tired of their games, or the audience of watching them, they turn to some woman who is known as a good story-teller and ask her to tell stories. All present assemble around her to listen. A story-telling session can last for hours with one story following another and with people demanding to hear their favourite ones.

Less frequently a woman will tell stories in the privacy of her house. It is always the children of the house who ask her to do so but the audience consists of all the people in the house and possibly a few visiting neighbours.

Telling stories is by no means a prerogative of old women; a woman of any age can be known as a good story-teller. Men too tell stories. They do so when they are among themselves, typically when relaxing after a communal meal and especially when there are visitors around. But their stories are different from those told by women; they are usually accounts of their various travels or narratives of other events in which they were involved.

References

ARDENER, E. (1972) Belief and the Problem of Women. In J. S. LaFontaine (ed.) *The Interpretation of Ritual: Essays in Honour of A. I. Richards*. London: Tavistock Publications.
— (1975) The 'Problem' Revisited. In S. Ardener (ed.) *Perceiving Women*. London: J. M. Dent & Sons.
AUGÉ, M. (1982) *The Anthropological Circle: Symbol, Function, History*. Cambridge: Cambridge University Press.
COHEN, R. (1971) *Dominance and Defiance: A Study of Marital Instability in an Islamic Society*. Anthropological Studies No. 6 Washington, D. C.: American Anthropological Association.
CRONIN, C. (1977) Illusion and Reality in Sicily. In A. Schlegel (ed.) *Sexual Stratification*. New York; Columbia University Press.
FRIEDL, E. (1975) *Women and Men: An Anthropologist's View*. New York: Holt, Rinehart & Winston.
HOLY, L. (1983) Symbolic and Non-Symbolic Aspects of Berti space. *Man* (NS) **18**: 269–88.
LAMPHERE, L. (1974) Strategies, Cooperation and Conflict among Women in Domestic Groups. In M. Z. Rosaldo and L. Lamphere (eds) *Woman, Culture and Society*. Stanford: Stanford University Press.
LÉVI-STRAUSS, C. (1966) *The Savage Mind*. London: Weidenfeld & Nicolson (quoted from the 1972 edition).
— (1967) The Story of Asdiwal. In E. Leach (ed.) *The Structural Study of Myth and Totemism*. ASA Monograph 5. London: Tavistock.
— (1970) *The Raw and the Cooked: Introduction to a Science of Mythology I*. London: Jonathan Cape.
MALINOWSKI, B. (1922) *Argonauts of the Western Pacific*. London: Routledge & Kegan Paul.
— (1948) *Magic, Science and Religion, and Other Essays*. Boston: Beacon Press.
PAULME, D. (1963) Introduction to D. Paulme (ed.) *Women of Tropical Africa*. Berkeley: University of California Press.
RABINOW, P. (1977) *Reflections on Fieldwork in Morocco*. Berkeley: University of California Press.
ROBINSON, M. S. (1968) 'The House of Mighty Hero' or 'The House of Enough Paddy?': Some Implications of a Sinhalese myth. In E. R. Leach (ed.) *Dialectic in Practical Religion*. Cambridge Papers in Social Anthropology 5: 122–52. Cambridge: Cambridge University Press.
ROGERS, S. C. (1975) Female Forms of Power and the Myth of Male Dominance: A Model of Female/Male Interaction in Peasant Society. *American Ethnologist* **2**: 727–56.
ROSALDO, M. Z. (1974) Woman, Culture and Society: A Theoretical Overview. In M. Z. Rosaldo and L. Lamphere (eds) *Woman, Culture and Society*. Stanford: Stanford University Press.

SANDAY, P. R. (1974) Female Status in the Public Domain. In M. Z. Rosaldo and L. Lamphere (eds) *Woman, Culture and Society*. Stanford: Stanford University Press.

SMITH, M. G. (1960) *Government in Zazau*. London: Oxford University Press.

STRATHERN, M. (1972) *Women in Between: Female Roles in a Male World: Mount Hagen, New Guinea*. London: Seminar Press.

ULLRICH, H. E. (1977) Caste Differences between Brahmin and non-Brahmin women in a South Indian village. In A. Schlegel (ed.) *Sexual Stratification*. New York: Columbia University Press.

WEINER, A. B. (1976) *Women of Value, Men of Renown: New Perspectives in Trobriand Exchange*. Austin: University of Texas Press.

WILLIS, R. G. (1967) The Head and the Loins: Lévi-Strauss and Beyond. *Man* (NS) **2**: 519–34.

Jonathan Parry

10 The Brahmanical tradition and the technology of the intellect[1]

The technology of the intellect

In *The Domestication of the Savage Mind* (1977), Goody takes up and develops a thesis which he had originally outlined in a joint article with Watt (1963), and which was further elaborated in his edited collection *Literacy in Traditional Societies* (1968a). *The Domestication* was published in the year after Goody's *Production and Reproduction*, and although the two volumes deal with quite different topics, their general inspiration is extremely close. In its barest outline the argument of the latter is that there is a causal relationship between the kind of agricultural technology (plough versus hoe) and the kind of inheritance rules present in a particular society, and between these inheritance rules and the forms of kinship and marriage. *The Domestication of the Savage Mind* assigns an equally prominent place to technology – 'the technology of the intellect'. It offers a view of human development in which literacy is the crucial variable with the potential for transforming social and mental life. The present paper provides a commentary on this view in the light of material on traditional Hindu India.

Many writers have discerned a radical contrast between the modes of thought characteristic of traditional and modern society. Though Goody speaks of a continuum rather than a dichotomy, he does not deny that this fundamental difference exists but seeks to explain it in terms of literacy. For Horton (1970) a critical distinction between traditional and scientific thought is the essential scepticism of the latter. But Africans, says Goody, are no more credulous than people in the industrial West. The real contrast is rather that in the absence of literacy they can neither accumulate nor reproduce scepticism. With writing a closer scrutiny becomes possible, and hence the perception of contradictions not immediately apparent in oral discourse. Writing is also a pre-condition of syllogistic reasoning, and of logic as a formalized set of analytic procedures (1977: 11). By contrast, pre-literate societies 'are marked not so much by the absence of reflective thinking as by the proper tools for constructive rumination' (1977: 44). With the heightening of critical activity made possible by literacy goes a movement from magic to science and from myth to history (which obviously depends on written records). Historical thinking in turn favours a stress on linear as opposed to cyclical conceptions of time; while scepticism promotes science, which encourages a process of secularization (1977: 150). Literacy further permits an enlargement of political scale and more depersonalized systems of government, lends itself to more anonymous modes of transmission of knowledge, and – by recording individual innovation – promotes the growth of individualism and stimulates creativity.

Book learning, however, has its costs. It leads to a 'restriction of spontaneity' (1977: 144). For Goody, knowledge in pre-literate societies seems to be an almost infinitely plastic resource. As in the Malinowskian view of myth, it is continually manipulated to serve as a charter for current social alignments. But 'ideas communicated by literary means can never be totally absorbed like those passed on orally, because the book always remains there as a check upon the transformations that have taken place' (1968b: 216).

To my mind the striking thing about this catalogue of corollaries that Goody derives from literacy is that – as I endeavour to document below – almost none of his predictions holds unambiguously good for traditional India. In part, perhaps, the problem derives from the fact that while he clearly recognizes the wide differences between literate traditions, he nevertheless seems at times to slip into an unconscious equation between literate societies and 'cognitive modernism', and between pre-literate societies and 'cognitive traditionalism'. Horton (1982) – from whom I borrow these terms – falls into the same trap when taking stock of, and refining, his earlier argument in the light of Goody and others. By revealing differences between past and present, he argues, literacy weakens the belief that existing knowledge is legitimated by an unbroken tradition stretching back to the time of the first ancestors, and encourages a theoretical pluralism which is likely to give rise to an 'inter-theoretic competition' which is one of the critical characteristics of cognitive modernism. At its most obvious level, however, the kind of data discussed below clearly suggest that literacy is quite as compatible with a thoroughgoing cognitive conservatism as with its converse, and that this cognitive orientation displays a remarkable tenacity in a context from which inter-theoretic competition has for many centuries been by no means absent.

But Goody is not, of course, unaware of the kind of situation I describe; he himself draws explicit attention to cases of 'restricted literacy' where writing is largely confined to religious uses and where 'the Book becomes less a means to further enquiry, a step in the accumulation of knowledge, than an end in itself, the timeless depository of all knowledge' (1968b: 237). So literacy may encourage 'criticism and commentary on the one hand and the orthodoxy of the book on the other' (1977: 37).

Given this second possibility, in what sense can literacy be seen as a critical causal factor in the emergence of the syndrome of mental attributes supposedly characteristic of modern society? It is, we are told, an enabling rather than a sufficient condition. In the sense of a general precondition for – as the Neolithic Revolution was a pre-condition for the Age of Steam – his argument would surely be as unexceptionable as it would be vacuous. But it is clear that Goody intends something far stronger. What I take him to mean is that the 'liberating effects' of literacy will almost inexorably lead in the direction I have outlined *unless* a powerful set of socio-cultural conditions inhibits this development. Exactly what these conditions would be is, however, left largely unspecified although attention is drawn to the restrictive practices of a religious literati anxious to preserve their monopoly over the sources of mystical power.

Adopting such a focus we might ask why literacy failed to promote 'cognitive modernism' in the kind of context I describe. By formulating the issue in these terms, however, we immediately concede to literacy a causal role in the transformation of mental life. In the concluding paragraphs of this paper I by contrast suggest that its significance as a dynamic force is questionable. Rather than providing a positive thrust towards the kind of rationality characteristic of modern science, all we can confidently endorse is the truism that it is a necessary prerequisite for such a development.

It is perhaps only natural that academics should have a propensity to exaggerate the unique significance of book learning, and Goody is by no means the only one who is prone to do so. In their manifesto 'For a Sociology of India', Dumont and Pocock (1957) insist on the postulate that sociologically India is one. 'The very existence, and influence', they claim, 'of the traditional higher, Sanskritic, civilization demonstrates without question the unity of India. One might think that it does not only demonstrate, but actually constitutes it' (p. 9). What is implied here, then, is that the unity of India is – in part at least – a consequence of the fact that all Hindus acknowledge the authority of the same set of texts and thus subscribe to the same set of fundamental ideas and values. We are therefore dealing 'not merely with a cultural unity' as among neighbouring African tribes (1957: 10). This last proposition – that in the pre-literate world continuities between neighbouring societies do not concern fundamental values but are 'merely cultural' – is, I would argue, a kind of optical illusion and would not be borne out by systematic regional comparisons of the sort being undertaken by Andrew Strathern for Highland New Guinea (e.g. Strathern 1982), or Adam Kuper for parts of Bantu Africa (e.g. Kuper 1982). More pertinent here, however, is that a textual tradition can surely only 'constitute' an ideological unity *if* one assumes that the texts themselves display a unity of ideas and values, and that all Hindus derive the same message from the same text. But when the scriptures themselves differ on such fundamental matters as monism, theism, vegetarianism, and caste (Singer 1972: 43), and when Tilak and Aurobindo

Ghose invoke the *Bhagavad-Gita* as justification for violence in the cause of nationalism while Gandhi makes it the cornerstone of his doctrine of non-violence (Cohn 1971: 55), there is surely good reason to doubt whether either of these assumptions is valid.

In line with their stress on the unity between text and the religion as it is actually practised, Dumont and Pocock reject the Great tradition/Little tradition dichotomy, and represent the relationship between textual and popular 'levels' as one of homologous structures and the local working out of a general idea. For the villagers themselves, they say in criticism of Marriott (1955) who implies otherwise, there are not two traditions but simply one. Hinduism on the ground is not conceptually separable into different elements (see Tambiah 1970: 369). For reasons I take up in the section after next, however, my own ethnographic experience leads me to believe that the facts are on Marriott's side.

The ethnographic context

The ethnographic experience referred to, and most of the observations reported here, derive from fieldwork in the city of Benares.[2] Benares is one of the most important centres of pilgrimage in India, and is inextricably associated in the Hindu mind with death and the transcendence of death. Each year scores of old and terminally sick people come to the city in order that they may die there; thousands of corpses are brought for cremation on one of the two principal burning *ghats*, and hundreds of thousands of pilgrims bring the ashes of a deceased relative to immerse in the Ganges or make offerings to their ancestors there. But what is also central to the identity of Benares is its ancient tradition of Sanskritic learning. A number of distinct theological traditions have at one time or another been influential in the city's religious history; though it is orthodox Brahmanism which remains the dominant influence.

With a population of little over half a million, and with an adult literacy rate of around 50 per cent (*India Year Book* 1974), the city now supports three independent universities, all of which pride themselves on a strength in Sanskrit studies and/or Hindu philosophy. More directly relevant to the present discusssion are the now dwindling number of traditional *pathasalas* (or schools), devoted to transmitting under the tutelage of a Brahman *guru* a knowledge of the sacred scriptures and an ability to recite the Vedic *mantras*. For Benares and its immediate environs I have a list of 142 of these, though the total number of students receiving this type of education is probably less than the 2,000 estimated by Saraswati (1975: 19).[3]

Numerically far more significant than the small, though highly prestigious, class of Sanskrit pedagogues attached to such institutions, are the vast array of different kinds of Brahman sacred specialist who cater to the religious needs

of the pilgrims, mourners, and inhabitants of the city: Vedic chanters, Funeral
Priests, Temple-priests, Pilgrimage-priests, and so on. This sacerdotal class
provides the ritual technicians of Sanskritic Hinduism rather than its theoreticians. It is they who actually conduct the rituals prescribed by the texts, who
expound their meaning, and who in this sense mediate between the textual
tradition and the theologically untutored. Not that they could (by their own
criteria) be appropriately described as prodigies of learning. Indeed their
reputation for avarice is at least as great as their reputation for scholarship.
Though all of them are literate in the vernacular, only a small minority have
any real command of Sanskrit. Though they learn to read, they do not on the
whole learn by reading. The majority rely principally for their religious
knowledge on the oral tradition of their communities, and secondarily on the
religious pamphlets and digests in Hindi which are sold throughout the city.
The Sanskrit *mantras* they recite have been learned by rote; they have little
idea of their 'real' meaning, and are often reduced to inaudible mumbling or
brazening it out with gobbledygook in the confident expectation that their
patrons will never know the difference. Though my most intimate contacts in
Benares are with priests rather than with scholars or laymen, I would claim
that the attitudes towards scriptural learning which I describe in what follows
are common to an extremely wide segment of the population.

The literate tradition of the Benarasi Brahman

For all my informants – whether priests, ascetics, or ordinary householders –
there is a sharp distinction, which brings me back to the Dumont-Pocock
criticism of Marriott, between the *shastrik* (or scriptural) and the *laukik* (or
popular). Belief and practice are visualized as a composite of both. The
shastrik elements are *pramanik* ('proven'), eternally valid and binding on all
Hindus, and in their interpretation the Brahman is pre-eminent. By contrast,
the *laukik* is ephemeral, a mere matter of local usage to be discarded if it
offends against contemporary canons of good sense, and here it is often the
women who are regarded as the repositories of tradition. Admittedly this
shastrik/laukik division is itself derived from the *shastrik* domain; but the fact
remains that it is internalized by many illiterate Hindus who clearly represent
their religious universe as composed of elements taken from two conceptually
separable traditions.

Debate on theological issues, or on correct ritual practice, always starts
from this distinction. If it can be established that a particular item is *shastrik*,
then there's an end of the matter, it is unquestionably authoritative. In 1981,
for example, a bitter controversy developed over whether to continue the
custom of cremating the corpses of the affluent next to the footprints left by
Lord Vishnu as he sat performing the austerities by which he created the
world at the beginning of time (see Parry 1981). Considerable financial

interests were generally held to be at the root of the matter. The debate – to which many column inches of the local press were devoted – was however couched entirely in terms of whether the practice was textually sanctioned.

While everybody agrees that the *laukik/shastrik* distinction is of fundamental significance, there is – as this last example shows – no general consensus on what belongs to which category. Moreover, some practices which in fact have no backing at all in the ancient texts (for example, the 50-mile circumambulatory pilgrimage of the city) are almost universally believed to be scriptural and are rated as *shastrik*, while others (like animal sacrifice) which do indeed have a respectable textual pedigree are generally regarded as merely *laukik*. The central point that I want to stress, however, is that that which is *believed* to be textual is – at least in principle – beyond debate, while that which belongs to the oral tradition is not. At the risk of labouring the point, the *textual* tradition is here accorded an ideological immunity to sceptical scrutiny, while the oral tradition is the focus of continual critical evaluation.

The equation I imply between the *shastrik* and the literate, and between the *laukik* and the oral is, however, only a first approximation. More precisely, the *shastrik* is that which is sanctioned – or held to be sanctioned – by the ancient Sanskrit texts[4] (a category which will itself require qualification in due course). Both their age and their language are crucial aspects of their authority.

Sanskrit is *deva-vani*, 'the speech of the gods'. Since many of the sacred texts purport to be a transcription of divine conversation or instruction, their original and most authoritative form is clearly Sanskrit. Sanskrit is far more than a language. It is a badge of civilization. Indeed the word itself means 'cultured' or 'refined'. When my Benares friends say – as they often do – that Europeans have no *sanskriti*, they are not merely referring to a linguistic deficiency but to the well-known fact that Europeans fornicate like dogs, never know who their fathers are, and have no religion and philosophy to speak of. In short, they are without culture – Sanskrit merely being the vehicle for *sanskriti*. It is only in this light that one can begin to appreciate the cultural appositeness of M. N. Srinivas's choice of the label 'sanskritization' for the process by which the lower castes come to take over the customs and style of life of their superiors. Sanskritization is something far more than is suggested by the dry sociological jargon 'reference group behaviour'. It took a Brahman anthropologist to coin a term which so perfectly captures the idea that it is above all a process of refinement and civilization (see van Buitenen 1966: 34).

The *shastras*, then, are written in the language of the gods and even at their dictation. Consistent with this, they are the repositories of all authentic knowledge. Knowledge, then, is not something to be *discovered*, as in the western scientific tradition, but something to be *recovered* from the texts (van Buitenen 1966: 35). The absolute truth has already been revealed and is there for man to appropriate if only he can penetrate their meaning. Sanskrit thus provides an essential handle on eternally valid knowledge.

But what kind of knowledge is that? The first thing to be said is that not all knowledge is equally worth while. One *aspect* of my informants' attitudes – which is strongly marked in the tradition at large – is a comparative devaluation of knowledge of the empirical world, which is after all the product of illusion (*maya*) and created by the divine play of the gods (*lila*). During my Benares fieldwork I was continually being upbraided for wasting my time with meaningless enquiries of a sociological character. I have no doubt that such admonishment was generally prompted by a certain uneasiness about what I might discover; but the reproach reflected and appealed to a deeply rooted cultural value that nothing of lasting worth is to be learnt from such matters. Real knowledge is knowledge of a metaphysical truth which liberates the soul from the endless cycle of existence – a knowledge which is revealed in the texts but which is generally thought to be obtained only by years of submission to a rigorous ascetic discipline. The theological premise that underlies such attitudes is that suffering and evil are not – as in mainstream Christianity – the consequence of original sin, but rather of ignorance of this truth. The obvious parallel is with the Christianity of the Gnostic Gospels (Pagels 1979). In both cases not only is man's problem located in ignorance, but the answer is to be found *within* the individual, who having found it becomes one with God – himself a Christ or a Siva.

But this is only one side of the picture. While what is of permanent value is knowledge which leads out of the world, the scriptures also provide the keys to an understanding by which it may be mastered while in it. They contain, that is, instructions of a pre-eminently practical kind which, properly understood, are the source of a fabulous power – a power which is conferred on those who travel the path which leads to liberation, but which must be renounced if liberation is to be obtained (though it is hard to suppress the suspicion that for a majority the real attraction is the journey rather than the destination). Continual play is made between the term *shastra* (i.e. the texts) and *shastr* (a weapon) – the *shastras* being the most powerful weapons at man's command. In Benares I have often been told – and I have heard variants of the same story elsewhere – that Max Muller stole chunks of the *Sama-veda* from India, and it was by studying these that German scientists were able to develop the atom bomb. The *rishis*, or ancient sages, not only knew all about nuclear fission, but as (what we would call) mythology testifies, they also had supersonic aeroplanes and guided missiles. Of a piece with such claims is the commonly made assertion that every ritual detail prescribed by the texts has some justification or other in terms of modern science, and if this scientific rationality remains obscure that is only because of the rudimentary state of our present knowledge. In reality, then, the *shastras* are a highly developed science which the *rishis* presented as religion (*dharma*) since they knew full well that in the degenerate times to come the wisdom they embodied would not be properly understood and could only survive as blind faith.

It is of course tempting to see in all this a kind of defensive reaction to the encounter with cosmopolitan science and British imperialism. Indeed my example of the stolen fragments of the *Sama-veda* immediately recalls the widespread Melanesian belief that the Europeans had excised various pages from the Bible in order to prevent them from obtaining cargo. I do not doubt that there is an element of this kind in what I have described, though it seems to me that there is more to it than that, and that the interpretation of religious texts as technical know-how is not the departure it might at first sight appear. The essential point is that in traditional Indian thought there is no conceptual divide between 'religious' and 'scientific' knowledge. Without any sense of incongruity the texts known as Puranas contain terrifying accounts of the fate of the souls of sinners, sandwiched between sections on – say – mineralogy and medicine. Again, in modern Hindi the term *shastra* elides what we would separate. The *shastras* are the sacred texts, but sociology is *samaj-shastra* – where the word has become a suffix which is used very much like the suffix '-ology' in our language, and conveys the idea of a theoretical discipline. A standard Hindi–English dictionary lists the following equivalents: 'scripture(s), a religious or scientific treatise, a composition of divine or secular authority, science. . . '.[5] The term thus broadly corresponds to the original meaning of the English word 'science' as knowledge in general.

While everything that I have said so far might seem to imply that the written is always privileged over the oral, it is important to stress that this written tradition is itself held to be based (at least in the case of certain texts) on an originally *spoken* revelation made by the gods, and to be preserved largely by oral transmission; and further that the most ancient and authoritative texts – the Vedas – are conventionally classified as *sruti*, that which is 'heard' (as opposed to *smriti* which is 'remembered'). Indeed, Brahman culture is very much a culture of the spoken word, and a desire to dominate verbally, to render others speechless by the force of one's own speech and erudition, is a striking aspect of the ethos of the Benarasi Brahman. It is institutionalized in the *shastrarth* – a kind of formalized verbal battle over the interpretation of the texts.

Given this premium on the spoken word, my earlier emphasis on the prestige of the written text may seem paradoxical. This apparent contradiction, I would argue, is more properly seen as a disjunction between principle and practice. While in theory oral transmission has ideological pre-eminence, in fact such knowledge may be suspect for its authority rests on that of its repositories. In these debased times human memory has supposedly become so fallible, and the pedagogical tradition of the Brahmans so enfeebled and corrupted, that the authenticity of knowledge transmitted by purely oral means can no longer be automatically accepted as axiomatic. Instead of a mere prop to memory, a supplement to the instruction of a teacher, the written text may now be regarded as a more reliable guide to an ancient wisdom once more fully apprehended through personalized transmission.

While Goody is clearly correct to note that literacy provides the potential for more anonymous modes of communicating knowledge, the Brahmanical tradition has gone as far as it possibly can to evade this possibility. It is uncertain when the Vedas were actually composed, or even when they were first written down. But what is generally agreed by Indologists (e.g. Winternitz 1927: 63; Staal 1961: 15) is that many centuries separated the two things, and that it was not for want of literacy that they were not written down earlier. Though Goody (in press) has recently challenged this claim in proposing that 'the role of writing in the composition or transcription of the Vedas must remain a serious possibility from the historical point of view', there can be no question about the consistent hostility of Brahmanical thought to the graphic reproduction of the Veda. Indeed some of the later texts condemn to hell those who reduce the Veda to writing (Kane 1976: 2: 349). It should be (and still is) preserved by direct transmission from teacher to pupil, a process involving the endless repetition of each verse until it has been completely mastered and an elaborate system of mnemonic checks and phonetic rules (*vyasa siksa*) designed to ensure the exact replication of the proper sound.

Rather than the essential character of oral discourse being modified by intellectual procedures inseparable from literacy, as Goody predicts for literate cultures, it would be nearer the mark to say that in traditional India it was literary expression which was subordinated to the demands of oral transmission, for much of the sacred literature was composed in a form and with a redundancy which was clearly intended to facilitate memorization and faithful replication.

A very high proportion of the Sanskrit corpus is written in verse rather than prose, and this applies to the texts on medicine, astronomy, and architecture, and to historical and biographical works, as much as to those which deal with such purely 'ritualistic' topics as sacrifice (Winternitz 1927: 3). Goody passes over the possible relevance of the distinction between prose and verse for his argument about the association between literacy and cognitive modernism. Its significance is, however, suggested by Merton's (1978: 19) observation that in seventeenth-century England the revolution in science went along with a marked shift of interest from poetry to prose – both developments revealing an increasing preoccupation with the exposition and description of empirical phenomena.

If verse is better suited than prose to the faithful memorization of the text and its exact verbal replication, then one might perhaps see these preoccupations as being in turn the typical product of a scribal (as opposed to a print) technology. In a scribal culture, the argument would go, much knowledge continually sinks into the sand as manuscripts disappear and as texts progressively 'drift' away from their original, and the overriding preoccupation tends therefore to be with the retention of what is already known. Books are scarce, their contents imparted to most only because they are read aloud, and memorization retains a significance it does not possess in a print culture where books are readily available (see Ong 1982: 119; Hirst and Woolley 1982: 36–8)

In India however – as in many other traditional cultures – this emphasis on the precise reproduction of the text has been motivated more by a concern with the precise reproduction of sound than by a concern with the retention of the meaning it conveys. The words in themselves have power once they are vocalized. For this power to become manifest they must be pronounced with precision and exactly the right inflection. Wrongly accentuated they may have an effect opposite to the one intended (see Kane 1976: 2: 347). I can best illustrate the importance of pronunciation by the case of a south Indian Brahman I know who earns his living performing mortuary rituals on Benares's principal cremation ground. He claims to have memorized three of the Vedas and to have learned to recite them with complete accuracy. Since Presidents Nixon and Ford short-sightedly overlooked his letters offering to put this remarkable skill at their disposal, he wishes me to make it known that he would be prepared to consider a post in the University of London, and that his appointment should be treated as a matter of urgency since it is only a question of time before he loses the full set of teeth essential for a flawless recitation. Seen in the light of all this, it is clearly irrelevant whether the written word exists in printed or manuscript form. In either case the memorization of its proper verbal manifestation remains an equally insistent need; and one which cannot therefore be wholly accounted for by the technical deficiencies of a scribal mode of communication.

The most powerful words of all are those of the Vedic *mantras* which are recited as an indispensable part of every major ritual and are what makes it efficacious. The *mantra* is not a prayer but a kind of sound form of the deity it embodies. More than a supplication it is a means of coercion.[6] By *japa* – the repeated muttering of Vedic passages – the Brahman chanter may achieve for his client success in litigation, the restoration of good health or the indefinite postponement of death – the more ambitious the project the larger the number of repetitions required.[7] The content of these passages is not, however, understood. Those ritual specialists who are competent in classical Sanskrit are quite unable to comprehend the archaic language of the Veda. Even amongst the traditional *scholarly* community of the city, and despite persistent enquiry, I experienced enormous difficulty in finding a Pandit who could confidently render any of the Vedic *mantras* used in the mortuary rituals into Hindi.

While all twice-born castes have in theory the right to study the Veda, it is only the Brahmans who are authorized to teach it. The stress on oral transmission and correct pronunciation clearly ensures that their indispensability in this role remains unthreatened by the potential literacy provides for circumventing pedagogical control by private study. Without the guidance of a *guru*, book learning is said to be without value and even an obstacle to the acquisition of knowledge (see Kane 1976: 2: 322, 349).

Power is with the word, and the word is with the Brahman; or – as my informants endlessly quoted – 'the gods control the world; *mantras* control the gods and the Brahmans control the *mantras*'. It was, after all, the Brahman who at the beginning of time emerged from the *mouth* of the sacrificial body of primeval man, while the progenitors of successively lower *varnas* emerged from successively lower parts of his body. It is they who are descended from the ancient *rishis* who originally received the divine revelation and expounded it for posterity. But above all it is the Brahman's purity that qualifies him for Vedic study – which must be suspended if either teacher or pupil is afflicted by the pollution of birth or death,[8] or if the place of study is in any way rendered impure.

Ideologically, Brahmanical pre-eminence is inseparable from their learning. The respectable Brahman is a scholar and a teacher rather than a priest. The priesthood is, as I have discussed at length elsewhere, regarded with equivocation since priests must necessarily accept the gifts (*dana*) of their patrons if the ritual is to work, but these gifts embody the sins of the donor (Parry 1980). Though in practice seen as an impossible ideal, the theory is that they can 'digest' these sins by the meticulous performance of certain rites and by passing on the gifts they have received, with increment, to a number of other Brahmans. The relevance of this here is that the transactional code it implies also obtains for learning. Indeed Stevenson (1920: 228) reports that the Brahman's teaching is assimilated to the category of gift (*dana*), and it is therefore not surprising that it should be governed by the same rules. These state that what the Brahman takes in, he must at all costs disgorge again, for if he fails to keep in circulation what he has received he will be required to pay the direst penalties in this and future lives. Here we are clearly in a quite different universe from those ideologies – like that of the Hindu Tantric or the New Guinea Baktaman (Barth 1975) – where the most powerful knowledge is the most highly secret and where access to it is as narrowly restricted as possible. Barring the Shudra – whose ears are to be filled with mercury if he hears the Veda – the Brahman's knowledge is theoretically something to be disseminated.

The specialists generally assert that over the centuries which separated their original composition from their commitment to writing, the Vedas were transmitted without significant alteration; and clearly this claim does not altogether square with Goody's characterization of oral knowledge as a highly volatile and malleable resource. The supposition of faithful oral transmission has recently – though in my view unconvincingly – been contested by Goody (in press) and Ong (1982: 65–6).[9] In any event the Veda must in certain respects be regarded as a special case. But attention has also often been drawn (e.g. Shulman 1980: 11) to the remarkable continuity between many classical myths and those of the contemporary village, where the presumption is that their transmission has been almost exclusively oral. Again, Wadley (1975) remarks on the lack of variation in the (unwritten) non-Sanskritic dialect '*mantras*' employed by the exorcists of Karimpur over the forty-year period since the Wisers' fieldwork; and Smith (1977) persuasively argues that the Pabuji epic of Rajasthan does not conform to Lord's findings for Yugoslavia, but is an example of an oral 'text' performed without improvisation or significant deviation from an original composition. The difference between the two traditions, he suggests, is related to the liturgical role of the Rajasthani epic; a suggestion which would receive support from Wadley's evidence (1978) that while in the case of those religious stories classed as *kissa* there is legitimate scope for a personal rendering, in the case of those which are classed as *katha* and which are distinguished by being recited within a *ritual* frame, the emphasis is on the careful reproduction of a set text. What seems clear at any rate is that oral knowledge of this kind may display a surprising resilience to change over long periods of time (see Ong 1982: 62–3).

Of more immediate interest here, however, is the other side of Goody's contrast – the relative immutability of knowledge which he associates with a literate tradition by contrast with an oral one, and which he sees as imposing a 'restriction on spontaneity'. On the contrary, I would like to emphasize its mutability, and its malleability to the requirements of practical life.

The Vedas, for example, are commonly cited as being the ultimate authority on matters of moral and religious duty (*dharma*). Yet the paradox is that these ritualistic texts do not contain any 'positive injunctions that could be used directly as rules of conduct' (Heesterman 1978: 81). In fact, to follow Heesterman's argument, their lack of any real bearing on the practical world is essential to their inviolability. Since they are not bound to the social world they are immune to the corrosive effects of the changes it undergoes. Given that the Vedas are the ultimate authority on matters they do not pronounce upon, the common recourse is to the 'transcendent vision', as Heesterman puts it, 'of a human authority' – a sage or a *guru*. But how is one to judge *his* credentials? The conventional answer is in terms of his knowledge of the scriptural revelation. It is his knowledge of texts that have nothing to say about *dharma* that authorizes him to rule on it. The way would seem to be open for him to say what he likes.

The content of the Veda is fixed; but its direct application to practical life is minimal. I now turn to a much later text where this situation is reversed. The *Garuda Purana* is one of the 18 so-called *Mahapuranas*, or Great *Puranas*, which were all supposedly composed by the legendary sage Vyasa at the beginning of the *Kali Yuga*,[10] the Black Age of historical time in which we actually live and which is the last and most degenerate of the four epochs of the world cycle. The text is one to which my informants continually refer; is regarded as the final word on matters relating to death, mourning, and the conduct of mortuary rituals; and it is with these matters that their version is exclusively concerned. During mourning it is read daily in the house of the deceased by a Brahman priest who is called in specially for this purpose.

An English translation of the *Garuda Purana* by an eminent Brahman Pandit has also been published from Benares. What is striking, however, is that virtually the only thing that the two versions have in common is the claim that unsurpassable benefits accrue to those who hear them, and the exhortation to give liberally to the Brahman who recites them. While the one deals only with matters related to death, the other has little to say on this topic, but ranges over a diffuse set of other subjects from aphrodisiacs to the medical treatment of horses. The translator of this version (1968: iii–iv) acknowledges the existence of the first as one of the parts, or *khandas*, of which the work has often been held to consist. But he goes on to say that 'it requires nothing more than average intellect to detect that (it) . . . is manifestly an interpolation . . . bad in reason and rhetoric'. This 'spurious portion' has been expunged in an attempt to restore the text to its original form. We therefore have at least two entirely different versions of the same work. According to a recent scholarly study, however, it is very doubtful whether either of them bears much relationship to the ancient texts of the same name, since the contents of none of the existing versions conform to what is said about the *Garuda Purana* in other better authenticated *Puranas* (Gangadharan 1971: 120, 124). It is, then, almost as if the *Garuda Purana* is an empty box into which an enormous range of possible contents might be poured by selecting from a vast array of manuscript sources of greater or lesser antiquity and authenticity.

A critical edition of the *Garuda Purana* is about to be prepared by the Kashi Raj Trust, a scholarly foundation set up and funded by the Maharaja of Benares to promote and disseminate knowledge of the Hindu texts. Amongst its most important projects is the publication of 'authorized' versions of each of the *Puranas*, restored as nearly as possible to their original form by 'scientific' principles of textual scholarship imported from the West. Manuscripts of the *Purana* in hand are collected from all over India, and are collated verse by verse. In the case of the *Garuda Purana*, for example, manuscripts have been obtained from as far afield as Kathmandu and Tamilnadu, Jammu and Calcutta. The oldest of these is probably no earlier than the beginning of the seventeenth century, and not one of them contains all of the three *khandas* (parts) of which the work is traditionally supposed to comprise. Variation within each *khanda* is itself enormous; and there are three quite different versions of the *preta-kalpa* – the part which relates to death and which my priestly informants unsuspectingly believe to be the complete and invariant work. In order to arrive at an authoritative text, the Trust's Pandits select the 'best' version of each passage, so that the new edition is a composite put together from quite different sources. In choosing between variants one of the rules applied is that the more impenetrable the verse the more authentic it is likely to be – clarity suggesting the intrusive hand and crude mind of later copyists. I need hardly say that the result of this procedure is likely to be an obscurity that lends itself to rival interpretations and requires a Brahman scholar for its elucidation.

Following Biardeau (1968), the more interesting point however is that what has been borrowed is a method which was developed in order to reconstruct, out of relatively minor variations between texts, the original written text of the author. But in the case of the *Puranas* it is very doubtful that there ever was a single original written text – the probability being that we are dealing with a number of quite different recensions which evolved out of the oral traditions of the regions from which each comes. What we have, then, is an attempt to restore something which probably never existed. Yet for the Brahman Pandits it is a matter of faith that it did exist, and that it was actually composed by Vyasa whom they regard as a historical individual rather than as a generalized symbol of tradition. In other words, the whole apparatus of the critical edition is directed – as Biardeau notes – to the essentially religious purpose of recovering as nearly as possible the divine inspiration of a purely mythical character. The objective result, however, is a completely new recension of the work.

As the Pandits are apt to see it, authentic fragments of Vyasa's revelation may have been preserved in the oral tradition as well as in the manuscript sources, and they therefore regard it as perfectly legitimate to supplement the latter from their own knowledge of the tradition as it was handed down to them. Here we can recall the experience of the great Sanskritist, Georg Buhler, who was presented with a copy of the *Nilamatapurana* by the Maharaja of Kashmir. When Buhler later visited Kashmir and checked the originals he discovered that the beginning of his text was the copyist's own insertion. Yet all the Pandits with whom he spoke rated his version as the best (Rocher 1983). Today, one of the most renowned Puranic scholars in Benares is quite forthright in the view that a new edition or translation of a text should be an original work incorporating details known to the Pandit but somehow missing from his sources. The implication here is clearly that the 'text' is not conceptualized as a purely literary document. Its 'authentic version' is rather an original and sacred revelation, the recovery of which may require recourse to *both* written and oral sources (the authenticity of the latter – if not also of the former – being validated only by the prestige and authority of its Brahman repositories).

Although everybody is aware that there are eighteen 'Great' *Puranas*, even amongst scholars there is no complete unanimity on which they are. Dozens of other works are also rated as *Puranas*, though not in the major league. More generally, the canon of sacred literature is by no means closed. Shulman (1980: 37–9) refers to a fascinating account written by a disciple of the nineteenth-century Tamil scholar Minatcicuntaram Pillai, who ran what Shulman appositely describes as a 'Purana-industry'. Commissioned by a wealthy patron, he would search out old manuscripts on the deity or shrine for whose glorification he was asked to work, make prose versions of any relevant mythology, and visit the temple itself. He then composed orally and at great speed while one of his pupils recorded his words. On one occasion he is reported as having reeled off 50 verses without preparation or hesitation. Clearly the style of composition was highly formulaic – and in this respect at least invites comparison with the bardic tradition which produced the *Odyssey* and *Iliad*. The obvious but significant difference, however, is that while Homer belonged to a pre-literate culture, not only did Minatcicuntaram Pillai belong to a literate one, he was also himself a man of letters. Once more, then, a pattern purportedly characteristic of oral cultures is seen to persist in a highly literate one. More germane to my present point, however, is that while the precise provenance of these particular texts is known, it is not hard to imagine that similar compositions of fairly recent date have in a relatively short space of time acquired an antiquity which links them with the direct inspiration of Vyasa at the beginning of the present world epoch.

Although in principle superior authority always resides with the most ancient texts, and although this might seem to promote an extreme religious conservatism, the notion of time as progressive degeneration in fact allows considerable scope for manoeuvre. Practices – like animal sacrifice and asceticism – which were appropriate in the Age of Truth at the beginning of time are no longer suitable to man's degraded nature in the Black Age. It is in precisely these terms that the Puranic texts often claim their equality with, or sometimes even their superiority to, the Veda (Kane 1977: 5: II: 914; Bonazzoli 1983). On the one hand they go out of their way to borrow its authority by presenting themselves as a kind of primer on the original revelation which the gods have provided out of compassion for the impoverished intellect of modern man. But they may on the other hand claim a pre-eminence in the degraded conditions of the present, and can justify quite radical innovation by reference to the exigencies of the Age (see Srinivasen 1980). The authority of the Veda is acknowledged as supreme, though Vedic precepts must perforce be modified in an epoch so debased.

One device by which the Puranic texts may be assimilated to Vedic revelation is by collapsing their mythological composers into one. The *Kashi Khanda*, which is a eulogy of Benares (and which probably dates from around the fourteenth century AD), opens with an account of how it came down to us from the gods. It is told here by Vyasa to the reciter (Sut) as it was told by the god Kartik to the sage Agastya, as Kartik himself heard it recounted to the goddess Parvati by his father Siva. What is obvious is that this elaborate pedigree is intended to establish a direct line of oral transmission from Siva to the reciter. But what is also happening here is that the *Kashi Khanda* is being equated with the *Rg-Veda*, the oldest of the Vedic texts. Agastya and his wife (Lopamudra) were the first human beings to hear it, just as in an earlier incarnation they are sometimes said to have been the first to receive the revelation of the *Rg-Veda*. In relation to Goody the more general point, however, is that the individuality of those who actually did compose these works must at all costs be suppressed since the authority of the text relies on establishing its direct transmission from the gods to a mythical sage who is credited with its preservation for posterity. So far from perpetuating individual achievement, the object here is to efface it. It is clearly not only oral communication which has a propensity to 'swallow up' the creative product of the individual 'in a body of transmitted custom' (Goody 1977: 27).

What this example might also alert us to is that the texts not only purvey a vision of time as progressive degeneration, but also as endlessly repeating itself. If it moves downwards it does so in spirals regularly returning to the same point, only lower down. In Puranic mythology, for example, the same characters keep reappearing in different incarnations, and re-enacting more or less the same events. Indeed, as my informants would appear to see it, these events continue to recur in the present. For example, the English – as I am ceaselessly reminded – are the descendants of Ravana, one of the main protagonists in the epic *Ramayana*. Ravana was the demon king of Lanka, the lustful abductor of the goddess Sita and a fallen Brahman whose knowledge gave him fantastic power. His wife, Mandodari, bore him a son at an astrologically disastrous moment. The boy was set to drift on the sea and was carried by the current to England, which is now populated by his descendants. In her next incarnation Mandodari, the mother, crops up again as Queen Victoria. In a similar vein I have several times been told that Mrs Gandhi was a reincarnation of the regenerate demoness Trijata, who befriended Sita in Lanka; and that the Americans are the descendants of Raja Bali – the explanation for which is perhaps provided by the fact his mythological comeuppance was the consequence of his interested and vainglorious donations. I cite all this not so much for its perspicacity about international relations, but to establish the point that the sacred texts purvey a model of time which is directly carried over into perceptions of present-day reality. There is, it seems to me, at least as good a case to be made for the argument that in traditional India literacy has promoted a cyclical conception of time, as for Goody's claim that it encourages a durational notion.

More generally, modern communications are – in the medium term at least – just as likely to reinforce 'traditional' religious values, to lend a helping hand to the 'civilizing' process of Sanskritization, as to contribute to a process of secularization. With the coming of the railways one of the most likely long-distance journeys for many a rural peasant is a pilgrimage; and with literacy and printing in the vernacular he is as likely to pick up a book or a pamphlet on a religious theme as one which promotes a secular 'disenchantment' of the world. Wadley (1978) reports, for example, that apart from schoolbooks, the only books which find their way to Karimpur are religious works published in the vernacular.

Another angle on the extent to which the literate tradition moulds, or constrains, knowledge would be to look at the way in which some of its key concepts are actually interpreted by the actors. The terms *moksha* and *mukti* mean 'liberation', which is conventionally described as the highest goal of human existence.The religious pre-eminence of Benares is associated with the fact that all who die there are held to achieve this goal. But the paradox is that nobody seems to be agreed on what exactly it is. The commonest view is that it is a 'cessation of coming and going' – that is, of rebirth. You no longer 'have to bear the pain of the womb', or have 'to wander between the 840,000 kinds of life form'. But some informants interpreted this as an extinction of the individual soul, which 'is absorbed into the universal Spirit as water mixes with water', while others took it to imply a perpetual and sybaritic residence in heaven. While either of these possibilities might find textual sanction, many people take the definitely unscriptural line that 'liberation' is here to be understood as the promise of a happy and prosperous rebirth (see Parry 1981).

It may at first sight appear tempting to see this as part of the process of 'parochialization' whereby 'the essentially unlearned and non-literate nature of the little tradition obstructs the direct transmission or spread of elements downward from great (tradition) to little' (Marriott 1961: 204). As the thoughts of the literati filter through to the masses their original meaning is diluted and transformed. The problem, however, is that the informants who interpreted the doctrine that 'death in Benares is liberation' in terms of a privileged rebirth included a number of sacred specialists, and I was as likely to get the doctrinally orthodox view from an illiterate pilgrim as from a professional priest. While I do not wish to discount the very real possibility of sheer ignorance of the *Shastric* tradition amongst the priesthood, I am inclined to look for the explanation of such variation as much in the con-tradictions inherent within textual Hinduism as in the adulterating influence of the so-called 'little tradition'. That is, the reason why some informants flatly rejected the claim that all who die in Benares are released from the cycle of rebirths may stem in part from the perceived inconsistency between this doctrine and other scripturally sanctioned beliefs – from a belief, for example, that the only way to escape the world is to renounce it.

With regard to matters of belief the kind of variation I have described is characteristic. But with regard to ritual practice – even allowing for the self-acknowledged incompetence of many of the priests and the surreptitious editing in which they indulge if the rewards look unpromising – there is much greater standardization. Unless he knows it by heart the priest more or less follows a printed manual (*paddhati*). But the manuals tell him only what to do and say, not what it means; and exegesis of the ritual is often highly discrepant. We are back, then, to my metaphor of the empty box into which quite different sets of contents can be put.

This contrast between the variability of belief and the constancy of ritual form is, however, far from absolute. For a start there are quite significant differences of form between, for example, the mortuary rituals laid down in the different manuals followed by the Maithila community of Benares, the South Indians and the indigeneous population of the city. The latter generally follow a *paddhati* known as the *Preta Manjari*. Even here the printed editions vary considerably not only in the number of errors which have crept into the Sanskrit text but also in length – the most extensive containing many details omitted from the shortest.

Moreover at least some of the priests creatively elaborate on what is laid down in the standard manual. A South Indian funerary priest once told me that when a woman of one of his client families dies in childbirth her corpse must be purified by bathing it 108 times before it is fit to be cremated. Intrigued by this information, I asked a large number of north Indian priests what they would do in such circumstances, and was consistently assured that no special rituals were required. One of these was my friend Sita Maharaj, with whom I discussed the matter at length, and to whom I told what I had heard from my south Indian informant. On visiting the cremation ground some weeks later I was intrigued to find Sita Maharaj presiding over the 108 purificatory baths of a female corpse. He had eventually tracked it down in an old book, he claimed, and had decided to adopt it into his repertoire. Incidentally his brother, Ram Maharaj, has often groused to me about Sita's insistence on doing things according to his own interpretation of the Shastras, even if it annoys their clients.

'But Ram Maharaj is not Sita. I do what they want. In my whole life I have only performed two or three *sraddhas* (mortuary rites) according to the *Shastras*. I emphasise *lokachar* (the popular tradition). What the women of the family say, that's the truth. Blowing our conch shells, we Brahmans throw dust in people's eyes.'

I conclude, then, that the 'restriction on spontaneity' imposed by reducing knowledge to a written form is in fact rather minimal. I have also suggested that in the context I have been discussing the written form – so far from promoting scepticism – provides a certain immunity against it; that the potential that literacy provides for the anonymous transmission of knowledge and the recording of individual innovation is evaded, and that textual knowledge is intimately bound up with the magical power of words and the pursuit of a metaphysical truth which is likely to inhibit any trend towards a more 'rational' scientific outlook. There is at least as much evidence to suggest that literacy promotes Sanskritization as secularization, and cyclical as against durational notions of time.

Literacy and 'cognitive modernism'

If we start from the (questionable) premise that literacy plays a crucial causative role in the transformation from 'cognitive traditionalism' to 'modernism', then the next obvious step is to ask why in some cases this 'take-off' apparently aborts. Why, in other words, do some literate societies (or part-societies) fail to realize its full potential?

One possible answer here would be in terms of the insufficient development of the technology of the intellect in the pre-print world, for in much of the recent literature it is the development of printing, rather than the development of literacy, which is seen as providing the crucial impetus for a revolution in human thought processes. Indeed it is striking that Eisenstein (1969, 1981, 1983) attributes to print almost exactly the same range of cognitive 'advances' as Goody attributes to literacy. Viewed from this perspective the crucial break is not that between pre-literate and literate, but that between scribal and print cultures.

In the former, texts not only have a tendency to 'drift' cumulatively away from their original source as they pass through the hands of generations of copyists, but many of them are lost or destroyed completely. Knowledge rests on a precarious foundation, and most of it is accessible only to the wandering scholar. In such a context the preoccupation is with retrieving what is already known; with recovering the wisdom of the ancients rather than with discovering something new. Before print it was in fact almost impossible to know whether a discovery was new. By vastly increasing the sheer quantity of knowledge available, print promoted a change in its qualitative character. Systematic cross-referencing became possible, thereby enhancing the likelihood of sceptical scrutiny and allowing for new intellectual combinations. What was known to the ancient world could now be established, could be found wanting and could provide the basis for a cumulative advance. In a scribal culture, by contrast, 'there could be no systematic forward movement, no accumulation of stepping stones enabling a new generation to begin where the prior one had left off' (Eisenstein 1969: 65). Associated with the development of print goes the shift from magic to science, and the growth of individualism. It was print technology that gave birth to the notion of intellectual property rights ('an absurdity . . . where every book copied is a minor victory over ignorance and wastage' (Hirst and Woolley 1982: 41)); 'which encouraged publishers to advertise authors and authors to advertise themselves' (Eisenstein 1969: 58), and which recorded individual achievement in a form and on a scale hitherto unknown. The transmission of knowledge became a more anonymous process, which allowed for the auto-didact. But in a scribal culture books remain relatively rare items, and most people are acquainted with their contents only by hearing them read aloud. As a result they tend to take the form of compendia covering a wide range of diffuse topics, and 'oral performance sets its demands on composition' (Hirst and Woolley 1982: 36). It was, in short, 'the shift from script to print (which) revolutionised Western culture', and which effected 'a shift in human consciousness' (Eisenstein 1969: 19, 56). Before print, literary products had a restricted circulation, and it is this simple fact that gave rise to the cognitive syndrome associated with 'restricted literacy'.

It might, in other words, be plausibly argued that many of the features I have described for traditional India are common to the pre-print world in general, and are a direct consequence of the technological deficiencies in a scribal mode of communication. Even such highly particularized cultural notions as the idea that knowledge is (or is like) a 'gift' which must be circulated if it is not to destroy its possessor, might be seen in terms of the necessary preoccupation of such a culture with the problem of preserving existing knowledge.

While the argument of the previous paragraph has a certain force, the causal proposition that printing promotes a spirit of sceptical scientific enquiry, a weakening of confidence in old theories and the development of new intellectual paradigms obviously presuppose a specific institutional context. If in early modern Europe access to the new means of communication had been monopolized by priests and rulers, and denied to 'free-wheeling urban entrepreneurs', then – as Eisenstein (1983: 273) herself explicitly acknowledges – the picture would have been significantly different. Far from being an instrument of intellectual liberation, under such conditions the printing press is far more likely to be an instrument of domination used to entrench the ruling paradigms. Moreover, the process of feedback from readers to publishers and authors which – on Eisenstein's showing – provided an important source of new information and facilitated a cumulative advance of knowledge in the early era of print, is clearly likely to occur only in a context where the submissions of the lay public are considered worthy of serious attention, and where the empirical knowledge they supply is highly valued. In short, the 'printing revolution' was revolutionary only because it was associated with a much wider 'democratization of society and learning' that was already under way. In a different institutional context (as for example in China and Korea) the implications of print technology were quite different (see Eisenstein 1983: 273); and the development of this technology is therefore manifestly insufficient to account for the 'great transformation' of mental life.

It has often been argued that the scientific revolution which took place in Western Europe in the sixteenth and seventeenth centuries was positively promoted by the religious climate created by the Reformation. All believers with the capacity to do so now had

> 'the right, and even the duty. . . to study Scripture without depending on the authority of tradition and hierarchy, together with the right and duty to study the other book written by God, the book of nature, without regard to the authority of the fathers of natural philosophy.' (Hooykaas 1977: 109)

Literacy itself became a moral obligation required of the believer so that he could directly receive the word of God (see Strauss 1981; Lockridge 1981). Though Newton and others saw themselves as retrieving knowledge which had been lost rather than discovering anything really new (Hall 1983: 14), the general expectation was that the wisdom of the ancients *would* be surpassed, for in science 'truth is the daughter of time' (Hooykaas 1977: 113). No pope was recognized in either religion or philosophy; the domain of science was freed from both ecclesiastical authority and that of the ancients, and was increasingly allowed to proceed by reference to its own autonomous rules and procedures. Since the Protestant God was remote and mysterious, he could only be known through his works and the investigation of his creation (Merton 1978; Parsons 1968: 523). 'The study of natural phenomena (was seen as) an effective means for promoting the glory of God' (Merton 1978: 71); empirical knowledge was highly valued and a premium placed on its practical utility – for what sweetens the lives of mortals is good in the sight of God (Merton 1978: 72). Painstaking observation and experiment became the scientific expression of the Puritan emphasis on labouring tirelessly in God's calling: and the relatively positive evaluation of both manual labour and artisan-type occupations favoured technological advance and the rise of experimental science. Made in the image of God, man moreover exercised dominion over nature and therefore had the right to master it by technological means.

The contrast between all this and the Brahmanical tradition I have described is radical. Far from a priesthood of all believers, the *shastras* are to be transmitted and interpreted only by those with the authority to do so, and literacy is not a requirement laid on the devout. Knowledge progressively degenerates with time, and is therefore something to be recovered from the sages of the past, whose wisdom cannot be surpassed in the present. Consistent with this is an emphasis on its faithful reproduction rather than on innovation and experiment; and on memorization over complete understanding. Since the *guru* provides a life-line to past tradition, his authority is paramount and a sceptical scrutiny of his teaching discountenanced. The *shastras* contain the last word on both science and salvation, and science does not constitute an autonomous domain apart from religion. Nor does the book of nature hold the keys to a transcendent truth. Knowledge of the empirical world is rather devalued – as is consistent with the notion that it is a world of illusion and an obstacle to salvation. 'The gods love the mystic'; they 'are fond of the obscure (and) detest direct knowledge', say the Satapatha Brahmana and the sage Yajnavalkya (quoted in Chattopadhyaya 1977: 272, 277). Real, eternally valid knowledge is of a soteriological nature; and in so far as one incidentally acquires a practical means of controlling the world by the acquisition of knowledge that leads out of it, this control is of an essentially magical nature associated above all with the power of the spoken word. The tradition moreover accords a relatively low status to manual labour and craft occupations, and offers little stimulus to experimentation and technological innovation.

I do not, of course, intend to claim that all this represents the *only* strand in traditional Hindu thought; nor to suggest that all the divergent traditions of Hinduism were equally antipathetic to that 'rational empiricism' which characterized the emergence of modern science in Western Europe. Nor is my objective to account for the failure of Indian science to sustain its early promise (though I do suggest that the authority of the particular tradition I describe would be *one* of the factors relevant for such an account). A proper exploration of these issues is both beyond the scope of this paper and the competence of its author; and would obviously demand a consideration of politico-economic constraints which have not been touched on here.

The point of juxtaposing the two situations is rather that it directs attention to the enormous disparity between the two cognitive worlds, and emphasizes the necessity of understanding the transformation of mental life to which Goody alludes in relation to the wider context in which it actually occurs. But once this wider context is brought into the picture, the assumption that literacy is an active agent in the process – an assumption that underlies the questions with which I opened this section – begins to look rather dubious. Literacy is certainly a general precondition for the transformation, but surely reveals as much about the specific conditions under which it is likely to occur as the Neolithic Revolution reveals about the conditions likely to produce Stephenson's 'Rocket'. Once we have recognized that it provides no more than a passive prerequisite for 'cognitive modernism', it comes as no surprise that the 'cognitive traditionalism' supposedly characteristic of preliterate societies is no less marked in most literate ones. In terms of types of rationality, any antithesis between oral and literate cultures is false.

Notes

1 An earlier draft of this paper was presented to 'The Patterns of History' seminar at the London School of Economics, the South Asian Anthropologists Group, and at the University of Sussex. I gratefully acknowledge the helpful comments received on these occasions. Thanks are especially due to André Béteille, Maurice Bloch, Mary Searle-Chatterjee, Chris Fuller, and Mick Mann for their critical scrutiny of a previous version of the text.

2 Fieldwork in Benares was carried out between September 1976 and November 1977 (supported by the Social Science Research Council) and in August 1978, August–September 1981 and March–April 1983 (supported by the London School of Economics and Political Science). I am deeply obligated to Virendra Singh for his language instruction, and to him and Om Prakash Sharma for their research assistance.

3 While the prestige and influence of these institutions is now much diminished, it is not clear that they catered for much larger student numbers in the pre-British period. Bernier observed that in the mid-seventeenth century 'the town contains no colleges or regular classes, as in our universities, but resembles rather the schools of the ancients, the masters being dispersed over different parts of the town in private houses. . . . Some of these masters have four disciples, others six or seven, and the most eminent have 12 or 15; but this is the largest number' (Bernier 1968: 334; originally 1670). From a much earlier date, however, we learn of an establishment with 500 students (Basham 1971; 165).

4 Technically the *shastras* are the 'law books' and compilations of the post-Vedic period. In everyday speech, however, the term *shastrik* is used indiscriminately to

cover beliefs and practices validated by the whole range of sacred texts from the Vedas to the Puranas and Dharmasastras.

5 For a body of scientific theory to rate as a *shastra* presupposes its unquestioned authority. Since it remains contentious, Darwin's theory of evolution would not be described as a *shastra*, but rather as a *siddhant* or 'doctrine'.

6 In the tradition at large the matter is not wholly unambiguous however; and even amongst my own informants there would be some who would stress an aspect of entreaty.

7 Not only the Veda but also the recitation of sacred texts of lesser prestige confers untold benefits. For the birth of a son the household priest will be asked to read the *Harivamsa Purana*; for the liberation of a soul who got stuck as a marginal ghost (*preta*) the *Shrimat Bhagavata Purana*. Though it is often said that it is necessary to listen to the text carefully if the desired result is to be obtained, and though the Sanskrit verses are accompanied by a Hindi commentary, attention tends to be rather fitful.

8 According to the ritual experts, Vedic *mantras* cannot in theory be chanted as part of the mortuary rituals of the first ten days after death which is the period of most intense pollution (though in practice this is not invariably true).

9 There is no way, they point out, that such stability could possibly be demonstrated in the absence of writing; and while it is certainly the case that Brahmanical dogma insists on the meticulous accuracy of oral transmission, this is no reason for accepting their testimony uncritically – a point which is brought home by Lord's (1960) work on Yugoslav bards, whose claims for the perfect repetition of their performance from one occasion to the next are both sincere and demonstrably false. The case of the Veda invites reassessment in the light of such findings. Ong (1982: 62–3) nevertheless cites some impressive evidence of stability in cases of purely oral transmission, and plausibly suggests that ritual recitations and those constrained by music and/or rigid metrical forms are least susceptible to distortion and drift. Why these considerations should be ignored in the case of the Vedas is left unclear.

What is incontrovertibly established is that the highly formalized, disciplined, and rigorous methods developed for teaching the Veda do result in a remarkably accurate reproduction of what has been taught by purely oral transmission. Goody suggests that what makes this possible is the application of mnemonic techniques that depend on the reduction of language to a visual form and therefore presuppose a literate culture – the implication being that verbatim reproduction of such accuracy could not be matched in a pre-literate one. This seems questionable. Is it really obvious that verbatim memorization *is* dependent on the visual representation of language, or that visual representation necessarily implies writing? Would not the commonplace observation that writing is destructive of memory suggest that oral knowledge is more likely to be faithfully reproduced in a pre-literate culture? While it is certainly the case that the elaborate theory of phonetics laid down in the Sanskrit texts which deal with the pronunciation and transmission of the Veda (e.g. Pattubhiram Sastri 1976) is inconceivable without literacy, is it equally clear that the actual teaching methods employed were wholly dependent on this theoretical apparatus and are unimaginable without it?

10 There are actually two slightly different traditions: the first that there is one *Purana* in heaven which Vyasa divided into eighteen on earth; the second that Vyasa transmitted only one *samhita* ('compilation') to his disciples, and it was subsequently subdivided.

References

BARTH, F. (1975) *Ritual and Knowledge among the Baktaman of New Guinea*. New Haven: Yale University Press.

BASHAM, A. L. (1971) *The Wonder that was India*. Fontana Ancient History.

BERNIER, F. (1968) *Travels in the Mogul Empire*. Delhi: S. Chand & Co.

BIARDEAU, M. (1968) 'Some More Considerations about Textual Criticism. *Purana* **10** (2): 115–23.

BONAZZOLI, G. (1983) Remarks on the Nature of Puranas. *Purana* **25** (1): 77–113.

CHATTOPADHYAYA, D. (1977) *Science and Society in Ancient India*. Calcutta: Research India Publications.

COHN, B. S. (1971) *India: The Social Anthropology of a Civilization*. New Jersey: Prentice-Hall Inc.

DUMONT, L. and POCOCK, D. F. (1957) For a Sociology of India. *Contributions to Indian Sociology* **I**: 7–22.

EISENSTEIN, E. L. (1969) The Advent of Printing and the Problem of the Renaissance. *Past and Present* **45**: 19–89.

— (1981) Some Conjectures about the Impact of Printing on Western Society and Thought: A Preliminary Report. In H. J. Graff (ed.) *Literacy and Social Development in the West*. Cambridge: Cambridge University Press.

— (1983) *The Printing Revolution in Early Modern Europe*. Cambridge: Cambridge University Press.

GANGADHARAN, N. (1970–71) *Garuda–Purana – A Study*. Printed as a supplement to *Purana* **13** (1): 1–112 and (2): 105–74.

GARUDA PURANA (n.d.) (Sanskrit with Hindi commentary by Sudama Misra Shastri). Varanasi: Bombay Pushtak Bhandar.

GARUDA PURANAM (1968) A prose English translation by Manmatha Nath Dutt Shastri (2nd edition). Varanasi: Chowkhamba Sanskrit Series vol. LXVII.

GOODY, J. (ed.) (1968a) *Literacy in Traditional Societies*. Cambridge: Cambridge University Press.

— (1968b) Restricted Literacy in Northern Ghana. In J. Goody (ed.) *Literacy in Traditional Societies*. Cambridge: Cambridge University Press.

— (1976) *Production and Reproduction: A Comparative Study of the Domestic Domain*. Cambridge: Cambridge University Press.

— (1977) *The Domestication of the Savage Mind*. Cambridge: Cambridge University Press.

— (in press) Oral Composition and Oral Transmission: The Case of the Vedas.

GOODY, J. and WATT, I. (1963) The Consequences of Literacy. *Comparative Studies in Society and History* **5** (3): 304–45.

HALL, A. R. (1983) *The Revolution in Science 1500–1750*. London: Longman.

HEESTERMAN, J. C. (1978) Veda and Dharma. In W. D. O'Flaherty and J. D. M. Derrett (eds) *The Concept of Duty in South Asia*. New Delhi: Vikas Publishing House.

HIRST, P. and WOOLLEY, P. (1982) *Social Relations and Human Attributes*. London: Tavistock Publications.

HOOYKAAS, R. (1977) *Religion and the Rise of Modern Science*. Edinburgh: Scottish Academic Press.

HORTON, R. (1970) African Traditional Thought and Western Science. In B. Wilson (ed.) *Rationality*. Oxford: Basil Blackwell.

— (1982) Tradition and Modernity Revisited. In M. Hollis and S. Lukes (eds) *Rationality and Relativism*. Oxford: Basil Blackwell.

India Reference Annual (1974) Delhi: Ministry of Information.

KANE, P. L. (1976) and (1977) *History of Dharmasastra*, vols 2 and 5. Poona: Bhandarkar Oriental Research Institute.

KUPER, A. (1982) *Wives for Cattle: Bridewealth and Marriage in Southern Africa*. London: Routledge & Kegan Paul.

LOCKRIDGE, K. A. (1981) Literacy in Early America 1650–1800. In H. J. Graff (ed.) *Literacy and Social Development in the West*. Cambridge: Cambridge University Press.

LORD, A. B. (1960) *The Singer of Tales*. Harvard Studies in Comparative Literature, 24. Cambridge, Mass.: Harvard University Press.

Manusmriti (*The laws of Manu*) (1969) (translated by Georg Buhler). New York: Dover Publications.

MARRIOTT, M. (1961) Little Communities in an Indigeneous Civilization. In M. Marriott (ed.), *Village India: Studies in the Little Community*. Bombay: Asia Publishing House.

MERTON, R. K. (1978) *Science, Technology and Society in Seventeenth-Century England*. New Jersey: Humanities Press. (Originally published in 1933 as vol. IV, Part 2 of *Osiris: studies on the history and philosophy of science, and on the history of learning and culture*).

ONG, W. J. (1982) *Orality and Literacy: The Technologizing of the Word*. London: Methuen.

PAGELS, E. (1979) *The Gnostic Gospels*. London: Weidenfeld & Nicolson.

PARRY, J. P. (1980) Ghosts, Greed and Sin: The Occupational Identity of the Benares Funeral Priests. *Man* (n.s.) **15** (1): 88–111.

— (1981) Death and Cosmogony in Kashi. *Contributions to Indian Sociology* (n.s.) **15** (1 and 2): 337–65.

PARSONS, T. (1968) *The Structure of Social Action*, vol. 2. Weber. New York: Free Press.

PATTUBHIRAM SASTRI, P. N. (1976) *Vyasa Siksha*. Varanasi: Veda Mimamsa Research Centre.

Preta Manjari (Samvat 2032. Compiled by Sudama Misra Shastri and revised by Mannalal Abhimanyu). Varanasi: Bombay Pushtak Bhandar.

ROCHER, L. (1983) Reflections on One Hundred and Fifty Years of Puranic Studies. *Purana* **25** (1): 64–76.

SARASWATI, BAIDYANATH (1975) *Kashi: Myth and Reality of a Classical Cultural Tradition*. Simla: Indian Institute of Advanced Study.

SHULMAN, D. (1980) *Tamil Temple Myths: Sacrifice and Divine Marriage in the South Indian Saiva Tradition*. Princeton: University Press.

SINGER, M. (1972) *When a Great Tradition Modernizes: An Anthropological Approach to Indian Civilization*. London: Pall Mall Press.

SMITH, J. D. (1977) The Singer or the Song? A Reassessment of Lord's Oral Theory. *Man* (n.s.) **12** (1): 141–53.

SRINIVASAN, A. (1980) Order and Event in Puranic Myth: An Analysis of Four Narratives from the Bhagavata Purana. In *Contributions to Indian Sociology* (n.s.) **14** (2): 195–212.

STAAL, J. F. (1961) *Nambudiri Veda recitation*. S'-Gravenhage: Mouton.

STEVENSON, S. (1920) *The Rites of the Twice-born*. London: Oxford University Press.

STRATHERN, A. (1982) Witchcraft, Greed, Cannibalism, and Death. In M. Bloch and J. Parry (eds) *Death and the Regeneration of Life*. Cambridge: Cambridge University Press.

STRAUSS, G. (1981) Techniques of Indoctrination: The German Reformation. In H. J. Graff (ed.) *Literacy and Social Development in the West*. Cambridge: Cambridge University Press.

TAMBIAH, S. J. (1970) *Buddhism and the Spirit Cults in North-east Thailand*. Cambridge: Cambridge University Press.

VAN BUITENEN, J. A. B. (1966) On the Archaism of the *Bhagavata Purana*. In M. Singer (ed.) *Krishna: Myths, Rites and Attitudes*. Chicago: Chicago University Press.

WADLEY, S. S. (1975) Folk Literature in Karimpur: A Catalogue of Types. *Journal of South Asian Literature* **11**: 7–17.

— (1978) Texts in Contexts: Oral Traditions and the Study of Religion in Karimpur. In S. Vatuk (ed.) *American Studies in the Anthropology of India*. New Delhi: Manohar Books.

WINTERNITZ, M. (1927) *A History of Indian Literature*. Calcutta: Calcutta University Press.

Michael Saltman

11 'The Law is a ass':
an anthropological appraisal

Anyone having had the misfortune to seek recourse to justice through the legal system cannot be impervious to the fact that, while the court aspires to arrive at a rational decision, the sought-after justice may be a purely coincidental consequence. The subject of this paper is the lawyers' belief in the rationality of the legal system. Many legal scholars appear to be quite distressed when the sacred groves of their domain are trampled upon by social scientists. Honoré (1973) accuses those sociologists, who have entered what he terms the 'World Cup' game between the proponents of natural law and the legal positivists, of never having learned the rules of the game. Auerbach (1966) takes social scientists to task for having the temerity to study such issues as the validity of laws. The list of accusations is long. But social scientists have their own disciplinary rules. From the perspective of these rules, they may legitimately study any social phenomenon, which by definition also encompasses the polemics of the legal philosophers. This holds true not only for the interactions between the protagonists but also for the substance of their debates.

This position derives in some measure from the present writer's own bias that social scientists may make, although not obligated to do so, critical assessments of social phenomena. Under this heading both the legal system and its practitioners become fair prey for critical evaluation. One can only concur with Ian Hamnett's concise and pointed statement that

> 'the specificity of the law then emerges as no more than the ideological charter of a particular professional group, and thus is subject to, rather than constitutive of the anthropologist's analysis.' (Hamnett 1977:4)[1]

Firmly entrenched in their ideologies and their own perceptions of what constitutes law, these practitioners as well as some of their philosophers function within and exert influence upon the network of social relationships in societies. By so doing they create social facts that warrant critical study.

The argument

Lawyers of the positivist persuasion perceive the formal system within which they operate as a rational system. For them, rationality means that a valid or correct judicial decision is logically deduced from predetermined rules that constitute the components of the *closed logical system*. By the same token, the arrival at a judicial decision by means not conforming to such logical derivations must be non-rational. In that case, either the decision is invalid, or the alternative system that generates such decisions is invalid. On these grounds jurists can dismiss what anthropologists have termed 'primitive law' or 'customary law' as 'defective law' (Hart 1961: 89–91), since they do not meet the requirements that Hart and others demand of a legal system.

From this we may learn that rationality is not some quality that comes into being *sui generis*, but is rather a function of certain requirements, in turn deriving from some axiomatic proposition. Employing an analogy familiar to anthropologists from the field of economics, the behavioural axiom underlying the rationality of formal economic systems is that of the 'economic man' – an ideal type apparently bent on profit maximization. Godelier asks what is meant by rationality, and in answer provides us with the following requirements, quoted from Maurice Allais:

> 'We have to have recourse to the definition which seems to emerge from scientific logic, by which a man is considered rational when:
> a) he pursues ends that are mutually coherent, and,
> b) he employs means that are appropriate to the ends pursued.'
>
> (Godelier 1972:11)

Maximization of profit is then the definitive criterion of rationality underlying the 'ends that are mutually coherent' in the formal western economic system.

In searching for the 'legal' equivalent of the economic man underlying positivist legal rationality, we find that the axioms relate in one way or another to concepts of power, authority, and sovereignty. For example, Austinian jurisprudence bases its logical consistency on the idea of the 'will of the sovereign' – a person or body above whom there is no higher authority. It is axiomatic that laws enacted by this person or body are valid laws. Hart, who rejects the Austinian position, provides an alternative model. For Hart a law obtains validity when it meets two requirements. First, a primary rule of obligation that reflects some shared understanding in a given society. Second, a secondary rule of recognition, which means authoritative criteria for identifying primary rules of obligation. Not all shared understandings have the force of law. Only those that are designated as law by the authorities achieve this status. Thus, Hart has not significantly deviated from a power-based axiom, since the second requirement demands the presence of an authority. For the purposes of this paper it will be assumed that the mutually coherent end defining rationality in a positivist legal system is the *exercise of sovereign power*. In the light of this assertion, the main objective of the paper now becomes to examine the process whereby concepts of social order become formalized into law-like propositions as components of a system.

The literature is replete with examples of polarities and dichotomies that may help to provide a useful framework of reference – Maine's status to contract, Weber's formal irrational to formal rational. Recent studies of a more concise nature have also posed continua extending between such polarities as customary law and enacted law (Fuller 1971); from order of custom to rule of law (Diamond 1971). A similar dichotomy to Diamond's has been proposed by Cairns (1959), but for quite different reasons. Cairns's differentiation between the concepts 'power' and 'order' becomes the theoretical point of departure for the present study. Cairns has differentiated between *formal systems* and *speculative systems* of law. 'The limits of the legal order in the formal systems are defined in terms of power'; for the speculative systems, 'the root idea is order, not power, and the ultimate postulate is the intelligibility of the world. In a word, the speculative systems are ontological in the traditional sense' (Cairns 1959: 25).

Cairns has inadvertently but elegantly reiterated the elements of the argument between Radcliffe-Brown and Malinowski as to what constitutes law. Radcliffe-Brown (1952: 208) did not deviate from the jurisprudential position assumed by Roscoe Pound that the law constitutes 'social control through the systematic application of the force of politically organized society'. By laying unqualified emphasis on the uses of power and force, Radcliffe-Brown falls squarely into Cairns's categorization of formal systems, and, ultimately, into the camp of the legal positivists. Malinowski is more problematic, since his views changed and shifted on this subject throughout his writings. But one theme seems to remain constant: that is the element of reciprocity as a postulate for all legal systems. This is indeed speculative, in that it assumes the form of a hypothesis about social order, and by so doing is also ascribing meaning to behaviour, or in Cairns's terms is discoursing on the intelligibility of the world. When people stop at red lights, it is not at all clear whether this is a consequence of the 'systematically applied force of politically organized society' or because *maybe* they have a reciprocal interest in so doing together with the drivers of traversing traffic.

An element of misnomer in Cairns's categorization is the apparently diametrical opposition between 'formal' and 'speculative', since this paper aims at demonstrating that speculative systems are also capable of undergoing formalization. The differentiation between these two types of system lies in the nature of the principle being formalized. While the true formal systems, in Cairns's sense, derive their logical rigour from an axiom concerning the uses of power and have committed their formalization to this direction, the speculative systems are concerned with different concepts relating to the social order, abstract concepts of justice and morality, ideological considerations, or even psychological assumptions about man's nature. All or any one of these factors can serve as a principle subject to formalization and there is no logical impediment to their systematization.

In many societies there is a parallel domain to the formal reality of lawyers' law. Moore (1973) has used the term 'semi-autonomous fields' to describe this domain. Within these fields are remedy agents that function outside the wider legal setting. The wider setting is characterized by the formal legal system at the state level, which is usually a western model in one form or another. In her own study Moore looked at such disparate groups, exemplifying semi-autonomous fields, as the International Ladies Garment Workers' Union and the traditional legal culture of the Chagga of Tanzania. These groupings have developed sets of rules that intimately evolve out of their own specific patterns of behaviour. In every society there are innumerable groups and institutions dispensing their own brands of justice on a daily basis – trade unions, co-operatives, disciplinary committees of institutions, ethics committees of professional associations, traditional societies undergoing social change, voluntary associations that subscribe to a given ideology.

The interactions and the independence of these parallel systems become the focal point of this paper. The relevant questions are as follows. First, how do speculative systems, based on some principle of social order, or even ideology, become transformed into a closed logical positivist system, based on the principle of the application of power? Second, do alternatives exist that enable speculative systems to undergo formalization without recourse to a power-based axiom? The answers are to be sought in the relationship obtaining between the semi-autonomous fields and the wider legal setting, and in particular the impingement of the formal legal system on its speculative counterpart.

The data

In order to answer the first question as to how a system, based on a principle of social order, becomes transformed into a logical system, based on the exercise of sovereign power and authority, a comparative ethnographic method is employed. Two apparently different situations relating to land law in eleventh- and twelfth-century England and in the recent history of the Busoga of Uganda, demonstrate a significant number of common features that allow for comparison.

The general structure in both instances is based on an ideal feudal concept of social order, whereby political and economic links are forged on the basis of personal bonds of loyalty of an inferior to a superior in an ascending hierarchy of rulers to the apex of a paramount ruler. The social order at the lowest levels rests on shared understandings about mutual rights and obligations, that include services rendered by the man to his ruler, for which he receives in return security and, still more important, rights in land. Rulers ruled over people rather than over land, a point constantly stressed by Fallers (1969) in reference to the Busoga. By the same token the feudal monarch in England was *Rex Anglorum* and not *Rex Anglie*. The legitimacy of rights and obligations was defined in terms of the meanings of social relationships, this being far removed from the rationale of formal logical rigour in contemporary land law.

In order to obtain an allotment of land, the subordinate in either instance had to pay homage to the ruler, and as long as he fulfilled his obligations throughout his lifetime, he had inalienable rights in that land. The non-fulfilment of obligations invoked the reversionary right of the ruler. The perpetuation of rights into subsequent generations was subject to the inferior's agreement to submit to the same obligatory conditions maintained by his ancestor. The legal system, both in England and Uganda, arrived at its decisions by interpreting the meanings of feudal relationships. In Cairns's terms this is a speculative system in so far as it sought intelligibility in the feudal order. In Malinowski's terms it is a system based on the principle of binding mutuality.

The shared understandings about social control in the feudal order provided the underlying rationale of the legal systems in both situations, and law-finding was achieved through the courts' interpretation of the meanings of the feudal order. But this rationale had to contend with changing social conditions. At the same time it suffered from a built-in inconsistency that became more apparent as time passed. The *lifetime* feudal relationship between a subject and his ruler was pitted against the principle of heredity that supposedly guaranteed rights of succession on the same terms, which in turn was pitted against the reversionary rights of rulers. While this in itself did not radically alter the basic substantive rationale of the legal system, the conflicting principles of heredity and reversionary rights, linked with ongoing political and economic change, ultimately emptied the legal relationship of its substantive content. Certainly, in the English example, the instance of land rights by knight's service was transformed into a cash nexus quite early on. When the heir was a woman or a person physically incapable of performing military service, a fee known as scutage was paid in lieu of service. Furthermore, and from the outset, the transfer of rights of succession was conditional on the payment of relief. Maine has pointed out the importance of the cash nexus as part of the process of depersonalizing legal relationships. But the cash nexus also provided a profit motive for the ruler to dispossess his tenant, and towards the end of the twelfth century in England rulers were asserting their reversionary rights at a considerably accelerated rate. Milsom (1981: 135), in describing this situation, states that 'the mischief originally aimed at was therefore not a disorder of which wrongdoers might take advantage, but an order in which lords might abuse their customary powers of control'. In Uganda the same type of abuse of reversionary right occurred. Chiefs and headmen, who had formerly subsisted in large measure from tax farming, had now become low-salaried civil service functionaries. One effective way of increasing income under these circumstances was to evict tenants, reallocate the land, and collect substantial entry fees from the new tenants. Litigation within this context rose sharply in both situations and the legal systems had to reinterpret the existing rationale of the feudal order in order to contend with the changing situation. The whole issue has to be transposed into the political context, wherein once again a common denominator in the English and Ugandan situations becomes apparent.

A political battle over sovereignty was being fought. In England the king was attempting to establish his sovereignty at the expense of his feudal lords, while in Uganda the African Local Government (established by the British colonial authorities) aspired to more than nominal sovereignty by reducing the traditional roles of chiefs and headmen. The establishment of royal courts in England and the African Local Government courts in Uganda, as an alternative form of access to justice, played a crucial role in the battle over sovereignty, but also had a profound effect on the rationality underlying legal decision making.

What emerges in both situations is a form of common law, that at one and the same time maintains continuity with past historical realities, and utilizes a different logic to achieve remedies for litigation. Fallers has described this for the Busoga by claiming that the sovereign source of power to allot headmanships and associated tracts of land had become a mere historic source of rights. What had formerly constituted political powers had now become a legal concept denoting powers not longer exercisable and the legal concept in this form became subject to interpretation by the courts. The courts' interpretation becomes that of analysing abstract property rights rather than searching for meanings of social relationships. In so far as the comparable English situation is concerned, the same phenomenon becomes evident. Milsom (1981: 124) has written 'litigants preferred to go directly to the king's court and its rules became rules about abstract property rights in which lords played no part. Seisin becomes like possession, a relation between one person and a piece of land; and the lord, the second person in the original idea vanishes.' Juxtaposing Milsom's contention with an additional clarification by Thorne (1959: 262), the process reveals itself in greater detail, 'the lord's interest in land, a real and undeniable one, was not taken from him; he was left his superior title; he and his heirs were simply barred from asserting it against the tenant and his heirs'.

A new logic was now imposed by the higher courts, the enabling factor being the sanctions of the central government. The court was obliged to provide an affirmative or negative answer to the questions based on an exclusively formal issue. Both in England and Uganda the question was whether the claimant had met all the necessary formal requirements for obtaining his initial rights in the land. This was established by the Assize of Mort d'ancestor in 1166 in England and in a landmark case cited by Fallers (1969: 274–75) for the Busoga – Asumani v. Musa.

The case of Asumani considers the criteria for abandonment as grounds for the headman to exercise his reversionary right. Asumani claimed that he was unjustifiably dispossessed of his land by the subsillage headman, Musa. The original allotment had been made by the village headman, Sowobi, but in 1938 Asumani moved his family into another subvillage, received a plot there, but nonetheless continued to cultivate his original allotment. Asumani's contention was that his continued cultivation of the disputed plot indicated non-abandonment, while the cultivation of the second plot in his new abode was a consequence of the low economic yield of the original plot. Musa's argument was based on the past historical reality that the allotment of a piece of land implies a personal relationship of allegiance between a man and his ruler. Therefore, the act of leaving the subvillage and living in another subvillage is tantamount to abandonment. The court found in favour of Asumani in the following terms – 'the holding which he claims from Musa is his. It was allotted to him by Sowobi.' Thus, the land was not subject to reversionary right. From this it may be concluded that the formal act of initial allotment constituted the test for the court in determining the legal status of the plot as long as the land was being actively cultivated. The issue remained one of *rights in holdings* deriving from the initial allotment and the question of *allegiance to a ruler* becomes irrelevant. In both instances (Mort d'ancestor and the Uganda court decision) the outcome is based on the examination of a series of formal acts rather than the interpretation of the meaning of a social relationship. If the formal requirements were met, the claimant could not be dispossessed. Any other questions appertaining to the patterns of behaviour between the litigants becomes totally irrelevant to the decision-making process.

Superimposing Weber's 'ideal types' on Cairns's differentiation between speculative and formal systems, there would appear to be here a shift in the nature of the rationality being employed. The transition, in Weber's terms, is from the substantive rational to the formal rational. The former state is that law-making and law-finding is 'guided by the principles of an ideological system other than that of the law itself (ethics, religion, power politics, etc.)', while the latter extrinsically ascribes 'significance to external acts observable by the senses' (in the cases under deliberation this would mean the act of the initial allotment of land). This is merely a transitional phase that ultimately brings law to express 'its rules by the use of abstract concepts created by legal thought itself and conceived of as constituting a complete system' (Weber 1954: xlii).

Having established the nature of the transformation from one rationality to another in a general trend towards legal positivism, it in no way follows that this is an inevitable process. The paper now goes on to address itself to its second question, that of the alternatives enabling speculative systems to undergo formalization without recourse to a power-based axiom. For this purpose, case material from the present writer's fieldwork will be discussed (Saltman: 1977, 1981).

The Kipsigis, a Kalenjin-speaking group in SW Kenya, were originally a cattle-herding people. They live in relatively autonomous territorial units known as *kokwotinwek* (sing. *kokwet*). Patrilineages tend to be dispersed as a consequence of preferred neolocal residence, and the main social grouping cross-cutting the families resident in a *kokwet* is the age-set system. In the absence of any traditional centralized political body above the level of the *kokwet*, the locus of power resides in the senior age sets of the *kokwet*. *Kokwet* elders perform an important judicial function in resolving local disputes. Because of the dispersed lineages litigants press their cases as individuals without the support of kinsmen, but in the absence of well-defined coercive sanctions the outcome of cases usually took the form of arbitrated compromises rather than adjudicated decisions.

In the initial state of almost exclusive commitment to cattle herding, land had no intrinsic value for the Kipsigis beyond its provision for pasture, and since land was plentiful, it never constituted a subject for litigation. The advent of the British at the end of the nineteenth century and the rapid imposition of the Pax Britannica had a profound effect on the Kipsigis relationship to land. By establishing buffer zones of British settlers between the Kipsigis and their traditional enemies – the Kisii and the Masai – the British restricted Kipsigis movement, confined them to 'Reserves', and by so doing, caused an effective shortage of land for cattle herders. Recognizing this latter problem, the British did all in their power to influence the Kipsigis to engage in cultivation and at the same time reduce the size of their herds. After some initial resistance to this idea, the Kipsigis eventually succumbed. Herds were indeed reduced but were maintained at a level to supply dairy needs and to fulfil traditional social obligations. But maintenance of herds at even this minimal level was incompatible with the ever growing commitment to cultivation without a radical change in the land usage patterns. Land now became a serious object for litigation, since it was imperative to enclose land in order to prevent encroachment of cattle on cultivated land. This resulted in the establishment of individual land-owning rights and accorded a concrete value to land, both of these being previously alien concepts to the Kipsigis mind.

It was inevitable under these circumstances that litigation over land would constitute a major legal quandary for the Kipsigis. The situation was quite different from that of the Busoga. There was no existing corpus of customary law that covered the new contingencies; there was no traditional hierarchy of chiefs and headmen that could legislate and enforce the new legislation; furthermore, the absence of any conflict between a traditional hierarchy and a civil-service bureaucracy removed the issue of sovereignty as a factor in the determination of legal rationality. Presumably for pragmatic reasons, the British were tolerant in respect of customary law and allowed Africans to litigate among themselves in accordance with customary law as long as it was not 'repugnant to justice or morality or inconsistent with the Order in Council or any written law'.[2] Thus, the decisions of *kokwet* elders were backed by the full authority of the colonial regime with rights of appeal to the District Officer and Provincial Commissioner. At a later stage, access to justice was granted through appeal to African courts, and today, magistrates' courts hear appeals from the *kokwet* level or accept civil cases, while stipulating quite categorically that these require a prior *kokwet* hearing before being admissible on the court's roster.

Given that no legislation on the land issue was forthcoming from the colonial authorities, the Kipsigis themselves were obliged to provide legal remedies. This was achieved by means of extrapolation from an indigenous shared understanding. In former times it had been customary that when a man cultivated a small plot of land close to his hut for growing millet used in the manufacture of beer, other people were liable for damages, if and when they allowed their cattle to stray on to this plot. It was understood that as long as a man actually cultivated this plot, he had rights to its use. When he ceased to cultivate it, the plot reverted to common grazing status. The principle was therefore one of usufructuary right. When, at the initial phase of establishing ownership over land conflicting claims were made, Kipsigis elders extrapolated from this usufructuary system a systematic set of qualifications that enabled them to resolve contending claims. The claimant who could prove actual usage or greater intent of usage in an ascending scale of more confining terms – fencing the land, clearing the land of stones, erecting a building on the land, domiciling a wife in that building – would win his case. All things being equal between the claimants, an additional test of 'necessity' was applied, and a claimant not having land or having significantly less land than his adversary could expect to win his case. It must be stressed here that in clear distinction to the traditional mode of dispute, wherein compromises were achieved, adjudicated and unilateral decisions were now being handed down systematically in land cases.

An examination of magistrate's courts' records revealed that in land cases the magistrate upheld 67 per cent of prior *kokwet* decisions, rejected only 12 per cent and in 21 per cent of the cases, accepted the *kokwet*'s decision in principle but modified its terms. It must also be borne in mind that hundreds of land cases are being settled at the *kokwet* level without recourse to the courts. What this means, in effect, is that the extension of sanctions by the state courts to the customary law process provides the legitimacy for the systemattization of an indigenous rationale. The intrusion of the element of sovereignty in this context is irrelevant and the legal rationale remains ʊ ʊin-fluenced by this extraneous factor. The Kipsigis example is demonstrative of Moore's *semi-autonomous field* from within which alternative forms of systematic legal reasoning can emerge.

The second example of a 'speculative' system, as an alternative to legal positivism, is in drawing the connection between ideology and legality. The field situation, from which the data are drawn, is the Israeli *kibbutz* movement. The prototype of the *kibbutz*, founded in 1910, was a small-scale, voluntary association bound together by an intensely shared ideological commitment to the notion of a new and just society. The founders of the movement synthesized many elements into the construction of this ideology – the secularism of the Jewish Enlightenment movement, the naturalism and altruism of Tolstoy and the social radicalism that stemmed from the Russian Revolution of 1905 as well as a strong streak of anarchism. Among its basic tenets was a well-defined anti-law ideology, that mirrored some of the early thinking of Soviet Jurisprudence as represented by Pashukanis and his followers. Common to both situations was the belief expressed by Pashukanis that the future communist society meant 'not the victory of socialist law, but the victory of socialism over any law. . . Public law is a bourgeois ideological weapon having its highest development under capitalism' (Pashukanis 1951: 127–29). Like Marx, the founding fathers of the *kibbutz* maintained that law would 'wither away' under the conditions of a just society. This has not proved to be the case either in the *kibbutz* movement or the Soviet Union, and almost 75 years after its establishment the *kibbutz* is saddled with a plethora of written rules and regulations.

It is obvious that a form of social control exists in the *kibbutz*. In the initial stages of its development the *kibbutz* based its social control on ideologically conditioned shared understandings. To clarify this, Honoré (1973: 27) has written,

> 'The understanding must relate to prescription. No prescription is necessary to tell people to do as they please. Natural liberty is the state of affairs existing in the absence of prescriptions. The understanding must relate to something which involves the curtailment of liberty.'

Without coercive sanction, this is the ideal Malinowskian position of mutuality being axiomatic to the legal system, perhaps even more so than in the Trobriands, since we are talking here of a voluntary commune. A second factor, of a more substantive nature, militating against positivist systematization, is the principle underlying resource allocation. In addition to the *kibbutz* having negated the private ownership of property, *kibbutz* distributive justice is linked with Marx's statement 'from each according to his ability, to each according to his needs' (Marx 1875, 1955). In his *Critique of the Gotha Programme*, Marx categorically relates this precept to the ultimate disappearance of bourgeois law. The absence of any utilitarian linkage between the two parts of Marx's formula does not lend itself easily to the formulation of legal statements about social obligations and resource allocation. Hart (1961: 121) has emphasized the generality of the classification which the law makes – classes of persons, categories of acts, things, and circumstances – and these classifications are essentially the basis of any kind of formal legal system. There is a clear contradiction between this process of classification and the built-in factor of individualism in Marx's formula. This argument will receive additional clarification below. The third relevant factor concerns the issue of sovereignty and the nature of sanctions in the *kibbutz*. The General Assembly of members is the sovereign body of each *kibbutz*. The individual *kibbutz* is federated within a *kibbutz* movement, but each and every General Assembly acting in a judicial capacity effectively deals with all internal matters of the *kibbutz*. Its ultimate sanction is expulsion, but a well-calibrated set of informal sanctions, relative to the offence and not determined by the General Assembly, is applied against the offender, ranging from joking relationships to total ostracism.

While all of this may be perfectly intelligible to the participants themselves, it is difficult for the observer to discover the underlying rationale for the system, that, for all intents and purposes, operates effectively. Shapiro (1976: 434) has provided a term, that on face value is confusing, but in fact is quite useful. He describes the rationality of the *kibbutz* legal system as 'individualized generality'. He claims that *generality* and *individuation* are not polar opposites. . . 'rather they are two axes defining the matrix within which the decision process operates'. The *kibbutz* General Assembly, in its judicial capacity, thus walks a tightrope between the maintenance of general principles and the recognition of individual characteristics. Case-to-case precedent is not created under these circumstances, and, apparently, we have an ideal type described by Weber as *substantive irrational*, whereby each case is decided solely on its own terms.

Behind this seeming confusion there is indeed a latent rationale. In analysing sets of judicial decisions handed down by the General Assembly, it emerges that the issue being judged is not solely the act of the individual, but the individual himself as a Whole Man. For example, it was noted that in two cases, within a two-year period, two men had been accused of utilizing funds from an outside source. There is a distinct rule forbidding members from having private sources of income. In one case the matter was glossed over by means of a compromise, while in the other, the individual was forced into a position whereby he had to leave the *kibbutz*. In the first instance the person was highly regarded by the membership in terms of his personality and his past contributions to the community, but in the second case, it was generally felt that the individual in question in the light of his overall past behaviour, had no redeeming features.

What occurs in the *kibbutz* bears many similarities to an anti-positivist school of jurisprudence known as Legal Realism, one of the main proponents being Karl Llewellyn. A summary of its main points would be:

1. There is no mandatory outcome to a given situation. The outcome is based on pragmatic considerations, either for a variety of reasons, or in order to achieve different kinds of effects.
2. Rules in the *kibbutz* do not constitute the basic premise of a syllogism, but are general propositions embodying a policy, the function of which is to guide rather than to control interpretation.

3. The General Assembly functions as a remedy agent, approximately in Llewellyn's terms, so as 'to resolve the doubt according to wisdom, justice and situation sense within the leeways accorded by the authoritative sources and to provide guidance for the future'.

In reiterating the main elements of *kibbutz* legal logic, it may be said that the rules of communal existence are shared understandings deriving from a common ideological position. These constitute the yardstick, against which the 'Whole Man' is constantly being measured and evaluated. Where shared understandings have to be restated in the form of rules, the intentions are universally known and a high degree of consistency can be maintained in contradistinction to the maintenance of consistency by case-to-case precedent. Rule making in the *kibbutz* today is designed to strengthen ideological positions in the face of growing individualism. This restatement of shared understandings as rules serves to balance between the two parameters of *individualized generality*. It may therefore be asserted that the *kibbutz*, which is also a semi-autonomous field, has managed to formalize its speculative axiom in order to meet ongoing contingencies.

Conclusions

Employing Allais's definition of rationality – pursuit of mutually coherent ends by appropriate means – it may be concluded that rationality is inextricably linked with and relative to specific substantive contexts. Mutual coherence denotes consistency, and the converse test for irrationality would be the affirmation of both p and not-p. If all the legal systems, described above, are double checked by these criteria of rationality and irrationality, they stand the test of consistency. But if, as claimed here, mutual coherence or p is a substantive variable, then it follows that no exclusive claims to any one rationale may be made.

Hart's criticism of customary law, or for that matter any non-positivist system of law, for being 'defective' law cannot be construed as an impeachment of customary law's rationality. His criticism rests on substantive issues. Without the power based secondary rule of recognition, Hart claims that 'the rules by which a group lives will not form a system, but will simply be a set of separate standards . . . which a particular group accepts. They will in this respect resemble our own rules of etiquette' (1961: 90). The data from the *kibbutz* case study speaks for itself and questions this assertion. Hart goes on to point out a second defect, which he calls the static character of the rules.

'There will be no means, in such a society, of deliberately adapting the rules to changing circumstances, either by eliminating old rules or introducing new ones; for, again, the possibility of doing this presupposes the existence of rules of a different type from the primary rules of obligation by which alone the society lives.' (Hart 1961: 90)

While Hart's position undoubtedly receives confirmation from the Busoga and English examples, it is, at the same time, challenged by the Kipsigis case, where law is shown to be adaptive without secondary rules of recognition. But this paper has argued that the Kipsigis were merely accorded a semi-autonomous status that allowed them to systematize their indigenous principles by their own criteria. This is quite different from the Busoga and English examples in which change took place over the secondary rule of recognition itself, and, consequently, emptied the primary rule of obligation of its meaningful content.

Hart's third and final criticism of what he terms defective law is its inefficiency. He bases this claim on the indeterminate sanctions of a non-centralized polity. But the case of the *kibbutz* demonstrates that when the law is based on shared understandings of an ideological nature, informal sanctions are not only the most appropriate but also are efficacious within the rationale of that given system. In so far as the Kipsigis are concerned, Abel (1970: 123) has pointed out that in a sample of 10 Kenyan tribes, the Kipsigis are among the least litigious in the national courts of Kenya. One hypothesis, among others, suggests that this may be the function of the efficient adaptive capacity of the indigenous law to resolve disputes in changing circumstances.

This paper began with a polemic and will conclude in a similar vein. The rationality of lawyers' law is upheld, in no small measure, by the vested interests of the legal profession. It has indeed become, in Hamnett's terms, an ideological charter for the legal profession. It is no longer clear whether the mutually coherent ends relate to the demands of the system itself or are a consequence of superfluous professionalization. At all events, law reform is the order of the day, before the legal system becomes an ass, totally removed from the realities of human behaviour.

Notes

Acknowledgement and thanks are due to the British Council for providing a travel grant that enabled the presentation of this paper at the ASA Conference.
1 Hamnett's conclusions, however, are different from those espoused in this paper.
2 Article 20. East Africa Order in Council, 1902.

References

ABEL, R. L. (1970) Case Method Research in the Customary Laws of Wrongs in Kenya – Part II: Statistical Analysis. *East African Journal of Law* **6** (1).
AUERBACH, L. (1966) Legal Tasks for the Sociologist. *Law and Society Review* **1**.
CAIRNS, H. (1959) The Community as the Legal Order. In J. Carl (ed.) *Community Nomos II*. The Liberal Arts Press: New York.
DIAMOND, S. (1971) The Rule of Law versus the Order of Custom. In R. P. Wolff, (ed.) *The Rule of Law*. New York: Simon & Schuster.

FALLERS, L. (1969) *Law Without Precedent.* Chicago: University of Chicago Press.

FULLER, L. (1971) Human Interaction and the Law. In R. P. Wolff (ed.) *The Rule of Law.* New York: Simon & Schuster.

GODELIER, M. (1972) *Rationality and Irrationality in Economics.* London: NLB.

HAMNETT, I. (1977) Introduction. In J. Hamnett (ed.) *Social Anthropology and Law.* ASA Monographs 14. London: Academic Press.

HART, H. A. L. (1961) *The Concept of Law.* Oxford: Oxford University Press.

HONORE, A. M. (1973) Groups, Laws and Obedience. In Q. W. B. Simpson (ed.) *Oxford Essays in Jurisprudence Second Series.* Oxford: Oxford University Press.

MARX, K (1875, 1955) Critique of the Gotha Programme. In *Karl Marx and Fredrick Engels, Selected Works.* Moscow: Foreign Languages Publishing House.

MILSOM, S. F. C. (1981) *Historical Foundations of the Common Law.* 2nd edition. London: Butterworths.

MOORE, S. F. (1973) *Law as Process.* London: Routledge & Kegan Paul.

PASHUKANIS, E. B. (1951) General Theory of Law and Marxism. In J. N. Hazard (ed.) *Soviet Legal Philosophy.* Cambridge, Mass.: Harvard University Press.

RADCLIFFE-BROWN, A. R. (1952) *Structure and Function in Primitive Society.* Glencoe, Ill.: Free Press.

SALTMAN, M. (1977) *The Kipsigis, A Case Study in Changing Customary Law.* Cambridge, Mass.: Schenkman Publishing Co.

— (1981) Legality and Ideology in the *Kibbutz* Movement. *International Journal of the Sociology of Law* **9**.

SHAPIRO, A. E. (1976) Law in the Kibbutz: A Reappraisal. *Law and Society Review* **10**.

THORNE, S. (1959) English Feudalism and Estates in Land. *Cambridge Law Journal.*

WEBER, M. (1954) *Law in Economy and Society* (M. Rheinstein, ed.). New York: Simon & Schuster.

Anne Salmond

---

12 Maori epistemologies

This paper focuses on the knowledge, speculations, and debates of tribal thinkers in Aotearoa, as these were first recorded between about 1840 and 1860 in Maori manuscripts and in the correspondence columns of Maori newspapers.[1] It also draws on the early accounts of European explorers, missionaries, and settlers, Elsdon Best's massive researches into tribal knowledge at the turn of the century, and my own attempts at understanding the knowledgeable talk of tribal elders between 1964 and 1984.

I will argue that *maatauranga* (Maori knowledge) was and still is a complex and 'open' system;[2] that European evaluations of Maori knowledge in Aotearoa have characteristically been ideological; and that much contemporary metropolitan speculation about 'traditional thought' is also evidently pre-formed and parochial – or as a Maori debater might say of another's doubtful account, '*he koorero i titoa ai i te roro o tana whare*' (a myth composed in the porch of his own house).

Maatauranga

Maatauranga, or reliable knowledge, is a term in Maori almost synonymous with *moohiotanga*, knowledge acquired by familiarity and the exercise of intelligence. A particular form of *maatauranga* is *waananga*, ancestral knowledge which enabled its possessor to communicate directly with the ancestor-gods and to activate their power. All of these forms of knowledge were stored in the belly (*puku*) where the various organs of thought and emotion were located; the *hinengaro* or spleen where thought, memory and emotions originated; the *ngaakau* or entrails where thought and feeling were given expression;[3] and the *manawa* or bowels, where thought and feeling associated with the life force or *manawa ora*. Thought (*mahara, whakaaro*) and desires (*hiahia, manako*) received their original impulse in the *hinengaro*, and welled up in the *ngaakau* or mind-heart to be expressed in words or actions; while the mind-heart received information about the phenomenal world through the senses: '*ka kite te kanohi, ka rongo te taringa, maatau ana ki te ngaakau*' (the eyes see, the ears hear, the mind-heart understands). The head had nothing to do with cognition in this account, but when a man talked with his ancestor-gods, their efficacy (*mana atua*) found a pathway to his body through his head, and especially his hair – a notion expressed in the patterns of the language:

uru =   head
          hair of head
          enter, possess as a familiar spirit
          chief

awe =   hair of head about the fontanelles
          essential, immortal power of atua
          strength, power, influence

A man's hair was linked quite literally with his descent lines (*kaka* – single hair, fibre, stalk; stock, line, lineage; main lines in tattooing), and the greater the *mana* of his ancestors, the greater the *tapu* of the head; so a chief's head had to be kept meticulously separate from contact with food, women's clothing, or the touch of commoners. For a woman, the link with descent lines was more particularly through the womb (*whare tangata*, or 'house of people'), and child-bearing women were kept away from certain potent forms of ancestral power, lest their fertility be attacked and the descent lines be broken; though older and high-born women acted as mediums and keepers of ancestral knowledge. Ancestral power for both men and women came to rest within the body in the *mauri*, the immaterial abiding-place for the *mana* of the gods; and the *mauri* protected the *hau*, an individual's characteristic vitality or breath of life, just as the *wairua* or immaterial self protected its physical basis the body (*tinana*). In fact all things in the phenomenal world had a *tinana*, a *wairua*, a *mauri* and a *hau*, for in Maori cosmological theory the same fundamental forces gave form and energy to all matter, and *tupu* or cosmic generative power already contained the potentiality for all forms of life.

Waananga

In this conception of the universe, men and women existed at a threshold or *pae* between sky and earth, life and death, light and dark, and exerted themselves to influence destiny.[4] Just as Tane, the ancestor of humanity, forced earth and sky apart to create a world of light, growth, and life, so people worked through ritual to focus ancestral and essential power (*mana atua*), and to harness it for their survival:

> *ihi* =   split, divide, separate
>   dawn, ray of sun
>   tendril of plant
>   spell, incantation, a form of altar (*tuuahu*)
>   essential force, power, authority, rank

At moments when this power entered the phenomenal world it was said, '*Te ihi, te wehi me te wana!*' (essential force, fearful force, awesome power!). Wild and extraordinary phenomena were attributed to the interventions of such power, and so were termed '*atua*'; (god, supernatural being: anything strange and extraordinary). *Tohu* or omens, on the other hand, were predictive indicators of the workings of the phenomenal world, and *tohunga* (priests or knowledgeable experts) were the skilled interpreters of such signs.

Waananga, or knowledge for activating ancestral power, included cosmological and ancestral histories – both expressed in a genealogical language of description since all matter proceeded from a common source; ritual practices; and *karakia* or formulae of power.[5] This sort of knowledge was regarded as a family treasure (*taonga*), and it was taught particularly to high-born boys[6] who were chosen for their intelligence and memory skills, either by their close relatives or in tribal Whare Waananga or Whare Kura, the district 'Schools of Learning'. As Shortland observed in 1851, 'the most important families of a tribe are in the habit of devoting one or more of their members to the study of this traditionary knowledge, as well as their "tikanga" or laws, and the rites connected with their religion. Persons so educated are their books of reference, and their lawyers' (Shortland 1851: 95).

Whare Waananga appear to have been held in most tribal districts, and many names of such schools occur in tribal histories. Among those known to have been active last century were Kahuponia at Maungapohatu (Best 1923: 5), Te Rawheoro at Uawa, where Te Matorohanga attended in 1836 (Ngata 1930: 25–28), Te Papa a Rotu at Whatawhata, where Potatau the first Maori King was taught (Jones 1959: 33), and Kirieke at Raukokore in the Bay of Plenty, where Eruera Stirling's teacher Pera te Kaongahau was taught (Stirling and Salmond 1980: 88–93).

Waananga sessions are still held in some tribal areas, although the teaching now focuses on tribal histories and the tapu teaching rules have been relaxed, a process that began with Christianization. As Te Matorohanga retorted in 1865, 'Well, what of the Whare Waananga! They are just like churches – nowadays we wash our heads in cooking-pots!' (Smith 1913: 1).

In the old days instruction was usually at night, in the dark, sometimes in a tapu house and sometimes out in the open;[7] and through these methods students were trained to remember vast amounts of information. Elsdon Best cites a Tuhoe elder, for instance, who dictated 406 songs to him from memory in 1896, and another, Tamarau Waiari of Ruatoki, who in the 1890s spent three consecutive days in the Native Land Court reciting the descent lines and accounts of Ngati Koura, an account which detailed in correct order, the names of over 1,400 ancestors (Best 1976: 48–9). Despite a number of vigilant critics also sitting in the court, Tamarau's recital was not faulted; and many examples could be given of similar, more recent feats of memory from elders trained in this tradition.

Each Whare Waananga had its own procedures. In the Ngai Tahu Whare Kura, according to a text collected by John White in the 1860s, about 20 or 30 high-born boys were chosen to attend a course of instruction held each winter over four or five years, in a *tapu* house built by their teachers and sanctified by the killing of a person or a dog. The boys were taught each night from sunset until midnight, attended by their fathers who had to keep them from 'crying, restlessness, whispering, or any act by which the attention of others would be distracted' (White 1887 I: 10). If a boy slept during that time it was a sign of his early death, and he had to leave the school. One expert sat by the door of the house on the right-hand side, the side of power, and began the teaching each night followed by others in order of rank, and listened to by a group of experts on the left-hand side, who corrected and amplified the accounts where necessary. Every night for a month, one section of the curriculum was rehearsed until the students knew it thoroughly (*kia tino mau puu ai te moohio o aua mea* (White 1887: 8)), then another section began. The teachings opened with a formula to 'make a path' for the *wairua* of the students so they could effectively master what they were taught, and then they were instructed in the emergence of Poo (darkness), Ao (light, world), down to Rangi (day, sky-father), and Tane the ancestor of humanity.

In each Whare Waananga the curriculum was somewhat differently organized. At the Waananga sessions taught by Te Matorohanga and Nepia Pohuhu at Wairarapa in 1865 for instance,[8] the teaching was divided into two main sections: the *kauae runga* ('upper jaw') or knowledge of ancestor gods, and the *kauae raro* ('lower jaw') or knowledge of human history from the earliest migration to 'Tawhiti' down to the migrations to Aotearoa. The *kauae runga* section began with a recital of the aeons of Poo (darkness) when Earth and Sky mated and produced the gods, who lived between their parents until Tane forced them apart so that light could enter the world. Then Tane ascended the twelve heavens on a whirlwind to obtain the three 'baskets' of knowledge, and he brought these down to earth with two god-stones to secure their power, and lodged them in the first terrestrial Whare Kura as a *taahu* (= origin, summit, direct line of ancestry, ridgepole, the commencement of knowledge) for knowledge in this world of light. After this he created the first woman and mated with her, and human life began. This section ended with the exploits of Mataora and Niwareka, a couple who visited the Underworld and returned with the knowledge of carving, tattooing, and ornamental weaving. The three *waananga* 'baskets', it was explained, held three main forms of knowledge as 'food' for people: *te kete uruuru matua* or knowledge of peaceful intention; *te kete urururangi* or knowledge of karakia or formulae for talking with the gods; and *te kete uruurutau*, or knowledge of worldly activity – war, wood-work, stone-work and earth-work (Smith 1913: Maori text 28); and each of these forms of knowledge was taught separately in this Whare Waananga. In other tribal accounts, however, where these baskets are mentioned they are differently described, and other gods – Tawhaki and Tiki, for instance – are said to be responsible for bringing them to earth.

The cosmogonic theories of different tribal districts and major thinkers also varied. Some accounts of cosmological formation began with original darkness, others with a void of primal negation or images of plant growth. There are several early texts which show thought as the first emergent principle in the cosmos, from which all intelligible order and matter proceeds; one of these is a very beautiful chant recorded by Te Kohuora of Rongoroa in 1854:

Na te kune te pupuke

From the source of growth the rising
       .*conception*   .*swelling*

Na te pupuke te hihiri
Na te hihiri te mahara
Na te mahara te hinengaro
Na te hinengaro te manako

From rising the thought
From rising thought the memory
From memory the mind
From the mind, desire
       .*spleen*

Ka hua te wananga

Knowledge became conscious
       . *was named, became fruitful*

Ka noho i a rikoriko

It dwelt in dim light
       .*mated with*

Ka puta ki waho ko te po

And darkness emerged
       .*was born*

Ko te po i tuturi, te po i
       pepeke
Te po uriuri,
       te po tangotango
Te po wawa, te po te kitea
Te po i oti atu ki te mate

The dark for kneeling,
       the dark for leaping
The intense dark,
       to be felt
The dark to be touched, unseen
The dark that ends in death

Na te kore i ai

From nothingness came the first cause
       .*primal void*   .*begetting*

Te kore te whiwhia
Te kore te rawea
Ko hau tupu, ko hau ora
Ka noho i te atea

Unpossessed nothingness
Unbound nothingness
The wind of growth, the wind of life
Stayed in empty space
       .*mated with*

Ka puta ki waho te rangi	And the atmosphere emerged
e tuu nei	*.was born*
Te rangi e teretere nei	The atmosphere which floats
I runga o te whenua	Above the earth
Ka noho te rangi nui e tu nei	The great atmosphere above us
Ka noho i a ata tuhi	Stayed in red light
Ka puta ki waho te marama	And the moon emerged
	.was born
Ka noho te rangi e tu nei	The atmosphere above us
Ka noho i a te werowero	Stayed in shooting light
Ka puta ki waho ko te ra	And the sun emerged
	.was born
Kokiritia ana ki runga	Flashing up
Hei pukanohi mo te rangi	To light the atmosphere
Te ata rapa, te ata ka mahina	The early dawn, the early day,
	the midday
Ka mahina te ata i hikurangi!	The blaze of day from the sky!

. . . and then the land was produced, then the gods, and man (Taylor 1855: 14–16)

The cosmological speculations presented in this chant and others like it raise in an acute form the problem of translation. Many of the words used here can be read on several levels at once, with ranges of significance that differ from anything in English semantics, and it is extremely difficult to sort out literal from figurative meanings in what they say. Assertions characteristically assume a world theory with certain presupposed conditions of possibility and a particular ordering of space and time, and if an expression makes claims that violate any of these fundamental orders, it is thought to be either absurd or metaphorical. So for instance, when Sir George Grey described the cosmological accounts which he collected in *Nga Mahi a Nga Tupuna* as 'fabulous', 'puerile', and 'absurd' (Grey 1884: ix–xvii), he was in effect saying that his literal reading of them violated his commonsense notion of the world. Elsdon Best, on the other hand, argued that creation accounts expressed in a genealogical language were essentially figurative (at least to knowledgeable tribal experts), and so could be regarded as rational and acceptable to Western thought (Best 1976: 34–5, 65). It is possible, however, that these accounts were neither simply figurative nor absurd; rather, they presupposed semantic and ontological orderings that are in some respects different, but not absolutely different, from our own. Nor should they be judged for reasonableness *until these conditions are thoroughly understood*; and this, given the linguistic and time limits on most fieldwork and some assumptions (particularly evolutionary ones) built into our own epistemology, is an extraordinarily difficult task.

Consider, for instance, the relationship between mind and matter described in the chant quoted above. A primal energy produces thought, memory, the mind, and then desire. From desire *waananga* (ancestral knowledge) generates darkness, and then the Kore – 'primal power of the cosmos, the void or negation, yet containing the potentiality of all things afterwards to come' (Best 1924: 60). From Kore, space emerges, and then light, land, the gods, and men. Thought and mind constitute phenomenal intelligibility in this account; they have efficacy in the phenomenal world. However, the translations 'thought' and 'mind' are inevitably misleading, for 'thought' and 'feeling' are not radically distinguished in Maori semantics.

aro =   mind, seat of feeling
              desire, inclination
              bowels
whakaaro = thought, intention, opinion
              understanding
              think, consider, plan
hiahia =   thought
              desire

They proceed alike from the mind-heart in the belly, and were activated together in the cosmos before matter received intelligible form. Mind-heart and mind-matter distinctions, presupposed in Western definitions of logic and philosophy, are differently understood in Maori theories of existence, and cannot be simply assumed in judging the reasonableness of Maori knowledgeable accounts (see Evens 1979).

This point can be illustrated further by looking at the genealogical description language used in Maori cosmological chants. Is it reasonable to speak of phenomena such as earth and sky 'mati.ig' and 'producing offspring'? Apparently not; and yet in the semantics of Maori, physical phenomena and people are held to proceed from a common primal source:

puu =   origin, cause, source
              root of a tree or plant
              base of a mountain
              heart, centre
              main stock of a kin group
              a learned person
pupuu =   bubble up
take =   origin, cause, reason
              root of a plant
              base of a hill
              incantation
              chief of a kin group
              ancestral source of a land-claim

and all things unfold their nature in a common dynamic process (*tupu*):

tupu =	spring, issue, begin
	shoot, bud, grow
	unfold essential nature
whakatupuranga =	generation
tupuna =	ancestor, grandparent
hika =	copulate, plant
whenua =	placenta, earth

'All things unfold their nature (*tipu*)), live (*ora*), have form (*ahua*), whether trees, rocks, birds, reptiles, fish, animals or human beings' (Smith 1913: 13). So words that appply to human generative activities can, without any great imaginative leap, also apply to the formation of natural phenomena – in *Maori*, but not in English. The interpretative problem arises in the possible translations, and not in the original texts. Even our habitual representations of genealogy can cause trouble in understanding these accounts. Pei te Hurinui records that according to Tainui learned men of last century, the process of creation is represented in carving as a double spiral marked by chevrons to show successive epochs (Jones 1959: 232), a double dynamism that moves into and out from a primal centre. This image links with the unfolding growth of fern-fronds, the twining tendrils of gourd plants painted on the rafters of meeting-houses, and the movement of whirlpools (an image of destruction) and whirlwinds (*toi huarewa* or *ara tiatia*, which carried Tane to the upper heaven), to give a spatial conception of genealogy which is quite unlike our own representation of descending vertical lines. The genealogical description language of the cosmological chants, then, cannot be simply assumed to fall in parallel with our notion of historical time, and our conceptions of Maori theories of cosmological formation have consequently to be rethought.

For reasons such as these I would argue that it is unwise to attempt to arrive at judgements of the reasonableness, absurdity, inconsistency, or intelligibility of assertions in language X simply by assessing the reasonableness, absurdity, etc. of their translations into language Y (see Gellner in Wilson 1979: 26–30). If the semantic and ontological order of X differs at certain points from that of Y, translation at these points will inevitably be problematic, and judgements of reasonableness at these points are likely to be radically misleading. What is more, they will also very likely be ideological (particularly where X is a Third World language and Y a language from the metropolitan 'centre'), for the differences allow plenty of room for political and epistemological interest to enter in the guise of dispassionate description.

So far I have focused on the teaching of *tapu* knowledge, in the Waananga tradition either by individuals to a chosen inheritor or in the schools of learning; and it may seem, given the emphasis on rote learning and accurate repetition in these situations, that there was not much room for argument and change. All the same, a great variety of accounts from different tribal districts and from particular authorities did (and does) exist, and it is clear that a great deal of speculation and debate did go on.

For the cosmological accounts it seems that discussion was mainly among learned experts, and for this reason they sought out other's company and on occasion travelled to the Whare Waananga of related tribes.[9] Te Matorohanga of Wairarapa, for instance, went to sessions of Te Rawheoro Whare Waananga among the people of Ngati Porou, and in his teachings he draws a number of explicit comparisons between their accounts and his own. Particular points of doctrine were often hotly debated, as an early Ngai Tahu source makes clear: '*Ki etahi tohunga e pono ana, ki etahi tohunga he whakakorekore atu ki etahi tohunga*' (What some experts believe, other experts dispute and deny: White I 1887 Maori texts 16–17), and this sort of debate was regarded as one of the great chiefly pleasures – '*Ko taa te rangatira kai, he koorero*' – talk is the food of chiefs. Another Ngai Tahu text describes a house where chiefs and experts gathered to discuss cosmological matters and compare their observations of the stars (White 1887 Maori texts: 13–14), and in the North during the summer, the learned experts would 'remain awake during the greater part of the night . . . observing certain stars and constellations which they are very fond of contemplating' (Nicholas 1817: 51). This ardent observation of the cosmos bore fruit in the various cosmological accounts, and there is no doubt at all that these tribal experts were well aware of competing accounts; as Te Matorohanga made clear when addressing his pupils in 1865:

> 'Attention! O Sirs! Listen! There was no one universal system of teaching in the Whare Waananga. For each tribe this was so; the teaching was led astray by the self-conceit of the priests which allowed of departure from their own doctrines to those of other schools of learning. My word to you is: Hold steadfastly to our teaching; leave out of consideration that of other (tribes). Let their descendants adhere to their teaching, and you to ours, so that if you are wrong (*hee*), it was we (your relatives) who declared it to you (and you are not responsible); and if you are right (*tika*), it is we who gave you this treasured possession (*taonga*).' (Smith 1913: Vol. I, 84)

This relativity of approach allowed tribal thinkers both to register episte-mological variation and to hold their own accounts to be true, for instance at the beginning of one cosmological account: 'We uphold the truth of our history . . . There are several versions of parts of our history but our belief is treasured in our hearts.' (White 1887: Maori texts 17.)

It is interesting, though, that the same truth claims do not seem to have been made, by some tribal thinkers at least, for accounts on the edge of cosmology and at the beginning of human history. The Maui stories, and those of Kae, and the *patupaiarehe* are said by several observers to have been commonly regarded as fables: 'We next meet with a variety of traditions respecting certain heroes, or demi-gods, who lived in very remote ages. As far as I am aware, these traditions are not considered sacred or worthy of credit; indeed, they are commonly called koorero tara, or fables' (Shortland 1856: 71, see also Best 1982: 198, Colenso 1869). Tribal histories, on the other hand, were regarded as factual accounts (Shortland 1856: 71).

Koorero: discourse

Koorero (translated as 'discourse' or simply 'talk'), is the form in which maatauranga was pre-eminently expressed, and it contrasts with *kupu* which is a smaller sketch of speech; a word, say, or an assertion. Thus the knowledge of tribal histories may be referred to as *ngaa koorero tuku iho* (talk handed down) or simply, *koorero*; so that a knowledgeable person is a *puu koorero* (source of talk), *whare koorero* (a house of talk), *maunga koorero* (talking mountain), *manu koorero* (talking bird, or orator). The great debating forum of Maori tribal life was, and still is, the *marae* or ceremonial courtyard, where kin groups meet in formal ritual and women exchange ceremonial calls (*karanga*) and male orators exchange speeches.[10] The art of formal speaking is termed *whaikoorero*, and contests of mana are fought out on the *marae* in displays of erudition, subtle historical allusion, or in moments of high excitement, insults being hurled and parried by a succession of striding, furious orators. In this tradition of knowledgeable debate, complex and precise judgements are made of the truth, consistency, and piquancy of accounts, and an elaborate vocabulary for these judgements has developed. Accounts that are regarded as reliable and thoroughly attested, for example, are called *koorero tuuturu* (permanent talk), while fables or idle stories are *koorero puuraakau* (ancient legend, myth, any incredible story), *koorero pakiwaitara* (fiction, legend, folklore, scandal), *koorero takurau* (a winter's tale, romance) or *koorero ahiahi* (fireside story, idle tale). A fictional account is *koorero tito* (a fabrication; *tito* – to compose, invent) or *koorero whaihanga* (lit. 'made-up talk'); while the terms for flattery, gossip, and deceit are numerous and detailed. According to Samuel Marsden 'the chiefs take their children from their mother's breast to all their public assemblies, where they hear all that is said upon politics, religion, war, etc., by the oldest men. Children will frequently ask questions in public conversation and are answered by the chiefs' (Marsden in Elder (ed.) 1932: 193). So high-born children learned the conventions and the characteristic scepticism of *koorero* from an early age.

Tribal histories (*koorero*) and genealogies (*whakapapa*) do not appear to have been taught in most early Whare Waananga, although more recent *waananga* sessions have focused on these accounts. From all accounts (Shortland 1856) these matters were openly discussed within the kin-group and were not particularly secret. I can only speculate that as Maori cosmo-logical theories gave way to Christianity and science, and as the Land Court forced tribal groups to assert their claims to land through *whakapapa* and histories, tribal histories became at once more contentious and less openly discussed. This knowledge has always been very important though, for just as ancestors could actively intervene in everyday life, so the accounts of their migrations, marriages, battles, and sayings constituted claims to mana and relationship that could be used to order everyday affairs. Names were the great object of this form of tribal scholarship – of ancestors, places, taonga (treasures), and events; they minutely marked the landscape, on hills, pools, cultivations, birding trees, fishing grounds, and rocks; they identified illu-strious forebears and the battles that made them famous; and commemorated important marriages, and past insults and defeats. Each group marked its complex of relationships in carvings, genealogies, placenames and historical accounts on the land, and so rendered its social and physical world intelligible. Tribal histories recounted relationships between named entities in genealogies and stories about how such relationships were made, changed, or broken. This relational mode of knowledge allowed probabilistic inter-pretations of *tohu* (signs, omens) in sickness, battle, and other meetings between people and ancestor gods, which could be reinterpreted if other information emerged; and it gave great resonance (of reference to landscape, carvings, gods, and people) to Maori knowledgeable talk. These accounts were intensely political and exuberantly various from one small kin-group to the next, and the differences were not accidental but often precisely reflected inter-group relations. This is still the case with tribal histories, and there is nothing more exciting than to hear these matters being debated on the *marae*.

The most critical judgement made of competing accounts then, in this and other contexts, is whether they are *tika*, or validated by reason, by precedent and experience:

tika =	straight, direct true, correct just, fair
tikanga =	custom, anything normal, usual rule, plan, method reasoning, meaning, significance correct, right

and so true or *pono*:

pono =	true, valid hospitable, bountiful
whakapono =	believe, admit as true ritually ratify

or whether they are false, or *hee*:

hee =   wrong, false
                     mistaken, at a loss
                     difficulty, trouble
                     dead

As Shortland records, 'the most certain method of prevailing with a New Zealander is to apply to his reason. Only get him to assert that your proposition is "tika" or straight, and you will soon obtain his consent to it. And it is notorious that, having once openly given his opinion, he will seldom retract' (Shortland 1851: 135). The meanings of *tika* shade from 'just' to 'customary' to 'true', and it was a judgement of propriety as well as of accuracy of account. *Hee* on the other hand, as one can see from the definitions, was a judgement with disastrous connotations; and between these two polarities lay *tito* or invention, whose meanings range from 'compose' to 'lie', so giving some room for political and artistic licence in the construction of accounts.

Perhaps the best way to demonstrate the use of these concepts in practical action is to quote extracts from early speeches, for instance those recorded in a debate between tribal elders over whose canoe first brought the *kumara* to Aotearoa (*c.* 1860). Major Ropata Wahawaha of Ngati Porou had recited his tribe's version of the coming of the kumara at an earlier meeting on the East Coast, and these speeches are commentaries upon his account:

HOANI NAHE of Hauraki
'Now my friends! When I heard those words spoken by Major Ropata, I did not take exception to them at that time, as I then thought his words were his own, and were a myth (tito) of his own invention, composed in the porch of his own house. But then I heard of the words of Iraia-tutanga-wai-o-nui . . . These two men are each confused (pooauau) and appear to think that their two tribes are the most learned of all the tribes who inhabit these islands of New Zealand, and that they two are the most learned men, and are the most able of all men to rehearse the genealogies and history of all the tribes who inhabit these islands.' (He tells his own tribal account, with a song insulting to the previous speakers.)
    'Now O Major Ropata and Iraia Tutanga! You say that the canoes Horouta and Aotea brought the kumara to these islands of New Zealand. You of all men, repeat the most absurd myth, falsehood and invention (papaki, tito, teka) . . . What makes me sad is that the lying words (korero titotito) spoken by you, friends, might be said to be true (kiia he pono). Truth is always truth, and here we are telling lies! (He pono ano te pono, ko tatou kei te korero tito).'

In this vigorous attack, the speaker ends by asserting a principle of absolute truth against which all accounts can be judged; but this argument is quickly disputed by a following speaker, Hohepa Te Poki-Tauwhitu-pore of Whanganui, who rebukes him for his arrogance.

'Friend Hoani Nahe, these are my words in answer to yours. You regard your words as correct. Do you think you are the only man who can rehearse our history from the first darkness (Poo), and is that why you assume such supreme knowledge? Why did you not remember that all men derive their origin from the gods, who first came from the Poo? By such knowledge you would have abstained from contradicting the assertions of other men. Perhaps you are deaf, as the fish in the water, the birds in the forest, the dogs in the scrub, have heard the history of these canoes (Aotea and Horouta), a history rehearsed by the old men of the days of ancient times.'

Oh, son! Here is a song of mine for the song which you chanted to us:

(He sings a song even more insulting than the first, which ends:

'But what canoe was yours? Or what did it contain? The scroll-marks on your nose, or slander spoken to all around? Or famine bulb and small black eel, the climax of your feast?')

His rebuke is joined by the next speaker, Tamati Tautuhi of Ngati Porou, who argues against Hoani Nahe that after all the truth of tribal accounts is essentially relative, since they are orally transmitted from one generation to the next and cannot be directly verified. He ends his speech with an ironic reflection on the nature of European history and its ideas of validation:

TAMATI TAUTUHI of Mata-ahu

'Now, my friend Hoani Nahe. I am the man who wrote down Major Ropata Wahawaha's words, and there were very many present (at Mata-ahu) to hear what he said – perhaps three thousand . . . No-one there disagreed with his words (whakahe), or disputed his account . . .

Now young fellow, the old men of this area tell these stories as well. The elders of the ancient past saw certain things, and they told them to others, and so on right down to this generation. It's not that Major Ropata saw Kahukura leave in his canoe; no, but he heard the elders telling the history of that voyage. Those accounts are still being told today and they can be laid clearly before you whenever you like. It is not right (tika) to say that Major Ropata conjured up this information (mohiotanga) by himself, for he didn't invent it – the old men taught him this knowledge (matauranga) and it was not a myth (tito) made up in the porch of his own house.

Now friend, you'd better think carefully before you take the words of your own ancestors as truth (he mea pono) while dismissing the words of our ancestors as lies (tito). For your similes (kupu whakarite) may turn against you, and if you then believe in (whakapono) things that *you* have heard and not seen, and that you cannot possibly verify (whakatikatika), everyone will know that you are quite mad.

You say that you're not sorry for what has been said about your canoe, because you are merely stating what was told to you by your ancestors. Well then, why do you contradict (whakahe) what Major Ropata has said? For he is only repeating the words of *his* ancestors.

As for me, I disagree with the accounts of the elders of my district, because although they say what they know, they can't give you the year, the month and the day – the precise date – that Kahukura came to Hawaiki. But you, friend, perhaps your elders can do better?' (White 1887 V: Maori texts 1–19).

In this 1860s debate, elders from a number of tribal districts entered the argument, and in the exchange of alternative versions numerous statements were made about truth, falsity, evidence, absurdity, and the nature of contradiction – an extended early example of the critical dialectics of *whaikoorero*. In these texts and on the *marae* today, the term '*tika*' is generally used to describe contextual truth judgements (true, proper, correct), while '*pono*' refers to assertions that the speaker firmly holds to be true (true, believed, ritually ratified). Always, though, there is a tendency towards a sceptical relativism, and an assessment of competing accounts as 'true for X'.

It seems to me indisputable, from the evidence of the *waananga* tradition and of debating on the *marae*, that Maori tribal thinkers were acutely aware of alternative cosmological and historical accounts, and that they had developed conventions for dealing with these. The prevalence of variant tribal epistemologies in Maori thought flatly contradicts the view, as presented by Horton for instance, that tribal thinkers invariably work in a 'closed' epistemological world:

'The traditional thinker, because he is unable to imagine possible alternatives to his established theories and classifications, can never start to formulate generalized norms of reasoning and knowing. For only where there are alternatives can there be choice, and only where there is choice can there be norms governing it.' (Horton in Wilson 1979: 160)

Nor can I find any evidence that Maori use of logic differs in any essential way from European reasoning: witness, for example, the final excerpt in this section, from a closely argued letter by Renata Tamakihikurangi of Ngati Kahungunu to the Superintendent of Hawkes Bay in 1861. The writer[11] is reproaching the Superintendent for refusing to accompany him to Taranaki to try to stop the fighting there, caused by a hasty Government purchase of disputed land:

Pawhakairo, February, 1861

'MR FITZGERALD Sir, – . . . Now then, I will answer your speech.

In reply to what you say about your grief for the war at Taranaki. If you felt genuine sorrow you would have been at Taranaki before this; your grief would have led you thither to put a stop to the war; then your word would have been heard beforehand in favour of stopping the evil; then you and I would have had nothing to discuss. I told you that the cause of our meeting was grief for the war at Taranaki, and proposed to go there and put a stop to it, to which you replied – that you could not influence the Governor. Then I thought, Eh! You are not sorry, your grief does not reach up to mine . . . This is your sort of sorrow. You wish that the Maoris only should be killed . . .

You say, "can chastisement be laid aside?" My reply is, Sir, what is the chastisement alluded to by you? Do you mean bloodshed? Do you mean shooting men down with guns? What part of the children do you mean to leave alive to feel your chastisement?. . . My idea of chastisement is investigation, that the child may survive to listen to your instructions in after days. These weapons of yours are not good things for teaching with; your teacher is a very bad kind of one; your children will run away. . .

You say, "that by fighting and division, the Maori King will be established in Waikato." . . . Sir, cease to cite this as a cause of quarrelling. For behold, the Treaty of Waitangi has been broken.[12] It was said that the Treaty of Waitangi was to protect the Maoris from foreign invasion. But those bad nations never came to attack us; the blow fell from you, the nation who made that same treaty. *Sir, it is you alone who have broken your numerous promises.*

You say, "The Maoris are not able to fight against the Queen of England and prevail against her." This is my answer. . . . who is the Maori that is such a fool as to be mistaken about the supremacy of the Queen of England? Or who will throw himself away in fighting for such a cause? No, it is for the land; for land has been the prime cause of war amongst the Maoris from time immemorial down to the arrival of the Pakehas in this island of ours. The Maori will not be daunted by his weakness, by his inferiority, or the smallness of his tribe. He sees his land going and will he sit still? No, but he will take himself off to resist.' (Hadfield 1861: 86).

Or as another chief said in another connection, 'The subject had been thoroughly discussed by themselves, and every knotty point argued according to principles recognized by Maori law, till they had arrived at conclusions which, as he quaintly expressed it, were as straight and even as a board planed by a carpenter' (Shortland 1856: 231).

Two worlds: the meeting of Maori and European thought

'Descriptions are never independent of standards. And the choice of such standards rests on attitudes which, because they can be neither logically deduced nor empirically proved, are in need of critical evaluation.' (J. Habermas, in *Knowledge and Interest* 1970: 48)

'The worst imperialisms are those of preconception.' (W. E. H. Stanner, in *White Man Got No Dreaming* 1979: 30)

In this section of the paper I will argue that historical descriptions of Maori thought were pre-formed by evolutionary ideas and political interest, and that contemporary theorists of 'traditional rationalities' too, must be wary of the epistemological and political context in which their arguments proceed. Sophisticated thinkers in any society are unlikely to want (or be able) to talk in any depth with outsiders whose command of the local language is perhaps unsubtle and whose local experience is brief; and even in a lifetime of dedicated fieldwork (as in the case of Elsdon Best), assumptions of superiority may serve to objectify the thought-world of others for scrutiny,[13] while closing off one's own. Under such conditions and particularly in colonial and neo-colonial contexts, accounts of 'traditional thought' are likely to be ethnographically insecure and ideologically distorted, and they are also likely to have damaging practical effects for those whose thought is being described.

From the first meetings of Maoris and Europeans, Europeans took the virtue of the imperial enterprise for granted. Aotearoa was on the wild edges of the world, to be 'discovered', named, and tamed by scientific exploration, evangelism, and colonization from the imperial centre. Abel Tasman was the first European to arrive at these islands in 1642, and his instructions from the Dutch East India Company spelt out the imperial argument:

'With what invaluable treasures, profitable trade connections, excellent territories, vast powers and dominions the kings by these discoveries (in America and Africa) and their consequences enriched their kingdoms and crowns; what numberless multitudes of blind heathen have by the same been introduced to the blessed light of the Christian religion: all this is well known to the expert, has always been held highly praiseworthy by all persons of good sense, and has consequently served other European princes as an example for the discovery of (other) regions.' (McNab 1914: 4–5)

Savages were held to be intellectually inferior to civilized men, and so could only benefit from contact with the West, as J. L. Nicholas declared in 1814:

'Though the savage does possess all the passions of Nature, pure and unadulterated, and though he may in many instances feel stronger and more acutely than the man of civilized habit, still is he inferior to him in every other respect: the former is the slave to the impulse of his will, the latter has learned to restrain his desires; the former stands enveloped in the dark clouds of ignorance, the latter goes forth in the bright sunshine of knowledge; the former views the works of his creator through the medium of a blind superstition, the latter through the light of reason and truth; the one beholds Nature and is bewildered, the other clearly "Looks through Nature up to Nature's God".' (Nicholas 1817: 86–7)

Thus Maoris were said to have no knowledge, only superstition and myth; and their thought was held to be inferior to European reason – by men who could not speak Maori, and knew nothing at all of Maori knowledge and thought. Maori thought was *prejudged* right from the time of European arrival in Aotearoa as unreliable and philosophically worthless, by people who were most profoundly ignorant of its qualities.

In the populist theories of the time, 'savages' and 'barbarians' were held to be like children, like ancestors (ancient Britons, Israelites, or Aryans in the Maori case), or like beasts to be tamed, exterminated, documented, or educated, according to the political philosophy of the writer. In all theories they were lesser beings, whose destiny could only be decided by 'civilized men'. The political interest in such prejudgements is evident in accounts of Maori thought written in England during the period of active colonization. A spokesman for the New Zealand Company, for instance, declared in 1838:

'The (Maori) is in a state of pupilage, and must be treated as we treat children. If you go into a country at all inhabited by savages and take possession of their land and become sovereigns of it, you infringe their rights only if you do not consider their benefit as well as your own . . . (But) they are themselves incapable of acquiring the arts and habits of civilized life; unless some influence that among civilized men would be considered unjust takes place, they never can, by themselves, rise to that higher position.' (Buick 1914: 72)

When the Treaty of Waitangi was negotiated with Maori chiefs in 1840, those who supported the Treaty, for whatever reason, argued that Maoris were intelligent and shrewd and that the chiefs were fully able to comprehend the Treaty and its implications; while those who opposed the Treaty claimed that Maoris were 'naked savages' or 'simple-minded' and, like idiots or minors, were Wards of Chancery, and thus incompetent to enter into legal contracts.

Comments on the intelligence of Maoris were commonplace in the early colonial literature, but these are accompanied by claims that Maoris were also devoid of knowledge, living in epistemological darkness and waiting only to be enlightened. Maoris were congratulated, however, for occupying a higher place in the Chain of Being than their neighbours, the Australian aborigines, as demonstrated in this column from a Maori newspaper published by the Government in 1849:

'If you knew what a proud people the English are, you too, would be proud to think that you, who but a few years since ate each other and were sunk in such utter mental darkness that you were looked upon by the rest of the world as the most brutal of men – you would be proud to think that the greatest nation in the world esteems you worthy of being admitted into enjoyment of all its privileges. . . You have reason to bless God, that your ignorance proceeds from no want of natural intelligence. It is attributable simply to a want of instruction, without which England, in times gone by, was as ignorant and so savage as you . . . Bad and designing men may tell, and we believe have told you that Englishmen are anxious to strip you of your lands. They may, to induce you to believe them, point to Australia, where the natives occupy no land. It is true they do not – but why? Because they are savages with no brains – no industry – no intellect – and like brutes, they but roam the surface of the earth.' (*Te Karere* English text, 19 Jan., 1849)

Intellectual evolutionism was (and is) a potent colonial ideology in Aotearoa, ratifying political inequality and disclaiming Maori knowledge by a complete epistemological prejudgement. As settler pressures for land increased, evolutionary ideology became more vicious, and the doctrine of survival of the fittest was invoked – for instance in this statement in the House of Representatives during the Land Wars in 1861:

'The Race, it is said, is irredeemably savage. It is also moribund. All that is wise, or safe to attempt, is to pacify or amuse them until they die out, – until the inscrutable physical law amongst them shall relieve the country from the incubus of a barbarous population, or . . . render it practicable to reduce them to the condition for which nature has intended them, of hewers of wood and drawers of water.' (AJHK 1861 EI: 4–5)
– a doctrine which was incorporated in the planning of Maori education for many years.

Not all writers were so violent in their condemnations of Maori intellect, and some (Edward Shortland, for instance) spoke in praise of Maori thought; but even Shortland was an evolutionist, describing Maoris as 'highly intellectual beings, who will eventually take their place side by side by the White man, as equals in civilization' (Shortland 1851: 41). There were liberal evolutionists, who regarded Maoris as intelligent pupils or children, to be taught and so 'raised' to civilization; and there were radical evolutionists, who thought it better that Maoris should die out, but there were virtually no non-evolutionary European theorists writing about Maori thought in the colonial period in Aotearoa. It was in the aftermath of the Land Wars and these discussions that Elsdon Best carried out his fieldwork from the 1870s until 1910, the descriptions of Maori thought used by Mauss and Lévy-Bruhl were written, and anthropological images of the 'Savage Mind' began to emerge.

Nothing is more certain, however, than that Maori thinkers throughout this period had their own reflections on Europeans and their claims. Very early after contact, Maoris enlisted as crew on European vessels and travelled to Australia, America, and Europe, and returned home to regale their relatives with their fieldwork experiences:

'(Moehanga) gave the surrounding chiefs an account of . . . London Bridge and the waterworks there, told them how the water was conveyed by pipes into different houses . . . and many other particulars relative to our mode of living, houses, carriages, shipping, churches, roads, agriculture, etc., and how the cooks dressed the food for the gentlemen's tables, and that they never ate it but only tasted it in the kitchen before it was served up. They heard him with great attention.' (Elder (ed.) 1932: 202).

The missionaries in their journals often refer to long conversations where they were questioned (sometimes all night) about astronomy, geography, agriculture, European marriage patterns, trade, law, and government; and of interested, reflective debates over European theology and its contradictory doctrines. Maori strategies for handling alternative cosmologies were evident in these discussions, for instance when Marsden tried to persuade a priestly expert and his companions that there was just one God, who had no notion of *tapu* requirements: 'They (answered) that our God and theirs were different. They said that I might violate their taboos, eat in their houses, or dress my provisions upon their fires – their gods would not punish me, but he would kill them for my crimes' (Elder 1932: 286); or again, in a discussion of heaven and hell with an elderly chief: 'He said that heaven and hell, taught by Europeans, might be very true; if so, he had been warring too much all his life to expect any transition from a better place than was appropriated to his ancestors, he had therefore made up his mind to go to the reinga and eat kumaras, as all his ancestors had done before him' (Polack 1838 II: 237). Another chief, in concluding a debate over the comparative virtues of Maori and European karakia, declared both theologies to be valid, or as Nicholas said 'allowing us to prize our own system, and himself and his countrymen to venerate theirs' (Nicholas 1817 I: 274).

Maori comments upon European practices were often critical and bemused, however, and it is clear that they were far from accepting any evolutionary scheme. When Te Pahi, chief of the Bay of Islands, visited Sydney in 1806, for instance, he 'never missed any opportunity of gaining the most particular information suspecting the cause and use of everything that struck his notice, and but few things there were of real utility that did not entirely engross his most serious attention. In communicating observations on his own country he was always very anxious to make himself understood, and spared no pains to convince us that the customs of his country were in several instances better than ours, many of which he looked on with the greatest contempt, and some with the most violent disapprobation' (McNab 1908: 264).

In brief, most Maoris were interested, but not intimidated by manifestations of western civilization, and they adopted European ideas and practices as it suited them. Most Europeans, on the other hand, learned little from Maoris and rapidly set about abolishing (while recording) Maori ideas and

practices. There is a harsh disparity between the evidence of Maori philosophical speculations and debates in the 1840s and 1860s, and European
accounts of Maori intellectual capacities in the same period; a disparity which
became institutionalized with the development of Native schools, and the
suppression of Maori language and culture in education and official life in
New Zealand (see Barrington and Beaglehole 1974). There is little in the
history of New Zealand to suggest that European thought, in contrast to
Maori thought for instance, is particularly 'open', nor does it offer much
support for Bryan Wilson's suggestion that traditional thought, in contrast to
European thought, is particularly 'closed':

> 'It is because he (the sociologist) has become conscious of the importance of
> eliminating emotional and evaluative elements in his concepts and has a
> tradition of enquiry that uses such concepts . . . that he is in a better
> position than primitive man to understand primitive society. He, after all,
> makes the attempt to understand other societies. They do not. His wider
> tolerance, his intellectual curiosity, and his willingness to criticize his own
> procedures are his initial advantages over men in other cultures. Other
> societies to them – but not to him – are bizarre, laughable, and "un-
> understandable." ' (Wilson 1979: xi)

This seems to me an extraordinary account, and self-contradictory as well;
one cannot claim both superiority and freedom from evaluation without
falling into paradox.

Contemporary literature on traditional thought is still bedevilled with
implicit, sometimes explicit, evolutionism. Ernest Gellner has argued that

> 'the philosophical significance of the scientific-industrial "form of life",
> whose rapid global diffusion is the main event of our time, is that for all
> practical purposes it does provide us with a solution of the problem of
> relativism – though a highly unsymmetrical one. . . The cognitive and
> technical superiority of one form of life is so manifest, and so loaded with
> implications for the satisfaction of human wants and needs – and, for better
> or worse, for power – that it simply cannot be questioned. If a doctrine
> conflicts with the acceptance of the superiority of scientific-industrial
> societies over others, then it really is out.' (Gellner 1973: 71–2)

It is true that guns, for instance, offered a retort to Maori reasoning that could
not be gainsaid, but this does not mean that Maori reasoning (see Renata
Tamakihikurangi's letter) was fallacious or unwise. Power in the sense of
control implies no necessary moral advantage;[14] Western science may have
achieved a measure of truth (and so efficacy) in its accounts of the physical
world, but this guarantees nothing whatsoever about its thoughts on other
matters. I do not accept the proposition that technological control is a final
form of wisdom, nor that other forms of thought simply do not count. That is
an old idea in New Zealand and a very destructive one indeed.

Conclusions

The ontological orders of Maori knowledge are not obvious; and in seeking to begin to understand *maatauranga*, a Western epistemology cannot be presupposed. The reasonableness of *maatauranga* rests within Maori language, and not in the partialities of translation; and gaps in translatability make room for political interest to enter discussions of Maori thought. It is for such reasons that short-term fieldwork on local intellectual traditions is not adequate; and armchair speculations on traditional thought within existing power relations between 'developed' and 'underdeveloped', and 'First' and 'Third' World countries are dangerous. Yet even the most recent ethnographies of traditional knowledge are based on relatively brief experience, and limited command of local languages (Barth 1975; Rosaldo 1980) and even the most recent discussions of traditional thought have evolutionary undertones. (Hallpike 1979; papers in Hollis and Lukes 1982.) In such a situation, descriptions of traditional thought as 'pre-logical', 'pre-philosophical', less abstract, and more mystical than our own are not surprising, for they are founded on 'facts' that have such judgements built into them in advance. In anthropology, the discipline where epistemological hazard and challenge could perhaps most readily proceed, Western thought is often closed by premises of intellectual superiority to radical cross-cultural reflection and thorough-going enquiry, and the process of opening Western knowledge to traditional rationalities has hardly yet begun.

Notes

1 For instance, in *Te Karere Maori, Te Waka Maori o Niu Tireni*, and *Te Wananga*.
2 See Horton 1970: 159–60.
3 'A native made the following singular remark to me: "The emotions may originate with the hinengaro and descend to the ngakau in order to find expression." ' (Best 1922: 53; see also Best 1982: 54–5).
4 See Salmond 1978.
5 Research on *karakia* is being carried out by Father Michael Shirres, who has been very helpful to me in discussing some of the ideas of this paper.
6 I have been unable to discover references to girls or women entering the Whare Waananga, and some references (e.g. White I 1887: Maori texts 5) explicitly state that girls were excluded. On the other hand, women did and do hold tribal knowledge (korero) and karakia (formulae of power).
7 'Whare' (house) in Whare Waananga is a metaphorical reference to a particular type of knowledge; see also whare maire ('house' of black magic), whare pora ('house' of weaving skills).
8 See Smith 1915.
9 See Jones's (1959: 153) discussion of the friendship between. Potatau, the first Maori King, and Te Heuheu, the high chief of Tuwharetoa.
10 See Salmond 1975. In East Coast tribes, senior high-born women may sometimes speak on the *marae*; and in other tribes they speak inside the meeting-house; but

usually a woman speaks directly to some issue (*take*, *kaupapa*) and without much ceremonial elaboration.

11 Renata became literate in his later years; he ends his letter by saying: 'That is my difficulty (writing). Had it been an exercise to which I had been accustomed in my youth, I should not have taken long to write an answer to what you have said; or had it been that which I understand properly – an oral discussion, it would not have taken me such a length to find a reply. That is all' (Hadfield 1861: 89). Many of the speakers reported in the transcripts of Maori gatherings during the 1860s were not literate, however; and there is no perceptible difference between their modes of reasoning in *whaikoorero* and those of literate speakers.

12 The Treaty of Waitangi, which was signed by a number of Maori chiefs and Governor Hobson as representative of Queen Victoria in 1840, guaranteed Maori chiefs the chieftainship of their lands, the absolute possession of their fisheries, lands, and settlements, and the rights of British subjects in exchange for British government in New Zealand and the Crown's pre-emptive control of land sales. The Land Wars were sparked in the 1860s by pressures from an increasing population of settlers on Maori lands, and the Maori King was established in the Waikato in this period as an attempt to create a Maori authority parallel to the Crown.

13 See Sissons 1984.

14 Note that 'superiority' in English is semantically slippery; it may refer to power advantage e.g. 'superior officer', or to moral advantage 'a superior person'. Power claims in English often slip insensibly into claims of moral advantage. (See also Salmond 1982: 79 for comment on metaphors of superiority.)

References

Appendices to the Journal of the House of Representatives. 1861, 1862, 1863.

ASAD, T. (1975) Anthropology and the Analysis of Ideology. *Man* **14**: 607–27.

BARRINGTON, J. M. and BEAGLEHOLE, T. H. (1974) *Maori Schools in a Changing Society.* Christchurch: Whitcoulls Ltd.

BARTH, F. (1975) *Ritual and Knowledge among the Baktaman of New Guinea.* Oslo: Universitetsforlaget.

BEST, E. (1922) *Spiritual and Mental Concepts of the Maori.* Dominion Museum Monograph No. 2. Wellington: Government Printer.

— (1922) *The Maori School of Learning.* Dominion Museum Monograph No. 6. Wellington: Government Printer.

— (1924) *Maori Religion and Mythology*, volume I. Wellington: Government Printer.

— (1982) *Maori Religion and Mythology*, volume II. Wellington: Government Printer.

BUICK, T. (1914) *The Treaty of Waitangi.* Wellington: S. & W. Mackay.

COLENSO, W. (1869) On the Maori Races of New Zealand. *TNZ Inst.* Vol. I: essays 5–75.

COOPER, D. (1975) Alternative Logic in Primitive Thought. *Man* **10**: 238–56.

CRUISE, R. (1824) *Journal of a Ten Months' Residence in New Zealand.* London: Longman, Hurst, Rees, Orme, Brown & Green.

EARLE, A. (1966) *Narrative of a Residence in New Zealand.* Oxford: Clarendon Press.

ELDER, J. R. (ed.) (1932) *The Letters and Journals of Samuel Marsden 1765–1838.* Dunedin: Coulls Somerville Wilkie Ltd.

EVENS, T. M. S. (1979) Mind, Logic and the Efficacy of the Nuer Incest Prohibition. *Man* **18**: 111–33.

GELLNER, E. (1973) *Cause and Meaning in the Social Sciences*. London: Routledge & Kegan Paul.

GOODY, J. (1977) *The Domestication of the Savage Mind*. Cambridge: Cambridge University Press.

GREY, Sir G. (1854) *Nga Mahi a Nga Tupuna*. London.

HABERMAS, J. (1970) Knowledge and Interest. In D. Emmet and A. Macintyre (eds) *Sociological Theory and Philosophical Analysis*. London: Macmillan.

HADFIELD, O. (1860) *One of England's Little Wars* . . . .London.

HALLPIKE, C. R. (1979) *The Foundations of Primitive Thought*. Oxford: Oxford University Press.

HESSE, M. (1978) Theory and Value in the Social Sciences. In C. Hookway and P. Petit (eds) *Action and Interpretation*. Cambridge: Cambridge University Press.

HOLLIS, M. and LUKES, S. (eds) (1982) *Rationality and Relativism*. Oxford: Basil Blackwell.

HORTON, R. and FINNEGAN, R. (1973) *Modes of Thought*. London: Faber & Faber.

JONES, P. te H. (1959) *King Potatau*. Polynesian Society.

LÉVY-BRUHL, L. (1923) *Primitive Mentality*. London: Unwin Brothers.

— (1926) *How Natives Think*. London: Unwin Brothers.

— (1979) *The Notebooks on Primitive Mentality*. Oxford: Basil Blackwell & Mott Ltd.

LIBERMAN, K. (1977) Ontology and Cultural Politics: Aboriginal versus European Australians. *Dialectical Anthropology* **2**: 245–51.

MCNAB, R. (1908) *Historical Records of New Zealand*. Wellington: Government Printer.

NGATA, A. T. (1930) He Tangi na Rangiuia. *Te Wananga*. Vol. II (I): 21–35.

NICHOLAS, J. L. (1842) *Narrative of a Voyage to New Zealand*. Volumes I and II. London: James Black & Son.

POLACK, J. S. (1838) *New Zealand, being a Narrative of Travels and Adventures*. London: Richard Bentley.

QUINE, W. V. (1969) *Ontological Relativity and Other Essays*. New York: Columbia University Press.

ROSALDO, M. (1980) *Knowledge and Passion*. Cambridge: Cambridge University Press.

SALMON, M. (1978) Do Azande and Nuer use a Non-Standard Logic? *Man* **13**: 444–54.

SALMOND, A. (1975) *Hui: A Study of Maori Ceremonial Gatherings*. Wellington: A. H. and A. W. Reed.

— (1978) Te Ao Tawhito: A Semantic Approach to the Traditional Maori Cosmos. *JPS* **87** (1).

— (1982) Theoretical Landscapes. In David Parkin (ed.) *Semantic Anthropology*. London: Academic Press.

SCHOLTE, B. (1978) On the Ethnocentricity of Scientific Logic. *Dialectical Anthropology* **3**: 157–76.

SHORTLAND, E. (1851) *The Southern Districts of New Zealand*. London: Longman, Brown, Green & Longmans.

— (1856) *Traditions and Superstitions of the New Zealanders*. London: Longman, Brown, Green.

— (1882) *Maori Religion and Mythology*. London: Longmans, Green & Co.

SIMMONS, D. R. (in press) Iconography of New Zealand Maori Religion. *Iconography of Religion*. Groningen, Netherlands: E. J. Brill.

SISSONS, J. (1984) 'Te Mana o Te Waimana : Tuhoe History of the Waimana Valley.' Unpublished Ph. D. thesis, University of Auckland.

SMITH, S. P. (ed.) (1915) *The Lore of the Whare Wananga*, Vols. I and II. New Plymouth: Polynesian Society.

STANNER, W. E. H. (1979) *White Man Got No Dreaming*. Canberra: Australian National University Press.

STIRLING, E. and SALMOND, A. (1980) *Eruera: The Teachings of a Maori Elder.* Auckland: Oxford University Press.

TAYLOR, REV. R. (1855) *Te Ika a Maui.* London: Wertheim & Macintosh.

TE RANGIKAHEKE. Grey manuscript 51, Auckland Public Library, Auckland.

THOMSON, A. (1859) *The Story of New Zealand.* London: John Murray.

WAKEFIELD, E. J. (1845) *Adventure in New Zealand.* Volumes I and II. London: John Murray.

WHITE, J. (1887) *The Ancient History of the Maori.* Volumes I, IV. Wellington: Government Printer.

WILSON, B. R. (1979) *Rationality.* Oxford: Basil Blackwell.

NEWSPAPERS

Te Karere Maori
Te Waka Maori o Niu Tireni
Te Wananga

Name index

Abel, R. L., 238
Allais, M. 227, 237
Althusser, L., 54
Apel, K.-O., 2
Ardener, E., 6, 10, 17, 21, 22, 47, 51, 55, 61, 63, 64, 66, 67, 68, 181
Arens, W., 136
Aristotle, 111, 115, 137, 176
Auerbach, L., 226
Augé, M., 196
Austin, J. L., 176
Averill, J. R., 12
Ayer, A. J., 115

Baier, A., 139
Bailey, F. G., 136
Banks, Joseph, 255
Barley, N. F., 106
Barnes, B., 9, 20, 25, 84, 87–92, 99–100, 101, 155
Barrington, J. M., 259
Barth, F., 210, 260
Barthes, R., 53
Basham, A. L., 221
Bastian, A., 44
Bateson, G., 67
Beaglehole, T. H., 255, 259
Bergson, H., 138
Bernier, F., 221
Best, E., 29, 240, 242–43, 245, 246, 249, 255, 257, 260
Bhaskar, R., 126
Biardeau, M., 213
Black, M., 25, 153, 154, 174, 176
Blacking, J., 142

Bloch, M., 113
Bloomsbury Group, 55
Bloor, D., 9, 20, 25, 85, 87–92, 100–01, 102, 155
Boas, F., 54
Bodin, J., 95
Bogatyrev, P., 53
Bohm, D., 126
Bonzaaoli, G., 214
Bourdillon, M., 44, 113
Boyd, R., 25, 159, 172, 173, 177, 178
Brown, S. C., 2
Buck, P., 29
Buhler, G., 213
Buick, T., 256
Burke, K., 5, 43

Cairns, H., 228, 230
Chapman, M., 136
Chattopadhyaya, D., 220
Chomsky, N., 51, 68, 129, 138, 176
Churchill, Winston, 55
Clausewitz, K. von, 125
Cohen, R., 186
Cohn, B. S., 203
Cohn, N., 93–4
Colenso, W., 249
Collingwood, G., 25
Covarrubias, M., 127
Crick, M., 64
Crocker, J. C., 5, 174, 176
Cronin, C., 186
Culler, J., 16, 25, 26, 153, 177

Davis, J., 44

Winternitz, M., 208
Wittgenstein, L., 129, 172, 176, 177
Wolfram, S., 6, 8, 9, 13, 24, 71, 82, 83, 117
Woolley, P., 102, 209, 218

Worsley, P., 60

Zilboorg, G., 95
Zoetmulder, P. J., 120, 129

Subject index